THE PEOPLE'S ALMANAC™
PRESENTS

THE BOOK OF LISTS

BY
DAVID WALLECHINSKY
IRVING WALLACE
AND
AMY WALLACE

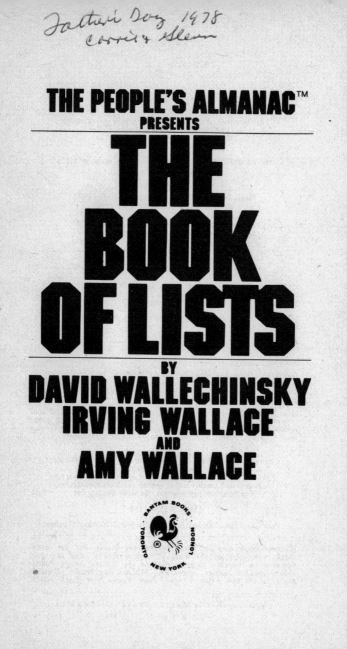

BANTAM BOOKS
TORONTO · NEW YORK · LONDON

*This low-priced Bantam Book contains the complete
text of the original hard-cover edition.*
NOT ONE WORD HAS BEEN OMITTED

THE PEOPLE'S ALMANAC™ PRESENTS THE BOOK OF LISTS
A Bantam Book

PRINTING HISTORY
*William Morrow edition published May 1977
24 printings through January 1978*

*Book-of-the-Month Club edition July 1977.
Playboy Book Club edition September 1977
Macmillan Book Club edition December 1977*

Excerpts appeared in SKY MAGAZINE/*June 1977,*
BOOK DIGEST/*July 1977,*
COMPANION MAGAZINE/*July 1977,*
NATIONAL ENQUIRER MAGAZINE/*July–August 1977,*
COSMOPOLITAN MAGAZINE/*October 1977.*

Serialized in New York Times *Special Feature/1977–1978.*
Chicago Daily News *and* DYNAMITE MAGAZINE
June–September 1977.

Bantam edition/February 1978

Grateful acknowledgment is hereby made to DC COMICS INC. *to
reprint the Superman illustrations on page 234 copyright 1938
Detective Comics, Inc., Renewed copyright © 1966 by National
Periodical Publications, Inc.*

MONOPOLY® *and the distinctive design of the game board and
component parts are trademarks for its real estate trading game
equipment of Parker Brothers, Div. of General Mills Fun Group
Inc., © 1935, 1946, 1961, and are used by its permission.*

ISBN 0-553-11150-7

Published simultaneously in the United States and Canada

PRINTED IN THE UNITED STATES OF AMERICA

0 9 8 7 6

For Flora,
with love
David

For Sylvia,
with love
David, Amy and Irving

THEY WROTE THE ORIGINAL MATERIAL

When "The Eds." is used it means the material has been
contributed by The Editors of *The Book of Lists.*

A.B.	Arthur Bloch	J.L.S.	Jeff L. Stolper
A.E.	Ann Elwood	J.M.	Joan Mooney
A.W.	Amy Wallace	J.N.	John Norment
B.F.	Bruce Felton	J.O.	Judy Osgood
B.F.G.	Bryan F. Griffin	J.T.	Jim Thebeau
B.H.	Bill Henkin	L.B.	Linda Bosson
C.H.	Cliff Hoffman	L.C.	Linda Chase
C.O.	Carol Orsag	M.A.A.	Malibu Authors
D.A.	Daniel Adams		Association
D.B.	Danny Biederman	M.B.T.	Marguerite B.
D.F.	David Frenkel		Thompson
D.G.	David Gunston	M.E.C.	Marion E. Colthorpe
D.M.F.	Dillman M. Furey, Jr.	M.G.R.	Marylee G. Rosenberg
D.M.S.	Darryl M. Stolper	M.MO.	Mark Mooney, Jr.
D.S.G.	David S. Goldman	M.S.M.	Michael S. Medved
D.W.	David Wallechinsky	M.W.J.	Melvyn W. Jones
E.D.	Eddie Dezen	N.C.D.	Nancy Courtman-
E.F.	Edward Fishbein		Davies
E.K.	Elizebethe	P.C.J.	Philip Cunliff-Jones
	Kempthorne	P.D.L.	Peter D. Lawrence
E.L.A.	Ernest L. Abel	P.F.	Pamela Fields
F.B.F.	Fern Bryant Fadness	P.S.H.	Paul S. Hagerman
F.C.D.	Frederick C. Dyer	R.H.	Robert Hendrickson
F.CH.	Flora Chavez	R.J.F.	Rodger J. Fadness
G.K.	Gary Kinder	R.O.	Richard O'Neill
H.A.K.	H. Arthur Klein	R.S.C.	R. S. Craggs
H.SI.	Helga Sitkin	R.T.	Richard Trubo
I.W.	Irving Wallace	S.B.	Stephanie Bernardo
J.B.	Jim Barnett	S.S.	Steve Sherman
J.BE.	Jeremy Beadle	S.ST.	Susie Stewart
J.BER.	Jeffrey Bernstein	S.W.	Sylvia Wallace
J.B.M.	Joseph B. Morris	W.A.D.	William A.
J.E.	Jim Eason		DeGregorio
J.EA.	John Eastman	W.H.	William Hammons
J.L.L.	Jeanne Lund Leleszi	W.K.	Walter Kempthorne

CONTENTS

Libel Cases . . . Melvin Belli's 10 Most Important Nonmurder Criminal Cases in History . . . 12 Famous Nonmurder Trials . . . Edgar Lustgarten's 10 Verdicts Still in Dispute . . . 10 Countries That Use Torture Today . . . 8 Remarkable Escapes From Devil's Island . . . 10 Doctors Who Tried to Get Away With Murder . . . 10 Possible Victims of 10 Possible "Jack the Rippers" . . . 13 Drops for the Working Hangman

4. WAR AND OTHER DISASTERS 77

10 of the Worst Generals in History . . . Gen. Omar Bradley's 10 Leading Military Leaders in History . . . Gen. George Patton's 6 Past Lives . . . Top 10 Air Aces of World War I . . . 12 Nazi War Criminals Still at Large . . . 10 Lethal or Incapacitating Drugs Stored by the CIA . . . Creasy's 15 Decisive Battles of the World . . . 10 Weapons Named After People . . . 10 Biggest Arms Importers . . . 10 Biggest Arms Exporters . . . 10 Nations With Largest Percentage of Persons in Armed Forces . . . 10 Nations With Smallest Percentage of Persons in Armed Forces . . . 10 Nations With Largest Military Expenditures Per Capita . . . 10 Nations With Smallest Military Expenditures Per Capita . . . 6 Nations That Receive Military Aid From China, the U.S.S.R. *and* the U.K. and the U.S. . . . The 10 Worst Motor Vehicle Disasters . . . The 10 Worst Famines . . . 35 Countries and Their Nuclear Bomb Capabilities

5. GOOD HEAVENS . . . WHAT ON EARTH 100

15 Prehistoric Things Alive Today . . . 20 Poisonous Plants—Don't Eat . . . 7 Famous Flowers of Fact and Fiction . . . 15 Islands for Sale . . . 20 Largest Islands in the World . . . 15 Longest Rivers in the World . . . 10 Highest Waterfalls . . . 20 Largest Lakes . . . 9 Great Rocks . . . 15 Largest Deserts . . . 13 Largest Producers of Crude Petroleum . . . 10 Unexplored Areas of the World . . . First 10 Men in Space . . . The 10 Most Spaced Astronauts . . . 4,007 Objects Orbiting the Earth . . . 12 Stellar Bodies and Phenomena . . . The 43 Major Members of our Solar System

6. INSIDE NOAH'S ARK—ANIMAL LIFE 125

9 Breeds of Dogs That Bite the Least . . . 9 Dogs That Bite the Most . . . 14 Celebrated Animals . . . And the Sheep Shall Inherit the Earth: 16 Sheep Majorities Around the World . . . 10 Birds That Could Not or Cannot Fly . . . 17 Animals With Pouches . . . Pregnancy or Gestation Periods of 20 Animals . . . Maximum Recorded Life Span of 94 Animals . . . 25 Wonderful Collective Nouns for Animals . . . 20 Endangered Species and Reasons for Their Decline

7. ON THE MOVE—TRAVEL AND TRANSPORTATION 138

9 Most Unusual Monuments in the World . . . Eugene Fodor's 10 Most Glamorous Cities in the World . . . Kate Simon's 10 Most Glamorous Cities in the World . . . 12 Countries Receiving the Largest Number of Tourists and Visitors . . . 11 Places to Spend a

Healthy Winter . . . Sydney Clark's 10 Favorite Overlooked Sights
in the World . . . Kate Simon's 10 Favorite Overlooked Sights in the
World . . . Temple Fielding's 7 Favorite Overlooked Sights in the
World . . . Temple Fielding's 13 Leading Places to Avoid in Your
Travels . . . 30 New Names for Old Places . . . 10 Countries With
Largest Areas . . . 25 Most Populous Countries . . . 11 Places With
Zero Population Growth . . . 12 Fastest-Growing Places . . . 15 Most
Populous Urban Areas in the Year 1975 . . . 15 Most Populous Urban
Areas in the Year 2000 . . . First 10 Transatlantic Flights . . . 15
Safest Airlines . . . 15 Most Dangerous Airlines . . . 9 Automobiles
That Made History

8. IN A WORD—COMMUNICATIONS   157

Wilfred J. Funk's 10 Most Beautiful Words in the English
Language . . . The 10 Worst-Sounding English Words . . . 10 Words
You Can't Pronounce Correctly . . . The 13 Longest Words in the
English Language . . . 12 Most Commonly Used Words in Written
English . . . Ten Tough Tongue Twisters Other Than Peter Piper
Picked a Peck of Pickled Peppers . . . 15 Semordnilap Palindromes
. . . 16 Names of Things You Never Knew Had Names . . . 15 People
Who Became Words . . . The Most Common Last Names in 10 Coun-
tries . . . 39 Non-Indo-European Languages Which Have Contributed
Words to the English Language . . . The 10 Languages of the World
With the Most Speakers . . . 7 Remarkable Messages in Bottles . . .
Charles Hamilton's 10 Rarest Autographs in the World Today—and
the Value of Each if Auctioned . . . Carey McWilliams's 10 Greatest
Muckrakers in the History of Journalism . . . Oriana Fallaci's 18
Persons in History She'd Most Like to Have Interviewed . . . John
C. Merrill's 10 Top World Newspapers . . . John Tebbel's 11 Most
Influential Newspapers in the World

9. ARTY FACTS   176

Rudy Vallee's 10 Best Popular Orchestra (or Band) Leaders of
All Time . . . Johnny Cash's 10 Greatest Country Songs of All Time
. . . David Ewen's 10 Best American Popular Songs . . . Dr. Demento's
10 Worst Song Titles of All Time . . . Bing Crosby's 10 Favorite
Performers of All Time . . . 15 Recording Artists With More Than
10 Albums that Have Sold a Million Copies . . . 10 Rare Rock-and-
Roll 45s From the 1950s . . . 12 Rare 45s by Rhythm and Blues Vocal
Groups . . . 10 Rare Records by Blues Artists . . . Dick Clark's 14 Music
Idols Worshipped by Teenagers Through the Years . . . Robert Mer-
rill's 10 Greatest Male Opera Singers of the Past . . . Regina Resnik's
10 Favorite Operas . . . Sir Rudolf Bing's 2 Favorite Operas . . . Sir
Rudolf Bing's Choice of the 3 Most Popular Operas . . . The 5 All-
Time Favorite Persons in the Arts . . . Gene Kelly's 11 Greatest
Dancers of the Past . . . Joshua Logan's 10 Best Stage Plays of All
Time . . . Joshua Logan's 12 Best Stage Actors of All Time . . . Sir
John Gielgud's 6 Greatest Hamlets of All Time . . . 20 Longest-
Running Broadway Shows . . . Samuel French, Inc.'s 15 Most Popu-
lar Plays Performed by Amateur Groups . . . Peggy Guggenheim's
10 Greatest Painters of the Past . . . Peggy Guggenheim's 10 Greatest

Modern Painters . . . 8 Fascinating Models and Artists . . . Rubén de Saavedra's 8 Famous Interior Designers . . . 9 Famous Magicians and a Feat for Which Each Was Renowned

With the Lowest Nicotine Content . . . The Deadliest Cigarettes: 10 Domestic Cigarettes With the Highest Tar Content . . . 12 Domestic Cigarettes With the Highest Nicotine Content . . . 10 Countries Where the Highest Percent of Men and Women Die Before the Age of 50 . . . 10 Countries Where the Highest Percent of Men and Women Live to be 85 Years Old . . . 16 of the Oldest People in the World . . . Dr. David Davies's 10 Tips for Longevity

20 Wonderful Boners . . . Coals to Newcastle: 7 Great British Export Sales . . . 15 Most Memorable Articles Ever Insured . . . 35 Countries and When They Extended the Vote to Women . . . 10 Famous Librarians . . . Dr. Margaret Mead's 10 Best Anthropology Books or Studies . . . 10 Top Financial Contributors to the U.N. . . . 10 Countries Which Have Gone the Longest Without a Census or Population Survey . . . 23 Typical Jobs Rated According to Boredom . . . 18 Unnatural Laws . . . 10 Great Impostors . . . 20 Favorite Scents of Men and Women . . . The Only 2½ Angels Mentioned by Name in the Bible . . . The Lord Thy God's 10 Commandments . . . The Authors' 7 Thoughts for You, The Reader

"I'VE GOT A LITTLE LIST"

"The human animal differs from the lesser primates in his passion for lists of Ten Best," wrote H. Allen Smith.

True. At least in our own experience. We have always been inveterate listmakers.

In fact, we can't believe there lives a person with a soul so dead, who never to himself has said, "I think I'll make a list." Everyone makes lists, whether they mean to or not. You make a list of New Year's resolutions, soon to be broken. You make up a shopping list, a laundry list, a party list. And if you are more thoughtful or competitive or crazy, at some time or other you graduate to making a list of the 10 best or worst movies you've seen or tennis players you've watched or military leaders you've read about.

Yes, everyone makes lists. The man or woman on the street. The Census Bureau. The pollster. The newspaper syndicates. The leading magazines. The president of the United States (remember Nixon's Enemies List?).

Lists are nothing new. They are as old as written history. Between 1792 and 1750 B.C., Hammurabi, king of Babylon, gave the world a list of 282 laws—a code of laws dealing with marriage, theft, slavery, and other civilized matters. Then, about 1200 B.C., Moses led the Israelites out of Egypt, seeking a homeland. Atop Mount Sinai, "Moses spake, and God answered him by a voice," and when Moses descended he had a list—the 10 Commandments, revered to this day by Jews, Christians, and Muslims.

Moving toward more modern times, in 1601 Shakespeare gave us his play *Hamlet* in which Polonius offers his son Laertes a list of pragmatic rules to live by, including, "Beware of entrance to a quarrel . . . Neither a borrower, nor a lender be . . . This above all: to thine own self be true,/And it must follow, as the night the day,/Thou canst not then be false to any man."

Throughout history, well-known people have made out shopping lists or kept expense lists in ledgers. Relatively few shopping lists have survived, but expense ledgers have proved less perishable. Lord Byron had such a ledger kept for him while in Italy. In March, 1822, he had listed 15 charitable gifts he had made, ranging from "Charity to four people, three old men, and a lame woman —two Pauls" to "Borrowed from Fletcher to give to a poor boy—one Paul, one Crazie."

In 1885, when Gilbert and Sullivan's *The Mikado* was introduced at the Savoy Theatre in London, Gilbert proved very list-conscious and offered the public a memorable one. Ko-Ko, the Lord High Executioner, had a list of "people whose loss will be a distinct gain to society at large." Ko-Ko sings out, "As some day it may happen that a victim must be found,/I've got a little list—I've got a little list/Of society offenders who might well be under ground,/And who never would be missed—who never would be missed!" Ko-Ko includes on his list of those who would not be missed—autograph hunters, people with flabby hands, piano organists, lady novelists, and ". . . the idiot who praises, with enthusiastic tone,/All centuries but this, and every country but his own."

Sixty-five years later, in 1950, people were still offering lists to the public. In this case it was U.S. senator Joseph McCarthy, who announced: "I have here in my hand a list of 205—a list of names that were known to the secretary of state as being members of the Communist party and who nevertheless are still working and shaping the policy in the State Dept." This eventually led to the Army-McCarthy hearings in 1954, which became the top television drama of the period, and resulted in McCarthy's downfall and his censure by the U.S. Senate.

Yes, indeed, everyone makes lists. But until now no one has ever done anything to bring them together. And so we decided to come forward and create what may be the first comprehensive book of lists in history—lists invented by us, by our associates, by our contributors, by celebrities we contacted, by well-known experts, authorities, and specialists in every field. We not only invented or invited the invention of lists, but we dug for them in new and old books, pamphlets, magazines, newspapers around the world, in an effort to compile and reprint the best lists that have ever appeared in print.

In short, for *The Book of Lists,* we have tried to assemble every fascinating list possible involving persons, places, happenings, things.

We felt that our findings and creations could be as exciting to other people as they were to us ourselves. We felt confident about that because we had already tried it out. Actually, that's how we got the idea for this book. To begin with, we were always fascinated by lists. Then in 1975, when we prepared *The People's Almanac,* we decided to test the entire appeal of lists—were other people really as interested in them as we were?—by including a light sampling of them. In Chapter 24 of our *Almanac,* we paraded 25 lists, ranging from "20 Celebrities Who've Been Psychoanalyzed" to "The 9 Breeds of Dogs That Bite the Most" to "The 5 Most Hated People in History" (based on an actual Madame Tussaud's Museum poll).

Since *The People's Almanac* contained over a million words, our handful of lists was buried away in this massive book. Nevertheless, readers and media alike found these lists and responded with overwhelming affirmation. At least a half dozen national magazines and syndicates reprinted many of our lists. When we were interviewed across the United States by television, radio, and newspaper reporters, again and again our lists were the focal point of discussions. On a two-hour radio show in Chicago, the host devoted his entire program to challenging his listeners to guess who was on our "5 Most Hated People in History" list. We were absolutely inundated by call-ins. Everyone wanted to play the game. From the time *The People's Almanac* was first published to the present day, readers' letters have poured in, coming by the hundreds from every corner of the continent, and writers of the largest percentage of these letters have wanted to discuss our lists, add to them, and suggest new ones.

And that's how *The Book of Lists* was born. Out of our interest. Out of public enthusiasm.

So we give you a book devoted entirely to lists. But to prepare it, we had to set ourselves some ground rules. First, we had to ask ourselves: What is a list? The Random House Dictionary defines a list as "a series of names or other items written or printed together in a meaningful grouping so as to constitute a record." Webster's Seventh New Collegiate Dictionary defines a list more concisely as a "roll, roster . . . a field of competition or controversy." Fair enough, but pretty dry stuff.

A list, we found, is more, much more. A list has flesh and blood, and is the stuff of life. A list such as "23 of the Busiest Lovers in History" reflects certain aspects of daily living, as does, "10 People Who Have Taken Cocaine."

A list, we found, is even more. A list can carry the weight of authority. We wrote to numerous well-known persons throughout the world for their lists, and their response was immediate and gratifying. As a result, we have a star-studded galaxy of lists written exclusively for this book. The contents of some of these celebrity lists provide ample fuel for controversy. To cite several examples: Gen. Omar Bradley's ranking of one of Hitler's favorite generals, Field Marshal Erwin Rommel, over any American or British military leader in history may cause some raised eyebrows. Malcolm Cowley's choice of Baroness Murasaki as one of the 10 greatest novelists of all time, and Henry Miller's choice of Élie Faure and Marie Corelli as two of the best 10 writers in history, may provoke some wonder. Peggy Guggenheim's omission of da Vinci in her list of 10 greatest painters of the past may invite some tongue-clucking. Clifford Irving's inclusion of Clifford Irving among the 10 best forgers of all time may cause no controversy whatsoever.

On the other hand, for our chapter entitled "Guess Who's Coming to Dinner" we asked a number of potential hosts around the world to tell us the 10 people (or more) in history they would most like to invite to dinner, and our hosts' ingenious replies often provided astonishment, amusement, or delight. To their festive tables, John Toland invited V. I. Lenin, Beverley Nichols invited Mary Baker Eddy, H. R. Haldeman invited Niccolò Machiavelli, Dr. A. L. Rowse invited Flannery O'Connor—and Art Buchwald invited not only Lizzie Borden but Richard M. Nixon. Mary Hemingway, to a table already attended by William Shakespeare and Samuel Johnson, invited—Ernest Hemingway.

In short, we learned that a list is a reflection of life—solemn or bizarre or amusing, a compilation that provides learning or fun or both, a gathering of information or opinion that invites participation or controversy or both. A list is a collection of facts that can surprise, stimulate, challenge.

Let's face it. We—all of us today—live in the Age of Lists—the 10 Best, the 15 Worst, the 20 Most, the 25 Least. Lists are a way of life around the world, and listomaniacs abound. And why not? In a busy, troubled time, a simple list is easy to read and digest and remember. A simple list diverts and relaxes. A simple list informs and educates. A simple list draws us into intellectual involvement, to extend it or improve upon it, to be part of it.

So we felt that this book was an original idea whose time has come—and now we hope you enjoy reading it as much as we enjoyed preparing it.

However, this is only a beginning. *The Book of Lists* will have offspring—many all-new, brand-new books of lists to follow it. And we want you, the reader, to join in on the next book. This is an invitation to you to participate.

We want the next edition to be more comprehensive, more entertaining than the first one. To achieve our goal, we need your help. Tell us what you liked most about this book. Tell us what we omitted, what we could do to improve the book. Most of all, tell us what you know that we don't know—the ideas or information you have that we would like to have for the next time around. Don't be listless, join in. Our address is:

> *The Book of Lists*
> P. O. Box 49699
> Los Angeles, Calif. 90049

Each of us says to each of you: "I've got a little list." We hope you have one, too.

Enjoy.

IRVING WALLACE
DAVID WALLECHINSKY
AMY WALLACE

THE
BOOK
OF LISTS

1
WHAT'S IN A NAME

THE 5 MOST HATED AND FEARED PERSONS IN HISTORY

Each year from 1970 to 1976, Mme. Tussaud's Waxwork Museum in London handed 3,500 of the international visitors to their exhibition a questionnaire which asked them which persons—past or present—they hated the most.

THE 1976 POLL

1. Adolf Hitler
2. Idi Amin
3. John Christie
4. Jimmy Carter
4. Count Dracula

THE 1975 POLL

1. Adolf Hitler
2. Idi Amin
3. Count Dracula
3. Richard M. Nixon
5. Jack the Ripper

THE 1974 POLL

1. Adolf Hitler
2. Harold Wilson
3. Richard M. Nixon
4. Jack the Ripper
5. Count Dracula

THE 1973 POLL

1. Richard M. Nixon
2. Adolf Hitler
3. Jack the Ripper
4. Moshe Dayan
5. Muammar el-Qaddafi

THE 1972 POLL

1. Richard M. Nixon
2. Idi Amin
3. Mao Tse-tung
4. Adolf Hitler
5. Satan

THE 1971 POLL

1. Adolf Hitler
2. Mao Tse-tung
3. Richard M. Nixon
4. Jack the Ripper
5. Enoch Powell
5. Count Dracula

THE 1970 POLL

1. Adolf Hitler
2. Mao Tse-tung
3. Enoch Powell
4. Richard M. Nixon
5. Spiro Agnew
5. Count Dracula
5. Edward Heath

THE 5 MOST BELOVED HEROES
OR HEROINES OF ALL TIME

Mme. Tussaud's Waxwork Museum also handed out 3,500 questionnaires asking visitors to indicate the people in history whom they admired most.

THE 1976 POLL

1. Joan of Arc
2. Winston Churchill
3. Jesus Christ
3. John F. Kennedy
3. Horatio Nelson

THE 1975 POLL

1. Winston Churchill
2. John F. Kennedy
3. Joan of Arc
4. Robin Hood
5. Napoleon

THE 1974 POLL

1. Winston Churchill
1. Horatio Nelson
1. Florence Nightingale
4. Joan of Arc
5. John F. Kennedy

THE 1973 POLL

1. Jesus Christ
2. Winston Churchill
3. John F. Kennedy
4. Joan of Arc
4. Moshe Dayan

THE 1972 POLL

1. Joan of Arc
2. Abraham Lincoln
3. Horatio Nelson
3. John F. Kennedy
5. Winston Churchill

THE 1971 POLL

1. Winston Churchill
2. Joan of Arc
3. John F. Kennedy
4. Napoleon
5. Horatio Nelson

THE 1970 POLL

1. Winston Churchill
2. Jesus Christ
3. John F. Kennedy
4. Horatio Nelson
5. Joan of Arc

20 FAMOUS PEOPLE
WHO DIED YOUNG

		Age at Death
1.	Anne Frank, German Jew and diarist	15
2.	Thomas Chatterton, English poet	17
3.	Tutankhamen ("King Tut"), Egyptian pharaoh	18

20 ACHIEVERS AT AN ADVANCED AGE

1. At 100, Grandma Moses was painting.
2. At 94, Bertrand Russell was active in international peace drives.
3. At 93, George Bernard Shaw wrote the play *Farfetched Fables*.
4. At 91, Eamon de Valera served as president of Ireland.
5. At 91, Adolph Zukor was chairman of Paramount Pictures.
6. At 90, Pablo Picasso was producing drawings and engravings.
7. At 89, Mary Baker Eddy was directing the Christian Science Church.
8. At 89, Arthur Rubinstein gave one of his greatest recitals in New York's Carnegie Hall.
9. At 89, Albert Schweitzer headed a hospital in Africa.
10. At 88, Pablo Casals was giving cello concerts.
11. At 88, Michelangelo did architectural plans for the Church of Santa Maria degli Angeli.
12. At 88, Konrad Adenauer was chancellor of Germany.
13. At 85, Coco Chanel was the head of a fashion design firm.
14. At 84, W. Somerset Maugham wrote *Points of View*.
15. At 83, Aleksandr Kerensky wrote *Russia and History's Turning Point*.
16. At 82, Winston Churchill wrote *A History of the English-Speaking Peoples*.
17. At 82, Leo Tolstoy wrote *I Cannot Be Silent*.
18. At 81, Benjamin Franklin effected the compromise that led to the adoption of the U.S. Constitution.

19. At 81, Johann Wolfgang von Goethe finished *Faust*.
20. At 80, George Burns won an Academy Award for his performance in *The Sunshine Boys*.

Grandma Moses. She was still painting at age 100.

ESTIMATED IQS OF
30 CELEBRATED PEOPLE

A normal intelligence quotient (IQ) ranges from 85 to 115. Only 1% of the people in the U.S. have an IQ of 140 or over. In 1926, psychologist Dr. Catherine Morris Cox—who had been assisted by Dr. Lewis M. Terman, Dr. Maud A. Merrill, Dr. Florence L. Goodenough, and Dr. Kate Gordon—published a study of 301 "of the most eminent men and women" who had lived between 1450 and 1850 to estimate what their IQs might have been. The resultant IQs were based largely on the degree of brightness and intelligence each subject showed before attaining the age of 17. Taken from this study, here are the projected IQs of 30 famous persons selected at random.

Experts believe John Stuart Mill had an IQ of 190.

		IQ
1.	John Stuart Mill, English writer, economist	190
2.	Johann Wolfgang von Goethe, German poet	185
3.	Thomas Chatterton, English poet and writer	170
4.	Voltaire (François-Marie Arouet), French writer	170
5.	George Sand (Aurore Dupin), French novelist	150
6.	Wolfgang Amadeus Mozart, Austrian composer	150
7.	George Gordon, Lord Byron, English poet	150
8.	Thomas Jefferson, U.S. president	145
9.	Benjamin Franklin, U.S. diplomat, statesman, and scientist	145
10.	Charles Dickens, English novelist and humorist	145
11.	Galileo Galilei, Italian physicist and astronomer	145
12.	Napoleon, French emperor	140
13.	Richard Wagner, German operatic composer and poet	135
14.	Charles Darwin, English naturalist	135
15.	Ludwig van Beethoven, German composer	135
16.	Leonardo da Vinci, Italian painter, scientist, and engineer	135
17.	Honoré de Balzac, French novelist	130
18.	Sir Isaac Newton, English mathematician	130
19.	Baruch Spinoza, Dutch philosopher	130
20.	George Washington, U.S. president	125
21.	Abraham Lincoln, U.S. president	125
22.	Robert Blake, English admiral	125
23.	Johann Sebastian Bach, German composer	125
24.	Joseph Haydn, Austrian composer	120
25.	Hernando Cortes, Spanish conqueror of Mexico	115
26.	Emanuel Swedenborg, Swedish religious writer	115
27.	Martin Luther, German religious reformer	115
28.	Rembrandt van Rijn, Dutch painter and etcher	110
29.	Nicolaus Copernicus, Polish founder of modern astronomy	105
30.	Miguel de Cervantes, Spanish poet and novelist	105

SOURCE: Catherine Morris Cox, *Genetic Studies of Geniuses,* Vol. II (Stanford, Calif.: Stanford University Press, 1926).

WILL DURANT'S
10 GREATEST THINKERS
OF ALL TIME

1. Confucius (K'ung Fu-tzu, 551?–479? B.C.), Chinese philosopher
2. Plato (427?–347 B.C.), Greek philosopher
3. Aristotle (384–322 B.C.), Greek philosopher
4. St. Thomas Aquinas (1225–1274), Italian theologian
5. Nicolaus Copernicus (1473–1543), Polish astronomer
6. Francis Bacon (1561–1626), English statesman-philosopher
7. Sir Isaac Newton (1642–1727), English mathematician-physicist
8. Voltaire (1694–1778), French author
9. Immanuel Kant (1724–1804), German philosopher
10. Charles Darwin (1809–1882), English naturalist

30 FAMOUS
LEFT-HANDED PEOPLE

1. Carl Philipp Emanuel Bach, German composer
2. Alphonse Bertillon, French anthropologist and criminologist
3. Thomas Carlyle, Scottish essayist and historian*
4. Charlie Chaplin, British actor and director
5. Jimmy Connors, U.S. tennis player
6. James J. Corbett, U.S. heavyweight boxing champion
7. Clarence Darrow, U.S. defense attorney
8. Leonardo da Vinci, Italian artist and inventor
9. Olivia de Havilland, U.S. actress
10. Marie Dionne, one of the Canadian quintuplets
11. Gerald Ford, U.S. president
12. James A. Garfield, U.S. president
13. Judy Garland, U.S. actress and singer
14. George II, king of England
15. Betty Grable, U.S. actress
16. Rex Harrison, British actor
17. Jack the Ripper, British murderer
18. Danny Kaye, U.S. actor and comedian
19. Sandy Koufax, U.S. baseball pitcher
20. Harpo Marx, U.S. comedian and harpist
21. Paul McCartney, British rock composer and singer
22. Michelangelo, Italian artist
23. Horatio Nelson, British naval hero*
24. Kim Novak, U.S. actress
25. Cole Porter, U.S. composer
26. Mandy Rice-Davies, British ex-call girl

27. Babe Ruth, U.S. baseball player
28. Terence Stamp, British actor
29. Tiberius, Roman emperor
30. Harry S Truman, U.S. president

    * Became left-handed after losing the use of his right hand.

—The Eds.

THE 5 MOST BEAUTIFUL
WOMEN OF MODERN TIMES

Each year from 1970 to 1976, 3,500 of the international visitors to Mme. Tussaud's Waxwork Museum in London were asked to select the most beautiful women of our time.

THE 1976 POLL

1. Twiggy
2. Brigitte Bardot
3. Marilyn Monroe
4. Elizabeth Taylor
5. Raquel Welch

THE 1975 POLL

1. Elizabeth Taylor
2. Sophia Loren
3. Raquel Welch
4. Twiggy
5. Brigitte Bardot

THE 1974 POLL

1. Sophia Loren
2. Raquel Welch
3. Twiggy
3. Elizabeth Taylor
3. Brigitte Bardot

THE 1973 POLL

1. Sophia Loren
1. Elizabeth Taylor
1. Raquel Welch
4. Brigitte Bardot
4. Princess Grace of Monaco

THE 1972 POLL

1. Raquel Welch
2. Sophia Loren
2. Elizabeth Taylor
4. Brigitte Bardot
5. Jackie Kennedy

THE 1971 POLL

1. Elizabeth Taylor
2. Sophia Loren
3. Brigitte Bardot
4. Raquel Welch
5. Julie Andrews
5. Audrey Hepburn
5. Princess Grace of Monaco
5. Twiggy

THE 1970 POLL

1. Elizabeth Taylor
2. Sophia Loren
3. Raquel Welch
4. Brigitte Bardot
5. Marilyn Monroe

LADIES' HOME JOURNAL'S POLL—
10 FAVORITE HEROES AND HEROINES
OF AMERICAN BOYS AND GIRLS

Who are the kids' heroes and heroines? That's what *Ladies' Home Journal* proposed to find out for their August, 1976, issue. They polled several hundred students from fifth grade through high school, in all parts of the country. The kids were asked to name names. High-school students, in addition, were given a checklist to rank. The results may surprise you.

GIRLS' TOP 10 HEROES AND HEROINES

1. O. J. Simpson
2. Neil Armstrong
3. Robert Redford
4. Elton John
5. Billie Jean King
6. Mary Tyler Moore
7. John Wayne
8. Chris Evert
9. Katharine Hepburn
10. Henry Kissinger

BOYS' TOP 10 HEROES AND HEROINES

1. O. J. Simpson
2. Elton John
3. John Wayne
4. Chris Evert
5. Neil Armstrong
6. Joe Namath
7. Henry Kissinger
8. Robert Redford
9. Gerald Ford
10. Mary Tyler Moore

SOURCE: Copyright 1976 *Ladies' Home Journal*. Reprinted with permission.

O. J. (Orenthal James) Simpson became the first runner in pro football history to rush 2,000 yards in a season.

DR. ASHLEY MONTAGU'S 10 WORST WELL-KNOWN HUMAN BEINGS IN HISTORY

Author, anthropologist, and social biologist, Dr. Montagu is an expert in the sciences that deal with human nature. His numerous books, among them *The Natural Superiority of Women*, and his frequent TV appearances have succeeded in popularizing formerly dull and esoteric scientific subjects.

1. Attila the Hun
2. Adolf Hitler
3. Kaiser Wilhelm II
4. Ivan the Terrible
5. Idi Amin
6. Heinrich Himmler
7. Joseph Stalin
8. Caligula
9. Richard M. Nixon
10. Comte J. A. de Gobineau

The Comte de Gobineau was a 19th-century French author, noted for his theory that the blond Aryan race is superior to all other races.

—Exclusive for *The Book of Lists*

10 RULERS WHO REIGNED THE LONGEST

	Reign	No. of Years
1. Pepi II, king of Egypt	c. 2566–2476 B.C.	90
2. Louis XIV, king of France	1643–1715	72
3. John II, prince of Liechtenstein	1858–1929	71
4. Franz Josef, king of Austria-Hungary	1848–1916	67
5. Victoria, queen of England	1837–1901	64
6. George III, king of England	1760–1820	60
7. Louis XV, king of France	1715–1774	59
8. Pedro II, emperor of Brazil	1831–1889	58
8. Wilhelmina, queen of the Netherlands	1890–1948	58
10. Henry III, king of England	1216–1272	56

THE 10 LONGEST-REIGNING
DICTATORS STILL IN POWER

"DICTATOR: A ruler or governor whose word
is law; an absolute ruler of a state."
—*Oxford English Dictionary*

		Nation	Gained Power
1.	Shah Mohammed Riza Pahlavi	Iran	Sept. 16, 1941
2.	Enver Hoxha	Albania	Nov. 29, 1944
3.	Marshal Tito	Yugoslavia	Mar. 5, 1945
4.	Marshal Kim Il Sung	N. Korea	May 1, 1948
5.	Prince Rainier III	Monaco	May 9, 1949
6.	King Hussein I	Jordan	Aug. 11, 1952
7.	Gen. Alfredo Stroessner	Paraguay	Aug. 15, 1954
8.	Habib Bourguiba	Tunisia	July 25, 1957
9.	Sékou Touré	Guinea	Oct. 2, 1958
10.	Fidel Castro	Cuba	Jan. 1, 1959

—D.A.

25 FAMOUS SLAVEHOLDERS

1. Hammurabi (c. 1955–1913 B.C.), king of Babylon
2. Aristotle (384–322 B.C.), Greek philosopher
3. Plutarch (46?–120?), Greek biographer and moralist
4. Constantine the Great (280?–337), Roman emperor
5. St. Thomas Aquinas (1225–1274), Italian theologian
6. Christopher Columbus (1451–1506), Italian navigator
7. Martin Luther (1483–1546), German Reformation leader
8. Hernando Cortes (1485–1547), Spanish conqueror of Mexico
9. John Calvin (1509–1564), French Protestant reformer
10. Sir Francis Drake (1540?–1596), English navigator and admiral
11. Catherine the Great (1729–1796), empress of Russia
12. George Washington (1732–1799), first U.S. president. Owned 216 slaves in 1773.
13. Patrick Henry (1736–1799), American political leader. In 1775, said, "Give me liberty, or give me death." Owned 65 slaves at the time of his death.
14. Thomas Jefferson (1743–1826), third U.S. president. Had 185 slaves in 1809.
15. James Madison (1751–1836), fourth U.S. president. At one time had 116 slaves.
16. Alexander Hamilton (1757–1804), U.S. statesman

17. **Andrew Jackson** (1767–1845), seventh U.S. president. Possessed 160 slaves when he became chief executive.
18. **John C. Calhoun** (1782–1850), U.S. vice-president
19. **Zachary Taylor** (1784–1850), 12th U.S. president. When elected to the White House, had 300 slaves.
20. **John Tyler** (1790–1862), 10th U.S. president
21. **James K. Polk** (1795–1849), 11th U.S. president. Owned 18 slaves.
22. **Jefferson Davis** (1808–1889), president of the Confederate States of America.
23. **Andrew Johnson** (1808–1875), 17th U.S. president
24. **Chang and Eng Bunker** (1811–1874), the original Siamese twins. Had 33 slaves between them on their farms in North Carolina.
25. **Ulysses S. Grant** (1822–1885), 18th U.S. president. The man who led the Union armies in the Civil War that ended slavery himself owned four slaves. In 1848, when he married Julia Dent in Missouri, she already owned one slave. She received a second as a wedding present, and later acquired a third one. Grant, in his own name, bought a slave named William Jones from his father-in-law and later freed him.

—A.B. & The Eds.

Gen. Ulysses S. Grant and family. He owned four slaves.

FORMER JOBS OF
30 FAMOUS PEOPLE

1. Desi Arnaz, bandleader	Bird-cage cleaner
2. Josephine Baker, dancer	Bessie Smith's maid
3. Carol Burnett, comedienne	Usherette
4. Robert Burns, poet	Tenant farmer
5. James Cagney, actor	Waiter
6. Johnny Carson, TV personality	Magician
7. Perry Como, singer	Barber
8. Sean Connery, actor	Bricklayer and truck driver
9. Howard Cosell, sports announcer	Lawyer
10. Albert Einstein, physicist	Patent office clerk
11. William Faulkner, author	House painter
12. W. C. Fields, comedian	Juggler
13. Gerald R. Ford, president	Male model
14. George Foreman, boxer	Electronics assembler
15. Clark Gable, actor	Lumberjack
16. Giuseppe Garibaldi, revolutionary	Sailor
17. Paul Gauguin, painter	Stockbroker
18. Adolf Hitler, dictator	Poster artist
19. Bob Hope, comedian	Boxer
20. Boris Karloff, actor	Real estate salesman
21. Dean Martin, entertainer	Steelworker
22. Golda Meir, prime minister	Schoolteacher
23. Marilyn Monroe, actress	Factory worker
24. O. Henry, author	Cowboy
25. Thomas Paine, political author	Corsetmaker
26. Elvis Presley, singer	Truck driver
27. Babe Ruth, baseball player	Bartender
28. Billy Sunday, evangelist	Baseball player
29. Henry David Thoreau, author	Schoolteacher and pencil maker
30. Harry S Truman, president	Haberdasher

—P.S.H. & E.D.

15 PROMINENT
HANDICAPPED PERSONS

1. JAY J. ARMES (b. 1937)

Born Julian Armas, he had both of his hands blown off at the age of 12. He has become a super private eye (fees as high as $100,000), using specially fitted hooks which enable him to fire a gun.

2. LUDWIG VAN BEETHOVEN (1770–1827)

Partly deaf at the age of 32, he became totally deaf at 46. He wrote his greatest music during his later years.

3. SARAH BERNHARDT (1844–1923)

Lamed by a knee injury in 1905, her leg amputated in 1914, she continued starring on the stage until just before her death. She is regarded by many as France's greatest actress—the Divine Sarah.

4. JORGE LUIS BORGES (b. 1899)

This great Argentine poet, story writer, and critic, many of whose works have been translated into English, is blind.

5. LOUIS BRAILLE (1809–1852)

Blinded at the age of 3, he became a teacher and developed the Braille system of printing and writing for the blind.

6. LAURA BRIDGMAN (1829–1889)

Deaf, blind, and mute, she was the first to be successfully educated using the raised-alphabet system of Dr. Samuel G. Howe, head of the Perkins Institution for the Blind. Later, she became a sewing teacher at the school.

7. MIGUEL DE CERVANTES (1547–1616)

He lost his left arm in the battle of Lepanto in 1571 and had to live in poverty on a farm. Such works as *Don Quixote* have made him the greatest figure in Spanish literature.

8. HOMER (flourished 850? B.C.)

This blind master-writer of epics is alleged to have created *The Iliad* and *The Odyssey*, which have greatly influenced world literature.

9. HELEN KELLER (1880–1968)

Blind and deaf from the age of 2, she became a successful lecturer, and the author of 10 books and many other works.

10. JOSEPH PULITZER (1847–1911)

Pulitzer was a journalist, publisher, and congressman who went blind at the age of 40, but continued his various activities during the remaining 24 years of his life. He left large endowments, including one for the Pulitzer prizes.

11. FRANKLIN D. ROOSEVELT (1882–1945)

When he was 39, both of his legs were paralyzed by polio. He became governor of New York State and was elected president of the U.S. four times.

12. CHARLES STEINMETZ (1865–1923)

A hunchback from birth, he was a well-known engineer-inventor (with over 200 patents for General Electric Co.), a professor at Union College, and an author.

13. JAMES THURBER (1894–1961)

After being blinded in one eye in a boyhood accident, he lost the sight of his other eye as an adult. He wrote for *The New Yorker* magazine and worked on plays and books, and produced sketches and cartoons, until the brightest lights and large magnifying glasses could no longer help him.

14. HENRI DE TOULOUSE-LAUTREC (1864–1901)

Deformed and crippled by falls at age 14, his growth was stunted. He was gifted as an artist; his lively lithograph posters of performers at the Moulin Rouge cabaret in Paris gave him enduring fame.

15. HENRY VISCARDI, JR. (b. 1912)

Born without legs, he is the president of the Human Resources Center and founder of Abilities, Inc., with 13 honorary degrees, nine books, and many articles to his credit. He is the chairman of the White House Conference on the Handicapped and director and/or member of numerous organizations.

—F.C.D.

DR. LAURENCE J. PETER'S 10 FAMOUS HISTORICAL PERSONS WHO ROSE TO THEIR LEVEL OF INCOMPETENCE

Author, educator, and consultant, Dr. Peter is best known for his discovery of the "Peter principle"—that an employee in a hierarchy tends to rise to the level of his incompetence. In addition to numerous scholarly articles written for professional journals, Dr. Peter is the author of two best-sellers, *The Peter Principle* (co-authored with Raymond Hull) and *The Peter Prescription*.

1. SOCRATES

A competent teacher who reached his level of incompetence when he became his own defense attorney.

2. JULIUS CAESAR

One of the greatest generals of all time, who was too trusting in his relationships with politicians.

3. NERO

A competent fiddler who achieved his level of incompetence as an administrator.

4. ALEXANDER HAMILTON

A brilliant scholar and financier—although at one time he was jealous of the combat record of his former law partner, Aaron Burr, he later challenged him to a duel.

5. BENEDICT ARNOLD

When his courage and competence as a patriotic officer were not appreciated, he reached his level of ineptitude by shifting allegiance to the British.

6. ULYSSES S. GRANT

Victorious U.S. general of the Union forces in the Civil War, he served two scandal-ridden presidential terms.

7. GEN. GEORGE ARMSTRONG CUSTER

Flamboyant glory seeker who achieved his level of incapacity when he attempted to wipe out an Indian encampment at Little Big Horn.

8. WARREN G. HARDING

A newspaper publisher who became president of the U.S. and gave dirty politics a bad name by surrounding himself with some of the most dishonest and corrupt chiselers of all time.

9. ADOLF HITLER

The consummate politician who found his level of incompetence as a generalissimo.

10. RICHARD M. NIXON

Author of a successful book, *Six Crises,* was later unable to communicate convincingly a simple message such as "I am not a crook."

—Exclusive for *The Book of Lists*

LEON URIS'S 12 GREATEST JEWS OF ALL TIME

Leon Uris, one of the world's most widely read novelists, is best known for *Exodus,* a story of Israel's beginnings. Among Uris's other novels are *Mila 18, QB VII,* and *Trinity.* He lives in Aspen, Colo., with his photographer-wife Jill.

1. Moses	6. Sigmund Freud
2. David	7. David Ben-Gurion
3. Solomon	8. Maimonides
4. Jesus Christ	9. The Rothschilds
5. Albert Einstein	10-12. Karl Marx, Heinrich Heine, Felix Mendelssohn (non-Jewish Jews)

—Exclusive for *The Book of Lists*

STEPHEN BIRMINGHAM'S 10 GREATEST IRISH MEN AND WOMEN IN HISTORY

Best-selling author Stephen Birmingham has written *Our Crowd, The Right People,* and *The Right Places.* His recent book *Real Lace* is a social history of Irish-Americans. He is currently writing a book about the life and times of Samuel Goldwyn.

1. William Butler Yeats	6. Sean O'Casey
2. George Bernard Shaw	7. Al Smith
3. James Joyce	8. Thomas E. Murray, Sr.*
4. Eugene O'Neill	9. John O'Hara
5. John M. Synge	10. Rose Fitzgerald Kennedy

* American engineer and inventor (1860–1929) known for his work with safety appliances.

—Exclusive for *The Book of Lists*

30 RENOWNED REDHEADS

1. Lucille Ball, U.S. actress and comedienne
2. Sarah Bernhardt, French actress
3. Lizzie Borden, American acquitted of murder
4. Winston Churchill, British prime minister
5. Oliver Cromwell, British lord protector
6. George Armstrong Custer, U.S. general
7. Emily Dickinson, U.S. poet
8. Elizabeth I, queen of England
9. Arthur Godfrey, U.S. TV personality
10. Harold "Red" Grange, U.S. football hero
11. Henry VIII, king of England

12. Katharine Hepburn, U.S. actress
13. Thomas Jefferson, U.S. president
14. Rod Laver, Australian tennis champion
15. Sinclair Lewis, U.S. novelist and playwright
16. Napoleon, French emperor
17. Nero, Roman emperor
18. Ignace Jan Paderewski, Polish pianist and statesman
19. Walter Reuther, U.S. labor union leader
20. Salome, biblical dancer
21. Margaret Sanger, U.S. feminist and birth-control advocate
22. William Shakespeare, British playwright and poet
23. George Bernard Shaw, British playwright
24. Beverly Sills, U.S. opera star
25. Svetlana Stalin, Russian writer, daughter of Joseph Stalin
26. Titian, Italian painter
27. Mark Twain, U.S. author and humorist
28. Martin Van Buren, U.S. president
29. George Washington, U.S. president
30. William the Conqueror, king of England

234 PEOPLE BORN THE SAME DAY, MONTH, AND YEAR

CAPRICORN (Dec. 22–Jan. 20)

Dec. 24, 1907	Cab Calloway (singer) and I. F. Stone (journalist)
Dec. 31, 1943	John Denver (singer) and Sarah Miles (actress)
Jan. 1, 1879	E. M. Forster (writer) and William Fox (film studio executive)
Jan. 1, 1909	Dana Andrews (actor) and Barry Goldwater (U.S. senator)
Jan. 6, 1920	Sun Myung Moon (evangelist) and Early Wynn (baseball player)
Jan. 9, 1941	Joan Baez (singer) and Susannah York (actress)
Jan. 10, 1883	Francis X. Bushman (actor) and Florence Reed (actress)
Jan. 17, 1863	David Lloyd George (British statesman) and Konstantin Stanislavski (drama coach)

AQUARIUS (Jan. 21–Feb. 19)

Jan. 22, 1909	Ann Sothern (actress) and U Thant (U.N. official)
Jan. 26, 1928	Eartha Kitt (singer) and Roger Vadim (film director)
Jan. 30, 1937	Vanessa Redgrave (actress) and Boris Spassky (chess player)
Jan. 31, 1923	Carol Channing (actress), Joanne Dru (actress), and Norman Mailer (writer)

Labor leader Jimmy Hoffa and clergyman James Pike:
Both born on February 14, 1913; both disappeared.

Feb. 2, 1923	James Dickey (writer) and Red Schoendienst (baseball manager)
Feb. 5, 1848	J. K. Huysmans (writer) and Belle Starr (horse thief)
Feb. 5, 1919	Red Buttons (comedian) and Andreas Papandreou (Greek politician)
Feb. 9, 1914	Carmen Miranda (singer), Ernest Tubb (country singer), and Bill Veeck (baseball team president)
Feb. 10, 1893	Jimmy Durante (comedian) and Bill Tilden (tennis player)
Feb. 10, 1898	Judith Anderson (actress) and Bertolt Brecht (playwright)
Feb. 11, 1925	Eva Gabor (actress) and Virginia E. Johnson (sexologist)
Feb. 11, 1934	Tina Louise (actress) and Mary Quant (fashion designer)
Feb. 12, 1809	Charles Darwin (naturalist) and Abraham Lincoln (U.S. president)
Feb. 12, 1926	Joe Garagiola (TV star) and Charles Van Doren (academician)
Feb. 14, 1913	Mel Allen (sportscaster), Jimmy Hoffa (labor leader), and James Pike (clergyman)
Feb. 18, 1920	Bill Cullen (TV personality) and Jack Palance (actor)

PISCES (Feb. 20–Mar. 20)

Feb. 22, 1900	Luis Buñuel (filmmaker) and Seán O'Faoláin (writer)
Mar. 1, 1917	Robert Lowell (poet) and Dinah Shore (singer)
Mar. 9, 1918	George Lincoln Rockwell (U.S. Nazi leader) and Mickey Spillane (writer)
Mar. 14, 1933	Michael Caine (actor) and Quincy Jones (jazz musician)

Mar. 17, 1938	Rudolph Nureyev (ballet dancer) and Monique Van Vooren (actress)
Mar. 20, 1922	Ray Goulding (comedian) and Carl Reiner (comedian)

ARIES (Mar. 21–Apr. 19)

Mar. 30, 1913	Richard Helms (former U.S. government official) and Frankie Laine (singer)
Mar. 31, 1926	Sydney Chaplin (actor) and John Fowles (writer)
Mar. 31, 1935	Herb Alpert (bandleader) and Richard Chamberlain (actor)
Apr. 3, 1898	George Jessel (actor) and Henry R. Luce (publisher)
Apr. 3, 1924	Marlon Brando (actor) and Doris Day (actress)
Apr. 3, 1942	Marsha Mason (actress) and Wayne Newton (singer)
Apr. 4, 1922	Robert Abplanalp (financier) and Elmer Bernstein (composer)
Apr. 5, 1908	Bette Davis (actress) and Mary Hemingway (writer)
Apr. 6, 1866	Butch Cassidy (outlaw) and Lincoln Steffens (writer)
Apr. 7, 1939	Francis Ford Coppola (filmmaker) and David Frost (TV personality)
Apr. 9, 1895	Mance Lipscomb (blues musician) and Michel Simon (actor)
Apr. 9, 1905	Ward Bond (actor) and J. William Fulbright (former U.S. senator)
Apr. 16, 1904	Clifford Case (U.S. senator) and Lily Pons (opera diva)

TAURUS (Apr. 20–May 20)

Apr. 29, 1947	Johnny Miller (golfer) and Jim Ryun (runner)
May 6, 1856	Sigmund Freud (psychoanalyst) and Robert Peary (arctic explorer)
May 6, 1902	Harry Golden (writer) and Max Ophuls (film director)
May 6, 1915	Orson Welles (actor and film director) and T. H. White (writer)
May 8, 1895	Fulton J. Sheen (clergyman) and Edmund Wilson (critic)
May 9, 1936	Albert Finney (actor) and Glenda Jackson (actress)
May 12, 1925	Yogi Berra (baseball player) and John Simon (critic)
May 17, 1911	Clark Kerr (educator) and Maureen O'Sullivan (actress)
May 20, 1908	James Stewart (actor) and "Commander" Edward Whitehead (soft-drink executive)

GEMINI (May 21–June 21)

May 21, 1904	Robert Montgomery (actor) and Fats Waller (jazz musician)
May 21, 1917	Raymond Burr (actor) and Dennis Day (singer)
May 25, 1898	Bennett Cerf (publisher) and Gene Tunney (boxer)
May 27, 1911	Hubert Humphrey (U.S. senator) and Vincent Price (actor)

May 27, 1912	John Cheever (writer) and Sam Snead (golfer)
June 1, 1926	Andy Griffith (actor) and Marilyn Monroe (actress)
June 2, 1941	Stacy Keach (actor) and Charlie Watts (rock musician)
June 3, 1926	Colleen Dewhurst (actress) and Allen Ginsberg (poet)
June 9, 1916	Robert McNamara (U.S. government official) and Les Paul (singer)
June 18, 1913	Sammy Cahn (songwriter) and Sylvia Porter (columnist)
June 20, 1924	Chet Atkins (guitarist) and Audie Murphy (actor)

CANCER (June 22–July 21)

June 22, 1906	Anne Morrow Lindbergh (writer) and Billy Wilder (film director)
June 23, 1894	Alfred Kinsey (sexologist) and the duke of Windsor (former king of England)
June 30, 1917	Lena Horne (singer) and Buddy Rich (drummer)
July 1, 1942	Karen Black (actress) and Genevieve Bujold (actress)
July 2, 1925	Medgar Evers (black leader) and Patrice Lumumba (Congolese premier)
July 4, 1902	Meyer Lansky (mobster) and George Murphy (actor)
July 4, 1918	Ann Landers (columnist) and Abigail Van Buren (columnist)
July 4, 1928	Steven Boyd (actor) and Gina Lollobrigida (actress)
July 12, 1895	Kirsten Flagstad (Wagnerian soprano), Buckminster Fuller (engineer and writer), and Oscar Hammerstein II (songwriter)
July 17, 1917	Lou Boudreau (baseball player) and Phyllis Diller (comedienne)
July 18, 1906	S. I. Hayakawa (U.S. educator and senator) and Clifford Odets (dramatist)
July 20, 1938	Diana Rigg (actress) and Natalie Wood (actress)
July 21, 1899	Hart Crane (writer) and Ernest Hemingway (writer)

LEO (July 22–Aug. 21)

July 22, 1898	Stephen Vincent Benét (writer) and Alexander Calder (sculptor)
July 28, 1943	Mike Bloomfield (blues musician) and Bill Bradley (basketball player)
July 29, 1905	Clara Bow (actress), Dag Hammarskjöld (U.N. secretary-general), and Thelma Todd (actress)
Aug. 2, 1924	James Baldwin (writer) and Carroll O'Connor (actor)
Aug. 10, 1928	Jimmy Dean (singer) and Eddie Fisher (singer)
Aug. 15, 1912	Julia Child (cookbook writer and TV personality) and Wendy Hiller (actress)
Aug. 16, 1930	Robert Culp (actor) and Frank Gifford (sportscaster)
Aug. 21, 1936	Wilt Chamberlain (basketball player) and Mart Crowley (playwright)

VIRGO (Aug. 22–Sept. 22)

Aug. 24, 1872	Aubrey Beardsley (artist) and Max Beerbohm (writer)
Aug. 25, 1909	Ruby Keeler (dancer) and Michael Rennie (actor)
Aug. 29, 1916	Ingrid Bergman (actress) and George Montgomery (actor)
Aug. 30, 1901	John Gunther (writer) and Roy Wilkins (black leader)
Aug. 30, 1943	R. Crumb (cartoonist) and Jean-Claude Killy (skier)
Aug. 31, 1918	Alan Jay Lerner (songwriter) and Ted Williams (baseball player)
Aug. 31, 1935	Eldridge Cleaver (writer and former Black Panther party advocate and recent religious convert) and Frank Robinson (baseball coach)
Sept. 1, 1922	Yvonne DeCarlo (actress), Vittorio Gassman (actor), and Melvin Laird (U.S. government official)
Sept. 2, 1918	Allen Drury (writer) and Martha Mitchell (Watergate celebrity)
Sept. 16, 1925	Charlie Byrd (guitarist) and B. B. King (blues singer and musician)
Sept. 18, 1905	Eddie Anderson (actor) and Greta Garbo (actress)
Sept. 19, 1926	Duke Snider (baseball player) and Lurleen Wallace (U.S. governor)

LIBRA (Sept. 23–Oct. 22)

Oct. 1, 1928	George Peppard (actor) and Laurence Harvey (actor)
Oct. 5, 1923	Philip Berrigan (militant priest) and Glynis Johns (actress)
Oct. 9, 1940	John Lennon (rock musician) and Joe Pepitone (baseball player)
Oct. 10, 1930	Harold Pinter (playwright) and Adlai Stevenson III (U.S. senator)
Oct. 22, 1925	Dory Previn (songwriter) and Robert Rauschenberg (artist)

SCORPIO (Oct. 23–Nov. 21)

Nov. 5, 1941	Art Garfunkel (singer) and Elke Sommer (actress)
Nov. 9, 1918	Spiro Agnew (U.S. vice-president) and Florence Chadwick (swimmer)
Nov. 11, 1904	Alger Hiss (onetime U.S. government official) and Sam Spiegel (film producer)
Nov. 15, 1887	Marianne Moore (poet) and Georgia O'Keeffe (painter)
Nov. 15, 1891	W. Averell Harriman (U.S. government official) and Erwin Rommel (German field marshal)
Nov. 20, 1925	Robert Kennedy (U.S. attorney general) and Maya Plisetskaya (prima ballerina)

SAGITTARIUS (Nov. 22–Dec. 21)

Nov. 29, 1933	John Mayall (blues singer) and David Reuben (physician and writer)

Nov. 30, 1924	Shirley Chisholm (U.S. representative) and Allan Sherman (comedian)
Dec. 1, 1935	Woody Allen (comedian) and Lou Rawls (singer)
Dec. 2, 1915	Adolph Green (songwriter) and William Randolph Hearst, Jr. (publisher)
Dec. 3, 1930	Jean-Luc Godard (filmmaker) and Andy Williams (singer)
Dec. 9, 1911	Lee J. Cobb (actor) and Broderick Crawford (actor)
Dec. 14, 1935	Abbe Lane (singer) and Lee Remick (actress)

—M.G.R. & D.W.

2

AMERICA THE BEAUTIFUL

30 GOOD PLACES TO LIVE—AND 30 NOT-SO-GOOD PLACES TO LIVE

In 1975 the Midwest Research Institute of Kansas City, Mo., published the results of a study to determine the relative "quality of life" in 243 urban areas. The final rankings are based on the compilation of 120 statistical factors concerning economics, crime, housing, pollution, weather, recreational facilities, health, education, racial and sexual equality, etc. In the first three lists, the cities—some of whose urban areas spill over into neighboring states—are ranked from 1 to 10, with the best as number 1. But in the lists of not-so-good places to live, the cities are ranked from 10 to 1, with the worst as number 10.

30 GOOD PLACES TO LIVE

Over 500,000 People

1. Portland, Ore.-Wash.
2. Sacramento, Calif.
3. Seattle-Everett, Wash.
4. San Jose, Calif.
5. Minneapolis-St. Paul, Minn.
6. Rochester, N.Y.
7. Hartford, Conn.
8. Denver, Colo.
9. San Francisco-Oakland, Calif.
10. San Diego, Calif.

Portland Ore., has the highest "quality of life"
rating of any large city in the U.S.

200,000–500,000 People

1. Eugene, Ore.
2. Madison, Wis.
3. Appleton-Oshkosh, Wis.
4. Santa Barbara, Calif.
5. Stamford, Conn.
6. Des Moines, Ia.
7. Lansing, Mich.
8. Kalamazoo, Mich.
9. Fort Wayne, Ind.
10. Ann Arbor, Mich.

Less Than 200,000 People

1. La Crosse, Wis.
2. Rochester, Minn.
3. Lincoln, Neb.
4. Topeka, Kans.
5. Green Bay, Wis.
6. Ogden, U.
7. Norwalk, Conn.
8. Sioux Falls, S.D.
9. Fargo, N.D.; Moorhead, Minn.
10. Bristol, Conn.

30 NOT-SO-GOOD PLACES TO LIVE

Over 500,000 People

10. Jersey City, N.J.
9. Birmingham, Ala.
8. New Orleans, La.
7. San Antonio, Tex.
6. Jacksonville, Fla.
5. Greensboro-Winston-Salem-High Point, N.C.
4. Norfolk-Portsmouth, Va.
3. Memphis, Tenn.-Ark.
2. Philadelphia, Pa.-N.J.
1. Tampa-St. Petersburg, Fla.

200,000–500,000 People

10. Mobile, Ala.
9. Charleston, S.C.
8. Macon, Ga.
7. Montgomery, Ala.
6. Columbus, Ga.-Ala.
5. Fayetteville, N.C.
4. Greenville, S.C.
3. Columbia, S.C.
2. Huntington, W.Va.; Ashland, Ky.
1. Augusta, Ga.-S.C.

Less Than 200,000 People

10. Laredo, Tex.
9. Pine Bluff, Ark.
8. McAllen-Pharr-Edinburg, Tex.
7. Fort Smith, Ark.-Okla.
6. Lawton, Okla.
5. Brownsville-Harlingen-San Benito, Tex.
4. Albany, Ga.
3. Tuscaloosa, Ala.
2. Savannah, Ga.
1. Gadsden, Ala.

SOURCE: *Quality of Life in the U.S. Metropolitan Areas, 1970* (Summary), by Ben-Chieh Liu (Kansas City, Mo.: Midwest Research Institute, 1975).

12 WINDIEST CITIES IN THE U.S.

Is Chicago, Ill., the Windy City, actually the windiest? Have a look. Here the National Climatic Center, U.S. Weather Bureau, ranks the leaders.

Average Wind Speed (mph)

1.	Great Falls, Mont.	13.1
2.	Oklahoma City, Okla.	13.0
3.	Boston, Mass.	12.9
4.	Cheyenne, Wyo.	12.8
5.	Wichita, Kans.	12.7
6.	Buffalo, N.Y.	12.4
7.	Milwaukee, Wis.	11.8
8.	Des Moines, Ia.	11.2
9.	Providence, R.I.	10.9
9.	Omaha, Neb.	10.9
9.	Dallas, Tex.	10.9
9.	Cleveland, O.	10.9

Becalmed Chicago ranks 16th, with a mere 10.4 mph.

—J.E.

7 MOST POPULAR NATURAL ATTRACTIONS IN THE U.S.

1. The Grand Canyon, Arizona
2. Yellowstone National Park, Wyoming
3. Niagara Falls, N.Y.
4. Mount McKinley, Alaska
5. California's "Big Trees": the sequoias and redwoods
6. Hawaii's volcanoes
7. Florida's Everglades

SOURCE: Poll of travel industry agents, U.S. Travel Service (Dept. of Commerce), 1975.

7 MOST POPULAR MAN-MADE ATTRACTIONS IN THE U.S.

1. Golden Gate Bridge, San Francisco, Calif.
2. Mount Rushmore National Memorial, South Dakota
3. Astrodome sports and convention center, Houston, Tex.
4. Statue of Liberty, New York Harbor
5. Hoover Dam, Arizona-Nevada
6. Walt Disney World, Lake Buena Vista, Fla.
7. Gateway Arch, St. Louis, Mo.

SOURCE: Poll of travel industry agents, U.S. Travel Service (Dept. of Commerce), 1975.

10 MOST POPULOUS INDIAN TRIBES IN THE U.S. AND CANADA

		U.S.	Canada	Total
1.	Navaho	96,743	—	96,743
2.	Chippewa	41,946	50,431	92,377
3.	Cree	2,169	70,403	72,572
4.	Cherokee	66,150	—	66,150
5.	Sioux	47,825	5,153	52,978
6.	Iroquois	21,473	21,263	42,736
7.	Pueblo	30,971	—	30,971
8.	Lummi	27,520	—	27,520
9.	Puget Sound Salish	2,810	20,989	23,799
10.	Choctaw	23,562	—	23,562

SOURCE: *Akwesasne Notes*, Autumn, 1973.

10 TOP AMERICAN ARABS —OR DIDN'T YOU KNOW?

"Arab," according to Ibrahim Abu-Lughod, professor of political science at Northwestern University, "is a cultural, not a racial or religious designation and it applies to anyone who is from an Arabic-speaking country and the product of Arab culture." There are 1 million to 2 million persons in the U.S. of Arab ancestry, 100,000 of them in Detroit alone. Here are 10 famous Arab-Americans.

1. Robert Abboud, vice-chairman, First National Bank, Chicago
2. James Abourezk, U.S. senator (S.D.)
3. Paul Anka, popular singer
4. William Peter Blatty, author of *The Exorcist*
5. Dr. Michael E. De Bakey, renowned heart surgeon
6. Abe Gibron, former football coach of Chicago Bears
7. Najeeb E. Halaby, former chairman of Pan American World Airways, Inc.
8. Ralph Nader, consumer advocate
9. Joe Robbie, owner of the Miami Dolphins football team
10. Danny Thomas, actor and entertainer

—T.W.

15 NOTED FOREIGN-BORN AMERICANS

1. JOHN JAMES AUDUBON

Painter, naturalist, ornithologist, and inceptor of the National Audubon Society. Born in Cayes, Haiti, on April 26, 1785; came to the U.S. in 1803.

2. ALEXANDER GRAHAM BELL

Inventor of the telephone. Born in Edinburgh, Scotland, on March 3, 1847; came to the U.S. in 1871.

3. IRVING BERLIN (Israel Baline)

Composer of popular music. Born in Temun, Russia, on May 11, 1888; came to the U.S. in 1893.

4. ANDREW CARNEGIE

Steel industry magnate, millionaire, and philanthropist. Born in Dunfermline, Scotland, on November 25, 1835; came to the U.S. in 1848.

5. ALBERT EINSTEIN

Physicist who revolutionized science with his theories of relativity. Born in Ulm, Germany, on March 14, 1879; came to the U.S. in 1933.

6. SAMUEL GOMPERS

Labor leader, founder and first president of American Federation of Labor. Born in London on January 27, 1850; came to the U.S. in 1863.

7. JAMES J. HILL

Railroad entrepreneur, owner of the Great Northern Railway Co. and the Northern Pacific Railroad. Born near Rockwood, Ont., Canada, on September 16, 1838; came to the U.S. c. 1856.

8. ALFRED HITCHCOCK

Film director. Born in London on August 13, 1899; came to the U.S. in 1939.

9. HENRY KISSINGER

U.S. secretary of state. Born in Furth, Germany, on May 27, 1923; came to the U.S. in 1938.

Rodolpho Alfonzo Rafaelo Pierre Filibert Guglielmi di Valentina d'Antonguolla migrated from Castellaneta, Italy, to the United States at 18—to become Rudolph Valentino in Hollywood.

10. JOHN MUIR

Naturalist, explorer, and conservation advocate. Born in Dunbar, Scotland, on April 21, 1838; came to the U.S. in 1849.

11. THOMAS PAINE

Revolutionist and author of *Common Sense*. Born in Thetford, England, on January 29, 1737; came to America in 1774.

12. JOSEPH PULITZER

Journalist, publisher, and founder of Pulitzer prizes. Born in Budapest, Hungary, on April 10, 1847; came to the U.S. in 1864.

13. KNUTE ROCKNE

Football hero and coach at Notre Dame University. Born in Voss, Norway, on March 4, 1888; came to the U.S. in 1893.

14. RUDOLPH VALENTINO

Silent-film actor. Born in Castellaneta, Italy, on May 6, 1895; came to the U.S. in 1913.

15. WERNHER VON BRAUN

Engineer and scientist who helped to develop German V-2 rockets and American guided missiles. Born in Wirsitz, Germany, on March 23, 1912; came to the U.S. in 1945.

—R.J.F.

15 LEADING SOURCES
OF NEWCOMERS TO THE U.S.

(based on immigrants legally admitted to U.S. in 1975)

1.	Mexico	62,205
2.	Philippines	31,751
3.	S. Korea	28,362
4.	Cuba	25,955
5.	Republic of China (Taiwan)	18,536
6.	India	15,773
7.	Dominican Republic	14,066
8.	Portugal	11,845
9.	Italy	11,552
10.	Jamaica	11,076
11.	United Kingdom	10,807
12.	Greece	9,984
13.	Canada	7,308
14.	Colombia	6,434
15.	Trinidad and Tobago	5,982

SOURCE: U.S. Immigration and Naturalization Service.

THE AP POLL OF
THE 20 MOST IMPORTANT
EVENTS IN AMERICAN HISTORY

What were the leading front-page stories in the history of the U.S. between 1776 and 1976? The Associated Press took a poll of newspaper editors and radio and television news directors. The 273 respondents ranked the big events in descending order of importance.

1. The American Revolution
2. Drafting of the U.S. Constitution
3. The Civil War
4. World War II
5. The U.S. moon landings
6. Development of the atomic bomb
7. The 1929 crash and the ensuing Great Depression
8. Watergate and the resignation of Richard M. Nixon
9. World War I
10. Henry Ford, the Model T, and the rise of the automobile
11. Abraham Lincoln's assassination
12. The development of television
13. The assassination of President Kennedy
14. Thomas Edison and the electrification of the nation
15. Vietnam
16. Franklin D. Roosevelt's New Deal
17. The changing role of women
18. The Wright brothers and the growth of aviation
19. The Louisiana Purchase
20. The 1954 Supreme Court decision outlawing segregation in U.S. schools

SOURCE: By permission of The Associated Press.

RANKING OF
31 U.S. PRESIDENTS

In 1962, Professor Arthur M. Schlesinger, Sr., chaired a group of 75 historian-observers of the presidency who evaluated 31 presidents and ranked them in categories ranging from "great" to "failures." Omitted from the list because of their brief presidential tenure were William Henry Harrison (one month in office) and James A. Garfield (six months in office); also omitted, of course, are the presidents after Dwight D. Eisenhower.

GREAT

1. Abraham Lincoln
2. George Washington
3. Franklin D. Roosevelt
4. Woodrow Wilson
5. Thomas Jefferson

NEAR GREAT

6. Andrew Jackson
7. Theodore Roosevelt
8. James K. Polk
9. Harry S Truman
10. John Adams
11. Grover Cleveland

AVERAGE

12. James Madison
13. John Quincy Adams
14. Rutherford B. Hayes
15. William McKinley

16. William Howard Taft
17. Martin Van Buren
18. James Monroe
19. Herbert Hoover
20. Benjamin Harrison
21. Chester A. Arthur
22. Dwight D. Eisenhower
23. Andrew Johnson

BELOW AVERAGE

24. Zachary Taylor
25. John Tyler
26. Millard Fillmore
27. Calvin Coolidge
28. Franklin Pierce
29. James Buchanan

FAILURES

30. Ulysses S. Grant
31. Warren G. Harding

THE HARRIS SURVEY
RATES LAST 7 U.S. PRESIDENTS

In March, 1976, Louis Harris published a poll revealing the American public's opinion about the last seven U.S. presidents. His nationwide sampling of 1,512 adults resulted in the following ranking of overall presidential performance:

1. Franklin D. Roosevelt
2. John F. Kennedy
3. Harry S Truman
4. Dwight D. Eisenhower
5. Gerald R. Ford
5. Lyndon B. Johnson
5. Richard M. Nixon

The poll also covered questions about presidential stature in more specific areas. These areas included:

1. Most Inspired Confidence: Kennedy first; Ford, L. B. Johnson, and Nixon tied for last
2. Most Personally Appealing: Kennedy first; Ford, L. B. Johnson, and Nixon tied for last
3. Best in Domestic Affairs: F. D. Roosevelt first; Nixon last
4. Best Administrator: Kennedy first; Ford and Nixon tied for last
5. Best in Foreign Affairs: Nixon first; Ford last
6. Set Highest Moral Standards: Eisenhower first; Nixon last

It is interesting to note that in the aftermath of Watergate, Nixon was in last place in four out of five categories but still scored highest in foreign affairs. It is worth mentioning that there was a definite breakdown according to age: Those under 30 overwhelmingly opted for John F. Kennedy as "best" in all categories, while those over 50 supported Franklin D. Roosevelt by the same margin.

13 PRESIDENTS WHO WON WITH LESS THAN 50% OF THE VOTE

	Candidates	Popular Vote	% of Popular Vote
1824	JOHN QUINCY ADAMS	108,740	30.5
	Andrew Jackson	153,544	43.1
	Henry Clay	47,136	13.0
	William H. Crawford	46,979	12.9
1844	JAMES K. POLK	1,338,464	49.6
	Henry Clay	1,300,097	48.1
	James G. Birney	62,300	2.3
1848	ZACHARY TAYLOR	1,360,967	47.4
	Lewis Cass	1,222,342	42.5
	Martin Van Buren	291,263	10.1
1856	JAMES BUCHANAN	1,832,955	45.3
	John C. Frémont	1,339,932	33.1
	Millard Fillmore	871,731	21.6
1860	ABRAHAM LINCOLN	1,865,593	39.8
	Stephen A. Douglas	1,382,713	29.5
	John C. Breckenridge	848,356	18.1
	John Bell	592,906	12.6
1876	RUTHERFORD B. HAYES	4,036,572	48.0
	Samuel Tilden	4,284,020	51.0
1880	JAMES A. GARFIELD	4,453,295	48.5
	Winfield Hancock	4,414,082	48.1
	James B. Weaver	308,578	3.4
1884	GROVER CLEVELAND	4,879,507	48.5
	James G. Blaine	4,850,293	48.2
	Benjamin F. Butler	175,370	1.8
	John P. St. John	150,369	1.5

1888	BENJAMIN HARRISON	5,447,129	47.9
	Grover Cleveland	5,537,857	48.6
	Clinton B. Fisk	249,506	2.2
	Anson J. Streeter	146,935	1.3
1892	GROVER CLEVELAND	5,555,426	46.1
	Benjamin Harrison	5,182,690	43.0
	James B. Weaver	1,029,846	8.5
	John Bidwell	264,133	2.2
1912	WOODROW WILSON	6,296,547	41.9
	Theodore Roosevelt	4,118,571	27.4
	William Howard Taft	3,486,720	23.2
	Eugene V. Debs	900,672	6.0
	Eugene W. Chafin	206,275	1.4
1916	WOODROW WILSON	9,127,695	49.4
	Charles Evans Hughes	8,533,507	46.2
	A. L. Benson	585,113	3.2
	J. Frank Hanly	220,506	1.2
1948	HARRY S TRUMAN	24,105,812	49.5
	Thomas E. Dewey	21,970,065	45.1
	J. Strom Thurmond	1,169,063	2.4
	Henry Wallace	1,157,172	2.4
1960	JOHN F. KENNEDY	34,227,096	49.9
	Richard M. Nixon	34,108,546	49.6
	Harry F. Byrd	440,298	0.6
1968	RICHARD M. NIXON	31,785,480	43.4
	Hubert Humphrey	31,275,165	42.7
	George Wallace	9,906,473	13.5

Note: In the 1976 presidential election, Jimmy Carter won with 50.06% of the popular vote.

IRVING STONE'S
10 LOSERS WHO WOULD HAVE
MADE BETTER PRESIDENTS
THAN THE WINNERS

Best-selling biographical novelist Irving Stone has drawn to life such notables as Michelangelo (*The Agony and the Ecstasy*) and Vincent van Gogh (*Lust for Life*). Among his widely read nonfiction works is *They Also Ran,* a study of defeated presidential candidates.

1. Hubert Humphrey over Richard M. Nixon (1968)
2. Alfred E. Smith over Herbert Hoover (1928)
3. John W. Davis over Calvin Coolidge (1924)
4. James M. Cox over Warren G. Harding (1920)
5. Winfield Hancock over James A. Garfield (1880)
6. Samuel J. Tilden over Rutherford B. Hayes (1876)
7. Horatio Seymour over Ulysses S. Grant (1868)
8. John C. Frémont over James Buchanan (1856)
9. Winfield Scott over Franklin Pierce (1852)
10. Lewis Cass over Zachary Taylor (1848)

—Exclusive for *The Book of Lists*

5 PORTRAITS
ON HIGHEST-DENOMINATION
U.S. PAPER CURRENCY

	Denomination
1. Woodrow Wilson, 28th president	$100,000
2. Salmon P. Chase, secretary of the treasury (1861–1864), chief justice of the Supreme Court (1864–1873)	10,000
3. James Madison, fourth president	5,000
4. Grover Cleveland, 22nd and 24th president	1,000
5. William McKinley, 25th president	500

The largest denomination in American currency is not circulated publicly.

13 FAMOUS AMERICAN LAWYERS WHO NEVER WENT TO LAW SCHOOL

1. Patrick Henry (1736–1799), member of the Continental Congress, governor of Virginia
2. John Jay (1745–1829), first chief justice of the Supreme Court
3. John Marshall (1755–1835), chief justice of the Supreme Court
4. William Wirt (1772–1834), attorney general
5. Roger B. Taney (1777–1864), secretary of the treasury, chief justice of the Supreme Court
6. Daniel Webster (1782–1852), secretary of state
7. Salmon P. Chase (1808–1873), senator, chief justice of the Supreme Court
8. Abraham Lincoln (1809–1865), president
9. Stephen Douglas (1813–1861), representative, senator from Illinois
10. Clarence Darrow (1857–1938), defense attorney in Scopes trial of 1925*
11. Robert Storey (b. 1893), president of the American Bar Association (1952–1953)
12. J. Strom Thurmond (b. 1902), senator, governor of South Carolina
13. James O. Eastland (b. 1904), senator from Mississippi

* While Clarence Darrow attended a law school for one year, he did not distinguish himself and preferred to study law on his own. He received the greater part of his education in a law office in Youngstown, O.

—C.H.

Clarence Darrow made headline news with his defense of evolution in the famous Monkey Trial of 1925.

14 U.S. GENERALS
RANKED IN THEIR WEST POINT
GRADUATING CLASSES

	Year Graduated	Rank
1. Creighton Abrams	1936	185th of 276
2. Omar Bradley	1915	44th of 168
3. George Armstrong Custer	1861	35th of 35
4. Jefferson Davis	1828	23rd of 33
5. Dwight D. Eisenhower	1915	61st of 168
6. Ulysses S. Grant	1843	21st of 39
7. Alexander Haig	1947	167th of 313
8. Robert E. Lee	1829	2nd of 46
9. Douglas MacArthur	1903	1st of 93
10. Benjamin McClellan	1903	55th of 93
11. George S. Patton	1909	46th of 103
12. John J. Pershing	1896	30th of 77
13. William Tecumseh Sherman	1840	6th of 42
14. William C. Westmoreland	1936	112th of 276

—A.B.

2 NOTABLE MEN
WHO DROPPED OUT OR WERE
THROWN OUT OF WEST POINT

1. EDGAR ALLAN POE (class of 1834)

Short-story writer and poet. Expelled for "gross neglect of duty" and "disobedience of orders" on March 6, 1831.

2. TIMOTHY LEARY (class of 1943)

Psychologist, educator, and LSD advocate. Dropped out in 1941 and entered the University of Alabama.

—P.S.H.

9 OUTSTANDING WINNERS OF THE CONGRESSIONAL MEDAL OF HONOR

The U.S. Congressional Medal of Honor has been awarded to 3,357 people since 1862, including 1 woman, 1 father and son, and 19 men who won 2 medals each.

The Congressional Medal of Honor is the highest military award for bravery in the U.S. It was first conceived by Adjutant Gen. Edward Townsend in 1861 and authorized by joint acts of Congress—the navy's medal in 1861 and the army's in 1862. The medal has had a colorful and turbulent history which has culminated in the requirement that its recipients display "bravery or self-sacrifice above and beyond the call of duty." Apart from the honor it conveys, its recipients can often obtain free military transportation, a 10% raise in retirement pay, and a special pension of $100 per month. Also, sons of Congressional Medal of Honor winners are eligible to enter U.S. military academies on a nonquota basis. As of the end of the Vietnam War, 3,376 medals had been awarded, including 1 to a woman, 19 to individuals who won medals twice, and 1 each to a father and son: Arthur MacArthur and his son Douglas MacArthur.

1. ANDREWS'S RAIDING PARTY (Civil War)

The first awards of the Congressional Medal of Honor went to the 6 surviving members of a group of 21 volunteers who, in April,

1862, penetrated almost 300 mi. into Confederate territory and captured a rebel train at Big Shanty, Ga. After a frantic railroad chase, they were captured by Confederate cavalry. Seven, including the party's leader, James J. Andrews, were executed. Eight others escaped in October, 1862. The remaining 6 were paroled in March, 1863, returned to Washington, and received the Medal of Honor, as well as a cash award of $100 each.

2. LT. COL. COUNT LUIGI PALMA DE CESNOLA (Civil War)

This fiery Italian was arrested and placed under guard before the battle of Aldie in June, 1863, after he had challenged an upstart (who had been promoted over him) to a duel. When the battle commenced, de Cesnola's regiment refused to fight without their leader. Realizing the predicament, the Italian ignored his guards, raced to the head of his troops, and—unarmed—led them in three gallant charges. Before the fourth charge, General Kilpatrick, who had arrested him, rode forward and handed de Cesnola his sword. De Cesnola was felled and captured in this charge, but later he was exchanged and fought again in the Shenandoah campaign.

3. MAJ. HARRY E. TREMAIN (Civil War)

A member of the U.S. Volunteers at Resaca, Ga., Tremain distinguished himself in 1864 by riding the length of the front between two Union brigades which were firing at each other, each believing the other to be the enemy. They were so intent upon shooting one another, and so oblivious to Tremain's cries, that he had to ride along the first ranks, knocking aside their muskets with his sword.

4. 1ST LT. MARION P. MAUS (Indian wars)

Maus was second in command of a raiding party of 100 Apache scouts sent by Gen. George Crook into Mexico to capture Geronimo. The leader of the expedition, Capt. Emmet Crawford, was wearied by the long journey, and it was Maus who led the attack when Geronimo's camp was finally found. In this battle, Geronimo and his men escaped, but their supplies were burned and the Apache women were captured and raped. Geronimo doubled back and was persuaded to meet with Gen. Crook to negotiate the release of the captured women and children. The old renegade crossed back into American territory where he spent the rest of his life in army custody. In 1886, Lt. Maus was awarded the Medal of Honor for his role in the affair.

5. PVT. JOSEPH DALY (China relief expedition)

On August 15, 1900—during the battle of Peking (Boxer Rebellion)—Private Daly, a marine, volunteered for an extraordinary mission. One flank of the American position had been exposed, and Daly's job was to keep away the encroaching Chinese while a barricade could be erected. Daly crawled forward alone along the Tartar Wall (100 yds. away from the rest of the troops) and single-handedly, with rifle blast, bayonet, and rifle butt, managed to protect the company. Not one Chinese got by him that night, and in the morning, the barrier erected, Daly was surrounded by the bodies of men he had killed. Later, Daly received another Medal of Honor—this in the Haitian campaign, and he was also recommended for a third.

6. SGT. ALVIN YORK (W.W. I)

York is probably the most famous of all Medal of Honor winners. His feat at Hill 223 in Argonne was indeed remarkable. Born and raised a backwoodsman, York's experience as a Tennessee fox hunter paid off in full on October 8, 1918, when he single-handedly shot and killed 28 Germans, thus persuading the rest of the enemy battalion (132 in all) to surrender. Upon returning to the U.S., York was treated to a ticker-tape parade in New York City and a suite at the Waldorf Astoria. He returned to his home county in Tennessee where the hero's welcome continued. York earned a considerable sum of money on the lecture circuit, most of which he put into the York Agricultural Institute. In 1941, Hollywood made a movie, *Sergeant York*, based on his life. The institute's share was over $200,000. In 1954, York was stricken with a cerebral hemorrhage. Not sympathetic to his condition, the IRS claimed he owed $25,000 in back taxes.

7. 1ST LT. AUDIE LEON MURPHY (W.W. II)

The U.S. awarded seven medals for heroism during W.W. II; Murphy won five. The other two medals were for extraordinary service not under combat conditions. Murphy was the most decorated soldier in the history of the U.S. The baby-faced recruit from Farmersville, Tex., who had to beg his way into the infantry and beg again for an overseas assignment, earned his Medal of Honor outside Holtzwihr, France, on January 25, 1945. With his company hopelessly outnumbered, and both of their tank destroyers out of commission, Murphy ordered his men to retreat. But he chose to remain at the front himself, giving coordinates to the artillery by telephone while keeping the enemy at bay with any weapons he could get his hands on. He mounted a burning tank destroyer, using its machine gun to fire upon the advancing Germans whenever the smoke cleared enough for a shot. At the same time he ordered artillery barrages dangerously close to his own position. The enemy could not believe that the harassing machine-gun fire was actually coming from a burning tank destroyer, and they were afraid to fire upon it in case they set off the explosives and gasoline. Murphy's last order was for an artillery blast directly upon his own position. He jumped clear of the destroyer just before the vehicle exploded, then finished off the remaining German troops. In June, 1945, the people of Farmersville gave Murphy $1,750 in war bonds as a gesture of esteem. He later became even better known as a Hollywood actor.

8. CORP. EINAR H. INGMAN (Korean War)

Ingman joined the army in 1948 at the age of 19. In February, 1951, his regiment was fighting a series of skirmishes with the Chinese when the squad leader was killed. Ingman assumed command. A few hours later the leader of another squad was wounded, and Ingman took over that squad as well. While he was leading the two squads against a machine-gun nest, a grenade exploded a foot away from his head, blowing off his left ear. Ignoring this, he charged ahead with his bayonet, only to be struck full in the face with a rifle bullet. Dazed, he leaped forward, killing 10 Chinese with bayonet and rifle. Then he staggered away and collapsed. Later he said: "That bullet through my head kind of made me quit thinking."

9. SPECIALIST 4 CARMEL B. HARVEY, JR. (Vietnam War)

In An Nhon Province on June 21, 1967, Harvey's platoon was ordered to secure a downed helicopter. While setting up a defensive perimeter, Harvey and two others found themselves under heavy enemy fire. The other two were wounded, and one round of enemy fire struck and armed a hand grenade on Harvey's belt. He tried unsuccessfully to remove the grenade. Realizing the danger to his companions, he raced toward the enemy machine-gun nest. He nearly reached the nest when the grenade exploded, stunning the enemy gunners. The Medal of Honor was awarded posthumously.

—A.B.

20 MEMBERS OF PRESIDENT NIXON'S ORIGINAL ENEMIES LIST

On June 27, 1973, President Nixon's former counsel, John W. Dean III, released to the Senate Watergate Committee a 1971 memo proposing the use of "available federal machinery to screw our political enemies." Accompanying it was a document listing the names of 20 persons who were viewed by the administration as being unsympathetic to the Nixon White House. These 20—who were given priority over 200 additional "enemies" on a separate list—were to be "screwed" with IRS audits, litigation, prosecution, or denial of federal grants. Next to each name appeared a comment—apparently written by then special counsel Chuck Colson—qualifying the action to be taken.

1. ARNOLD M. PICKER (United Artists Corp., New York, N.Y.)

"Success here could be both debilitating and very embarrassing to the Muskie machine. If effort looks promising, both Ruth and David Picker should be programmed and then a follow-through with United Artists."

2. ALEXANDER E. BARKAN (national director, AFL-CIO Committee on Political Education)

"Without a doubt the most powerful political force programmed against us in 1968 . . . We can expect the same effort this time."

3. ED GUTHMAN (national editor, *Los Angeles Times*)

"It is time to give him the message."

4. MAXWELL DANE (member of Doyle Dane Bernbach, a top New York, N.Y., advertising agency which had worked for Democrats)

"They destroyed Goldwater in '64. They should be hit hard starting with Dane."

5. CHARLES DYSON (Dyson-Kissner Corp., New York, N.Y.)

". . . deeply involved in the Businessmen's Educational Fund which bankrolls a national radio network of 5-min. programs—anti-Nixon in character."

6. HOWARD STEIN (Dreyfus Corp., New York, N.Y.)

"Heaviest contributor to [Sen. Eugene] McCarthy in '68."

7. ALLARD LOWENSTEIN (ex-congressman)

"Guiding force behind the 18-year-old 'dump Nixon' vote drive."

8. MORTON HALPERIN (leading executive at Common Cause)

"A scandal would be most helpful here."

9. LEONARD WOODCOCK (United Auto Workers, Detroit, Mich.)

"No comments necessary."

10. S. STERLING MUNRO, JR. (aide to Sen. Henry "Scoop" Jackson)

"We should give him a try. Positive results would stick a pin in Jackson's white hat."

11. BERNARD T. FELD (president, Council for a Livable World)

"Heavy far left funding. They will program an 'all court press' against us in '72."

12. SIDNEY DAVIDOFF (top aide to Mayor John Lindsay, New York, N.Y.)

"A first class SOB, wheeler-dealer, and suspected bagman. Positive results would really shake the Lindsay camp . . ."

13. JOHN CONYERS (congressman, Detroit, Mich.)

"Coming on fast. Emerging as a leading black anti-Nixon spokesman. Has known weakness for white females."

14. SAMUEL M. LAMBERT (president, National Education Association)

"Has taken us on vis-à-vis federal aid to parochial schools—a '72 issue."

15. STEWART RAWLINGS MOTT (Mott Associates, New York, N.Y.)

"Nothing but big money for radic-lib candidates."

16. RONALD DELLUMS (congressman, Berkeley, Calif.)

"Had extensive EMK [Sen. Edward M. Kennedy]-Tunney support in his election bid. Success might help in California next year."

17. DANIEL SCHORR (CBS reporter, Washington, D.C.)

    "A real media enemy."

18. S. HARRISON DOGOLE (president, Globe Security Systems)

    "Fourth-largest private detective agency in the U.S. Heavy Humphrey contributor. Could program his agency against us."

19. PAUL NEWMAN (actor)

    "Radic-lib causes . . . '72 involvement certain."

20. MARY McGRORY (Washington, D.C. columnist)

    "Daily hate-Nixon articles."

—D.B.

SOURCE: "Plans for 'Political Enemies'—and Mills's Response," *Watergate: Chronology of a Crisis,* Vol. I (Congressional Quarterly), p. 153.

Richard Nixon's "enemy," Paul Newman,
accused of supporting "Radic-lib causes . . ."

THE 10 WORST INSURANCE
RISKS IN THE U.S.

		*Extra Deaths per 1,000 per Year**
1.	Astronauts	30 (est.)
2.	Drivers of Gold Cup hydroplanes	25 (est.)
2.	Drivers of Indianapolis race cars	25 (est.)
2.	Drivers in Grand Prix auto race	25 (est.)
5.	Aerial performers (without nets)	8 (est.)
5.	Professional prizefighters	8 (est.)
7.	Lumbermen and woodchoppers in the Pacific area	6.18
8.	Professional divers (helmet or skin)	4 (est.)
9.	Electrical power line constructors, tower erectors, and linemen	3.44
10.	Steeplejacks	2.78

* For example, for each 1,000 lumbermen insured there will be 6.18 more annual deaths than expected. Some of the extra death figures are estimates, due to the scarcity of statistics.

As a base for comparison, the death rate for all U.S. men aged 25–29 is about 2 per thousand per year.

—R.T.

Source: *1967 Occupational Study* (Chicago: Society of Actuaries).

11 MAJOR CORPORATIONS
WHICH PAID NO FEDERAL INCOME
TAXES IN THE U.S. IN 1975

1. Ford Motor Co.
2. Delta Air Lines, Inc.
3. Northwest Airlines, Inc.
4. Chemical New York Corp.
5. Manufacturers Hanover Corp.
6. Western Electric Co.
   (a subsidiary of American
   Telephone & Telegraph Co.)
7. Bethlehem Steel Corp.
8. Lockheed Aircraft Corp.
9. National Steel Corp.
10. Phelps Dodge Corp.
11. Freeport Minerals Co.

In 1975, the nation's 148 largest corporations paid $20 billion in taxes to foreign governments and only $10 billion to the U.S. government. The eight largest banks in the nation all showed a profit for the year, but none paid taxes. Ford Motor Co., by taking advantage of foreign tax credits and investment tax credits, not only was able to avoid paying U.S. income tax for 1974 and 1975, but actually received a $189 million refund for those years at the taxpayers' expense.

Source: *Facts on File,* Nov. 13, 1976.

21 U.S. CITIES WHICH HAVE ELECTED SOCIALISTS TO PUBLIC OFFICE

1. Barre, Vt. (1916)
2. Berkeley, Calif. (1911)
3. Birmingham, Ala. (1915)
4. Bridgeport, Conn. (1932–1954)
5. Butte, Mont. (1911, 1913)
6. Cedar City, U. (1911)
7. Cleveland, O. (1915)
8. Daly City, Calif. (1912)
9. Davenport, Ia. (1911, 1920)
10. Duluth, Minn. (1917)
11. Flint, Mich. (1911)
12. Kalamazoo, Mich. (1911)
13. Longmont, Colo. (1913)
14. Lorain, O. (1911)
15. Mascoutah, Ill. (1918)
16. McKeesport, Pa. (1917)
17. Milwaukee, Wis. (1910, 1916, 1918, 1920)
18. Minneapolis, Minn. (1916)
19. Minot, N.D. (1913)
20. Schenectady, N.Y. (1911, 1915)
21. Watts, Calif. (1911)

Source: John H. Laslett and Seymour Martin, eds., *Failure of a Dream?* (New York: Doubleday, 1974).

3
CRIME AND PUNISHMENT

CLIFFORD IRVING'S
10 BEST FORGERS OF ALL TIME

Born in New York City, the son of a well-known cartoonist, Clifford Irving attended Cornell U. He became a full-time writer, publishing such novels as *On a Darkling Plain, The Losers, The Valley, The 38th Floor,* and a widely read nonfiction book, *Fake!* He became world-famous in 1971 and 1972 when he sold an autobiography—purportedly written by Howard Hughes with Irving's assistance—which proved to be a fantastic forgery. In his list of the greatest forgers of all time, Irving picks himself as one of them, and tells his version of the Hughes caper.

1. THE SEE OF ROME

For audacity, simplicity, and widespread effect over the centuries, no forgery can equal that of the *Constitutum Constantini,* the so-called Donation of Constantine. Constantine, the first Roman emperor to become a Christian, not only legalized his religion throughout the empire but, sometime between 315 and 325 A.D., gave to the See of Rome spiritual command over the entire world and secular authority over Europe. He did this in a 3,000-word document, the Donation; although, oddly, it was not made public by the Church until the ninth century, when Rome was at odds with the Eastern Orthodox Church. The Donation was cited by various popes throughout the Middle Ages and used to buttress many of the Church's temporal claims. The first doubts were cast in the 15th century, and by the 18th century, Voltaire could openly and without serious contradiction call it "that boldest and most magnificent forgery." For one thing, it had come to light that Constantine had given Rome authority over his capital, New Rome (which later became Constantinople and, still later, Istanbul), at least a decade before New Rome was founded. The actual author of the text of the *Constitutum Constantini* remains unknown.

2. WILLIAM HENRY IRELAND (1777–1835)

The son of a London printer and Shakespearean scholar, young Ireland, at the age of 19, "discovered" in an English country manor an extraordinary treasure: love letters from Shakespeare to his mistress, a new version of *King Lear,* a fragment of *Hamlet,* various legal and other documents, and, even more marvelously, in time, two "lost" and unknown complete Shakespearean plays, *Vortigern,* a love story of the Saxon conquest, and *Henry II*—both handwritten by the Bard. Most scholars, including James Boswell, examined them and were ecstatic. *Vortigern* was performed in 1796, but somehow by then, doubts had arisen and the public at the Drury Lane Theatre howled with scorn toward the end of the performance. It was a one-night stand and within a year Ireland had confessed that the entire collection of Shakespeareana was a forgery, composed and written by him on old paper stained with a clear dye to simulate even greater age. Ireland received no punishment other than the angry disdain of critics when he went on to publish several novels.

3. ALCIBIADES SIMONIDES (1818–1890)

An Albanian artist and chemist, this little-known but prolific forger wins the prize for industriousness and perseverance in the face of constant exposure. He began his career in 1853 by selling an ancient manuscript of Homer to the king of Greece, who consulted scholars at the University of Athens before making his purchase. The Homer was soon discovered to be a forgery, but Simonides had vanished. Some years later he sold to a consortium of Turkish scholars, for the handsome sum of $40,000, a collection of ancient Greek, Assyrian, and Egyptian manuscripts. Microscopic examination in Berlin determined that they were fake, but Simonides had vanished. Several times, using other names, Simonides excavated rare manuscripts in Turkey and sold them to local pashas. Finally he turned up in London with letters reputedly written by Belisarius to the Emperor Justinian and by Alcibiades to Pericles, for which the duke of Sutherland eventually paid over $4,000. They were found to be forgeries, but Simonides had vanished. He was banished once from Spain, but never imprisoned, and he died old.

4. CHARLES DAWSON (1864–1916)

This English attorney and amateur geologist was the discoverer of Piltdown man, the bones of the so-called "missing link" between man and ape which were unearthed in 1912 from a gravel pit near Piltdown Common in East Sussex, England. Experts from the British Museum authenticated the find and the scientific world was so thrilled—for it seemed a confirmation of basic Darwinian theory—that it bestowed upon Dawson a high honor by naming the new species *Eoanthropus dawsoni*. In 1949, however, the English geologist Kenneth Oakley subjected the famous Piltdown bones to some new chemical tests and announced that there was doubt as to their authenticity. Finally, in 1953, newer and more sophisticated tests proved that the jaw of *Eoanthropus dawsoni* was that of an orangutan; its teeth had been filed with modern instruments and then stained in a crucible. Piltdown man was one of the more amusing forgeries of history. Charles Dawson—one might think, luckily—died many years before its exposure.

5. FRITZ KREISLER (1875–1962)

The famous Viennese violinist, clearly a genius as an interpretive performer, was also the most successful known musical forger. Because he believed that the concert violinist's repertory of unaccompanied pieces was too small, and therefore insufficient to display his talents, Kreisler created a repertory of his own. Beginning in the late 1890s, he wrote pieces and ascribed them to then little-known composers such as Couperin, Pugnani, Francoeur, Padre Martini, Porpora—even Vivaldi—claiming that he had found the hitherto unknown manuscripts "in libraries and monasteries while visiting Rome, Florence, Venice, and Paris." Critics called them "little masterpieces." In 1935, casually, he confessed his brilliant forgeries to Olin Downes, music critic of *The New York Times*. There was an uproar but, of course, no penalty.

6. HANS VAN MEEGEREN (1889–1947)

The forgeries of this erratic, hard-working Dutch painter might never have been revealed had it not been for a quirk of fate: Reichsmarschall Hermann Göring owned one of them, which had been bought for him in the Netherlands during W.W.II. Called *Christ and the Adulteress*, it was signed Jan Vermeer, and it was one of the 14 Dutch 17th-century "masterpieces" by Vermeer and Pieter de Hooch that had been laboriously painted and most carefully aged by Hans van Meegeren. Dutch authorities accused van Meegeren of collaboration with the Nazi enemy in selling works of national importance. He was jailed, and to evade the consequences of the worse crime he confessed to the lesser: forgery. To prove his point, in his prison cell he painted one more Vermeer, and in addition produced some of the rare pigments he had used in the forgeries. Van Meegeren had been paid the astounding sum of over $3 million in Dutch gulden for his paintings, and six of his Vermeers hung in museums and galleries. At his trial he was given a year's imprisonment, but before the sentence could be carried out, frail, penniless, and depressed, he died of a heart attack.

7. ARTURO ALVES REIS (1896–1955)

Labeled by one biographer as *The Man Who Stole Portugal*, mild-mannered, visionary Alves Reis was indisputably history's boldest known forger of money. With several confederates, including a then famous Dutch actress, he forged documents and letters which convinced the famous London firm of Waterlow & Sons, which printed money for the Bank of Portugal, that he was empowered to personally receive over $10 million worth of Portuguese 500-escudo banknotes destined—he said—for the Portuguese colony of Angola. The money flowed so smoothly and steadily into Alves Reis's hands that he not only founded his own private bank in Lisbon, but, with the forged notes, bought so many shares in the Bank of Portugal that in time he threatened to become its majority stockholder. A duplication of serial numbers led to his arrest in 1925. He finally confessed in 1930, spent the next 15 years in prison, and died a pauper.

8. ELMYR DE HORY (1906–1976)

Born Josef Hoffman, also known as Louis Raynal, Jean Cassou, and Elmyr Dory-Boutin, this Hungarian Jewish émigré homosexual was probably the greatest and certainly the most prolific art forger of all time. He was a failed expressionist painter, but hundreds of his works hang in famous museums and art galleries throughout the world, and thousands are in private collections; they are all signed Matisse, Modigliani, Dufy, Chagall, Derain, Picasso, Vlaminck, Gauguin, Braque, or Cézanne. De Hory was finally exposed in 1967 through the greed and flamboyance of two men who had sold 44 of his fake postimpressionist canvases to a Texas oil millionaire. After 1962, de Hory lived and painted on the island of Ibiza, Spain; he was the subject of a biography, *Fake!* by Clifford Irving, and a recent feature-length documentary film by Orson

Welles. In 1976, harassed, constantly threatened by the two men who had grown rich as salesmen of his fakes, and facing almost certain extradition to France, where he feared he would die of cold in a prison cell, de Hory killed himself on Ibiza with an overdose of barbiturates. The current market value of his lifework has been estimated at over $30 million.

9. CLIFFORD IRVING (b. 1930)

A novelist, Irving perpetrated the most widely publicized hoax of this century when, in 1971, he convinced his New York publisher, McGraw-Hill, that he had been commissioned to ghostwrite the autobiography of the famous elusive billionaire Howard Hughes. With Richard Suskind, a friend and author of children's books, Irving not only wrote a wildly imaginative 1,200-page book "by Hughes" which veteran newsmen and men who knew Hughes well swore "had to be authentic," but he forged over 20 pages of handwritten letters and contracts by Hughes to buttress his claim. These forgeries, done by a complete amateur who had never seen an original specimen of the handwriting he was reproducing, were submitted to five of the finest handwriting experts in the U.S., who, after close examination, unanimously declared them to be genuine. For Irving to have forged such a mass of material, said expert Paul Osborn, "would be beyond human ability." Despite the furor and publicity, Irving's essentially absurd scheme would never have been discovered and proved a hoax if Swiss banks had not broken their traditional secrecy and revealed that the holder of a Zurich bank account in the name of H. R. Hughes was in fact a woman—Irving's wife. The author returned what was left of the $765,000 he had received from McGraw-Hill and went to prison for 17 months.

10. MR. X (?–?)

By definition, the identity of the greatest forger of all time, whether man or woman, is unknown to us. For he (or she) must have been—or must be—far too clever and skillful to ever have been suspected or exposed. *Caveat emptor.*

—Exclusive for *The Book of Lists*

10 PRISONERS ELIGIBLE FOR PAROLE IN THE NEXT 13 YEARS

Although these prisoners will be legally eligible for parole in the years indicated, their applications may be turned down. It is also possible that some of them will successfully appeal their sentences and be released earlier.

1. CHARLES MANSON (1978)

The leader of a pseudo-religious cult with headquarters at a ranch near Los Angeles, Manson inspired his "family" to commit the execution-style murders of movie actress Sharon Tate and six others on August 9–10, 1969.

2. JOHN EHRLICHMAN (1979)

Richard Nixon's former domestic counselor was sentenced in 1974 for his connection with the 1971 burglary of Daniel Ellsberg's psychiatrist's office and in 1975 for his involvement in the Watergate cover-up. It is possible that Judge John Sirica may reduce Ehrlichman's sentence as he did with several other Watergate figures.

3. JUAN CORONA (1980)

Allegedly one of the most prolific murderers in American history, Corona is said to have killed 25 migrant farm workers in 1970–1971. In 1973, he was sentenced to 25 consecutive life terms.

4. EDMUND E. KEMPER III (1980)

While in his teens, Kemper killed his grandparents and was committed to a state hospital. After his release in 1970, he killed his mother, a friend of hers, and six hitchhiking coeds in Santa Cruz, Calif.

5-6. WILLIAM and EMILY HARRIS (1983)

These Symbionese Liberation Army members were convicted of armed robbery, kidnapping, and auto theft. The crimes stemmed from their activities with Patricia Hearst in 1974.

7. SARA JANE MOORE (1986)

A onetime FBI informer, Moore fired at President Gerald R. Ford as he walked out of the St. Francis Hotel in San Francisco on September 22, 1975. She pleaded guilty and was sentenced to life imprisonment.

8. SIRHAN B. SIRHAN (1986)

While campaigning for the Democratic presidential nomination, Robert F. Kennedy was shot by Sirhan, a native of Jordan, in Los Angeles on June 5, 1968.

9. ARTHUR H. BREMER (1988)

On May 15, 1972, Bremer shot and seriously wounded Governor George Wallace at a Maryland shopping center. According to a diary produced by the FBI, allegedly in Bremer's handwriting, he had previously stalked Richard M. Nixon and Hubert Humphrey. On August 4, 1972, he was sentenced to 63 years in jail, but the sentence was later reduced by 10 years.

10. LYNETTE ALICE FROMME (1990)

"Squeaky" Fromme, a member of Charles Manson's "family," was sentenced to life imprisonment for trying to kill President Ford on September 5, 1975, in Sacramento, Calif. She now performs housekeeping chores as a prison orderly in San Diego.

—L.B.

10 INDIVIDUALS WHO HAVE REMAINED ON THE FBI'S "10 MOST WANTED FUGITIVES" LIST FOR THE LONGEST PERIODS OF TIME

		Date Placed on List	Date of Removal
1.	Frederick J. Tenuto, murder	May 24, 1950	Mar. 9, 1964
2.	David Daniel Keegan, murder; interstate transportation of stolen property	June 21, 1954	Dec. 13, 1963
3.	James Eddie Diggs, murder	Aug. 27, 1952	Dec. 14, 1961
4.	Charles Lee Herron, murder; assault with intent to commit murder	Feb. 9, 1968	At large
5.	Eugene Francis Newman, robbery	May 28, 1956	June 11, 1965
6.	Henry R. Mitchell, bank robbery	Mar. 17, 1950	July 18, 1958
7.	Benjamin Hoskins Paddock, escaping from a federal prison; bank robbery	June 10, 1969	At large
8.	John William Clouser, interstate transportation of a stolen motor vehicle	Jan. 7, 1965	Aug. 1, 1972
9.	Katherine Ann Power, murder; theft of government property; bank robbery	Oct. 17, 1970	At large
10.	Cameron David Bishop, sabotage; destruction of war utilities	Apr. 15, 1969	Mar. 12, 1975

Frederick Tenuto was on the FBI's "Most Wanted" list for over 13 years when murder charges against him were finally dismissed by local authorities.

50

10 SENSATIONAL THEFTS

1. THE BRITISH CROWN JEWELS (Tower of London, c. 1675)

During the reign of King Charles II, a swashbuckling high-wayman, Col. Thomas Blood, posed as a clergyman to gain access to the royal treasure room high atop the Tower of London. Overpowering an unwary guard, Blood stashed the gem-encrusted crown and dozens of other jewels in a sack and fled, but he was captured before clearing the Tower. Blood's daring venture so intrigued King Charles that he commuted the automatic death sentence and instead conferred upon the royal burglar a lifetime annual pension of £300.

2. THE CENTRAL PACIFIC EXPRESS (Verdi, Nev., Nov. 5, 1870; Independence, Nev., Nov. 6, 1870)

In one of the nation's first train robberies, six men, led by Big Jack Davis, hopped aboard the eastbound express for Reno, forced the train to a stop, and rode off to Virginia City with $40,000 in minted coin. Ten hours later, as the delayed engine chugged into Independence, six army deserters jumped aboard to take $4,490 that the Davis gang had overlooked. Within days, authorities captured all 13 bandits, who were sentenced variously from 10 to 15 years in prison.

3. THE FIRST NATIONAL BANK (Northfield, Minn., Sept. 7, 1876)

This bungled holdup destroyed the notorious James-Younger gang after 15 years of outlawry. The eight-man crew stormed the tiny town of 4,000 in hopes of taking the fat payroll of the Ames Flour Mill. Instead, an alert citizenry shot it out with the bandits and drove them into the hills with only $12 in stolen currency. Two of the armed robbers lay dead in the streets. Five others, among them Frank and Jesse James, suffered gunshot wounds. During their escape, the James brothers split off from the other four and found refuge across the border in the Dakotas. The three Younger brothers (Bob, Cole, and Jim) were captured two weeks later and received life terms in the Minnesota State Penitentiary. Jesse was murdered for bounty in 1882. That same year Frank surrendered voluntarily, was twice tried and acquitted, and retired to his Missouri farm where he died in 1915.

4. *THE DUCHESS OF DEVONSHIRE* (London, May 25, 1878)

Gentleman burglar Adam Worth engineered the theft from art dealers Agnew and Agnew not for profit, but rather as a bargaining wedge with which to secure the release of his employee George Thompson, who had been arrested for check forgery. Using a thick London fog to cover his entry through a second-story window, Worth scrambled in and out of the Agnew building in five minutes. But by the time he sent a note to authorities promising restoration of the Gainsborough masterpiece in exchange for his colleague in crime, Thompson had already been freed on a technicality. Worth, unwilling to give up the painting for nothing, shipped it to America where it spent the next quarter of a century in Brooklyn and Boston warehouses. In 1901, broke and dying from tuberculosis, Worth sold *The Duchess* back to Agnew and Agnew for an undisclosed sum.

5. THE FIRST NATIONAL BANK and THE CONDON BANK
   (Coffeyville, Kans., Oct. 5, 1892)

After three years of horse stealing and train robbery, the three cocky Dalton brothers and two other outlaws returned to their hometown of Coffeyville intent on simultaneously knocking over two banks. Bob Dalton, 25, and brother Emmet entered the First National Bank, while Grant Dalton and the other two stormed the Condon Bank. Detected in progress, the twin holdups collapsed before massive local resistance. When the smoke cleared, only Emmet Dalton remained alive. Surviving multiple gunshot wounds, the youngest Dalton brother stood trial and was found guilty. After serving 14 years of a 25-year sentence, he was granted a full pardon by President Theodore Roosevelt.

Onetime baseball player and navy deserter John Dillinger
robbed more banks in 1 year than Jesse James did in 16 years.
Author Jay Robert Nash has made a strong case to prove that in 1934
the FBI killed a small-time hoodlum named Jimmy Lawrence
instead of Dillinger, and that Number One remained alive and free.

6. THE MONA LISA (the Louvre, Paris, Aug. 21, 1911)

On a cleaning day when the museum was closed to the public, Vicenzo Peruggia, a Louvre employee, cut the priceless *Mona Lisa* from its gilt frame and headed for the exit. Since Leonardo da Vinci had painted the smiling lady on wood instead of canvas, Peruggia couldn't just roll it up and run. Still, he managed to spirit it to his apartment where it remained in the false bottom of a trunk for two years. After the furor in the press died down, he attempted to sell the painting to his native Italy for $95,000. Italian officials promptly arrested him and returned the 300-year-old masterpiece to France without a scratch. At his trial in Florence, Peruggia convinced the tribunal that his act was one of patriotism—that his sole motive was to return the portrait to the land of its creator. Thus, he received the relatively light sentence of 1 year and 15 days.

7. THE FIRST NATIONAL BANK (Mason City, Ia., Mar. 13, 1934)

While designated "public enemy number one" by the FBI, John Dillinger, age 31, along with trigger-happy Baby Face Nelson and four others, burst into the bank brandishing pistols and machine guns. A guard perched in a glass booth above the tellers' cages fired off a tear-gas pellet at the bandits before taking a bullet himself. With tears streaming down their faces, the gang ordered the vault opened. Assistant cashier Harry Fisher handed over a huge sack of pennies and slowly produced stacks of $1 bills. The delaying tactic worked, for Dillinger's crew fled with barely $50,000 of the $240,000 on hand. Although Dillinger and a few others were wounded in the escape, the gang eluded the police and finally found refuge in a Wisconsin resort. Later that year Dillinger was betrayed by a girl friend and gunned down in Chicago by FBI agents on July 22. Nelson met a similar end four months later.

8. BRINK'S HEADQUARTERS (Boston, Mass., Jan. 17, 1950)

For two full years, 11 middle-aged Bostonians plotted out a scheme to break into the headquarters of the famed armored car company. On numerous occasions prior to the actual robbery, they entered the building after midnight to study the alarm system and the safe. After a complete dress rehearsal in December, 1949, they felt ready for the real thing. Thus, on the appointed day, seven of the heretofore petty thieves—dressed in simulated Brink's uniforms, rubber Halloween masks, and overshoes—slipped into the counting-house and emerged just 15 minutes later with $2.5 million in cash, checks, and securities. The bandits kept a low profile for nearly six years, but less than a week before the expiration of the statute of limitations, one of them confessed to the police. As a result, 8 of the 11 men went to prison under a life sentence.

9. THE BANK OF NOVA SCOTIA (Montreal, P.Q., Canada, July 1–2, 1961)

Veteran Canadian burglar Georges LeMay chose the weekend of Dominion Day—a national holiday—to blast a 200-sq.-in. hole through the 2-ft. concrete vault floor. After prying open almost 400 safe-deposit boxes, LeMay was able to crawl back to daylight with what bank officials conservatively estimated to be $633,605 in cash, jewelry, stocks, bonds, traveler's checks, and rare stamps and coins. Although he evaded authorities for four years, LeMay in 1965 became the first known criminal to be captured with the help of the Early Bird satellite, which relayed his photo to TV screens all over the world. Nabbed in Miami, he immediately married his girl friend so that she could not be forced to testify against him. He nevertheless stood trial in Montreal and was convicted on the testimony of his accomplice, Jacques LaJoie. On January 17, 1969, LeMay began serving an eight-year term. The loot has never been recovered.

10. THE GREAT TRAIN ROBBERY (near Cheddington, England, Aug. 8, 1963)

In a grand scheme timed down to the second, 12 masked Englishmen converged on a preselected site in two Land Rovers, a 3-ton army truck, two Jaguars, and a motorcycle. They quickly switched the railroad signals and, like clockwork, the Glasgow-to-London mail train ground to a halt before them. In less than 45 minutes they fled with $7,368,715 in cash. In spite of all their well-laid plans, the thieves blew the otherwise perfect crime when they failed to wipe off their fingerprints at a nearby drop house. They are now serving an aggregate sentence of about 300 years. Less than $1 million of the haul has thus far been recovered.

—W.A.D.

8 IMPORTANT LIBEL CASES

1. *WHISTLER* v. *RUSKIN* (1878)

Outraged by John Ruskin's insulting, reputation-damaging critique of his impressionistic paintings, American-born James McNeill Whistler initiated the most famous libel case in art history. At issue was the question: "What is art?" Ruskin, a traditionalist, had accused Whistler of presenting "unfinished pictures" lacking composition and detail, in a London gallery, and of "Cockney impudence" in overcharging for "flinging a pot of paint" not only against his canvases but "in the public's face." Too emotionally upset to appear in court, Ruskin declared through counsel that he would offer no retraction and, if he lost, would retire forever from writing criticism. Ruskin lost. Dishonored and shattered, he withdrew from his Oxford professorship as well and lived out his years in seclusion. Whistler, technically triumphant, was stung by the award —a mere farthing—and had to abandon his house and sell personal possessions to meet his court costs.

2. *REG.* v. *PARKE* (1890)

The brothel situated at 19 Cleveland Street in London was no ordinary house of prostitution. Catering to men of aristocratic standing, its specialty was providing the services of other males. The proprietor, one Charles Hammond, on learning the police planned a raid, promptly left the country. Two men, a clergyman and an 18-year-old clerk, did fall into police clutches. They confessed to "acts of impropriety" and received light sentences. The mildness of their sentences and the timely escape of Hammond intrigued a crusading reporter, Ernest Parke. Parke suspected the authorities were part of a conspiracy to protect certain prominent patrons, among them Lord Arthur Somerset, an intimate friend of the prince of Wales who had hurried off to France to avoid the breaking scandal. Soon after Lord Somerset's departure, Parke, still bird-dogging the case, published an article in *The North London Press* naming a second aristocrat, the earl of Easton, as a former patron of the now notorious male brothel. Protesting his innocence, Lord Easton brought Ernest Parke to trial. Admitting a single visit to the Cleveland Street house, Lord Easton contended it had been a ghastly error. True, he had, on a dull evening, entered the brothel hoping to view female nudes, but when the real nature of the establishment was revealed he had fled and never returned. Parke's defense offered witnesses to support his accusation that Lord Easton had returned to the brothel five or six times, but these witnesses—largely male prostitutes—were a scruffy lot who contradicted each other's testimony. Parke yielded to the charge of libel and was sentenced to 12 months' imprisonment.

3. *MONSON* v. *TUSSAUD'S* (1895)

To prepare him for the army, young Cecil Hambrough was sent by his father to live in the home of Alfred John Monson and his wife Agnes, there to be tutored by Alfred, the hard-drinking, extravagant, bankrupt member of a distinguished British family. Three years later, Cecil joined Monson on a rowboat excursion. The boat capsized and Cecil narrowly escaped drowning. The following day Cecil accompanied Monson on a hunting excursion and was shot to death. Suspicion fell on Monson, whose wife was beneficiary to Cecil's two insurance policies. Monson was brought to trial in Edinburgh for both the attempted murder and the successful murder of Cecil. The court decision was "not proven," a unique Scottish verdict meaning neither innocent nor guilty, and Monson was freed. The sensational trial inspired Madame Tussaud's famous waxworks to construct a wax likeness of Monson. Injudiciously, Tussaud's displayed Monson in the company of a convicted poisoner and forger, adjacent to its famed exhibit of murderers called the Chamber of Horrors. Monson sued, arguing correctly that visual images as well as words can constitute libel. He won his case. To compensate him for damage to his reputation, the jury—after deliberating for 15 minutes—awarded him a farthing.

4. *STOPES* v. *SUTHERLAND* (1923)

Marie Stopes, doctor of philosophy, Quaker, author of *Married Love* and *Radiant Motherhood*, believed that artificial birth control was essential to marital joy. There could be no happiness, she contended, if sexual expression was curtailed by fear of parenthood, or if flocks of unplanned children accrued as a result of normal lovemaking. At her own expense, she opened a clinic in a London slum from which she dispensed birth-control information and rubber diaphragms to working-class women. H.G. Sutherland, a medical doctor and recent convert to Catholicism, attacked her by inference in his book *Birth Control*, stating that the poor were her "natural victims," and the subject of experiment in this "monstrous campaign of birth control." Dr. Stopes had a writ issued for libel. The case was heard before a judge who influenced the jury to bring in a verdict against Dr. Stopes. On appeal, the decision was reversed. However, the House of Lords restored the original decision and—after a 2½-year battle—Dr. Stopes lost her case. But only in the courts. Years later, disguised as "a work-grimed charwoman," she had the satisfaction of being fitted with a contraceptive device by the very gynecologist who, at the trial, had condemned her for advocating use of the diaphragm.

5. *CROWLEY* v. *CONSTABLE AND CO., LTD.* (1934)

Aleister Crowley, satanic magician, poet, exponent of pagan sex orgies, and self-styled drug fiend, was widely known to the British press and public as "The Beast," "The Wickedest Man in the World," and "The King of Depravity." To his disciples he was "The Messiah." After dubious adventures abroad, he returned to England. Broke and ignored, he sought new fame and funds through litigation. Constable and Co. had published *Laughing Torso*, a memoir which hinted Crowley was a practitioner of black magic. Crowley sued. In court, he insisted he practiced white magic, not black. Revolted by Crowley's testimony, especially his admission that he had kept a human skeleton in his London flat and "fed" it human blood and small birds, the jury turned against him. Crowley lost the suit and an appeal as well. Soon after, he disappeared from the limelight he loved. He died in 1947.

6. *PRINCESS IRINA ALEXANDROVNA YUSUPOV* v. *MGM PICTURES, LTD.* (1934)

On December 29, 1916, Prince Feliks Yusupov murdered the infamous peasant mystic Grigori Rasputin. Rasputin, while secretly serving the German Army, maintained a hypnotic influence over the czar and czarina. This influence, in the judgment of the prince, threatened the future of imperial Russia. When his crime was discovered, the prince and his wife—the Princess Irina—were sent into exile and eventually found permanent refuge in Paris. In 1932, MGM released a film entitled *Rasputin and the Empress*. Although names were changed, Prince Yusupov was unmistakably portrayed. His princess, called Natasha in the film, confessed to having been ravished by the repulsive Rasputin. Deeply shocked by the implication, Princess Irina—who had never met Rasputin—brought action to have scenes with the defiled Natasha eliminated from the picture. Princess Irina won her case. She was awarded libel damages of £25,000 and the fictional Natasha was cut from the film.

7. *WRIGHT* v. *GLADSTONE* (1937)

William Ewart Gladstone, four times prime minister under Queen Victoria, had been in his grave for 40 years when, in 1937, he became the central figure in a case of libel. Capt. Peter Wright in *Portraits and Criticism* stated that the deceased Gladstone, while pretending piety, had actually wished to "pursue and possess every sort of woman." The prime minister's surviving sons, both in their 70s, were appalled. Having no legal recourse, but determined to bring Captain Wright into court where the accusations could be aired and their father's reputation vindicated in the annals of history, the two sons contrived to get Captain Wright to sue *them*. They wrote libelous letters to the press calling Wright a "coward, liar, and fool"— and eventually succeeded in having the monocled captain expelled from his club. Captain Wright fell into their trap. Charging that expulsion from his club, as well as the libelous letters, had "gravely injured his credit and reputation," he brought suit. In the witness box, Wright expanded his charges, accusing the prime minister, who had died at 89, of having been faithless to his wife for 60 years. He linked Gladstone with the actress Lillie Langtry (from Monte Carlo, Langtry wired indignant denial). And he revived rumors, abundant in the prime minister's lifetime, that Gladstone had consorted with prostitutes. The canards were refuted with the reminder that the dead man had been a founder of the Association for the Reclamation of Fallen Women and that his charitable concern had caused him to approach prostitutes on the street and to visit their rooms at night. The jury sided with the sons and the dead prime minister's reputation was restored.

8. *LIBERACE* v. *DAILY MIRROR AND CONNOR* (1959)

"Winking." "Sniggering." "Snuggling." "Quivering." "Giggling." "Mincing." "Fruit-flavored." These epithets were heaped upon Liberace on his first trip to England in 1956. All came from one man, William Connor, a vitriolic, aggressive journalist who dispensed his views in the London *Daily Mirror* under the pseudonym "Cassandra." To Liberace, and to his mother who accompanied him, Cassandra's attack spelled one word: *homosexual*. Mrs. Liberace immediately took to her bed under a physician's care. When it was recommended she leave England, she refused, fearful her departure would give credence to the vile suggestion of her son's unorthodox sexuality. The Liberaces were not alone in their interpretation. Huge audiences were almost unanimously adoring, but a sprinkling of gallery viewers, presumably spurred by the words of Cassandra, greeted Liberace's appearances with catcalls of "Queen," "Fairy," and "Go home, queen." Liberace promptly consulted counsel and brought suit against the *Daily Mirror* and William Connor. Three years later, when Liberace took the stand as plaintiff, two questions were put to him bluntly: "Are you a homosexual?" "No, sir." "Have you ever indulged in homosexual practices?" "No, sir, never in my life." The defense claimed its comments fell in the legitimate realm of criticism, and insisted it was unaware of the implication of the word *fruit* to Americans. It did, however, make caustic references to Liberace's gaudy costuming and unveiled a witness who stated Liberace had confided that he intended, when in Paris, to buy perfume for himself. After a six-day trial and several hours of deliberation, the jury awarded victory and £8,000 plus costs to the pianist.

—s.w.

MELVIN BELLI'S
10 MOST IMPORTANT NONMURDER
CRIMINAL CASES IN HISTORY

Attorney and author Melvin Belli has counseled such notables as Mae West, Errol Flynn, Tony Curtis, and Jack Ruby. He specializes in tort cases, and at least 100 of his clients have been awarded over $100,000 each. In addition to his syndicated column and numerous scholarly articles for professional journals, Mr. Belli has written several books, including *The Adequate Award, Modern Trials*, and *Melvin Belli: My Life on Trial*.

1. Jesus
2. Socrates
3. Sir Thomas More
4. Galileo Galilei
5. Joan of Arc
6. Captain Dreyfus
7. Sacco and Vanzetti
8. Scopes "Monkey Trial"
9. Japanese War Crimes Trial (General Yamashita)
10. Jack Ruby

Mr. Belli is aware that three of his great nonmurder trials did involve killing, but he states murder was not their main issue. "The Sacco and Vanzetti case involved alleged anarchist bombings of which they were not accused," says Mr. Belli. "Although the pair were tried for murdering guards, it was mainly a social problem that was being dealt with in the trial. The Japanese War Crimes trial stressed the policy of a country in a postwar situation and the treatment of prisoners—mainly torture. The Jack Ruby trial focused upon the political assassination syndrome."

—Exclusive for *The Book of Lists*

Anarchists Nicola Sacco (L) and Bartolomeo Vanzetti, executed in Massachusetts on August 23, 1927, for a crime they may not have committed. Protests against their deaths came from Albert Einstein, H. G. Wells, George Bernard Shaw, and 250,000 silent marchers in Boston.

12 FAMOUS NONMURDER TRIALS

1. SOCRATES (399 B.C.)

At age 70, Socrates stood accused of two crimes: impiety (not recognizing the gods recognized by the state) and corrupting the youth of Athens. Both charges were trumped up in an attempt to rid Athens of its most outspoken citizen. At the trial before 501 jurors, Socrates' three accusers testified that he continuously criticized established institutions and their leaders, and that he encouraged the youth of Athens to do the same. Socrates spoke in his own behalf (as Plato recounted in his *Apology*), but instead of refuting the nebulous charges, he defended his position as a seeker of truth. By a margin of 60 votes he was convicted and sentenced to death. His friends provided for his escape, but Socrates refused—the death penalty offered an opportunity for martyrdom. He spent his last moments consoling friends, then drank the fabled hemlock potion.

2. GALILEO GALILEI (1633)

When Galileo published *Dialogue on the Two Greatest Systems in the World*, he advanced the Copernican theory that the sun, not the earth, was the center of the universe, and defied an order by the Catholic Church to regard the theory as a mere hypothesis, not as truth. The theory was considered heretical because it contradicted the Bible, which said that God created the earth in five days and the rest of the universe in one. Such blasphemy could only lead to further questioning of the Scriptures. *Dialogue* was banned in Italy and all foreign countries, and Galileo was summoned to Rome at age 69, brought before the Court of Inquisition, threatened with torture, and —on June 22, 1633—forced to confess the falsehood of the Copernican theory.

3. SALEM WITCHES (1692)

The cry of "Witch!" began innocently enough when a West Indian servant named Tituba began teaching the native occult arts of palmistry, fortune-telling, and black magic to excitable young girls in Salem, Mass. The group of about 10 girls, ranging in age from 9 to 20, became so adept at the rituals that they were pronounced "bewitched" and pressured to name those responsible. "For sport," the girls accused certain men and women of bewitching them. Their word was rarely questioned. If the accused had an alibi, the girls swore that the accused's "specter" had afflicted them. Almost 150 "witches" were arrested, but only 31 were tried in 1692. All 31 (6 of them men) were sentenced to death. Nineteen were hanged, 2 died in jail, and 1 man was slowly pressed to death under heavy stones. None were burned. By May, 1693, all such trials had ceased, and the untried witches were released.

4. JOHN PETER ZENGER (1735)

The trial of John Peter Zenger, which took place over half a century before the U.S. Constitution was written, struck a heavy blow for freedom of the press. Zenger was arrested for "seditious ibel," after publishing true accounts of the corrupt tactics of the appointed governor of the colony of New York, William S. Cosby. The trial opened August 4, 1735. The court proclaimed that the mere publication of slanderous remarks against a sacred government office was sufficient to constitute libel. But Zenger's lawyer, the wily Andrew Hamilton, claimed that truth was a defense to libel, and in arguing the point with the court made it clear to the 12 jurors that to deny the right to publish true statements about government officials was a restriction of expression the citizens could ill afford. The jury adjourned for 10 minutes, then returned with a verdict of not guilty.

5. REV. HENRY WARD BEECHER (1875)

One of the biggest scandals of the 19th century was the charge of adultery leveled at the pious, beloved, and highest-paid preacher in the U.S., Rev. Henry Ward Beecher. Unbeknownst to his admiring congregation, Beecher had engaged in a number of extramarital trysts, but he erred when he seduced Elizabeth Tilton, wife of his best friend, editor Theodore Tilton. Although Elizabeth confessed to her husband, the matter would have ended there if free-love advocate Victoria Woodhull had not found out and publicly blasted Beecher for his hypocrisy. After Woodhull's accusations, Tilton brought charges against Beecher for having alienated his wife's affections, and demanded $100,000 in damages. The trial opened on January 11, 1875, and lasted 112 days. After 52 ballots, the jury was hung in a 9-3 split against Tilton. The scandal ended Beecher's aspirations of becoming President, but did little to lessen the esteem his devoted followers felt for him.

6. CAPT. ALFRED DREYFUS (1894 and 1899)

French army officer Capt. Alfred Dreyfus—a Jew—was alleged to have committed an act of espionage for the Germans in 1894. Tried in a star chamber proceeding (closed to the public and press), Dreyfus was convicted by a "secret file" containing forgeries, irrelevancies, and hearsay. He was imprisoned and shipped to Devil's Island. When evidence was disclosed that a French officer, Major Esterhazy, was the guilty collaborationist, a wave of agitation swept across France. The famed French novelist Émile Zola wrote a scathing attack against the army cover-up, hoping to be sued for libel to expose the whole matter. Zola was not only sued but was found guilty. However, the publicity provided Dreyfus with a new trial in 1899. Dreyfus was again found guilty, but was pardoned 10 days later. In 1906, his innocence officially proclaimed, he was elevated to the rank of general and made a chevalier of the French Legion of Honor.

7. OSCAR WILDE (1895)

In 1895, when the literary genius and homosexual libertine Oscar Wilde wooed the son of the marquess of Queensberry, Lord Queensberry retaliated by addressing a circulated note: "For Oscar Wilde, posing as a somdomite [sic]." Wilde sued Lord Queensberry for libel, but after three days of the trial Wilde realized that the truth was working against him, and he dropped his case. The following day Wilde and his procurer of young paramours, Alfred Taylor, were charged with violating the Criminal Law Amendment Act by procuring males for "acts of gross indecency." Treated to a display of Wilde's wit on the witness stand, but confronted with a string of boys intimate with Wilde in the past, the jury was unable to agree on a verdict. At a second trial, Wilde and Taylor were found guilty and sentenced to two years at hard labor, which they each served.

8. GEORGE ARCHER-SHEE (1910)

In the fall of 1908, 13-year-old George Archer-Shee, a cadet at the Royal Naval College in Osborne, England, was expelled for heisting a 5-shilling postal order from another boy's locker. There was no hearing, and the case was immediately closed. Young George denied the charges. Believing in his son's innocence, Martin Archer-Shee set out to discover why there was never an investigation into the matter. Blocked at every turn by haughty and unconcerned bureaucrats, Archer-Shee's solicitor finally got the case (now a cause célèbre) into court on July 26, 1910. On the fourth day of the trial, the solicitor general, realizing there had never been sufficient evidence against the boy, proclaimed the boy's innocence and dropped the case. The Admiralty reluctantly paid £7,120 to Archer-Shee and swore that no boy's rights would ever again be so summarily dispensed with at the college.

9. JOHN T. SCOPES (1925)

The famous "Monkey Trial" occurred when a biology teacher at Dayton, Tenn., John T. Scopes, was persuaded to violate a Tennessee statute which forbade the teaching of ". . . any theory that denies the story of the Divine Creation of man as taught in the Bible, and to teach instead that man has descended from a lower order of animals." The trial pitted William Jennings Bryan against Clarence Darrow. Since the violation of the law, not its validity, was the only issue, testimony was dull, until Darrow called Bryan as a defense witness. Firing questions on the origins of the earth and Adam and Eve, Darrow reduced the aging orator to raging contradictions, proving his point that the Bible, in light of scientific knowledge, cannot be interpreted literally. Nevertheless, the jury found Scopes guilty and he was fined $100. (The decision was later reversed on a technicality.) In spite of Scopes's conviction, academic freedom had been advanced.

10. ALGER HISS (1948)

In 1948, Whittaker Chambers, a senior editor for *Time* magazine, testified before the House Committee on Un-American Activities that Alger Hiss, a top-ranking member of the State Dept., had been a Communist and had engaged in high-level espionage. Hiss denied even knowing Chambers, but one committee member, Rep. Richard M. Nixon, pressed the issue. A series of accusations and denials ensued, which resulted in Hiss suing Chambers for libel. During a pretrial hearing, Chambers introduced incriminating documents in Hiss's own hand. Although the statute of limitations for espionage had run out, a federal grand jury indicted Hiss for perjury before the committee. The first trial ended in a hung jury, but in the second trial Chambers's testimony, plus evidence that some documents had been typed on Hiss's personal typewriter, led to Hiss's conviction. He was sentenced to five years in prison. Some authorities still feel that

Hiss was framed. In August, 1975, he became the first disbarred lawyer in the state of Mass. ever to be readmitted to the bar.

11. JULIUS and ETHEL ROSENBERG (1951)

In 1951, Julius and Ethel Rosenberg were charged with transmitting U.S. atomic secrets to the Russians and found guilty, in what is remembered as the greatest "political" trial of their generation. The case against the Rosenbergs was pockmarked with glaring inconsistencies, but it was their fate to be tried during the height of McCarthyism. The chief evidence against them was the testimony of Ethel's brother, David Greenglass, a convicted coconspirator. After their conviction, demonstrations demanding clemency erupted throughout Europe and South America, but to no avail. They were electrocuted on June 19, 1953, the first husband-and-wife team ever executed in the U.S. An alleged accomplice, Morton Sobell, was sentenced to 30 years in prison with a recommendation against parole. Doubt as to the guilt of the Rosenbergs and Sobell still exists.

12. THE GREAT SOUL TRIAL (1967)

The famous "Ghost Trial of the Century" began 18 years after a dusty old prospector, James Kidd, disappeared in Arizona's Superstition Mountains in 1949, leaving $250,000 to "research for some scientific proof of a soul of the human body which leaves at death. . . ." During a trial that lasted 90 days, 133 claims by neurological foundations, parapsychology groups, and various other organizations and individuals were carefully considered. Defining the word *soul* and deciding whether the soul lends itself to scientific examination were major considerations in attempting to carry out the intent of the will. The money was eventually awarded (pending appeal) to the Barrow Neurological Institute of Phoenix, Ariz. Allegedly, when the renowned New York medium Douglas Johnson contacted Kidd later, the old prospector observed, "I should have done things better, I don't think much of the result . . . [but] I'm very glad that I'm not a puff of smoke. I'm quite solid."

—G.K.

EDGAR LUSTGARTEN'S 10 VERDICTS STILL IN DISPUTE

Edgar Lustgarten, English barrister turned author, is one of the world's leading writers of true crime cases. One of his most famous books, *Verdict in Dispute,* covers the murder trials of Florence Maybrick, Steinie Morrison, Norman Thorne, Edith Thompson, William Herbert Wallace, and Lizzie Borden. Each of those verdicts is still debatable. Now, Edgar Lustgarten presents 10 more cases to ponder.

1. NICOLA SACCO and BARTOLOMEO VANZETTI (1927)

Two "Reds" (actually anarchists) executed for murder in the course of a Massachusetts robbery.

2. MADELEINE SMITH (1857)

Escaped (in Scotland) with a verdict of "not proven" on the charge of poisoning her lover (who was blackmailing her). She died in America in 1928.

3. WILLIAM KIRWAN (1852)

Dublin artist, with a mistress who had borne him seven children, convicted of murdering his wife. The death sentence was commuted. When he was finally released, he joined his mistress in America.

4. DONALD MERRETT (1926)

Eighteen-year-old student charged with murdering his mother. He escaped (in Scotland) with a verdict of "not proven" and was therefore discharged. In 1954, after having adopted another name, he murdered his wife and mother-in-law and committed suicide.

5. GASTON DOMINICI (1954)

French peasant farmer in his late 70s who was convicted of murdering a notable British biochemist and his wife and 11-year-old daughter. The death sentence was commuted, and he was released in 1960 on the grounds of old age.

6. TONY MANCINI (1934)

Acquitted at Lewes (England), of murdering a prostitute with whom, and off whom, he had admittedly been living.

7. THE HALL-MILLS CASE (1927)

The wife and her male relatives were acquitted of murdering a New Jersey Episcopalian minister and his choir singer mistress.

8. JESSIE McLACHLAN (1862)

A domestic servant sentenced to death (commuted) for the murder of another female domestic servant. It seems likely that the real culprit was an old man of higher social station.

9. JULIUS and ETHEL ROSENBERG (1951)

American husband and wife executed for conspiracy to commit espionage at the Los Alamos atomic plant.

10. ADELAIDE BARTLETT (1886)

Acquitted at the Old Bailey of murdering her husband by administering liquid chloroform. A famous Harley Street specialist said afterward: "Now that it's all over, in the interests of science she should tell us how she did it."

—Exclusive for *The Book of Lists*

10 COUNTRIES
THAT USE TORTURE TODAY

"I do not deny that torture continues to be used in this country, but there are strict orders to the army not to use torture."
—Ernesto Geisel, president of Brazil

1. BRAZIL

Army, air force, navy, and Dept. of Public Safety personnel use every contemporary torture technique on political and criminal suspects. Documented cases since 1964. Recent reports that torture has ended have already been proved false—locations of the centers were simply changed.

2. CHILE

DINA (military government secret police) uses burning with cigarettes and acid, electric shock, rape of both sexes, floggings, and beatings with metal rods and rubber hoses. The victims include Communists, socialists, workers, students, and supporters of the Allende regime. Documented cases since 1969, but wholesale torture began after the overthrow of Allende in 1973.

3. INDIA

Indian police and army secret service agents use burning with cigarettes and candles, beatings, starvation, and rape of both men and women who are suspected Communists, regional separatists, or opponents of the present regime. Documented cases since 1970.

4. IRAN

SAVAK (Iranian secret police) uses beatings, electric shock treatment to the rectum and sexual organs, and the "electric grill" on political dissidents and terrorists. Documented cases since 1963.

5. PARAGUAY

The Ministry of the Interior and the Dept. of Crimes and Vigilance use water torture, extraction of fingernails, and sexual abuse on suspects to obtain political information and to extort money. Documented cases since 1966.

6. PHILIPPINES

The army, constabulary, and antinarcotics unit use beatings, electric shock, and floggings on political dissidents and narcotics suspects. Documented cases since 1972.

7. SPAIN

The Guardia Civil and the Brigada Político-Social (secret police) use flogging of the soles of the feet, water torture, running the gauntlet, and solitary confinement without food on dissident students, workers, and Basque separatists. Documented cases since 1963—Franco's death has not put an end to these practices.

8. TURKEY

Army secret police and MIT (Turkish secret service) use starvation, beatings while the victim hangs by his wrists, and electric shock on political dissidents and Greek Cypriots. Documented cases since 1971.

9. UGANDA

Police Criminal Investigations Dept. uses floggings, beatings with rifle butts, and mutilation on political and tribal opponents. Documented cases since 1967.

10. URUGUAY

National police and Armed Forces Ministry of Defense use water torture, electric shock, rape with trained dogs, and beatings on suspected Tupamaro terrorists and political dissidents. Documented cases since 1965.

The peculiar case of NATO: During NATO war games in 1971, 6 Belgian commandos "captured" 12 Belgian "enemy" soldiers and tortured them with beatings, electric shock, and exposure to the cold for 24 hours, before an officer put an end to their activities. When the 6 commandos were brought to trial, their defense was that NATO armies not only taught resistance to torture but also taught torture techniques.

—R.J.F.

8 REMARKABLE ESCAPES FROM DEVIL'S ISLAND

The penal colony in French Guiana, known as *le bagne*, had a long and black history. There were scattered camps on the mainland, as well as on the three "Isles of Salvation," one of which is Devil's Island. In time, the whole colony was referred to as Devil's Island, and escape was on the mind of all who were unlucky enough to find themselves imprisoned there.

1. RENÉ BELBENOÎT

Sentenced to eight years at hard labor for the theft of a necklace when he was 22, Belbenoît escaped from *le bagne* by boat in 1936 along with several other prisoners. They were recaptured in Colombia, but before the French authorities could retrieve their prisoners, Belbenoît escaped from the Colombian jail (with the help of a sympathetic prison commandant). He is the author of *Dry Guillotine* and *Hell on Trial*.

2. HENRI CHARRIÈRE ("Papillon")

Convicted of murdering a "pimp and a stool pigeon" in 1931, Papillon was condemned to hard labor for life, when he was 25. He escaped from Île du Diable in 1941 (his ninth escape attempt). He and another prisoner, Sylvain, used bags of coconuts for rafts, riding out on a large wave. Sylvain died in quicksand upon reaching the shore. Papillon, assisted by natives, made his way to Georgetown, British Guiana, where he ran a restaurant, caught and sold butterflies, and operated a striptease joint. From there, he went to Venezuela, where he was befriended by fishermen and subsequently arrested for "vagrancy" by corrupt police officials. He finally gained his freedom as a result of a military and civilian coup d'etat. It was October 18, 1945.

3. DIEUDONNÉ

He was convicted of assisting in the robbery of a bank messenger in 1913, at the age of 27. In 1928, after several unsuccessful attempts to escape, Dieudonné convinced an Indian to sail him from *le bagne* to Brazil, a long ocean voyage in a canoe designed for streams and rivers. He was captured in Pará, Brazil, but was released because of strong public sentiment. He was eventually pardoned and returned to France a free man.

4. JEAN DOUVERNAY

This ingenious Frenchman enlisted 10 prisoners, 4 from

Cell in punishment block on Royale, one of the group
of islands that includes Devil's Island.

Royale Island, 4 from St. Joseph's, and 2 from Devil's Island. With money he had stashed away, Douvernay had bought a 16-ft. canoe. The men swam through shark-infested water to reach this canoe and then spent 32 days at sea before meeting up with a British freighter. The freighter renewed their supplies, which had run out days before, and they set off again, landing in Trinidad. Leaving from there in a new craft, they were wrecked in Curaçao, where kindly folks took them in and gave them a 14-ft. fishing boat. They went from there to Aruba in the Dutch West Indies, where they came to the attention of the world press.

5. GERARDIN

After being chained to a leper for a year, Gerardin feigned leprosy by pretending numbness in his legs, and cutting off fingers and an ear. He was put on St. Louis (Leper's Island), where the lepers treated him as a brother and helped him escape to Pará. In Brazil, he masqueraded as a dentist in little towns, making a good living. Then, in São Paolo, he went to the Prevention Bureau and discovered that he really did have leprosy. The Prevention Bureau realized from his accent and tattoos that he was from *le bagne,* but no ship would carry him back there. So the bureau built him a small prison of his own, where he grew fruit and raised pigs and chickens.

6. GERMAIN JOLITON

Convicted in 1919 of stabbing his sweetheart when he caught her with another lover, Joliton arrived at Port of Spain, Trinidad, in 1937, in the company of seven exhausted, sun-blistered convicts. In the group there were three murderers, a bank robber, and a jewel thief. Joliton and the others had escaped from the colony in an Indian dugout and had traveled 750 mi. on the open sea before drifting ashore in Trinidad. There, he was placed in the care of the Salvation Army. It was Joliton's third escape attempt.

7. LOUIS LEGARDE

With Legarde as their leader, 12 prisoners escaped while they were assigned to the job of ferrying timber. The men hid out in the jungles of French Guiana for a month, avoiding the guards and the paid native informants, while they built a raft from torn clothing and the green boughs of trees. They lost track of the time they were at sea, but eventually 5 weary men landed on Santa María de Venezuela. The other 7 had died and been eaten by sharks.

8. CHARLOT PAIN

Sentenced to six years at hard labor for setting fire to a $5 army tent while suffering from sunstroke in 1907, Pain attempted escapes in 1913, 1917, 1926, and 1931. His and similar military offenses were annulled in France in 1925. However, according to the rules of the French penal colony, he was required to remain in Guiana as a *libéré* (involuntary settler) for several years after his sentence had expired. Each of his escape attempts forced him to serve more years as an exile. Thus, 32 years after his noncrime, Charlot Pain was still a prisoner in French Guiana.

—A.B.

10 DOCTORS WHO TRIED
TO GET AWAY WITH MURDER

"Wherever the art of medicine is loved,
there also is love of humanity."
—Hippocrates, c. 400 B.C.

1. JOHN WEBSTER (U.S.; 1791–1850)

A distinguished Harvard professor, Webster was deeply in debt to Dr. George Parkman of the Massachusetts Medical School. Angered over Parkman's demands for repayment, Webster killed him by a blow to the head, then dismembered the body. Charred bones were found beneath Webster's laboratory, along with a set of false teeth which a dentist identified as Parkman's. Webster was convicted on this circumstantial evidence and, prior to hanging, confessed to the crime.

2. EDME CASTAING (France; 1796–1824)

Castaing was the first to use the newly discovered drug morphine to commit murder. He poisoned a patient, the wealthy Hippolyte Ballet, so that the victim's brother Auguste would inherit a fortune. Then, after getting Auguste to make out a will in his behalf, Castaing poisoned him, too. He was suspected almost immediately and arrested. At his trial, medical opinions differed as to the nature of the poison used. Castaing was convicted of Auguste's—but not Hippolyte's—murder. He was executed, protesting his innocence to the last.

3. ALFRED WILLIAM WARDER (England; 1820–1866)

All three of Warder's wives died under suspicious circumstances, but he was held responsible for the murder of only one—his third wife, Ethel. She died suddenly after their secret wedding. Warder, an authority on forensic toxicology, admitted prescribing a tincture of aconite—to be taken orally for her bladder trouble—although he knew the remedy was strictly for external use. Before the jury at the inquest could return its verdict of guilty, Warder committed suicide by taking prussic acid.

4. WILLIAM PALMER (England; 1824–1856)

In his youth, Palmer was a thief and a gambler. Heavily in debt, he took out insurance policies on his wife and brother. Both died soon after. When the insurance company refused to honor the brother's policy, Palmer faced financial ruin, as he had borrowed against his expectations. To save himself, he falsely appropriated the gambling winnings of his friend John Cook, and then poisoned Cook with strychnine. Convicted for just this one murder, he was believed to have committed 12-15 others, including those of his mother-in-law and an illegitimate child. He went to the gallows.

5. EDWARD WILLIAM PRITCHARD (Scotland; 1825–1865)

A vain, pathological liar and seducer of young women, the only motive Pritchard had for the slow poisoning of his wife was his egotistical desire to get away with murder. He killed his wife's mother for no better reason, and it was thought he had murdered a young girl some years before. His was the last public execution in Scotland and allegedly was attended by 100,000 people.

6. PHILLIP CROSS (Ireland; 1825–1888)

Cross was an aging Lothario and a bungler. To dispose of the wife he no longer wanted, he used arsenic, the most detectable of all poisons. Then—only two weeks later—he married his mistress, a girl young enough to be his granddaughter. The gossip this started led to the exhumation of Mrs. Cross's body. The arsenic was traced to Cross and a jury took only 10 minutes to find him guilty. His young wife abandoned him, and he died on the gallows, a very bitter man.

7. HAWLEY HARVEY CRIPPEN (England; 1862–1910)

The American-born Crippen prescribed an overdose of hyoscine, a drug used to lessen the sex drive, to kill his vain, nymphomaniac wife, who was a music hall artist. He then dismembered her body and hid parts of it in his cellar, where they were discovered. He sailed for Canada with his young mistress, Ethel Le Neve, whom he hoped to marry. She was disguised as a boy. In the first such use of wireless telegraphy, Crippen was identified while aboard ship and arrested upon landing in Quebec. He was convicted and hanged in England. Le Neve was acquitted of complicity.

Hawley Harvey Crippen, who murdered his nymphomaniac wife in London. This is a wax likeness of the infamous doctor.

8. TOM DREHER (U.S.; c. 1882–1929)

Aided by his mistress, Ada Le Boeuf, and a hired accomplice, Dreher shot Ada's husband and dropped his body into a Louisiana lake. Though it was weighted, and had been slashed across the stomach to release any buoyant gases, it was discovered. The doctor's affair with Ada was common bayou gossip, so he was immediately suspected. He confessed and all three murderers were convicted. Ada and her doctor-lover were hung together despite a plea to Governor Huey Long for clemency in her case.

9. ROBERT GEORGE CLEMENTS (England; c. 1885–1947)

Clements's first wealthy wife died of "sleeping sickness" in 1920, his second of "endocarditis" in 1925, his third of "cancer" in 1939, and his fourth of "myeloid leukemia" in 1947. He had signed the first three death certificates, but the fourth was signed by Dr. James Houston, a colleague who had accepted Clements's diagnosis. But other doctors suspected morphine, and it was found in an autopsy. Both Clements and Houston committed suicide after writing notes: Clements's, a last disclaimer of guilt; Houston's, a sad admission of his error.

10. GEZA DE KAPLANY (U.S.; b. 1926)

De Kaplany was an arrogant Hungarian womanizer practicing in San Francisco. He poured acid over his estranged wife, a former showgirl, then mutilated her further, using a knife. She died in agony a month later, on September 30, 1962. De Kaplany claimed insanity, and defense psychiatrists called him a paranoid, a latent homosexual, and a transvestite. However, he was declared legally sane and sentenced to life imprisonment and committed to a California prison medical facility.

—J.B. & S.ST.

10 POSSIBLE VICTIMS OF 10 POSSIBLE "JACK THE RIPPERS"

". . . I am down on whores and shant [sic] quit ripping them . . ." warned the writer of an anonymous letter to London's Central News Agency on September 28, 1888. The letter may have been a hoax, but it gave a lasting nickname to the murderer of several prostitutes in the slums of London's East End in 1888—and possibly later. Jack the Ripper has inspired at least a dozen movies and stage plays; two operas, Alban Berg's *Lulu* and *The Threepenny Opera* by Bertolt Brecht and Kurt Weill; and several hundred books, both fact and fiction. Estimates of the Ripper's victims range from the "dozens" of popular belief down to the 10 selected by serious criminologists. The 10 "most likely" victims are listed here in chronological order, with the 6 "favorites" starred.

THE VICTIMS

1. EMMA ELIZABETH SMITH (Apr. 3, 1888)

Forty-five-year-old prostitute; died in hospital from stab wound in abdomen inflicted by a "sharp spike." No mutilations.

2. MARTHA TURNER* (or Tabram) (Aug. 7, 1888)

Thirty-five-year-old prostitute; found with throat slit and 39 wounds on body; autopsy suggested ambidextrous killer.

3. MARY ANN ("Polly") NICHOLLS* (Aug. 31, 1888)

Forty-two-year-old prostitute; throat cut and body mutilated, almost disemboweled; examination suggested left-handed expert with "surgical" knife.

4. ANNIE CHAPMAN* (Sept. 8, 1888)

Forty-seven-year-old prostitute; nearly decapitated; kidney and ovaries removed "by an expert hand."

5. ELIZABETH ("Long Liz") STRIDE* (Sept. 30, 1888)

Forty-five-year-old prostitute; throat cut but body unmutilated. The killer may have been disturbed at his work (at 1:00 A.M.).

6. CATHERINE EDDOWES* (Sept. 30, 1888)

Forty-three-year-old prostitute; *found only 45 minutes after discovery of Stride's body*, some 15 minutes' walk away; throat cut, face and body mutilated, left kidney and other organs missing.

7. MARY JANE ("Jeanette") KELLY* (Nov. 9, 1888)

Twenty-four-year-old prostitute; body found in her room, horribly mutilated but no organs missing.

8. ELIZABETH JACKSON (June, 1889)

Prostitute, age unknown; headless trunk and other parts of body taken from the Thames.

9. ALICE ("Clay Pipe Alice") MACKENZIE (July 17, 1889)

Forty-seven-year-old prostitute; body found near site of Nicholls slaying, throat cut and abdomen mutilated.

10. FRANCES ("Carrotty Nell") COLES (Feb. 13, 1891)

Twenty-five-year-old prostitute; found dying of stab wounds in East End.

THE SUSPECTS

1. DR. THOMAS NEILL CREAM (1850–1892) and "ANOTHER"

Born in Scotland, Cream was taken to Canada by his parents in 1854. He was graduated as a doctor of medicine in Montreal in 1876, having already begun his criminal career with theft, arson, attempted blackmail—and the possible murder of his wife following an abortion. In 1876–1878 he continued his medical studies in England and was admitted as a member of the Royal College of Physicians and Surgeons in Edinburgh. Cream practiced medicine in Ontario, Canada, but an unsuccessful blackmail attempt, plus suspicion of his having murdered his mistress with chloroform, caused him to move to Chicago, where he was arrested for murder after a patient of his died following an abortion in 1880. He beat the rap, as well as another for attempted poisoning and blackmail the same year. Convicted of second-degree murder—strychnine poisoning of his mistress's husband—in 1881, Cream served 10 years in Joliet penitentiary, going to England on his release. In 1891–1892, for the sheer joy of killing, Cream murdered at least five London prostitutes by strychnine poisoning. He was hanged on November 15, 1892. Billington, the executioner, stated that Cream's last words were: "*I am Jack the* . . ."! Although Cream was in Joliet when the main Ripper murders were committed, reliable evidence suggests he had a "double," also a criminal. Cream once beat a bigamy rap by claiming that he was in Sydney, Australia, at the relevant time; he never was in Australia, but was identified as a former prisoner by the governor of Sydney prison. The famous advocate Marshall Hall, who defended Cream—or his double—on the bigamy charge, believed Cream and his "twin" had an alibi pact and that one of them was the Ripper. The Australian con man and murderer Frederick Bailey ("Mad Fred") Deeming (1853–1892) also confessed on the scaffold to being the Ripper: he would have had little opportunity to commit the crimes and, although both men were spectacularly ugly, he was not Cream's double.

2. JOHN DRUITT MONTAGUE (1857–1889)

Oxford-educated Montague was a brilliant but unstable young man. Failing in his career as a lawyer (not a doctor, as sometimes stated), in 1888 he was teaching at a shabby private school near London. A month after the killing of Mary Kelly, he attempted suicide by drowning; a second attempt a month later was successful. In March, 1889, an anti-Ripper vigilante group was persuaded to disband when secretly informed by the police that "the Ripper drowned himself two months ago." Montague was a strong police suspect, according to the assistant chief of London's Criminal Investigation Department (CID) in 1889.

3. "THE GENERAL'S SECRETARY" (unnamed man)

"General" William Booth (1829–1912), founder of the Salvation Army, believed that his former secretary was Jack the Ripper. In February, 1891, a few days before the slaying of Frances Coles, the young secretary told Booth: "Carrotty Nell will be the next to go"; immediately after that murder, he vanished. Booth was no liar—but the secretary probably was. Some writers say the secretary *may* have "ripped" Coles, but others state that she was almost certainly killed by Thomas Sadler, a drunken railroadman, who was arrested earlier but released for lack of evidence after the murder of Alice MacKenzie.

4. "JILL THE RIPPER"

There has to be one theory that Jack was a Jill. Author William Stewart believes the murders were committed by a psychopathic midwife, who may have walked the East End disguised as a man. The thin evidence rests on the fact (not revealed at the time) that Mary Kelly was three months pregnant at the time of her killing, and that ashes in the fireplace of her room may have been the remains of the Ripper's disguise. Others point out that the "mad midwife" could hardly have escaped in Kelly's spare clothes. The unfortunate woman had pawned them.

5. JAMES KENNETH STEPHEN (1859–1892)

J. K. Stephen, whose humorous verse is still to be found in many anthologies, was the cousin of Sir Leslie Stephen, who was the tutor of Prince Albert Victor and the father of the novelist Virginia Woolf. He was a friend of John Druitt Montague, another suspect. Basing his evidence on a detailed comparison of Stephen's poetry and the "Ripper letters," author Michael Harrison regarded the poet as the slayer. In spite of Stephen's undoubted eccentricity and his connection with other suspects, this theory seems exploded by the fact that of the hundreds of letters to the police and newspapers supposedly sent by Jack the Ripper, only two are accepted by Jurgen Thorwald and other reliable criminologists as genuine.

6. "LEATHER APRON"

Among the police suspects named by crime writer Maj. Arthur Griffiths, "an insane Polish Jew" figures strongly. This unfortunate man, variously called Pizer or Kosminski, was a mentally deranged shoemaker (who got his nickname of "Leather Apron" from his working dress), and appears to have been the victim of local gossip which linked him with the killings as early as the Turner slaying. He was arrested, questioned, and freed—after the murder of Nicholls. A slogan chalked on a wall near Eddowes's body—"The Jewes [sic] Are The Men What Wont Be Blamed For Nothing"—was probably the work of an anti-Semitic troublemaker, although both Sir Robert Anderson, appointed head of the CID in 1889, and Maj. Sir Henry Smith, then head of the City of London police, seem to have believed "Leather Apron" was guilty. Another authority also suggests the Ripper was a Jew—not a cobbler, but a *shochet,* employed to slaughter animals by the approved Jewish ritual method.

Which of the 10 wrote this letter?

7. PRINCE ALBERT VICTOR, DUKE OF CLARENCE
(1864–1892)

Although he would have been king of England had he lived, "Prince Eddy," elder son of Edward, prince of Wales (later King Edward VII) and brother of the future King George V, was admittedly weak-minded and almost certainly a sexual degenerate. Contemporary gossip connected "a member of the royal family" with the Ripper slayings, but the prince's possible guilt was not aired until Dr. Thomas Stowell, a surgeon of international repute, published evidence in 1970 pointing to "Eddy" as the possible killer. (Stowell later denied that the prince was his suspect.) Other attempts have been made to link "Eddy" with the case.

8. SIR WILLIAM WITHEY GULL (1816–1890)
and "OTHERS"

Gull's rise in the medical profession was assured when he cured the prince of Wales of typhoid in 1871; he was made a baronet and appointed physician in ordinary to Queen Victoria. The famous spiritualist medium Robert James Lees (consulted by the mourning queen in 1868, after the death of her husband) claimed in the 1890s that he had "dreamed" of the Ripper and had identified "a distinguished physician"—fairly obviously meaning Gull—to the police. The main case against Gull was put by Dr. Benjamin Howard in a sensational interview with the *Chicago Sunday Times-Herald* on April 28, 1895, claiming that Gull, who had "died" in 1890, was really still alive, a raving madman in a London asylum to which he had been confined after a private "trial" by 12 eminent physicians (Howard himself being one). A more circumstantial attempt to establish Gull as the Ripper was made by author Stephen Knight in 1976. He argued that a bastard child sired by "Prince Eddy" had been nursed by Mary Kelly, last of the "probable" Ripper victims. Having fallen from the status of nursemaid to that of harlot, Kelly attempted to blackmail the royal family, whereupon Prime Minister Salisbury, with the queen's approval, ordered the "elimination" of Kelly and her closest associates. The murders were carried out by Gull, police chief Sir Robert Anderson, and "Eddy's" former private carriage driver John Netley—the trio stalking their prey in a horse-drawn cab into which the women were lured, "ripped," and later dumped. The painter Walter Richard Sickert (1860–1942), said to have been the guardian—and later the lover—of "Eddy's" illegitimate daughter, is also alleged to have played an active part in the conspiracy.

9. GEORGE CHAPMAN (1865–1903)

In the opinion of three authorities, George Chapman is the likeliest of the named suspects. Born in Poland—his real name was Severin Klosowski—Chapman served an apprenticeship to a barber-surgeon before departing hurriedly to England (he was suspected of the decapitation of a woman) in 1887. At the time of the Ripper slayings, Chapman was working as a barber in the area. Early in 1890, he left suddenly for New York; attempts to link him with a supposed series of Ripper-type murders in Jersey City in 1891–1893 have been discounted. Back in London by 1895, Chapman turned tavernkeeper, and in the following years murdered a succession of barmaid-mistresses by antimony poisoning. He was arrested in 1902. Chief

Inspector Abberline, formerly a top detective on the Ripper case, told the inspector who collared Chapman: "You've got Jack the Ripper at last!" Chapman was hanged for the murder of three mistresses. Much circumstantial evidence points to him as the Ripper; the main objection, that he was a poisoner by inclination and that mass murderers rarely vary their method, seems inconclusive.

10. "THE RUSSIAN DOCTOR"

A theory with more weight than some, supported by authors Sir Harold Scott and Richard Deacon, attributes the Ripper murders to "an insane Russian doctor" named Alexander Pedachenko, also known as Vassily Konovalov, Andrey Luiskovo, and Mikhail Ostrong (or Ostrog). Pedachenko was employed at a clinic for London's East End poor, where Martha Turner, Mary Nicholls, Annie Chapman, and Mary Kelly all received treatment early in 1888. Deacon suggests that Pedachenko, who had already "ripped" a Parisian prostitute, was deliberately introduced into England by the Okhrana, the Russian czarist secret police, who hoped his activities might discredit the Russian radicals living in exile in east London. After the Ripper murders, Pedachenko returned to St. Petersburg (now Leningrad), where he died in an asylum after murdering yet another woman. Sir Basil Thompson, assistant head of the CID, was convinced of Pedachenko's guilt.

—R.O.

13 DROPS FOR THE WORKING HANGMAN

In the early days, hanging consisted of placing a noose around the culprit's neck and having the executioner pull on the other end of the rope until strangulation occurred. Later, the drop system came into use, with the height of the drop regulated in order to: (1) cause instantaneous death by dislocation rather than strangulation; and (2) prevent any visible mutilation of the victim. James "Hangman" Barry, author of *The Business Side of Hanging*, discussed at length the particulars of hanging and prepared the following table of proper drop heights for persons of average build with no unusual physical problems. He noted, however, that when executing "persons who had attempted suicide by cutting their throats . . . to prevent reopening the wounds I have reduced the drop by nearly half."

	Culprit's Weight	Drop
1.	14 stone (196 lbs.)	8 ft. 0 in.
2.	13½ stone (189 lbs.)	8 ft. 2 in.
3.	13 stone (182 lbs.)	8 ft. 4 in.
4.	12½ stone (175 lbs.)	8 ft. 6 in.
5.	12 stone (168 lbs.)	8 ft. 8 in.
6.	11½ stone (161 lbs.)	8 ft. 10 in.

7.	11 stone (154 lbs.)	9 ft. 0 in.
8.	10½ stone (147 lbs.)	9 ft. 2 in.
9.	10 stone (140 lbs.)	9 ft. 4 in.
10.	9½ stone (133 lbs.)	9 ft. 6 in.
11.	9 stone (126 lbs.)	9 ft. 8 in.
12.	8½ stone (119 lbs.)	9 ft. 10 in.
13.	8 stone (112 lbs.)	10 ft. 0 in.

SOURCE: Charles Duff, *Handbook on Hanging* (Boston: Hale, Cushman & Flint, 1929).

4
WAR AND OTHER DISASTERS

10 OF THE WORST GENERALS IN HISTORY

1. MARCUS LICINIUS CRASSUS (115?–53 B.C.)

In 54 B.C., the Roman general Crassus was collecting tribute money and enriching himself in Syria, while his enemy—the Parthians—massed their forces for battle. In 53 B.C., Crassus, with 50,000 men, finally marched into Parthia. Crassus entrusted himself to a guide who led him into the middle of the Mesopotamian desert where the whole Parthian army awaited him. The Parthians, who fought on horseback, rode in circles around his Roman infantrymen, firing deadly volleys of arrows. Crassus was bewildered by this unorthodox form of warfare. He sent his men running after the enemy cavalry, which simply retreated, drawing him into an ambush. The result was one of Rome's greatest defeats. Crassus was killed, and only two-fifths of his army escaped.

2. PHILIP VI OF FRANCE (1293–1350)

At the battle of Crécy (1346), the inept Philip annihilated his own army. He sent 4,000 mercenary Genoese crossbowmen against the English line. They were promptly cut down by the English longbowmen. Seeing the surviving Genoese retreating, the enraged Philip ordered his knights forward to kill them. While the French cut down their allies—the Genoese—the English rained down arrows on both. Philip then ordered 15 charges of mounted knights, all of which were stopped by English arrows. At the end of the day, Philip had lost one-third of his army (4,000 men) while killing less than 100 Englishmen.

3. GEN. HORATIO GATES (1728?–1806)

At the battle of Saratoga, the American commanding general Gates fought more with his subordinate, Benedict Arnold, than with the British. Gates (who had almost no military experience), had received his command due to political intrigue in Congress. During the fighting, Gates refused to leave the safety of his fortified camp and ordered his men to remain inactive. Arnold disobeyed him and engaged the British. During the critical battle of Bemis Heights, Gates sat in his tent and argued the merits of the American revolutionary cause with a captured British officer, while Arnold defeated the British army. Gates later lost the battle of Camden (1780) and was dismissed from the army.

4. GEN. WILLIAM H. WINDER (1775–1824)

In the War of 1812, the American general Winder proved his incompetence with disastrous consequences. In 1813, he lost the battle of Stony Creek even though he had three times as many men as the British. He was captured but, unfortunately for the Americans, the British released him. In 1814, he commanded the American forces protecting Washington, D.C., against the invading British. One charge routed Winder's army, and he fled for safety. The British proceeded to the American capital and burned it.

5. GEN. ANTONIO LÓPEZ DE SANTA ANNA (1795?–1876)

The Mexican general Santa Anna, who considered himself the Napoleon of the Americas, lost two wars for Mexico. In 1836, in the Texas War, Santa Anna wasted men and time storming the Alamo. Then he marched north and encamped his army at the San Jacinto River—unaware that a Texan army was only a few miles away. The Texans attacked while Santa Anna and his men were taking their siestas. The Mexican army was destroyed and Santa Anna was captured. In the Mexican-American War (1846–1848), Santa Anna lost every battle he fought.

6. GEN. AMBROSE BURNSIDE (1824–1881)

The Union general Burnside's blunders were innumerable. At the battle of Antietam (1862), he sent masses of men across a narrow bridge where Confederate gunners slaughtered them. If Burnside had reconnoitered, he would have discovered that the river beneath the bridge was only waist deep, and his men could have forded it anywhere, thus avoiding the deadly bridge. At Fredericksburg (1862), Burnside ordered a hopeless, suicidal attack which left 1,284 Union soldiers dead. At the siege of Petersburg (1865) he had a tunnel dug beneath the enemy trenches, and filled it with explosives. The powder was detonated, leaving a huge crater. Burnside ordered his troops into the crater where they were entrapped and shot down by Confederates along the crater's rim. President Lincoln remarked on this battle: "Only Burnside could have managed such a coup, wringing one last spectacular defeat from the jaws of victory."

7. GEN. SIR IAN HAMILTON (1853–1947)

During W.W. I, the Allies launched an attack on the Turkish Gallipoli Peninsula in April, 1915, in order to capture Constantinople. The British and French soldiers who landed on the peninsula never got off the beaches, and were finally evacuated in January, 1916. The Allied commander, General Hamilton, spent his time on the Greek islands or aboard British battleships. He mismanaged the entire operation, allowing subordinates to do as they pleased, and giving no direct, comprehensive orders to anyone. Stirring from his inactivity in August, 1915, Hamilton devised an attack which was changed and modified so often that it was totally confusing and doomed to fail. In the end, the campaign cost the Allies 250,000 casualties.

8. GEN. ROBERT NIVELLE (1856–1924)

In 1917—during W.W. I—the French general Nivelle became the commander in chief of the French Army. He promptly planned a grand offensive. The French government tried to dissuade him, since the recent battle of Verdun had nearly bled the French Army to death. But Nivelle paid no attention—he launched his attack. It was soon apparent that the offensive was a failure. Nevertheless, Nivelle continued pouring men onto the battlefields, ignoring casualty reports and refusing to accept defeat. Finally, the French soldiers had had enough—mutiny spread throughout the army and Nivelle was dismissed from his command.

9. GEN. ALEKSANDER SAMSONOV (1859–1914)

At the start of W.W. I, the Russian general Samsonov was given command of the Russian Second Army. He had never been a front-line commander, but always a bureaucrat, serving in the rear. Pushing his army into East Prussia, Samsonov had no idea where the Germans were or what he was supposed to do. He completely lost control of his forces, and the Germans easily smashed his disorganized army at the battle of Tannenberg (1914). Samsonov gave up all hope for his army, and rode off to the front to die in battle. Failing to accomplish even that, he committed suicide.

10. GEN. MAURICE GAMELIN (1872–1958)

In 1940—during W.W. II—General Gamelin, the French Army commander in chief, kept his army safely behind the Maginot Line. When the Germans launched their blitzkrieg through Belgium, Gamelin believed it was just a diversionary attack. Failing to send troops to the Ardennes sector of the Belgian front, Gamelin ensured the success of the German blitzkrieg there. When the Germans plunged into France, Gamelin was relieved of his command. The English evacuated their army at Dunkirk while Paris and all of France fell to the Germans.

—R.J.F.

GEN. OMAR BRADLEY'S 10 LEADING MILITARY LEADERS IN HISTORY

General of the Army Bradley, himself one of the great military leaders of modern times, was born in 1893. During W.W. II he led American troops in the North African campaign and the Sicilian invasion. On D day, June 6, 1944, he commanded the First Army's landing in Normandy. His forces symbolically liberated Paris. He commanded the 12th Army Group, the largest force ever under an American leader, in the sweep through Europe that ended with Germany's surrender. After the war, he was the first chairman of the Joint Chiefs of Staff.

Tutored by Aristotle, ruler of Macedon, Alexander the Great
conquered much of Asia in the 4th century B.C.

1. ALEXANDER THE GREAT

King of Macedonia, military conqueror who helped spread
Greek culture from Asia Minor and Egypt to India.

2. HANNIBAL

Carthaginian general who crossed the Alps to invade Italy in
the Second Punic War.

3. NAPOLEON

French military leader and emperor of France.

4. FIELD MARSHAL ERWIN ROMMEL

The Desert Fox, German W.W. II general.

5. **GEN. ROBERT E. LEE**

   Commander in chief of the Confederate Army.

6. **GEN. ULYSSES S. GRANT**

   Commander in chief of the Union Army.

7. **GEN. WILLIAM TECUMSEH SHERMAN**

   Union general in the U.S. Civil War.

8. **GEN. OF THE ARMIES JOHN J. PERSHING**

   Commander in chief of American Expeditionary Forces in W.W. I.

9. **GEN. GEORGE WASHINGTON**

   Commander in chief of the Continental Army and first president of the U.S.

10. **GEN. SIR HAROLD ALEXANDER**

    First earl of Tunis, British general and statesman, governor-general of Canada (1946–1952).

—Exclusive for *The Book of Lists*

GEN. GEORGE PATTON'S 6 PAST LIVES

Patton had "subconscious memories" of these previous incarnations:

1. A prehistoric warrior who "battled for fresh mammoth" and "warred for pastures new."
2. A Greek hoplite who fought the Persians of King Cyrus.
3. A soldier of Alexander the Great at the siege of Tyre.
4. A legionnaire with Julius Caesar in northern Gaul.
5. An English knight at the battle of Crécy during the Hundred Years' War.
6. A Napoleonic marshal at a time "when one laughed at death and numbers, trusting in the emperor's star."

—Farago, Ladislas, *Patton: Ordeal and Triumph* (New York: I. Obolensky, 1964).

TOP 10 AIR ACES OF WORLD WAR I

Name, Combat Years, and Country	Type of Plane Flown Most	Victories
1. Rittmeister Manfred Richthofen (1915–1918; Germany)	Fokker Dr I	80
2. Capitaine René P. Fonck (1914–1918; France)	Caudron G. IV	75
3. Maj. Edward Mannoch (1916–1918; Great Britain)*	S.E. 5a	73
4. Maj. William Avery Bishop (1915–1918; Great Britain)	Nieuport 17	72
5. Oberleutnant Ernst Udet (1915–1918; Germany)	Siemens-Schuckert D III	62
6. Maj. Raymond Collishaw (1916–1918; Great Britain)	Sopwith Triplane	60
7. Maj. J. T. R. McCudden (1916–1918; Great Britain)*	S.E. 5	57
8. Capt. A. W. Beauchamp-Proctor (1915–1918; Great Britain)	Nieuports	54
8. Capt. D. R. MacLaren (1916–1918; Great Britain)	S.E. 5	54
8. Capitaine Georges-Marie Guynemer (1914–1917; France)*	Nieuports	54

* Killed in action.

—A.B.

The Red Baron, Manfred von Richthofen, leading air ace of W.W. I.

12 NAZI WAR CRIMINALS
STILL AT LARGE

1. DR. ANDRIJA ARTUKOVICH

Minister of justice in the Nazi state of Croatia. Deported 25,000 Jews to concentration camps. Living in California as of 1976, although deportation hearings for his return to Yugoslavia—to face charges of mass murder—have been pending since 1959.

2. KLAUS BARBIE

A Gestapo chief in Lyons, France. Ordered the torture of prisoners and deported Jews to concentration camps. Sentenced to death in absentia in France. Currently a businessman living in La Paz, Bolivia.

3. MARTIN BORMANN

Chief of the Nazi party chancellery and Hitler's secretary. Sentenced to death in absentia at Nuremberg trials. In April, 1973, a West German court declared him dead and ordered that all search warrants be revoked. However, there were reports that he was alive in Argentina in 1974.

4. RICHARD GLÜCKS

SS general and inspector general of all concentration camps. Disappeared in 1945.

5. ROLF GÜNTHER

Berlin deputy of Adolf Eichmann. Probably living in Argentina as of 1960.

6. DR. LUDWIG HAHN

SS colonel and chief of the Warsaw Gestapo. Deported 500,000 Jews to Treblinka concentration camp. Rumored to be living in Hamburg, West Germany, as of 1961.

7. DR. JOSEPH MENGELE

Auschwitz concentration camp doctor who Anne Frank called "the angel of extermination." Conducted gruesome "medical experiments" and murdered camp inmates. Indicted on charges of mass murder in Germany. Living in Paraguay as of 1972.

8. HEINRICH MÜLLER

Chief of the Gestapo; after Bormann, Müller is the most wanted Nazi. Presumed killed in 1945, but his grave was opened in 1963 and the skeleton proved not to be his. Reported to be estate manager living in Córdoba, Argentina, as of 1974.

9. WALTER RAUFF

SS colonel at Auschwitz. Devised "gas trucks" which channeled exhaust fumes into the rear compartment, killing the occupants. Charged with the murder of 97,000 people, he was a fish cannery manager living in Chile as of 1975.

10. ALFONS WILLEM SASSEN

SS captain wanted for mass murder in the Netherlands. He was a businessman and former Ecuadorian police officer living in Ecuador as of 1975.

11. FRIEDRICH SCHWEND

SS colonel who used concentration camp laborers to counterfeit $500 million worth of British banknotes. Sentenced to prison in absentia in Italy for murder. As of 1975, living in Lima, Peru, where he was arrested for illegal currency transactions but was quickly released.

12. CHRISTIAN WIRTH

Supervisor of Polish concentration camps and commandant at Belzec, where 1 million Jews were exterminated. Disappeared in 1945.

—R.J.F.

10 LETHAL OR INCAPACITATING DRUGS STORED BY THE CIA

1. ACONITINE NITRATE

More commonly known as wolfsbane, legend has it that this drug will cure lycanthropy (the werewolf disease). It causes severe abdominal discomfort in small doses and death in large doses.

2. BZ

An experimental drug, BZ blocks nerve impulses and causes death.

3. CARBACHOL

This drug produces a wide variety of symptoms among which are flushing, colic, diarrhea, salivation, and nausea.

4. CINCHONINE

This drug is used in medicine to treat malaria. Overdoses cause severe nausea, vomiting, and heart malfunction.

5. COBRA VENOM

This is the deadly poison obtained from the snake. It kills by paralyzing the nervous system.

6. COLCHICINE

A drug, overdoses of which cause muscle paralysis and respiratory failure resulting in death.

7. CYANIDE

The suicide drug (sodium or potassium cyanide) used by spies during W.W. II to escape being tortured into revealing secret information. The drug blocks the absorption of oxygen and death occurs rapidly as a result of asphyxiation.

8. S-341

An experimental drug similar to BZ but even more powerful.

9. SAXITOXIN

More commonly known as shellfish toxin, saxitoxin produces death in seconds by causing failure of the body's respiratory, cardiovascular, nerve, and muscle systems.

10. STRYCHNINE

Once used by doctors as a nerve stimulant, in anything but small doses it paralyzes nerve-muscle junctions and causes death.

—E.L.A.

SOURCE: Hearing Before the Select Committee to Study Governmental Operations with Respect to Intelligence Activities of the U.S. Congress (Washington, D.C.: U.S. Government Printing Office, 1976).

CREASY'S 15 DECISIVE BATTLES OF THE WORLD

More often than not, whenever military affairs are discussed, reference is made to Creasy's 15 Decisive Battles. Yet who is the little-known creator of this authoritative, oft-quoted list? Sir Edward S. Creasy, born in England in 1812, educated at Eton and Cambridge, became professor of ancient and modern history at London University when he was 28. He served as an assistant judge in London, and later chief justice of Ceylon. He was knighted in 1860, and he died in 1878. He wrote four books in his lifetime, and one of these, published in 1851, *The 15 Decisive Battles of the World*, became a minor classic. Yet this early Victorian scholar, this student of ancient Greece, never witnessed nor experienced a battle in his life. He was never a soldier, never connected with the military in any way. But he knew his history, and the conflicts that were turning points in history. Creasy's battles were selected, according to him, "on account of their enduring importance, and by the reason of the practical influence on our own social and political condition."

1. THE BATTLE OF MARATHON (Persian-Greek Wars, 490 B.C.)

A Persian force of 100,000 led by King Darius I landed in Greece to enslave that country. They were met by 10,000 Athenians who drove them into the sea, slaughtering 6,400 Persians.

2. DEFEAT OF THE ATHENIANS AT SYRACUSE (Great Peloponnesian War, 413 B.C.)

A powerful Athenian fleet of 134 war galleys sailed off to conquer Sicily. The Greeks laid siege to Syracuse, but the Syracusans broke out of their city and overwhelmed the Athenians. The dominace of Athens was ended forever.

3. THE BATTLE OF ARBELA (Macedonian conquests, 331 B.C.)

Alexander the Great of Macedonia set out to crush an oriental dynasty and replace it with Greek rule. With 47,000 troops, Alexander moved against the Persian Empire, defeated the forces of King Darius III, and spread Greek culture to the Indus River.

4. THE BATTLE OF THE METAURUS (Second Punic War, 207 B.C.)

After 10 years of fighting, Hannibal and his brother Hasdrubal hoped to win a decisive victory against the Roman Army. At the Metaurus River, 7,000 Romans led by Nero (Gaius Claudius, not the later emperor) attacked Hasdrubal's force and killed 10,000 men, dooming the Carthaginians' dreams of conquest.

5. VICTORY OF ARMINIUS OVER THE ROMAN LEGIONS UNDER VARUS (Germanic wars of the Roman Empire, 9 A.D.)

The Roman general Varus was led into a trap by the German chief Arminius in the Teutoburg Forest. All 50,000 Romans were killed or enslaved and Varus himself committed suicide. The disaster put an end to Roman expansion into Germany.

6. THE BATTLE OF CHÂLONS-SUR-MARNE (Wars of the western Roman Empire, 451)

Flavius Aëtius, military commander of the western Roman Empire, and Theodoric I, Germanic Visigoth king, joined forces against Attila the Hun's 40,000-man army. They drove Attila across the Rhine, thus ending the Hun threat to western Europe.

7. THE BATTLE OF TOURS (Muslim invasion of France, 732)

The army of the Frankish king Charles Martel defeated the 60,000-man Muslim army and permanently broke the Muslim hold on western Europe beyond Spain.

8. THE BATTLE OF HASTINGS (Norman Conquest of England, 1066)

The Norman duke William landed a force of 7,000 men in

The battle of Hastings, the most important conflict ever fought on English soil. Here is the death of Harold, his two brothers having fallen before him.

England to attack Harold II. After a long and bloody battle, Harold was killed and the victorious William was crowned king of England.

9. JOAN OF ARC'S VICTORY OVER THE ENGLISH AT ORLÉANS (Hundred Years' War, 1429)

Charles VII provided Joan of Arc with a French army to try to break the English siege of Orléans. Joan's army routed the English and inspired a string of victories which ensured French independence.

10. THE DEFEAT OF THE SPANISH ARMADA (English-Spanish wars, 1588)

The 34-ship fleet of Queen Elizabeth I successfully deflected Philip II's Invincible Armada, whose aim had been to secure the English Channel and then attack England itself. England's stunning victory made the nation a first-class naval power.

11. THE BATTLE OF BLENHEIM (War of the Spanish Succession, 1704)

The 52,000-man allied armies of John Churchill, duke of Marlborough, and Prince Eugene of Savoy decisively defeated the 60,000-man Franco-Bavarian force, thus ending the prospect of French dominance of Europe.

12. THE BATTLE OF POLTAVA (Great Northern War, 1709)

Charles XII, king of Sweden and, in effect, ruler of an empire, invaded Russia and besieged the Ukrainian city of Poltava. Czar Peter the Great's army—with a three-to-one numerical superiority—routed the Swedes and killed all but 1,500 of them. Poltava marked the end of Swedish military might.

13. VICTORY OF THE AMERICANS OVER BURGOYNE AT SARATOGA (American Revolution, 1777)

In the first major American victory, Gen. Horatio Gates's American army, led by Benedict Arnold, encircled British Gen. John Burgoyne at Saratoga and forced him to surrender. Saratoga gave the Americans real hope of winning their independence from England and helped persuade France to lend its support to the rebels.

14. THE BATTLE OF VALMY (Wars of the French Revolution, 1792)

French forces commanded by Charles Dumouriez and François Kellermann succeeded in halting the duke of Brunswick's Prussian column and forcing it back across the Rhine. The victory at Valmy greatly bolstered the lagging morale of the French revolutionaries.

15. THE BATTLE OF WATERLOO (Napoleon's Hundred Days, 1815)

In a final bid for victory, Napoleon attacked the allied Prussian and English forces, led by the duke of Wellington. Although the French launched an all-out assault, the English line held and the French Army was forced to fall back. Napoleon abdicated and Louis XVIII was restored to the French throne.

—I.W. & F.B.F.

10 WEAPONS NAMED AFTER PEOPLE

1. BIG BERTHA

This name was given to several German W.W. I weapons—at first, to large but short-barreled mortars, and later to the gargantuan cannon which shelled Paris in 1918. The name originated from the resemblance between the mortars and the short, stocky build of Bertha Krupp von Bohlen und Halbach (1886–1957). Her father, Friedrich Alfred Krupp, committed suicide in 1902 after the Italian police had released photographs of him performing homosexual acts. Bertha then inherited the Krupp armaments empire and was provided with a husband, Gustav von Bohlen und Halbach, by order of the German emperor. Bertha survived both wars and politics, dying in W. Germany at the age of 71.

2. BOWIE KNIFE

A popular weapon of the American West, the Bowie knife was named after Jim Bowie (1796–1836), the hero of the Alamo. Bowie popularized the 9–18-in. stabbing and cutting knife, but according to the most reliable sources, his brother Rezin Bowie (1793–1841) was the actual inventor. Rezin drew a diagram of the knife, then had a blacksmith forge it from a large metal file. The knife was given its first trial soon afterward in 1827, when brother Jim baptized it in a duel.

3. COLT REVOLVER

The celebrated "six-shooter" of the American West was named after its inventor, Samuel Colt (1814–1862). At 16, Colt ran away to sea and, aboard ship, carved a wooden model of his revolver. He produced the revolver and patented it in 1836. In 1855, Colt began mass production of the gun and became one of the wealthiest men in America.

4. DERRINGER

This short-barreled, large-caliber pistol was named after its inventor, Henry Deringer, Jr. (1786–1868). A Philadelphia gunsmith, Deringer began making pistols in 1825 and later specialized in derringers. His guns were widely imitated. One such imitation was inscribed with the double *r* spelling, which became the accepted form.

5. GARAND RIFLE (M-1)

This semiautomatic rifle served as the basic weapon for American soldiers in both W.W. II and the Korean War. It was named after John Cantius Garand (1888–1974) who developed it while he was an employee of the U.S. Armory at Springfield, Mass. Garand perfected the rifle in 1930 and, six years later, the U.S. Army issued it as the standard infantryman's rifle. Garand first became interested in guns while running a shooting gallery. As a government employee, he received neither a patent for the rifle nor any royalties from its sale.

6. GATLING GUN

A crank-operated prototype of the modern machine gun, it was named after its inventor, Dr. Richard Jordan Gatling (1818–1903). Though he studied medicine, Gatling never practiced as a doctor. Instead, he became an inventor of agricultural machinery, which made him wealthy. He patented the Gatling gun in 1862 during the Civil War. After initial rejection of his gun by northern military men, Gatling hired a civilian crew and personally demonstrated the effectiveness of his invention on the battlefield.

7. MAUSER RIFLE

The first practical bolt-action rifle was named after its German inventors, the brothers Peter Paul Mauser (1838–1914) and Wilhelm Mauser (1834–1882). Following in their father's footsteps, both boys became gunsmiths. In 1867, they moved to Liège, Belgium, and after two years' work they perfected the Mauser rifle, which they sold to the Prussian Army in 1871. Returning to their hometown of Oberndorf, Germany, the brothers built the enormous Mauser rifle factory.

8. MAXIM GUN

This first modern machine gun was named after Sir Hiram Maxim (1840–1916). Born an American, Maxim worked as an engineer, draftsman, and inventor in the U.S. before going to England in 1881. He created the Maxim gun in 1883 and formed a company for its manufacture. In 1900, Maxim became a British subject and was knighted by Queen Victoria. This prolific inventor received 122 U.S. patents and 149 British patents during his lifetime.

Sir Hiram Maxim demonstrating his product.

9. THOMPSON SUBMACHINE GUN (tommy gun)

This famous machine gun, used by gangsters and W.W. II G.I.s, was named after its inventor, Col. John Taliaferro Thompson (1860–1940). A West Point graduate, Thompson served in the U.S. Army's Ordnance Dept. from 1890 to 1914, when he retired. W.W. I brought him out of retirement and, in 1920, he invented the "tommy gun." The gun was lethal at short range, as the U.S. Marines demonstrated when they landed in Nicaragua in 1926.

10. WINCHESTER RIFLE

The favorite repeating rifle of the American frontiersman and the Indian was named after its manufacturer, Oliver Fisher Winchester (1810–1880). Winchester started his career as an industrialist by manufacturing men's shirts. This proved profitable, allowing him to buy the Volcanic Repeating Arms Co. in 1857. By 1867, business was booming, and he founded the Winchester Repeating Arms Co. By hiring inventors and buying up patents, Winchester nearly monopolized the repeating rifle industry.

—R.J.F.

10 BIGGEST ARMS IMPORTERS

	Millions of U.S. Dollars (1975)	Major Supplier
1. Iran	1,110	U.S.
2. Vietnam	1,061	U.S.
3. Israel	711	U.S.
4. W. Germany	483	U.S.
5. Iraq	451	U.S.S.R.
6. E. Germany	370	U.S.S.R.
7. Libya	361	U.S.S.R.
8. Poland	275	U.S.S.R.
9. Saudi Arabia	245	U.S.
10. Egypt	231	U.S.S.R.

SOURCE: *World Military Expenditures and Arms Transfers 1966–1975* (Washington, D.C.: U.S. Arms Control and Disarmament Agency, 1977).

10 BIGGEST ARMS EXPORTERS

		Millions of U.S. *Dollars (1975)*
1.	U.S.	4,850
2.	U.S.S.R.	2,610
3.	France	504
4.	United Kingdom	378
5.	W. Germany	257
6.	People's Republic of China	191
7.	Czechoslovakia	118
8.	Italy	99
9.	Canada	73
10.	Belgium	67

SOURCE: *World Military Expenditures and Arms Transfers 1966–1975* (Washington, D.C.: U.S. Arms Control and Disarmament Agency, 1977).

10 NATIONS WITH LARGEST PERCENTAGE OF PERSONS IN ARMED FORCES

		% in Armed Forces (1975)
1.	Israel	5.53
2.	Qatar	3.57
3.	United Arab Emirates	3.21
4.	Republic of China (Taiwan)	3.14
5.	Syria	3.12
6.	Cyprus	2.98
7.	N. Korea	2.85
8.	Portugal	2.55
9.	Mongolia	2.49
10.	Kuwait	2.48

SOURCE: *World Military Expenditures and Arms Transfers 1966–1975* (Washington, D.C.: U.S. Arms Control and Disarmament Agency, 1977).

10 NATIONS WITH
SMALLEST PERCENTAGE OF
PERSONS IN ARMED FORCES

		% in Armed Forces (1975)
1.	Fiji	—
1.	Barbados	—
1.	Iceland	—
4.	Jamaica	0.048
5.	Kenya	0.066
6.	Upper Volta	0.084
7.	Niger	0.088
8.	Rwanda	0.094
9.	Lesotho	0.096
10.	Benin	0.097

SOURCE: *World Military Expenditures and Arms Transfers 1966–1975* (Washington, D.C.: U.S. Arms Control and Disarmament Agency, 1977).

10 NATIONS
WITH LARGEST MILITARY
EXPENDITURES PER CAPITA

		U.S. Dollars (1975)
1.	Israel	1,110
2.	Oman	782
3.	Qatar	692
4.	U.S.S.R.	428
5.	U.S.	390
6.	Saudia Arabia	257
7.	Sweden	221
8.	W. Germany	216
9.	Kuwait	213
10.	E. Germany	211

SOURCE: *World Military Expenditures and Arms Transfers 1966–1975* (Washington, D.C.: U.S. Arms Control and Disarmament Agency, 1977).

10 NATIONS
WITH SMALLEST MILITARY
EXPENDITURES PER CAPITA

	U.S. Dollars (1975)
1. Mozambique	—
2. Costa Rica	—
3. Lesotho	—
4. Botswana	—
5. Guinea—Bissau	—
6. The Gambia	—
7. Swaziland	—
8. Surinam	—
9. Iceland	—
10. Nepal	0.66

SOURCE: *World Military Expenditures and Arms Transfers 1966–1975* (Washington, D.C.: U.S. Arms Control and Disarmament Agency, 1977).

6 NATIONS THAT RECEIVE
MILITARY AID FROM CHINA,
THE U.S.S.R., <u>AND</u> THE U.K.
AND THE U.S.

1. Iraq
2. Pakistan
3. Sudan
4. Syria
5. Tanzania
6. Zambia

SOURCE: *World Military Expenditures and Arms Transfers 1966–1975* (Washington, D.C.: U.S. Arms Control and Disarmament Agency, 1977).

THE 10 WORST
MOTOR VEHICLE DISASTERS

1. SOTOUBOUA, TOGO (Dec. 6, 1965)

More than 125 people died when two trucks crashed into a crowd of dancers on a congested street during a festival.

2. TERPATE, PHILIPPINES (Jan. 6, 1967)

Two homemade buses, really no more than open trucks with wooden benches lining their flatbed bodies, collided on a winding mountain road and plummeted over a cliff, killing 84 passengers and injuring another 140. The buses were part of a 57-bus caravan carrying Catholic pilgrims from Batangas Province to the town of Terpate in Cavite Province. The shrine of the Infant Christ in that town was thought to have miraculous powers, and the peasants were reenacting the visit of the Three Kings on the Feast of the Epiphany. As the buses slowly traversed the narrow zigzag route through the mountains, the brakes failed on the ninth vehicle in the long line. This vehicle rammed the bus ahead, and, each carrying 150 passengers, both tumbled into a 100-ft. ravine. Most of the dead were in a bus that landed upside down on its canvas and wood-frame top. Known locally as "rolling coffins," the jerry-built buses were a national scandal. Just a week earlier, in downtown Manila, the brakes had failed on one such bus and it had crashed through the gates of the presidential palace.

3. ALWAR, INDIA (July 7, 1973)

At least 78 people were drowned when a flash flood washed away the road and swept a bus into a swollen river about 100 mi. southwest of Delhi. Only 8 passengers survived. Supposedly, the passengers belonged to two different high-caste communities and refused to share the one rope that might have pulled many to safety.

4. LE MANS, FRANCE (June 13, 1955)

The worst accident in the history of auto racing occurred near the start of the annual 24-hr. endurance race at Le Mans, when a car went out of control, hit a retaining wall, and exploded in midair, killing 77 people, including the driver, as parts of the car shot into the crowd. According to reconstructions of the accident, the leading car, a Jaguar, cut sharply into the pit area, thus cutting off an Austin-Healy, which went into a spin. French driver Pierre Levegh, traveling at more than 180 mph in a Mercedes Benz, attempted to swerve away from the Austin, clipped several other cars, and then slammed into the wall and exploded over the crowd. The accident occurred near the start of the race, and the Le Mans officials refused to cancel the remaining program. Horrified by this apparent callousness, nearly four-fifths of the crowd of some 250,000 left Le Mans before the race's completion and the German government withdrew all Mercedes entries. The French, in turn, publicly reminded the Germans of their atrocities during the recent war years and thereby touched off a series of heated debates in the press over technological

95

progress, human nature, and the philosophy of auto racing. Most interesting, perhaps, was the body of folklore and legend that developed around the character of Pierre Levegh, the ill-fated driver. According to the popular press, he was a hero, having saved famed Argentine racer Juan Fangio with a last-minute warning signal. Some accounts claimed he swerved away from even greater crowds and thus prevented worse carnage. Among the working class of the Paris bistros, however, there was another version of the Levegh legend. They claimed Levegh had a choice of hitting Fangio or going into the crowd and he chose the latter. For the common people, at least, this proved that the elite have loyalty only for one another.

4. S. KOREA (May 10, 1972)

One other motor vehicle disaster took 77 lives. A South Korean bus carrying 100 passengers, or 45 more than its legal capacity, plunged off a road into a reservoir and killed 77 aboard.

6. CAIRO, EGYPT (Nov. 1, 1965)

A huge electric bus (trackless trolley) traveling on one of the streets bordering the Nile veered out of control and plunged down a 20-ft. embankment into the river. Seventy-four of the passengers drowned in the waters; another 19 survived.

7. BELÉM, BRAZIL (July 28, 1974)

Sixty-nine people were killed and 10 were injured when a packed bus struck a heavy transport truck 250 mi. south of Belém.

7. AHMADABAD, INDIA (May 30, 1962)

Sixty-nine people also were killed in a bus crash in Ahmadabad, India.

9. POONA, INDIA (May 19, 1975)

A farm truck jammed with guests on their way to a wedding was struck by a train, killing at least 66 persons and injuring another 18. All the dead and injured were on the truck, which was rammed as it crossed the railway tracks about 40 mi. from Poona, in central Maharashtra State.

10. TURVO RIVER, BRAZIL (Aug. 24, 1960)

Some 60 people died when a bus fell from the bridge over the Turvo River near São José do Rio Prêto.

Reprinted by permission of Charles Scribner's Sons from *The Great International Disaster Book* by James Cornell. Copyright © 1976 by James Cornell.

THE 10 WORST FAMINES

1. RUSSIA (1914–1924)

Famine and influenza left 20 million people dead.

2. NORTH CHINA (1876–1879)

Three years of drought resulted in a famine that affected a total of 70 million Chinese. The populace turned to slavery, murder, and cannibalism; children were sold as food in marketplaces. Mass graves, known as "10,000-man holes," were created to house the carcasses. Due to the reclusiveness of the Manchu Dynasty, word of the disaster didn't spread to the West until an entire year had passed. Even then, political and physical obstacles frustrated relief missions. The tragedy took the lives of between 9.5 million and 13 million people.

3. CHINA (1333–1337)

This widespread famine was probably the result of an extensive drought, and possibly the source of the greatest human catastrophe of all time: Europe's Black Death. Six million people died of starvation; about 75 million died from the ensuing Black Death.

3. INDIA (1876–1878)

The lack of a monsoon in the north and an overabundance of rain in the south ruined crops and brought about mass starvation, coupled with widespread cholera. Several foreign-aid efforts were hampered by the Indian government. Death count: 6 million.

5. INDIA (1896–1897)

Drought was followed by famine and disease. Although relief efforts were somewhat successful, there were 5 million casualties.

5. U.S.S.R. (1932–1934)

Two factors triggered the famine that led to the deaths of 5 million Russians. First, the Soviet government went overboard and exported 3.5 million tons of grain during a two-year period. Second, peasants killed 50% of the country's livestock during an uproar over forced farm collectivization. Because the facts were kept so secret, it was some time before the West learned how grave the situation really was.

5. WEST CHINA (1936)

Five million people died of starvation during a lengthy drought.

8. HINDUSTAN, INDIA (1769–1770)

An 18-month drought triggered a great famine that left 3 million dead.

8. CHINA (1928–1929)

Three million people starved to death when a heavy drought hit the provinces of Honan, Kansu, and Shensi. The delivery of relief supplies was expedited by a refurbished railroad system. Starvation continued through 1931.

8. INDIA (1669–1670)

India's earliest recorded famine produced a death toll of 3 million.

—D.B.

35 COUNTRIES AND THEIR NUCLEAR BOMB CAPABILITIES

According to the intelligence findings of the Joint Committee on Atomic Energy, these are the countries which appear technically capable of detonating a nuclear device as of April, 1976.

A-bomb over Nagasaki. This explosion on
August 9, 1945, killed 74,800 people.

6 NATIONS THAT CAN BLOW UP THE WORLD RIGHT NOW

1. People's Republic of China
2. France
3. India
4. United Kingdom
5. U.S.S.R.
6. U.S.

9 NATIONS THAT CAN BLOW US UP IN 1–3 YEARS

7. Canada
8. Republic of China (Taiwan)
9. Israel
10. Italy
11. Japan
12. South Africa
13. Spain
14. Sweden
15. Switzerland

11 NATIONS THAT CAN BLOW US UP IN 4–6 YEARS

16. Argentina
17. Austria
18. Belgium
19. Brazil
20. Czechoslovakia
21. Denmark
22. E. Germany
23. Netherlands
24. Norway
25. Poland
26. S. Korea

9 NATIONS THAT CAN BLOW US UP IN 7–10 YEARS

27. Egypt
28. Finland
29. Iran
30. Mexico
31. Pakistan
32. Portugal
33. Romania
34. Turkey
35. Yugoslavia

SOURCE: U.S. Congress, Joint Committee on Atomic Energy.

5
GOOD HEAVENS ...
WHAT ON EARTH

15 PREHISTORIC
THINGS ALIVE TODAY

1. COELACANTH (fish)

A 6-ft. fish discovered alive in 1939 in the Indian Ocean off South Africa. Existed 400 million years ago. Previously thought to have become extinct 70 million years ago.

2. AUSTRALIAN LUNGFISH (fish)

Discovered alive in 1869. Was on this earth 200 million years ago.

3. LINGULA (marine animal)

Member of the phylum Brachiopoda. Has been in existence half a billion years. Longest lived of all animals.

4. GINKGO (tree)

Darwin called it a "living fossil." Dates back to the time of the dinosaurs. May still be found in China and elsewhere.

5. PERIPATUS (worm)

Goes back 500 million years. Found in tropics.

6. HORSESHOE CRAB (crustacean)

Still exists unchanged after 300 million years.

7. DAWN REDWOOD (tree)

Also known as Metasequoia. Was found in China in 1946 and has since been propagated in California. Goes back 100 million years.

8. TUATARA (reptile)

Unchanged for 200 million years. May be seen on islands near New Zealand.

9. OKAPI (African mammal)

Related to giraffe. Goes back 30 million years and remains almost unchanged.

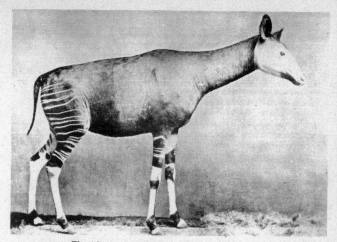

The African okapi has survived 30 million years.

10. WELWITSCHIA (desert plant)

Was on the earth millions of years ago. May still be found in southwest Africa.

11. BRISTLECONE PINE (tree)

Was on the earth in 6200 B.C. Is on the earth today. One specimen, known as Methuselah (it started growing at the time the pyramids were built), is 4,600 years old and may be seen 9,000 ft. up on one of the White Mountains in California.

12. STEPHENS ISLAND FROG (amphibian)

It is believed that this frog is the one from which all living frogs have descended. From 170 to 275 million years old. First found in 1917 in New Zealand, its present home. Unlike most frogs, it does not have webbed toes.

13. CROCODILE (reptile)

From 160 to 195 million years old. Found all over the world. Twenty-one species known today.

14. DUCKBILL PLATYPUS (aquatic mammal)

First seen in Australia in 1797. At least 150 million years old.

15. TURTLE (reptile)

About 275 million years old. Can be found in most parts of the world. From 200 to 250 species.

—I.W.

20 POISONOUS PLANTS
—DON'T EAT

		Where Found	Poisonous Part	Result
1.	Buttercup	Fields	All	Indigestion
2.	Cherry	Trees, shrubs	Twigs, foliage	Death
3.	Crocus, autumn	Flower garden	Bulbs	Vomiting
4.	Daphne	Ornamental plant	Berries	Death
5.	Elderberry	Trees, shrubs	Shoots, leaves, bark	Nausea
6.	Foxglove	Flower garden	Leaves	Irregular heartbeat
7.	Hemlock	Fields	All	Death
8.	Hyacinth	House plant	Bulbs	Nausea; death
9.	Iris	Flower garden	Underground stems	Indigestion
10.	Jimsonweed	Fields	All	Death
11.	Larkspur	Flower garden	Young plant, seeds	Indigestion; death
12.	Lily of the valley	Flower garden	Leaves, flowers	Irregular heartbeat
13.	Nightshade	Fields	All, especially berry	Death
14.	Oak	Trees, shrubs	Foliage, acorns	Kidney injury
15.	Oleander	House plant	Leaves, branches	Indigestion; death
16.	Red sage	Ornamental plant	Green berries	Death
17.	Rhododendron	Ornamental plant	All	Death
18.	Rhubarb	Vegetable garden	Leaf blade	Death
19.	Wisteria	Ornamental plant	Seeds, pods	Indigestion
20.	Yew	Ornamental plant	Berries, foliage	Death

SOURCE: CIBA-GEIGY Corp. (Ardsley, N.Y.).

7 FAMOUS FLOWERS
OF FACT AND FICTION

1. THE CAMELLIA

In the famous *La Dame aux Camélias*, Alexandre Dumas fils created the Lady of the Camellias, Marguerite Gautier. The story is based on the life of Marie Duplessis, a beautiful French courtesan of the 1840s, who had a great love for flowers of all kind. When Marie died of tuberculosis at the age of 23, Dumas, who had been one of her lovers, recalled their days together and her particular attraction to camellias. In the novel, Marguerite was never seen with any flower other than the camellia. For 25 days of the month she wore white camellias and for 5 she wore red.

2. THE AFFAIR OF THE CARNATION

On August 28, 1793, a carnation was used in a final attempt to rescue Marie Antoinette from the guillotine. She was being held at the Conciergerie in Paris when the Chevalier de Rougeville, a royalist nobleman who was willing to risk anything to save her, entered her cell with the inspector (a secret friend). He threw a carnation behind the stove and signaled to Marie. When she was left alone, she picked up the flower and found among the petals a tiny note. Money was being raised to bribe her guard, Gilbert. Having no pen or ink, she used a needle to prick out an answer on a scrap of paper, which she handed to Gilbert. The guard, confused by the offer of such a substantial amount of money, waited five days before he finally filed an official report of the incident to his superiors. Marie Antoinette was placed under heavier guard and on October 16, 1793, she was executed. The queen had torn up the note she received, but her response is now preserved in the National Archives in Paris.

The upper sheet is a transcription of the message which Marie Antoinette pricked on the lower sheet in an attempt to bribe a guard.

3. THE CHRYSANTHEMUM

Although the chrysanthemum is popular throughout Japan, it is not cultivated in the city of Himeji, and the local people consider it unlucky even to carry one. According to legend, long ago there lived in a castle a servant girl named O-Kiku ("Chrysanthemum Blossom"). Among her responsibilities was the care of 10 gold plates. One day she discovered that one of the plates was missing. Fearing she would be blamed for its disappearance, she threw herself into a well and drowned. It is said that on that night, and every night thereafter, her spirit returned to count the plates. Each time the ghost reached nine it let out a scream and began counting again. The inhabitants of the castle were forced to leave and, as a gesture of respect to O-Kiku's troubled spirit, the people of Himeji agreed not to grow chrysanthemums in their city.

4. THE WARS OF THE ROSES

In 1455, the houses of Lancaster and York opposed each other in what was to be a 30-year struggle for the throne of England. The duke of Lancaster used the red rose for his badge, and his brother adopted the white rose as the emblem of York. In 1486, Henry Tudor—a Lancaster—married Princess Elizabeth of York, thus ending the fighting and uniting the two houses. In 1551, Nicholas Monardes named the damask hybrid rose (*Rosa damascena versicolor*) "York and Lancaster," to memorialize what had already become known as the Wars of the Roses.

5. THE TALKING TIGER-LILY

Among the live flowers in the garden of Lewis Carroll's *Through the Looking-Glass*, the Tiger-lily is the most loquacious. The Tiger-lily claims that all flowers can talk, "when there's anybody worth talking to." When Alice inquires why she has never heard flowers talk in other gardens, the Tiger-lily explains, "In most gardens they make the beds too soft—so that the flowers are always asleep."

6. TULIPMANIA

Today the tulip is considered a relatively common flower. However, during the height of "tulipmania" which swept Holland from 1634 to 1637, tulip bulbs commanded astronomical sums. An unnamed buyer delivered as payment for a single bulb of a rare variety of tulip called "Viceroy": 8,000 lbs. of wheat, 16,000 lbs. of rye, 4 fat oxen, 8 fat swine, 12 fat sheep, 2 hogsheads of wine, 1,000 gals. of beer, 500 gals. of butter, 1,000 lbs. of cheese, a complete bed, a suit of clothes, and a silver drinking cup. Collecting tulips became fashionable among the wealthy because the flowers were so rare and so delicately beautiful. The fad soon spread to the middle and lower classes, and the possession of tulips became a status symbol as well as a means of turning a quick profit. Money poured into Holland from all directions. People invested their entire life savings in the buying and selling of tulips which were being traded at exorbitant prices. But, as quickly as the craze had begun, it ended, and many people who thought they had achieved financial security found themselves with bulbs which couldn't be sold for the high price at which they had been purchased. The bottom had fallen out of the market, and the Dutch economy was left badly scarred.

7. CORPORAL VIOLET

Napoleon's favorite flower was the violet. When he left France for Elba, he told his friends that he would "return with the violets." The flower, as well as the color, became the symbol of the Bonapartists and the means by which they were able to recognize one another. Napoleon was secretly referred to as General Violet or Corporal Violet by his followers. On March 20, 1815, he returned to the Tuileries in Paris, just as he had promised, while the violets were in full bloom. The violet continued to be the flower of the empire until the battle of Waterloo. Then it became dangerous to wear a violet or even to be overheard admiring one.

—F.CH.

15 ISLANDS FOR SALE

1. CLARK ISLAND

Location: Cape Breton, N.S., Canada, in Bras d'Or Lake, a protected saltwater inland sea. *Description:* 16 acres surrounded by white sand beach with a central warm salt pond. *Price:* $16,000.

2-4. MOSS CAYS

Location: Near George Town, Exuma Island, the Bahama Islands. *Description:* Three small islands totaling 5 acres with fine swimming beaches. Located in the middle of the Bahama Islands' finest yachting and diving areas. *Price:* $30,000.

5. SHEEP ISLAND

Location: Off Steuben, Me. *Description:* 6 acres with beautiful evergreen and white birch trees and a pink granite shoreline. The island has good protected anchorage. *Price:* $49,500.

6. PATONU ISLAND

Location: Tahiti, French Polynesia, approximately 350 mi. from Papeete. *Description:* This 20-acre island features a white sand beach and is covered with coconut palms. *Price:* $78,000.

7. CANDY ISLAND

Location: Cedar Keys, Fla., in the Gulf of Mexico. *Description:* 7 acres with fertile soil and large cedar trees. The island once supported three fishing families. *Price:* $110,000.

8. SKEWWELL ISLAND

Location: Knight Inlet, B.C., Canada. *Description:* Beautiful evergreen trees cover 160 acres of tillable land with pebble beaches. *Price:* $160,000.

9. M'BEKANA ISLAND

Location: Off Vanua Levu, Fiji's second-largest island. *Description:* This 30-acre island features a white sand beach, deepwater anchorage, coconut palms, and two freshwater springs. *Price:* $225,000.

10. CALIVIGNY ISLAND

Location: Grenada, Windward Islands. Situated just ¼ mile off the mainland with good roads leading to the takeoff point from St. George's, the main city of Grenada. *Description:* A 70-acre island with an excellent sandy beach, several protected anchorages, a small pond, and a partly restored 10-room house. *Price:* $275,000.

11-13. PALMETTO CAY

Location: Off Monkey Point, Nicaragua. *Description:* There are approximately 65 acres on these three islands featuring lush vegetation and some of the Caribbean's best jumbo shrimp waters. There are docking facilities and three small bungalows. *Price:* $375,000.

14. NANUYA LEVU

Location: Yasawa Islands, Fiji. *Description:* This 450-acre gem is the largest freehold island in the best climatic region of Fiji. The island has 12 white beaches, 7 freshwater springs, and a small stream. The owner has planted the island in coconut palms and Caribbean pine trees. *Price:* $1.3 million.

15. PALMYRA ISLAND

Location: About 1,000 mi. south of Hawaii. *Description:* Technically administered by the U.S. government as a trust territory, this 1,200-acre island is privately owned. It is covered with giant (100-ft.-high) coconut palms and includes an airstrip large enough to land a 727 jet. *Price:* $14 million.

Information on islands for sale can be obtained from:

Rare Earth Real Estate, Inc., Kappas Marina, Sausalito, Calif. 94965; Boehm and Vladi, Ballindamm 9, Hamburg 2,000, W. Germany; Bob Douglas, Douglas and Associates, Mahone Bay, N.S. BOJ 2C0, Canada; H. G. Christie Real Estate Ltd., 309 Bay St., Nassau, Bahama Islands; Henry Roethel, 345 Quebec St., Suite 1209, Victoria, B.C. V8V 1X5, Canada; Previews, Inc., International Real Estate Marketing Realtors, Greenwich Office, 51 Weaver St., Greenwich, Conn. 06830; and Private Island Unltd., 17538 Tulsa St., Granada Hills, Calif. 91344.

20 LARGEST ISLANDS
IN THE WORLD

		Ocean or Sea	Area (sq. mi.)
1.	Greenland	Arctic	839,999
2.	New Guinea	W. Pacific	319,713
3.	Borneo	Indian	290,320
4.	Madagascar	Indian	226,657
5.	Baffin Island	Arctic	183,810
6.	Sumatra	Indian	182,561
7.	Great Britain (incl. Scotland)	N. Atlantic	88,146
8.	Honshu, Japan	N.W. Pacific	86,246
9.	Ellesmere Island	Arctic	82,119
10.	Victoria Island	Arctic	81,930
11.	Celebes	Indian	69,225
12.	South Island, New Zealand	S.W. Pacific	59,439
13.	Java	Indian	51,007
14.	North Island, New Zealand	S.W. Pacific	44,297
15.	Cuba	Caribbean	44,218
16.	Newfoundland	N. Atlantic	43,359
17.	Luzon	W. Pacific	41,765
18.	Iceland	N. Atlantic	39,702
19.	Mindanao	W. Pacific	38,254
20.	Ireland (incl. Northern Ireland)	N. Atlantic	32,052

Australia is regarded by geographers as a continental land-mass, as are Antarctica, Afro-Eurasia, North and South America, and Africa.

15 LONGEST RIVERS
IN THE WORLD

		Length (mi.)
1.	Nile, Africa	4,145
2.	Amazon, South America	4,000
3.	Mississippi-Missouri, U.S.	3,710
4.	Ob-Irtysh, U.S.S.R.	3,460
5.	Yangtze, China	3,400
6.	Huang Ho, China	3,000
7.	Congo, Africa	2,718
8.	Amur, Asia	2,700
9.	Lena, U.S.S.R.	2,680

10.	Mackenzie-Peace, Canada	2,635
11.	Mekong, Asia	2,600
11.	Niger, Africa	2,600
13.	Parana, South America	2,530
14.	Murray-Darling, Australia	2,310
15.	Volga, U.S.S.R.	2,290

SOURCE: *National Geographic Atlas of the World* (Washington, D.C.: National Geographic Society, 1975).

10 HIGHEST WATERFALLS

Angel Falls on the Río Caroní in eastern Venezuela.

		Height (ft.)
1.	Angel, Venezuela	3,212
2.	Tugela, South Africa	3,110
3.	Yosemite, California	2,425
4.	Cuquenán, Venezuela	2,000
5.	Sutherland, New Zealand	1,904
6.	Eastern Mardalsfoss, Norway	1,696
7.	Takkakaw, B.C., Canada	1,650
8.	Cascade de Giétroz, Switzerland	1,640
9.	Ribbon Falls, California	1,612
10.	King George, Guyana	1,600

Niagara Falls is only 167 ft. high.

20 LARGEST LAKES

		Area (sq. mi.)	Area (sq. km.)
1.	Kaspiskoye More (Caspian Sea), U.S.S.R.-Iran	152,084	393,898
2.	Superior, U.S.-Canada	31,820	82,414
3.	Victoria, Tanzania-Uganda-Kenya	26,828	69,485
4.	Aralskoye More (Aral Sea), U.S.S.R.	26,518	68,682
5.	Huron, U.S.-Canada	23,010	59,596
6.	Michigan, U.S.	22,400	58,016
7.	Tanganyika, Zaire-Tanzania-Zambia-Burundi	12,700	32,893
8.	Great Bear, Canada	12,275	31,792
9.	Ozero Baykal (Lake Baikal), U.S.S.R.	12,159	31,492
10.	Great Slave, Canada	10,980	28,438
11.	Erie, U.S.-Canada	9,940	25,745
12.	Winnipeg, Canada	9,398	24,341
13.	Malawi (Niassa), Malawi-Mozambique-Tanzania	9,000	23,310
14.	Lago de Maracaibo, Venezuela	8,296	21,487
15.	Ontario, U.S.-Canada	7,540	19,259
16.	Ozero Balkhash, U.S.S.R.	7,050	18,260
17.	Ladozhskoye Ozero (Lake Ladoga), U.S.S.R.	7,000	18,130
18.	Lac Tchad (Chad), Chad-Nigeria-Niger-Cameroon	6,000	15,540
19.	Ozero Onezhskoye, U.S.S.R.	3,800	9,842
20.	Eyre, Australia	3,700	9,583

SOURCE: *The Times Atlas of the World* (London: The Times, 1975).

9 GREAT ROCKS

1. BLACK STONE

Said to have been given to the Hebrew patriarch Abraham by the angel Gabriel. It is kept in the Kaaba, a small sanctuary which is in the courtyard of the Great Mosque at Mecca, Saudi Arabia.

In the center of Mecca, covered by a black camel's hair cloth, is the holy Kaaba, the stone cube-shaped temple built by Abraham.

2. BLARNEY STONE

According to legend, those who kiss it will be endowed with great powers of persuasion. Difficult to reach, the inscribed slab rests high (up 127 steps) on Blarney Castle at County Cork, Ireland.

3. GRANITE BOULDER (unnamed)

One of the few uncut statue bases in the world, it supports the equestrian memorial to Theodore Roosevelt's "Rough Riders" at Prescott, Ariz. The sturdy rock symbolizes U.S. power following victory in the Spanish-American War (1898).

4. PLYMOUTH ROCK

Pilgrims from the ship *Mayflower* took their first steps on this boulder when they landed at Plymouth, Mass., on December 21, 1620. When raised for enshrinement in 1774, the rock split into two pieces.

5. ROCK OF GIBRALTAR

A natural fortress of limestone, it forms a peninsula on the southern coast of Spain, at the east end of the Strait of Gibraltar. It is 3 mi. long, ¾ mi. wide, and its highest elevation is 1,396 ft.

6. ROSETTA STONE

Inscribed in 196 B.C. in hieroglyphic, demotic characters, and Greek, this slab of black basalt enabled Jean-François Champollion to decipher Egyptian hieroglyphics in 1821–1822. Now in the British Museum in London, it was discovered near Rosetta, Egypt, in 1799.

7. SHIP ROCK

This towering monolith is on the Navaho reservation in northwestern New Mexico. Indian tradition says the "rock with wings" was once a bird which brought their people there.

8. STONE MOUNTAIN

The world's largest granite rock in isolation, Stone Mountain is located near Atlanta, Ga. It is 825 ft. high and has a volume of 7 billion cu. ft. Carved upon its northeastern face are heroic figures of the Confederacy.

9. STONE OF SCONE

Also called the Stone of Destiny, it was brought to a monastery at Scone, Scotland, in the eighth century. Irish and Scottish kings sat upon it while being crowned until 1296. It was then stolen by King Edward I and moved to Westminster Abbey where it was placed beneath the seat of the coronation chair.

—D.M.F.

15 LARGEST DESERTS

		Continent	Area (sq. mi.)
1.	Sahara	Africa	3,500,000
	Libyan		650,000
	Nubian		105,000
2.	Australian	Australia	600,000
	Great Sandy		160,000
	Great Victoria		127,000
	Simpson (Arunta)		120,000
	Gibson's		85,000
3.	Arabian	Asia	500,000
	Rub al-Khali		250,000
	Syrian		125,000
	An Nafud		50,000
4.	Gobi	Asia	400,000
5.	Kalahari	Africa	275,000
6.	Patagonia	South America	260,000
7.	Takla Makan	Asia	127,000
8.	Sonoran	North America	120,000
9.	Kara Kum	Asia	105,000
9.	Thar	Asia	105,000
11.	Kyzyl Kum	Asia	90,000
12.	Atacama	South America	68,000
13.	Mojave	North America	25,000
14.	Dasht-e-Lut	Asia	20,000
15.	Dasht-e-Kavir	Asia	18,000

13 LARGEST PRODUCERS OF CRUDE PETROLEUM

		Millions of Metric Tons Produced (1975)
1.	U.S.S.R.	490.0
2.	U.S.	485.5
3.	Saudi Arabia	337.3
4.	Iran	268.2
5.	Venezuela	124.0
6.	Iraq	111.3
7.	Kuwait	93.3
8.	Nigeria	87.8
9.	Canada	80.0
10.	People's Republic of China	78.0

11. Libya	71.0
12. Abu Dhabi	64.6
13. Indonesia	63.0

SOURCE: John Paxton, *The Statesman's Year-Book 1976/1977* (New York: St. Martin, 1976).

10 UNEXPLORED AREAS
OF THE WORLD

1. ALASKA

Northern Alaska's great Brooks Range, called the gates of the arctic, is the largest remaining expanse of untouched terrain in the U.S. Although the state is being overwhelmed with development activity, the Noatak River and Squirrel River basins in the Brooks Range, constituting about 7.6 million acres, are virtually devoid of human influences. Government geologists have mapped the rivers, a few prospectors have poked about, and there have been a few hunters in the area, but as a whole it has escaped serious attention. It was recently proposed as a site for a national park.

2. AMAZON BASIN

Covering a territory of about 2.7 million sq. mi., mainly in northern Brazil, the Amazon River basin is the largest river basin in the tropical world. Its average population density is less than 2 persons per sq. mi. Here immense tropical jungles contain mankind's greatest reserve of natural resources. Few have dared to penetrate these forests, and some have been lost on short trips. Even the Indians who live near the riverbanks are afraid of becoming lost if they stray too far from their settlements. They also fear the legendary inhabitants of the forests: At campfires one still hears stories of cultures—in which women dominate—that are hidden in the depths of the jungle. Insect pests abound, boa constrictors and anacondas reach 20-ft. lengths, rodents and bats flourish. Some Indian tribes living there, probably numbering 100,000 people in all, are still in the Stone Age. Scientific exploration is now going on under the auspices of the U.S. National Geographic Society, the Brazilian Petrobras Co., and research institutes in Brazil.

3. ANTARCTICA

With an area of more than 1 million sq. mi., less than 100 sq. mi. of the antarctic continent is free from a permanent blanket of ice. It is virtually lifeless, lacking so much as a shrub, let alone a human population. Except from December through March, ships cannot reach or leave the continent because of frozen bays and coastal waters. Although crisscrossed and honeycombed by explorers and scientists of many nations since the signing of the Antarctic Treaty in 1959, not all the surface terrain has been seen or reached by men on the ground. Few of the mountainous regions, though photographed from the air, are known in detail. Least known is the bedrock terrain that lies under the ice sheets.

4. THE ARCTIC

Drifting ice, 10 ft. thick, covers much of the 5,541,000 sq. mi. of the Arctic Ocean, which is surrounded by the northern portions of Canada, Alaska, Scotland, Russia, and such polar islands as Greenland, Iceland, and Spitsbergen. Averaging 10°F. warmer than the antarctic, it is less violent and less inhospitable, supporting a human population of over a million, along with polar bears, seals, reindeer, caribou, and a great variety of birds. Although airplanes have flown over most of the far north and it is laced with a network of radar warning stations served by military and technical personnel, there are still some blank spaces on the map. The governments of the U.S., Canada, and the U.S.S.R. have been engaged since the late 1950s in a continuous program of investigation in the arctic region, using drifting stations in addition to airlifted expeditions.

5. GREENLAND

The largest island in the world, owned by Denmark, Greenland has the greatest ice mass outside of Antarctica. Of its 840,000 sq. mi., 700,000 are ice-covered. Vegetation consists of tundra, the climate is bleak, and impenetrable blizzards are common. Greenland entered the 1970s with 154 inhabited places (19 towns, 117 villages, and 18 weather stations), all confined to the coastal fringe. Much of the interior has been crossed on the surface only by Eskimo. Greenland's climate was temperate until the onset of an ice age a million years ago. It is not known what might lie under the ice, the average depth of which is 5,000 ft.

6. GUIANA HIGHLANDS

South of the Orinoco River are the Guiana Highlands. Comprising about 45% of the total area of Venezuela, they are the least known and most sparsely inhabited portion of that country. A desolate region of rocky outcrop and dense jungle, the Guiana-Highlands are famous as the setting for two novels, A. Conan Doyle's *The Lost World* and W. H. Hudson's *Green Mansions*. Angel Falls, highest in the world, is in the northeastern part. So forbidding is the landscape that in many places the canoe with outboard motor is the only means of transportation and communication. Fauna include crocodiles, lizards, caymans (largest and fiercest of crocodilians), striped rattlesnakes, and bushmasters (largest venomous snakes in the Americas).

7. HIMALAYAS

India, China, and Pakistan now have sovereignty over the Himalayan Range of Asia, which stretches uninterrupted for about 1,550 mi. covering an area of about 229,500 sq. mi. Perpetually snow-covered, with 30 peaks attaining 24,000 ft. above sea level (including Mount Everest, highest mountain in the world), the Himalayas are characterized by soaring heights, stupendous glaciers, and steep-sided jagged peaks. The range is potentially rich in natural resources, which as yet remain inaccessible. Hundreds of peaks over 20,000 ft. remain unchallenged and unexplored, awaiting future generations of mountaineers.

8. MICRONESIA

Micronesia consists of the Mariana, Marshall, Caroline, and Gilbert island groups, located east of the Philippines and north of the equator. Politically, Guam and the Trust Territory of the Pacific Islands are administered by the U.S.; the Gilbert Islands are administered by the British; and Nauru is independent. Their combined land area (about 1,055 sq. mi.) is only a little larger than the land area of the state of Rhode Island, but is scattered over 3 million sq. mi. of ocean. There are more than 2,000 of these islands, with human populations living on 90 of them. Most of the islands are uninhabited wilderness. Although the presence of the American military is felt here, Micronesia entered the last quarter of the 20th century with its wilderness largely intact.

9. NEW GUINEA

The second-largest island in the world, about 320,000 sq. mi. in area, New Guinea is located north of Australia. Extending from the northwest to the southeast is an almost impenetrable range of mountains. The highest point on the island is over 16,000 ft., and many peaks are over 12,000 ft. Rivers, steep gorges, humid jungles, and high mountains have made normal movement impossible. There are few roads and most of these require a jeep or tractor. In the western half of the island, population density is 5 per sq. mi.; in the eastern half, 17 per sq. mi. Because of persistent cloud cover, only about 85% of the mainland had been photographed from the air by 1970.

10. RUB AL-KHALI

The Arabic name for this part of the Arabian Desert means "the Empty Place," but the Bedouins who travel over it call it "the Sand." Containing the most arid part of Arabia, it covers about 250,000 sq. mi. Hot days produce mirages and dust storms, while gale winds carry tons of sand in the windy season. Aerial photography finally enabled the region to be accurately mapped in 1965, but large expanses of the desert have been seen only from the air. Since 1950, the U.S. State Dept. and the U.S. Geological Survey have cooperated with the kingdom of Saudi Arabia in conducting surveys of the area's mineral resources.

—M.B.T.

FIRST 10 MEN IN SPACE

Cosmonaut Yuri Alekseyevich Gagarin, waving good-bye
before becoming the first man to be shot into space.

1. YURI ALEKSEYEVICH GAGARIN (U.S.S.R.; *Vostok 1;*
   Apr. 12, 1961)

   Set first world space record of 203.2 mi. up.

2. ALAN B. SHEPARD (U.S.; *Freedom 7;* May 5, 1961)

   Reached altitude of 115 mi.

3. VIRGIL IVAN GRISSOM (U.S.; *Liberty Bell 7;* July 21, 1961)

   Reached altitude of 118 mi. Spacecraft sank on splashdown,
   but he scrambled to safety.

4. GHERMAN STEPANOVICH TITOV (U.S.S.R.; *Vostok 2;*
   Aug. 6–7, 1961)

   Carried out study on effects of prolonged weightlessness.

5. JOHN HERSCHEL GLENN (U.S.; *Friendship 7;* Feb. 20,
   1962)

   First time an American manned spacecraft orbited the earth.

6. MALCOLM SCOTT CARPENTER (U.S.; *Aurora 7;* May 24,
   1962)

   Reenacted Glenn's first flight and achieved a speed of 17,532
mph.

7. **ANDRIAN GRIGORIEVICH NIKOLAYEV** (U.S.S.R.; *Vostok 3;* Aug. 11–15, 1962)

First astronaut-operated television in space. Flight of 1.64 million mi.

8. **PAVEL ROMANOVICH POPOVICH** (U.S.S.R.; *Vostok 4;* Aug. 12–15, 1962)

An essential purpose was to "obtain data on establishing contact" with *Vostok 3.*

9. **WALTER MARTY SCHIRRA** (U.S.; *Sigma 7;* Oct. 3, 1962)

A near tragedy occurred due to a malfunctioning space suit.

10. **LEROY GORDON COOPER** (U.S.; *Faith 7;* May 15–16, 1963)

After the automatic control system failed, a successful manually controlled splashdown was achieved.

THE 10 MOST SPACED ASTRONAUTS

The following astronauts have spent the most time in space:

	Flights	Time in Space and Name of Spacecraft
1-3. Gerald Carr; Edward G. Gibson; William R. Pogue	1	2,017 hrs. 16 mins. (Nov. 16, 1973–Feb. 8, 1974; *Skylab 4*)
4. V. Sevastianov*	2	1,936 hrs. (1970, 1975)
5. P. Klimuk*	2	1,700 hrs. (1973, 1975)
6. Alan L. Bean	2	1,671 hrs. 45 mins. (Nov. 14–24, 1969; *Apollo 12.* July 28–Sept. 25, 1973; *Skylab 3*)
7-8. Owen K. Garriot; Jack R. Lousma	1	1,427 hrs. 9 mins. (July 28–Sept. 25, 1973; *Skylab 3*)
9. B. Volynov*	1	1,182 hrs. (1976)
10. Charles Conrad, Jr.	4	1,179 hrs. 37 mins. (Aug. 21–29, 1965; *Gemini 5.* Sept. 12–15, 1966; *Gemini 11.* Nov. 14–24, 1969; *Apollo 12.* May 25–June 22, 1973; *Skylab 2*)

* Exact time in space and name of spacecraft are not available for these Russian astronauts.

—J.BER.

4,007 OBJECTS
ORBITING THE EARTH

	Earth Satellite Vehicle Payload	Earth Satellite Vehicle Junk	Total
U.S.	402	2,274	2,676
U.S.S.R.	379	837	1,216
France	13	43	56
Japan	8	8	16
United Kingdom	7	4	11
Canada	8	0	8
People's Republic of China	3	3	6
W. Germany	2	4	6
NATO	3	0	3
France/W. Germany	2	0	2
Australia	1	0	1
European Space Agency	1	0	1
European Space Research Organization	1	0	1
India	1	0	1
Indonesia	1	0	1
Netherlands	1	0	1
Spain	1	0	1
	834	3,173	4,007

The payloads are the instrument packages. The vehicle junk includes spent rocket stages, bolts, tether cables, separation springs, de-spin weights, and other fragments. In addition, there are 54 deep-space probes that have escaped earth's orbit together with 46 pieces of space junk. Approximately 1,132 payloads and 4,245 pieces of space junk have fallen back to earth or burned up in the atmosphere.

—M.MO.

12 STELLAR BODIES
AND PHENOMENA

1. ASTEROID

The minor planets orbiting between Mars and Jupiter are called asteroids. An unproved hypothesis, Bode's law, led to the prediction, in the late 18th century, that a planet might be found between Mars and Jupiter. Using calculations based on this prediction, Giuseppi Piazzi, an Italian astronomer, discovered the first asteroid,

Ceres, in 1801. Since then, thousands have been found, and the orbits of 2,000 have been calculated. Ceres, with a diameter of 480 mi., is the largest. Most asteroids are small lumps of rock a few miles in diameter.

2. BLACK HOLE

Near the end of a star's lifetime, the energy radiating from its center becomes insufficient to overcome its gravitational field, and it collapses on itself. As it shrinks, it becomes smaller and hotter, ending as a ball of matter only a few miles across, which has the mass of the star before it collapsed. If the star was large enough, the gravitational field of this ball of matter is so strong that nothing—not even light—can escape to reveal its presence. This is a black hole. Astrophysicists estimate there may be a billion in our galaxy alone, and they may constitute as much as 90% of the mass of the universe. According to David Brand in *The Wall Street Journal:* "At first glance any theory that talks of a hole in space, where time stands still so that a fraction of a second becomes eternity and where all things simply disappear from sight, would seem to belong to the more fantastic realms of science fiction. But to astronomers it is far from fantasy."

3. COMET

A member of the solar system, moving around the sun in an orbit which is usually highly eccentric. The nucleus of the comet may be several kilometers in diameter and is composed of frozen gases and particles of dust. The comet's tail always points away from the sun. Edmund Halley (1656–1742) first explained what comets are, identified the comet named after him, and correctly predicted its reappearance in 1758. Mark Twain's name is often associated with Halley's Comet because it shone in the skies when he was born, and it shone again in 1910 when he died. Halley's Comet appears on the average every 77 years and it will shine again in 1986.

4. GALAXY

A huge system of stars. Our galaxy, called the Milky Way, is a group of some 100 billion stars. Our sun is just an average-sized member of this vast assemblage. Approximately a billion galaxies are within photographic range of the Mount Palomar Observatory in California, but this number is probably a small fraction of the total number of galaxies in the universe—the number of stars is virtually infinite.

5. METEOR

A small particle of rock or metal attracted to earth by gravity, a meteor streaks toward the ground at speeds up to 45 mi. per sec. Friction with the air heats the meteor to such high temperatures that it usually disintegrates before reaching the ground. (If it does reach the ground, it is called a meteorite.) As it falls, the meteor leaves behind it a fiery trail that we recognize as a "shooting star."

6. NOVA

When a previously unobservable or inconspicuous star suddenly flares up to many times its normal brightness, it is called a nova. This "new" star fades after a period of time—from a few months to several years.

7. PLANET

A nonluminous body orbiting a star. There are nine planets in our solar system; earth is one of them. Irregularities in the motion of nearby stars indicate they also may have planets.

8. PULSAR

Pulsars are formed from the collapsed remnants of supernova explosions. When first formed, pulsars may rotate up to 1,000 times per sec. Their diameter is typically 12 mi. When the first pulsar was discovered in 1967, the remarkable regularity of its pulse rate was initially interpreted as a meaningful signal from another intelligent civilization.

9. QUASAR

Imagine a flashlight that shines with the combined brilliance of the lights of a large city, such as Los Angeles. That is how concentrated a quasar's energy output is. Quasars are about the size of large stars, but they emit an energy equivalent to the output of a thousand galaxies. One newly discovered quasar, OQ172, is believed to be the object most remote from earth thus far discovered—some 10 billion light-years away.

10. SATELLITE

An object orbiting a planet. Known natural satellites vary in size from Mars' tiny moon Deimos, only 5 mi. across, to Jupiter's massive Ganymede, 3,120 mi. in diameter. Mercury, a full-fledged planet, is only about 3,000 mi. in diameter.

11. STAR

A self-luminous gaseous body. Our sun is a star.

12. SUPERNOVA

A cataclysmic stellar explosion in which a star sends most of its material into space. At its height, a supernova is as bright as 10 million to 100 million suns. What we see today as the Crab Nebula is the debris of a supernova that was first seen on July 4, 1054. For two years it was so bright that it could be seen with the naked eye by day, then it faded and blinked out. Many Europeans took it as a warning that the millennium had ended and Judgment Day was at hand.

—J. BER.

THE 43 MAJOR MEMBERS
OF OUR SOLAR SYSTEM

Celestial Body/ Satellite	Diameter; Orbit Diameter (mi.)	
1. Sun	864,950	The sun rotates on its axis once each 25.38 days. It is a medium-sized star, of a color type called yellow.
2. Mercury	3,000; 36,000,000	Mercury rotates on its axis once each 58.5 days and orbits the sun once each 87.9 days. Its maximum surface temperature is a blazing 770°F.
3. Venus	7,700; 67,200,000	Venus rotates on its axis once each 243 days and orbits the sun once each 224.7 days. Under the planet's thick cloud cover of carbon dioxide and nitrogen, heat accumulates to produce temperatures over 750°F.
4. Earth	7,927; 93,000,000	Life thrives on this planet because it has water, and the earth is just the right distance from the sun so that water can exist here as a liquid. Temperatures: −126.9°-136.4°F.
5. Moon	2,158; 238,840	Earth, for its size, has the largest satellite of any planet in the solar system
6. Mars	4,219; 141,600,000	Mars' day is 24.6 hours long. It is the most likely of all the planets to have life on it, with a sparse atmosphere of carbon dioxide and traces of water. The maximum temperature on Mars is 80°F. on the equator at noon. Average temperature is −60°F. Lows range below −100°F.
7. Deimos	5; 14,600	Smallest known satellite in the solar system.

8. Phobos	8; 5,800	
9. Asteroids	1-429; 300,000,000 (average)	The asteroids are huge chunks of rock orbiting the sun between Mars and Jupiter. They are minor planets. There may be as many as 40,000 of them.
10. Jupiter	88,700; 484,300,000	Jupiter's atmosphere is largely hydrogen and helium. It is believed that Jupiter would have become a companion star to the sun had it been a little larger.
11. Amalthea	150; 113,000	
12. Io	2,310; 262,000	
13. Europa	1,950; 417,000	
14. Ganymede	3,120; 666,000	This satellite is larger than the planet Mercury.
15. Callisto	2,770; 1,170,000	
16. Hestia	100; 7,120,000	
17. Hera	35; 7,290,000	
18. Demeter	15; 7,300,000	
19. Adrastea	14; 13,000,000	
20. Pan	19; 14,000,000	
21. Poseidon	35; 14,600,000	
22. Hades	17; 14,700,000	
23. Saturn	75,100; 886,000,000	Known since ancient times, Saturn is the only planet with rings. After Galileo introduced the telescope, many theories were proposed about the form of Saturn. It was finally described correctly by Christian Huygens in 1659.

24.	Janus	190; 98,000
25.	Mimas	300; 115,000
26.	Enceladus	350; 148,000
27.	Tethys	600; 183,000
28.	Dione	600; 234,000
29.	Rhea	800; 327,000
30.	Titan	3,000; 758,000

A peculiar combination of circumstances gives Titan a fighting chance for supporting life. Its atmosphere traps and holds what little warmth reaches it at nearly a billion miles from the sun. The greenhouse effect might allow Titan to achieve temperatures similar to those on Mars, within the range suitable for life. The answer may come when an unmanned space vehicle takes a closer look.

31.	Hyperion	300; 919,000
32.	Iapetus	1,000; 2,210,000
33.	Phoebe	130; 8,040,000
34.	Uranus	29,300; 1,780,000,000

It's cold on Uranus: all-time high is −310°F. Uranus is the first "discovered" planet, found by accident in 1781 by William Herschel, an amateur astronomer at the time. When the German chemist Martin Klaproth discovered a new metallic element in 1789, he named it for the new planet: uranium.

| 35. | Miranda | 190;
76,000 |
| 36. | Ariel | 500;
119,000 |

37.	Umbriel	370; 166,000
38.	Titania	680; 272,000
39.	Oberon	620; 364,000

40. Neptune 31,200;
2,790,000,000

Neptune was the first planet whose existence was predicted theoretically before it was discovered. Urbain Leverrier, a French astronomer, completed his calculations in 1846, and the planet was discovered within the year.

41.	Triton	2,300; 220,000
42.	Nereid	190; 3,500,000

43. Pluto 3,700;
3,670,000,000

Pluto was discovered in March, 1930, by Clyde Tombaugh, a U.S. astronomer. The calculations used to predict Pluto's position had been done by another American, Percival Lowell.

—J. BER.

The Martian landscape as seen from the *Viking 1* lander at 7:30 A.M. (Mars Standard Time) on August 3, 1976. The boulder is about 1 by 3 meters (3 by 10 feet) in size and is 8 meters (25 feet) away from the spacecraft.

6
INSIDE NOAH'S ARK
—ANIMAL LIFE

9 BREEDS OF DOGS
THAT BITE THE LEAST

1. Golden retriever
2. Labrador retriever
3. Shetland sheepdog
4. Old English sheepdog
5. Welsh terrier
6. Yorkshire terrier
7. Beagle
8. Dalmatian
9. Pointer

—E.L.A.

9 DOGS THAT BITE THE MOST

This list was so popular in *The People's Almanac* that we thought we would run it again for those who may have missed it. After a 27-year study of the canine population of New York, N.Y., Dr. Robert Oleson of the U.S. Public Health Service came up with the nine bitingest dogs. He found that the time of year in which you will most likely be bitten is not July or August, the "dog days," but the middle of June. And the dogs most likely to do it, ranked in order of their biting averages, are:

1. German police dog
2. Chow
3. Poodle
4. Italian bulldog
5. Fox terrier
6. Crossed chow
7. Airedale terrier
8. Pekingese
9. Crossed German police dog

No, Dobermans didn't make it. And neither did mongrels.

14 CELEBRATED ANIMALS

1. BARRY

Barry, the legendary St. Bernard who rescued over 40 snow-bound people in his lifetime (1800–1814) can still be seen, thanks to the art of taxidermy, in the National Museum in Bern, Switzerland. Barry had remarkable sensory gifts. He could predict imminent avalanches and he could lead the monks of the Hospice of St. Bernard to travelers buried beneath the snow. The monks continued to name their lead dog "Barry" as a tribute to the original after his death.

2. BIBS

Heroic canaries are surely rare. One of them, Bibs, lived—and died—in Hermitage, Tenn. Bibs belonged to an elderly woman known as Old Aunt Tess. When Old Aunt Tess fell and injured herself severely, Bibs went winging down the road for help. She banged against the window of a neighboring house until she aroused the occupant. Old Aunt Tess survived but Bibs died from excessive tapping.

3. CHECKERS

While running for vice-president with Eisenhower in 1952, Richard M. Nixon's career was almost shattered by an exposé revealing that he had a secret $18,000 personal fund (mostly contributions from oilmen) stashed away under another name. Asked to resign, Nixon decided to defend himself on television. Told to make disclosures of any gifts he had received, Nixon remembered how FDR had defended his dog, Fala, in 1944, and he decided to do likewise. In his speech, Nixon said that he had received a gift from a Republican in Texas. "It was a little cocker spaniel dog . . . Black and white spotted. And our little girl—Tricia, the 6-year-old—named it Checkers. And you know, the kids (like all kids) love the dog, and I just want to say this right now, that regardless of what they say about it, we're gonna keep it." After the speech, Nixon wept, saying, "I was an utter flop . . . Well, at least I won the dog vote tonight." The speech was a success. Nixon stayed on the ticket, writing later, "Checkers emerged from the campaign the best-known dog in the nation since Fala."

4. COMANCHE

Gen. George Armstrong Custer and the 225 men of his 7th Cavalry were attacked by Sioux and Cheyenne Indians at Little Big Horn, Mont., in 1876. The troop's only survivor at the scene was Capt. Myles W. Keogh's horse, Comanche. The horse had suffered seven wounds, including three serious ones in the neck, lung, and groin. The horse, three-quarters American, one-quarter Spanish, survived to become a legend. He was sent to Fort Lincoln, Dakota, and a special order prevented anyone from riding him. He was paraded at all ceremonies and was allowed to wander free at each post he attended. Comanche died of colic at Fort Riley, Kans., on November 9, 1893. He was 30 years old.

Comanche. Embalmed, he now stands on display at the University of Kansas.

5. DAISY

A family summering in northern New York State temporarily
—they thought—adopted a cat and called her Daisy. They abandoned
her when they returned to their home in New York City and were
startled when she appeared on their doorstep a month later, carrying
one of her kittens. Their astonishment grew when Daisy made four
more trips to her old home, returning each time with another kitten.
Inquiries have yielded no explanation for Daisy's extraordinary hom-
ing instinct.

6. FLUSH

Because Flush has been portrayed on both stage and screen,
Elizabeth Barrett Browning's red cocker spaniel is better known than
the Brownings' son, Robert Wiedemann Barrett. Flush was the only
companion allowed the invalid Elizabeth by her tyrannical father.
When Robert Browning visited Elizabeth for the first time in the
house on Wimpole Street, the jealous Flush bit him. Flush was kidnapped on three occasions but ransomed each time.

7. INCITATUS

Caligula, emperor of Rome from 37 to 41 A.D., was one of the
most depraved and monstrous rulers of all time—but he lavished love
on his horse, Incitatus. Caligula made the horse a consul of the empire and supplied him with a marble manger, ivory stall, gold drinking goblet, furniture, and a retinue of slaves. Caligula even held
parties at which Incitatus was the host.

Jack operating the railway signal levers.

8. JACK THE BABOON

Jack was living proof that some animals are as intelligent as people. A chacma baboon, Jack belonged to James Wide, a legless railroad switchman in South Africa. Each day, Jack pushed his wheelchair-bound owner to work and gradually learned to assist the handicapped man by doing small chores in the signal box before moving on to operating signal levers by himself, as his master looked on. Jack died in 1890 after a nine-year career as a switchman's assistant.

9. JACK THE PORPOISE

Sailors bringing their ships through French Pass, a waterway near D'Urville Island off the coast of New Zealand, learned to depend upon a porpoise named Jack to guide them through the dangerous currents. From 1871 to 1903, Jack met and piloted every boat that appeared. In 1903 a drunken passenger on *The Penquin* shot and wounded him. Jack recovered, resumed his self-appointed job, and for nine more years guided all ships—except *The Penguin*.

10. JUMBO

The world's most famous elephant resided in the London Zoo for 17 years, sustained by a daily ration of 200 lbs. of hay, five pails of water, and a quart of whiskey, before P. T. Barnum contracted to bring him to the U.S. England was in an uproar over losing Jumbo. Queen Victoria, the prince of Wales, and John Ruskin—protesting that Jumbo was a national treasure—demanded that the contract be broken. But in 1882, after a 15-day Atlantic crossing during which he was soothed with beer, Jumbo arrived in New York. During his 3½ years with the circus, an estimated million children rode on his back. On a September evening in 1885, as Jumbo was being led across seldom used railroad tracks, an unscheduled freight train struck and killed him. Examination of his bones revealed that this marvelous animal who weighed 6½ tons had not yet achieved his full growth.

11. LAIKA

This sad-eyed Samoyed husky bitch was the first living sacrifice to the space age. In November, 1957, the Soviet Union launched *Sputnik 2* with Laika its sole passenger. No recovery system had yet been invented, so Laika traveled 1,050 mi. from the earth's surface to face certain doom.

12. MOIFAA

In 1904, the ship carrying this massive 8-year-old racehorse from New Zealand to England was lost in a storm. Moifaa almost drowned but was washed ashore on a desert island. There he roamed for two weeks before being rescued. Sent on to England, he was entered in the Grand National Steeplechase against 25 other horses. He won by eight lengths in 9 min., 59 sec.

13. MORRIS

The finicky cat who disdains all cat food except 9-Lives in television commercials should count his blessings. Morris was 20 minutes away from extinction in a suburban Chicago cat shelter when he was rescued and started on an enviable career. Today he has round-the-clock guards to protect him from kidnappers—and his picture hangs on the wall of the local pound.

14. MUHAMED

A mental wizard, Muhamed was part of a stable of horses in Elberfeld, Germany, trained and owned by Karl Krall in the late 19th century. Blindfolded by a sack, Muhamed could calculate cube roots after only four months of training. He could also add, subtract, multiply, and divide. To give an answer to a math problem—say, 54—he would tap his left foot five times, his right four times. Scientific observers came and went without proving that any trickery had occurred.

—S.W., I.W., C.O., & R.T.

AND THE SHEEP SHALL INHERIT THE EARTH: 16 SHEEP MAJORITIES AROUND THE WORLD

(based on 1974 data)

	Sheep	Humans
1. Australia	145,304,000	13,339,000
2. New Zealand	55,883,000	2,726,000

3.	South Africa	31,000,000	24,920,000
4.	Peru	17,300,000	15,383,000
5.	Iraq	15,500,000	10,765,000
6.	Uruguay	15,373,000	3,028,000
7.	Mongolia	14,077,000*	1,403,000
8.	Yemen	11,600,000	3,730,000
9.	Bulgaria	9,765,000	8,679,000
10.	Namibia	4,400,000	692,000
11.	Ireland	3,999,000	3,086,000
12.	Somalia	3,906,000	3,090,000
13.	Libya	3,200,000	2,346,000
14.	Mauritania	2,800,000	1,290,000
15.	Lesotho	1,600,000	1,016,000
16.	Iceland	846,000	215,000

* Unofficial.

World sheep population: 1,032,667,000.

SOURCE: *F.A.O. of the United Nations Production Yearbook 1974.*

And the sheep shall inherit the earth.

10 BIRDS THAT COULD NOT OR CANNOT FLY

1. CASSOWARY

A large bird, exceeded in size only by the ostrich and emu, the cassowary inhabits the forests of Australia and islands in Papua where it forages for fruit and small animals. The razor-sharp nail on the innermost of its three toes provides it with a deadly kicking weapon.

2. CORMORANT

While all other species of cormorant can fly at least short distances, the Galapogas cormorant, restricted to Isabela Island, is entirely flightless. It nests near the shore, and although clumsy and vulnerable on land, it is a good swimmer and diver. The Galapagos cormorant has been the victim of hunting and is now considered an endangered species.

3. DODO

This large bird, closely related to the pigeon family, once inhabited the island of Mauritius, east of Madagascar. The arrival of the Portuguese on Mauritius and their introduction of hogs heralded the demise of the dodo. Relatively slow and uncoordinated, the dodo was hunted into extinction by 1700.

4. EMU

This flightless Australian plains bird is second in size only to the ostrich, which it adaptationally resembles in many ways. The emu can run at 30 mph and fight effectively by kicking with its three-toed feet. Because it was once nearly exterminated, it is now legally protected.

5. KIWI

A resident of New Zealand, the kiwi is related to the extinct moa. Although flightless, it has a pair of 3-in. vestigial wings. It has had to adapt itself to life in the open country due to the destruction of much of its original forest habitat. This destruction, coupled with its inability to produce fertile eggs in captivity, has placed the kiwi on the verge of extinction.

6. MOA

This extinct bird, native to New Zealand, once comprised 25 species, ranging in size from that of a turkey to as tall as 10 ft. Hunted for food by the early Polynesian peoples of New Zealand, most species of moa were extinct by the end of the 17th century, though a few of the smaller varieties may have survived into the 19th century.

7. OSTRICH

The ostrich is the largest living bird and the fastest-moving of the flightless birds. It lives in bands of 10–50, primarily in the southern and eastern African plains. Because of its speed and keen eyesight, the ostrich can outrun and outmaneuver most of its enemies.

8. PENGUIN

All 18 species of penguin live in the southern hemisphere, ranging from Antarctica to the Galapagos Islands. With their wings transformed into flippers and their bodies protected by insulating layers of blubber, down, and close-set feathers, penguins are completely adapted to a life of swimming and diving. They leave the water to mate, raise young, and molt.

9. RAIL

There are over 100 species of rail throughout the world, and although most species are marsh birds with the full ability to fly, several near flightless varieties exist. These include the white-throated rail of the Aldabra Islands in the Indian Ocean, which can—with difficulty—fly a short distance; the Gough Island rail, which can flutter a few feet; and the tiny Inaccessible Island rail, which is totally unable to fly.

10. RHEA

The largest bird in the New World, the common rhea once roamed the Brazilian and Argentinian pampas in huge flocks, though now it is greatly reduced in number due to the spread of agriculture. The smaller Darwin's rhea inhabits the wild areas of the eastern foothills of the Andes from Peru to the Strait of Magellan. Although the rhea's wings are useless, on the ground it can outdistance the fastest horse.

—F.B.F.

17 ANIMALS WITH POUCHES

1. Anteater
2. Bandicoot
3. Cuscus
4. Echidna
5. Glider
6. Kangaroo
7. Koala
8. Marsupial cat
9. Opossum
10. Pouched mouse
11. Quokka
12. Sea horse (pipefishes)
13. Tasmanian devil
14. Tiger cat
15. Wallaby
16. Wallaroo
17. Wombat

—M. MO.

PREGNANCY OR GESTATION PERIODS OF 20 ANIMALS

		Gestation Period (days)
1.	African elephant	640
2.	Rhinoceros	560
3.	Giraffe	450
4.	Porpoise	360
5.	Horse	337

6.	Cow	280
7.	Orangutan	275
8.	Human being	267
9.	Reindeer	246
10.	Polar bear	240
11.	Honey badger	180
12.	Panther	93
13.	Cat	64
14.	Dog	64
15.	Fox	54
16.	Kangaroo	40
17.	Rabbit	31
18.	House mouse	19
19.	Hamster	16
20.	Opossum	13

—J.O.

MAXIMUM RECORDED
LIFE SPAN OF 94 ANIMALS

		Years/Months
1.	Lake sturgeon	152
2.	Tortoise	116
3.	Human being	113/7
4.	Turtle	88
5.	Whale	87
6.	Condor	72
7.	Elephant	70
8.	Raven	69
9.	Freshwater mussel	60
10.	Alligator	56*
11.	Orangutan	54
12.	Hippopotamus	51
13.	Ostrich	50
14.	Sponge	50
15.	Horse	46
16.	Seal	46
17.	Chimpanzee	44/6
18.	Vulture	41/5
19.	Trout	41
20.	Halibut	40
21.	Rhinoceros	40
22.	Gorilla	39/3

23.	Boa constrictor	39*
24.	Pigeon	35
25.	Tapeworm	35
26.	Monkey	34/9
27.	Polar bear	34/8
28.	Cat	34
29.	Giraffe	33/6
30.	Lobster	33
31.	Dolphin	32
32.	Cattle	30
33.	Chicken	30
34.	Goldfish	30
35.	Camel	29/5
36.	Swan	29/5
37.	Dog	27/3
38.	Leech	27
39.	Swine	27
40.	Deer	26/6
41.	Parakeet	25
42.	Gila monster	24/7
43.	Bat	24
44.	Canary	24
45.	Jaguar	23
46.	Swift	21
47.	Duck	20/6
48.	Sheep	20
49.	Sparrow	20
50.	Kangaroo	19/7
51.	Rattlesnake	19/5
52.	Herring	19
53.	Goat	18
54.	Starling	15/10
55.	Frog	15/8
56.	Mackerel	15
57.	Squirrel	15
58.	Toad	15
59.	Raccoon	13/9
60.	Abalone	13
61.	Ant (queen)	13
62.	Salmon	13
63.	Cobra	12/4
64.	Turkey	12/4
65.	Oyster	12
66.	Electric eel	11/5
67.	Mink	10
68.	Hummingbird	8
69.	Mouse	8
70.	North American porcupine	7/6
71.	Tuna	7
72.	Opossum	6/10
73.	Earthworm	6

	Years/Months
74. Snail	6
75. Honeybee (queen)	5
76. Starfish	5
77. Rat	4/8
78. American cockroach	4/7
79. Seahorse	4/7
80. Hamster	4
81. Octopus	4
82. Spider	4
83. Squid	4
84. Tick	4
85. Periwinkle	3
86. Scallop	2
87. Silverfish	2
88. Mosquito	1/6
89. Slug	1/6
90. Honeybee (worker)	0/11
91. Bedbug	0/6
92. Honeybee (drone)	0/6
93. Housefly	76 days
94. Roundworm	12 days

* Still alive.

SOURCE: Philip L. Altman and D. S. Dittner, eds., *The Biology Data Book* (Bethesda, Md.: Federation of American Societies for Experimental Biology, 1972).

25 WONDERFUL COLLECTIVE NOUNS FOR ANIMALS

Although not frequently heard in conversation, these terms are fully correct and appropriate ways of describing the animals listed.

1. A murder of crows
2. A clowder of cats
3. A leap of leopards
4. A sloth of bears
5. A rafter of turkeys
6. A smack of jellyfish
7. A skulk of foxes
8. A labor of moles
9. A peep of chickens
10. A crash of rhinoceroses
11. A paddling of ducks
12. A siege of herons
13. A rag of colts
14. A drift of hogs
15. A charm of finches
16. A trip of goats
17. A knot of toads
18. A shrewdness of apes
19. A parliament of owls
20. A troop of kangaroos
21. A gaggle of geese
22. A pride of lions
23. A watch of nightingales
24. A muster of peacocks
25. An exaltation of larks

—The Eds.

20 ENDANGERED SPECIES
AND REASONS FOR THEIR DECLINE

1. NUBIAN WILD ASS (northeastern Sudan)

Gradual deterioration and extinction through interbreeding with domesticated donkeys. *May be extinct.*

2. SOMALI WILD ASS (Ethiopia)

Severe competition for limited water and pasture; Somalis hunt wild asses for their fat which is regarded as a medicine against tuberculosis; early 20th-century military campaigns in Ethiopia and Somalia. *Doubtful that the total population exceeds 700.*

3. MEXICAN GRIZZLY BEAR (crest of Sierra Madre Mountains, Mexico)

Shooting by loggers, miners, ranchers, and sportsmen. *Several dozen remain.*

4. BRANDER'S SWAMP DEER (Kanha National Park, Madhya Pradesh, India)

Heavy and continuous illegal hunting. *Seventy-three survive.*

5. McNEILL'S DEER (Tibetan plateau)

Hunted by natives because the Chinese believe there is an aphrodisiac contained in antler velvet. *Unknown how many survive.*

6. NORTHERN KIT FOX (Cypress Hills, southwest Saskatchewan)

Trapping, poison, and capture by dogs. *No record, but appears extinct in Canada.*

7. NORTHERN SIMIEN FOX (Simien Mountains, Ethiopia)

Shooting; reputation as a sheep killer caused it to be persecuted. *One or two survive.*

8. SAN JOAQUIN FOX (San Joaquin Valley, Calif.)

Large numbers killed for fur; victim of poison campaigns directed against coyotes. *There are 113 active dens in Kern County, Calif.*

9. GOLDEN LION MARMOSET (southeast Brazil)

Deforestation resulting from development of sugar cane, coffee, and banana plantations; also housing projects. *Survivors: 400–600.*

10. WOOLLY SPIDER MONKEY (southeast Brazil)

Reduction of habitat forests by encroachment of agriculture and human occupation. *Unknown how many survive.*

11. **GIANT OTTER** (eastern rivers of Brazil, Venezuela, Peru, and Colombia)

Commercial hunting for skins. *Unknown how many survive.*

12. **NOVAYA ZEMLYA REINDEER** (Novaya Zemlya, Island, U.S.S.R.)

Hunting. *Less than a few dozen are left.*

13. **JAVAN RHINOCEROS** (Java and Sumatra)

Horn trade; also, excluded from land by agriculture. *Numbers surviving: 42–56.*

14. **NORTHERN SQUARE-LIPPED RHINOCEROS** (southwest Sudan, Uganda, northeast Congo, west Nile Province)

Disintegration of law and order in Zaire (1960s) and occupation of area by rebel forces. *Less than 100 left.*

15. **SUMATRAN RHINOCEROS** (Burma, Thailand, Malaya, Sumatra, Sabah, and possibly India)

Hunted because of belief in the medicinal, religious, or magical value of its various parts, e.g., hide, toenails, and blood. *About 100–170 left.*

16. **JAPANESE SEA LION** (Takeshima Island)

Korean settlement of the island (which is in the Sea of Japan) following the Korean War. *Probably none left.*

17. **CARIBBEAN MONK SEAL** (Caribbean area)

Slaughtered for their oil. *Nearly extinct.*

18. **MEDITERRANEAN MONK SEAL** (Mediterranean area)

Unceasing pursuit by fishermen, and disturbance of caves—their last remaining refuge—by skin divers. *Population: 500.*

19. **BLUE WHALE** (antarctic)

Overexploitation of the species for commercial purposes—one blue whale can yield 140 barrels of oil. *Estimated population: 650–1,950.*

20. **RED WOLF** (Gulf coast of Texas)

Heavy trapping and hunting pressures; habitat favors the coyote with which red wolves readily hybridize; it cannot compete with the more aggressive coyote. *Unknown how many survive.*

SOURCE: *Red Data Book* (Morges, Switzerland: International Union for the Conservation of Nature and Natural Resources, 1975).

7
ON THE MOVE —TRAVEL AND TRANSPORTATION

9 MOST UNUSUAL MONUMENTS IN THE WORLD

Monument to the boll weevil. The dreaded pest can be seen on the very top of the monument—as far from the ground as possible.

1. MONUMENT TO THE BOLL WEEVIL (Enterprise, Ala.)

Around the turn of the century, an attack of boll weevils devastated the cotton crop and virtually destroyed the economy of Alabama. As a result, farmers began diversifying their crops and planting peanuts, a much more stable and profitable crop. The farmers of Alabama rapidly reached new heights of prosperity and, in appreciation, erected a statue of the hated boll weevil.

2. FIVE STATUES FILLED WITH CIGARS IN THE AUSTRIA FOUNTAIN (Vienna)

The sculptor Ludwig von Schwanthaler attempted to earn some extra money by smuggling cigars through customs, hiding them inside the hollow bronze statues. However, he died before he could remove the cigars, and the statues were erected in 1844–1846 with the cigars still inside.

3. STATUE TO A POET (Guayaquil, Ecuador)

The statue is in honor of the Ecuadorian poet José Olmedo, but it is actually a secondhand statue of Lord Byron, purchased because it would have cost too much to commission a statue of Olmedo himself.

4. STATUE DEDICATED TO THE MEMORY OF WILLIAM HUSKISSON (London)

Huskisson was a popular member of Parliament who, on September 15, 1830, became the first man to be run over by a railroad train. Contemporary accounts note that the elderly Mr. Huskisson had "a peculiar aptitude for accident," and at the opening ceremonies of the Manchester and Liverpool Railway, in 1830, he neglected to look both ways before crossing the tracks to speak to the duke of Wellington. The bereaved public erected a memorial to him in Pimlico Gardens in London. It was an 8-ft.-high marble statue of Huskisson clad in a Roman toga.

5. STATUE DEPICTING KING CHARLES II ON HORSEBACK TRAMPLING HIS ENEMY OLIVER CROMWELL (Ripon*)

The Italian statue originally depicted the king of Poland trampling a Turkish soldier underfoot. Unfortunately, the Poles could not afford the monument, so the sculptor was stuck with a large and unusual statue. He made some minor changes in the statue and succeeded in selling it to the British as a statue of Charles II and Oliver Cromwell. However, he neglected to change one detail: Cromwell is wearing a turban.

6. TEMPLE OF THE BUTCHERED COW (Shimoda, Japan)

It was erected shortly after Japan opened its doors to Westerners in the 1850s. It honored the memory of the first cow slaughtered in Japan and marked the first violation of the Buddhist tenet against the eating of meat.

* Moved in 1738 from London to Yorkshire.

7. MODEL EXHIBITED AT THE NEW YORK WORLD'S FAIR (1939–1940)—A PROPOSED STATUE HONORING CAPT. HANSEN GREGORY, THE PURPORTED INVENTOR OF THE DOUGHNUT HOLE

The full statue was to have been 250–300 ft. high and would have been located on the summit of Mount Battie, Me. Plans called for it to be lit by huge floodlights so that it could be seen 50 mi. out to sea. Needless to say, the statue was never built.

8. BAS-RELIEF OF BENEDICT ARNOLD'S LEFT BOOT (Saratoga, N.Y.)

Although Arnold later became a traitor, he served bravely in the American Revolution and was wounded in the thigh at the battle of Saratoga in 1777. The marble memorial was erected in recognition of Arnold's bravery but, since he was a traitor, it depicts only a cannon, a military boot for his left leg, a major general's epaulet, and a wreath. It is called the "Boot Monument."

9. STATUE OF POCAHONTAS'S FATHER, CHIEF POWHATAN (Cuzco, Peru)

The Peruvians had commissioned a statue of Atahualpa, the last king of the Incas, but the foundry accidentally sent them the wrong statue. The people couldn't afford to ship the statue back to the U.S., so they kept it and erected it in the town square.

—P.S.H.

EUGENE FODOR'S 10 MOST GLAMOROUS CITIES IN THE WORLD

Eugene Fodor, whose travel books have won the Grand Prix de Littérature de Tourisme and the Award of the National Association of Travel Organizations, publishes widely read guides to almost every tourist-oriented nation on earth.

1. Paris, France
2. New York, N.Y.
3. London, England
4. Rio de Janeiro, Brazil
5. Hong Kong
6. Rome, Italy
7. Madrid, Spain
8. Sydney, Australia
9. Kyoto, Japan
10. Stockholm, Sweden

—Exclusive for *The Book of Lists*

KATE SIMON'S
10 MOST GLAMOROUS
CITIES IN THE WORLD

Kate Simon, whom Phyllis McGinley has called "a public benefactor," is known for her witty and entertaining books. Among the most popular of her travel guides are *Paris—Places & Pleasures* and *London—Places & Pleasures*.

1. Venice, Italy
2. Leningrad, U.S.S.R.
3. New York, N.Y.
4. San Francisco, Calif.
5. Kyoto, Japan
6. Siena, Italy
7. Guanajuato, Mexico
8. Bourges, France
9. Barcelona, Spain
10. York, England

Kate Simon adds: "The word *glamorous* is the catch here. I don't quite know what it means to you and your book. I've listed those that I find most alluring or vivacious or lovely, or all three."

—Exclusive for *The Book of Lists*

12 COUNTRIES RECEIVING
THE LARGEST NUMBER OF
TOURISTS AND VISITORS (1974)

1. Spain — 30,343,000
2. W. Germany — 15,229,000
3. U.S. — 14,123,000
4. Canada — 13,759,000
5. Italy — 12,442,000
6. Czechoslovakia — 11,786,000
7. Austria — 10,886,000
8. France — 9,838,000
9. United Kingdom — 7,935,000
10. Poland — 7,893,000
11. Belgium — 7,477,000
12. E. Germany — 6,951,000

SOURCE: *United Nations Statistical Yearbook, 1975.*

11 PLACES TO
SPEND A HEALTHY WINTER

For most of the nations of the world, including the U.S., Mexico, and most of Europe, the deadliest months of the year are December and January. Here is a list of places which experience their lowest death rates during December and January.

1. Barbados
2. Cape Verde Islands
3. Dominica, Windward Islands
4. Greenland
5. Nicaragua
6. Pakistan
7. Sabah, Malaysia
8. Sarawak, Malaysia
9. Surinam
10. Togo
11. Wallis and Futuna Islands, Melanesia

SOURCE: *United Nations Demographic Yearbook 1974.*

—D.W.

SYDNEY CLARK'S
10 FAVORITE OVERLOOKED
SIGHTS IN THE WORLD

Sydney Clark, named "Dean of the Travel Writers," devoted a lifetime to producing authoritative information books about the numerous nations throughout the world which he visited. Mr. Clark died in April, 1975, and his son, Donald E. Clark, supplied this list in his father's name.

Dubrovnik, Yugoslavia. No motor vehicles are allowed within the walls of this Croatian port.

1. Dubrovnik, Yugoslavia—steeped in beauty and history
2. Liechtenstein—postage stamp principality
3. Hallstatt—Tyrolean treasure town
4. Alkmaar, Holland—and its Dutch cheeses
5. Rovaniemi, Finland—rebuilt capital of Lapland
6. Heidelberg, W. Germany—with its university life
7. Geirangerfjord, Norway—for breathtaking beauty
8. Annecy, France—and its charming lake
9. The Channel Islands, England—within sight of France
10. Conimbriga—Roman mosaics in northern Portugal

—Exclusive for *The Book of Lists*

KATE SIMON'S
10 FAVORITE OVERLOOKED
SIGHTS IN THE WORLD

1. City of Lincoln, England
2. The compound of Fatehpur Sikri not far from the Taj Mahal in India
3. Place des Vosges, Paris
4. Castel del Monte near Andria, Italy
5. Cathedral of Autun, France
6. Central square of Todi, Italy
7. Old section of Stockholm at night
8. Greek temple at Segesta, Sicily
9. Houses by Antonio Gaudí in Barcelona, Spain
10. Moors of northern Yorkshire, England

—Exclusive for *The Book of Lists*

TEMPLE FIELDING'S
11 FAVORITE OVERLOOKED
SIGHTS IN THE WORLD

Travel writer Temple Fielding focuses on the more practical aspects of vacationing—where to eat, favorite entertainment spots, hotels—rather than museum statistics and history. His popular approach to travel has won him much acclaim and an enormous audience. The best-selling *Fielding's Travel Guide to Europe* is produced annually. His other travel books include *Fielding's Currency Guide* and *Fielding's Low-Cost Guide to Europe*.

1. MALDIVES (near Sri Lanka)

Over 1,000 lush coral islands which are totally uninhabited. Skinny-dip in the picture postcard lagoon from its magnificent white beaches as king and queen of *your* private realm until the fisherman returns in the late afternoon to pick both of you up.

2. THE DUPLEX PENTHOUSE SUITE AT THE HOTEL BRISTOL, PARIS

Three bedrooms, three baths, a glorious sweep of the City of Light from the wraparound terraces, and a private elevator between the two floors—for only $500 per day.

3. NORWAY'S PEER GYNT MOUNTAIN COUNTRY

Only three hours north of Oslo, with a handful of good, scenically sited exchange-plan hotels above pristine lakes. Excellent skiing in winter and a panoply of sports facilities and walking trails in summer, inexpensive prices, and water so pure that you can dip your drinking cup into any natural font anywhere.

4. THE OUTER SEYCHELLES

A fascinating chain of tropical islands 1,000 mi. east of Kenya in the Indian Ocean, whose most seductive features are the untouched bird and turtle sanctuaries and the wide variety of exotic fish, some of them still unclassified by ichthyologists.

5. THE BUFFET LUNCH AT COPENHAGEN'S HOTEL ROYAL

Your choice of 55 different platters, dishes, and baskets— lobster, caviar, a galaxy of fish, pâtés, salads, at least 10 sliced cold meats, a battery of hot casseroles, pastries, desserts, cheeses, and much more—for only $12.10 per appetite.

6. A PRIVATE FLIGHT OVER THE SAVAGE, UNINHABITABLE, NEARLY IMPENETRABLE ONE-QUARTER OF TASMANIA

Charter a light four-seater plane with a bush pilot at Hobart Airport, and be sure to land on the eerily serene and beautiful shores of Lake Pedar for your picnic lunch.

7. SPAIN'S PICOS DE EUROPA

Twenty-five miles west of Santander, this spectacularly beautiful coastal range is as high as the Swiss Alps but steeper. The only lodgings of consequence are three small government-operated hostelries, the best of which is the Fuente de Parador deep in the wilderness.

8. JAPAN'S MATSUSHIMA

Translated as Pine Tree Island, it is referred to in the singular after the small island which bears its name, but it also embraces a cluster of 260 other islands which are sheltered in Matsushima Bay, about 230 mi. northeast of Tokyo. You will enjoy cruising through the quaintness of this fairyland archipelago.

9. KENYA'S MASAI MARA LODGE

A snug oasis on the Mara River, in lion, Cape buffalo, and leopard country where, accompanied by guides, you'll be able to watch the animals on their native ground.

10. THE POUSADA DE RAINHA SANTA ISABEL, PORTUGAL

Situated above medieval Estremoz, 110 mi. from Lisbon and 20 mi. from the Spanish border, this magnificent 13th-century bastion has been lavishly restored and refurnished with an eye-boggling collection of antique Portuguese objets d'art.

11. THE MAIN TERRACE OF VILLA FIELDING AT FORMENTOR, MAJORCA

A 180° panorama of mountains, scented pine trees, snow-white sands, the sweeping turquoise Mediterranean bay, and limit-less skies. May it never change!

—Exclusive for *The Book of Lists*

TEMPLE FIELDING'S 13 LEADING PLACES TO AVOID IN YOUR TRAVELS

Cartagena, a city of 147,000 in southeast Spain, is a naval base and site of important smelting works.

1. Brindisi, Italy
2. Calcutta, India
3. Cardiff, Wales
4. Cartagena, Spain
5. Djibouti, Afars and Issas
6. Essen, W. Germany
7. Monrovia, Liberia
8. Paramaribo, Surinam
9. Punta Arenas, Chile
10. Rangoon, Burma
11. Seoul, S. Korea
12. Shanghai, People's Republic of China
13. Tirana, Albania

Fielding adds: "It would be easy to list 75 or 100 less prominent places which are as wretched and inhospitable, mostly in the second and third worlds."

—Exclusive for *The Book of Lists*

30 NEW NAMES FOR OLD PLACES

Old	*New*
1. Abyssinia	Ethiopia
2. Basutoland	Lesotho
3. Batavia, Dutch East Indies	Djakarta, Indonesia
4. Bechuanaland	Botswana
5. Belgian Congo	Zaire
6. British Honduras	Belize
7. Ceylon	Sri Lanka
8. Christiania, Norway	Oslo
9. Ciudad Trujillo, Dominican Republic	Santo Domingo
10. Constantinople, Turkey	Istanbul
11. Dahomey	Benin
12. Danzig	Gdansk, Poland
13. E. Pakistan	Bangladesh
14. Edo, Japan	Tokyo
15. Fort Dearborn, Indian Territory	Chicago, Ill.
16. Fort Rouillé, New France	Toronto, Ont., Canada
17. Gold Coast	Ghana
18. New Amsterdam, New Netherland	New York, N.Y.
19. Northern Rhodesia	Zambia
20. Nyasaland	Malawi
21. Peiping	Peking
22. Persia	Iran
23. Saigon, S. Vietnam	Ho Chi Minh City, Vietnam
24. St. Petersburg, U.S.S.R.	Leningrad
25. Siam	Thailand
26. South-West Africa	Namibia
27. Stalingrad, U.S.S.R.	Volgograd
28. Tanganyika and Zanzibar	Tanzania
29. Tenochtitlán, Mexico	Mexico City
30. Ubangi-Shari	Central African Empire

—The Eds.

10 COUNTRIES
WITH LARGEST AREAS

		Area (sq. mi.)
1.	U.S.S.R.	8,647,250
2.	Canada	3,851,809
3.	People's Republic of China	3,691,502
4.	U.S.	3,615,122
5.	Brazil	3,286,470
6.	Australia	2,965,368
7.	India	1,229,737
8.	Argentina	1,072,067
9.	Sudan	967,491
10.	Algeria	919,951

25 MOST POPULOUS COUNTRIES
(July 1, 1975, estimates)

1.	People's Republic of China	842,545,000
2.	India	613,957,000
3.	U.S.S.R.	254,300,000
4.	U.S.	213,631,000
5.	Indonesia	139,421,000
6.	Japan	110,944,000
7.	Brazil	106,976,000
8.	Bangladesh	80,645,000
9.	Pakistan	69,307,000
10.	Nigeria	63,022,000
11.	W. Germany	62,040,000
12.	Mexico	59,238,000
13.	United Kingdom	56,075,000
14.	Italy	55,845,000
15.	France	52,876,000
16.	Vietnam	45,067,000
17.	Philippines	43,408,000
18.	Thailand	42,223,000
19.	Turkey	40,284,000
20.	Egypt	37,066,000
21.	S. Korea	36,245,000
22.	Spain	35,596,000
23.	Iran	34,903,000
24.	Poland	34,022,000
25.	Burma	31,183,000

SOURCE: "World Population: Recent Demographic Estimates for the Countries and Regions of the World" (U.S. Bureau of the Census, International Statistical Programs Center, 1975).

11 PLACES WITH ZERO POPULATION GROWTH
(July 1, 1975, estimates)

	Annual growth rate (%)
1. Panama Canal Zone	−1.5
2. Falkland Islands	−1.0
2. Malta	−1.0
4. Montserrat	−0.6
5. Portugal	−0.4
6. Barbados	−0.3
6. E. Germany	−0.3
6. Turks and Caicos Islands	−0.3
9. Austria	0.0
9. Channel Islands	0.0
9. W. Germany	0.0

SOURCE: "World Population: Recent Demographic Estimates for the Countries and Regions of the World" (U.S. Bureau of the Census, International Statistical Programs Center, 1975).

12 FASTEST-GROWING PLACES
(July 1, 1975, estimates)

	Annual growth rate (%)
1. Western Sahara	10.4
2. U.S. Virgin Islands	9.6
3. Kuwait	5.9
4. Guam	5.0
5. Bahamas	4.1
6. Libya	4.05
7. Pacific islands	3.8
8. New Caledonia	3.6
9. Gaza Strip	3.5
9. Honduras	3.5
9. Jordan	3.5
9. Mexico	3.5

SOURCE: "World Population: Recent Demographic Estimates for the Countries and Regions of the World" (U.S. Bureau of the Census, International Statistical Programs Center, 1975).

15 MOST POPULOUS
URBAN AREAS IN THE YEAR 1975

1.	Tokyo-Yokohama	17,317,000
2.	New York-northeastern New Jersey	17,013,000
3.	Mexico City	10,942,000
4.	Shanghai	10,888,000
5.	London	10,711,000
6.	São Paulo	9,965,000
7.	Rhine-Ruhr (Dusseldorf-Essen-Cologne)	9,701,000
8.	Los Angeles-Long Beach	9,502,000
9.	Buenos Aires	9,332,000
10.	Paris	9,189,000
11.	Osaka-Kobe	8,684,000
12.	Peking	8,487,000
13.	Rio de Janeiro	8,328,000
14.	Calcutta	8,077,000
15.	Moscow	7,609,000

SOURCE: U.N. Population Division estimates.

15 MOST POPULOUS
URBAN AREAS IN THE YEAR 2000

1.	Mexico City	31,616,000
2.	Tokyo-Yokohama	26,128,000
3.	São Paulo	26,045,000
4.	New York-northeastern New Jersey	22,212,000
5.	Calcutta	19,663,000
6.	Rio de Janeiro	19,383,000
7.	Shanghai	19,155,000
8.	Greater Bombay	19,065,000
9.	Peking	19,064,000
10.	Seoul	18,711,000
11.	Djakarta	16,933,000
12.	Cairo-Giza-Imbâba	16,398,000
13.	Karachi	15,862,000
14.	Los Angeles-Long Beach	14,795,000
15.	Buenos Aires	13,978,000

SOURCE: U.N. Population Division projections.

FIRST 10
TRANSATLANTIC FLIGHTS

1. *LAME DUCK* (U.S. NC-4 flying boat)

Lt. Comdr. Albert "Putty" C. Read and a crew of five
Trepassey Bay, Nfld., Canada, to Plymouth, England
May 16–27, 1919

Lame Duck was regarded by many as a jinxed plane. Just prior to takeoff, Chief Mechanic E. H. Howard lost a hand in the propellers. During the flight, one crew member became severely airsick and two of the plane's four engines broke down. As a result, the NC-4 spent about as much time on the ground and water as it did in the air. Nevertheless, Read—commander of the first transatlantic flight—became a national hero.

2. A BRITISH VICKERS CONVERTED VIMY NIGHT BOMBER

Capt. John Alcock and Lt. Arthur Whitten Brown
St. John's, Nfld., Canada, to Clifden, Ireland
June 14–15, 1919

The first nonstop crossing was laced with superstition. Accompanying Alcock and Brown on their journey were Lucky Jim and Twinkletoes—two stuffed black cats. It is debatable whether these charms proved lucky, for a series of disasters befell the flight. First, a heated-up exhaust pipe turned to liquid and blew away. Later, a blinding fog so disoriented the men that a potential nose dive into the Atlantic wasn't noticed—and avoided—until visibility suddenly increased just 100 ft. above the ocean. And following a snowstorm, Brown—with a crippled leg—had to climb out onto the wing to chip away ice that had frozen the plane's instruments. Miraculously, the two war veterans landed safely in Clifden, completing the first nonstop transatlantic flight. However, six months later Alcock was killed when a plane he was flying in a Paris show crashed in the fog. After that tragedy, Brown refused to fly again. His son, though, became a pilot and was killed in W.W. II.

3. *R-34* (English airship)

Maj. G. Scott and a crew of 30
East Fortune, Scotland, to Mineola, N.Y.
July 2–6, 1919

The R-34 was the first dirigible to cross the Atlantic. It also had the distinction of carrying with it—in addition to high officials—the first transatlantic aerial stowaway. William Ballantine, a crew member who had been grounded to lighten the load, had slipped aboard and hidden himself, but he made his presence known when he got airsick. (A court-martial eventually followed.) Before the R-34 could return to earth, Maj. J. Pritchard had to parachute to the ground to organize a new landing party. Since there was no radio on the airship, the original ground crew could not be notified that heavy winds were causing a change in descent plans.

Capt. John Alcock (L) and Lt. Arthur Whitten Brown
made the first nonstop flight across the Atlantic eight years
before Lindbergh's historic solo crossing.

4. *LOS ANGELES* (German Z-R3 airship)

Dr. Hugo Eckener and a crew of 33
Friedrichshafen, Germany, to Lakehurst, N.J.
Oct. 12–15, 1924

The successful delivery flight by the German crew mended
postwar relations between Germany and the U.S. At the same time,
the accomplishment helped unite a politically troubled Germany by
creating in its people a sense of national pride.

5. *PLUS ULTRA* (Dornier Wal tandem-engined flying boat)

Ramon Franco, Druan, R. De Alda, and Prata
Palos, Spain, to Buenos Aires, Argentina
Jan. 23–Feb. 5, 1926

Franco became known as the "Columbus of the air" because
his flight originated at the port from which Christopher Columbus
had set out for the New World. Although it was the first successful
aircraft crossing of the south Atlantic, the event attracted little
attention.

6. *SANTA MARIA* (Savoia-Marchetti 55)

Francesco Marquis De Pinedo, Capt. Carlo Del Prete, and Lt.
Vitale Vacchetti
Sardinia, Italy, to Pernambuco, Brazil
Feb. 13–24, 1927

The goodwill tour joining Fascist Italy with South America and the U.S. ended in disaster. After the journey across the South Atlantic, the *Santa Maria* stopped in Arizona to refuel at a lake. A local teenager who was assisting the crew lit a cigarette and then casually threw his match into the lake where De Pinedo—minutes earlier—had dumped some excess fuel. The *Santa Maria* caught fire and sank, and Rome was soon up in arms blasting the U.S. with charges of an anti-Fascist plot. The uproar died down a short time later when an Arizona news reporter unearthed the facts behind the incident.

7. *SPIRIT OF ST. LOUIS* (single-engine Ryan high-wing monoplane)

Capt. Charles Lindbergh
Garden City, N.Y., to Paris, France
May 20–21, 1927

Lindbergh stripped all nonessentials from his plane, including the front window. Instead, a massive instrument panel faced the pilot and a periscope was installed for forward viewing. Also, the fuel tank was located at the nose of the plane so that Lindbergh wouldn't be crushed by its weight in case of a crash. "Lucky Lindy" was airborne for 33½ hrs. and, even after landing in Paris, it was another 30 mins. before his feet were allowed to touch the ground. Cheering crowds lifted him into the air; collectors took fuselage fabric and engine parts from the *Spirit*. A reporter, having donned Lindbergh's helmet, was mistaken for the pilot and taken to the official reception committee where he was introduced to U.S. Ambassador Herrick. The flight made Lindbergh a legend for the rest of his lifetime. Even today, most people think his was the first transatlantic flight. It was the first *solo* transatlantic flight.

8. *SANTA MARIA II* (Savoia-Marchetti 55)

Francesco Marquis De Pinedo, Capt. Carlo Del Prete, and Lt. Vitale Vacchetti
Trepassy Bay, Nfld., Canada, to Lisbon, Portugal
May 23–June 11, 1927

Flying against heavy winds, the *Santa Maria II* ran out of fuel and landed 300 mi. short of its destination. A passing ship towed it ashore. News of De Pinedo's second transatlantic crossing was buried beneath the talk of Lindbergh's flight.

9. *COLUMBIA* (Giuseppe Bellanca)

Clarence Chamberlain and Charles A. Levine
New York, N.Y., to Eisleben, Germany
June 4–6, 1927

The Bellanca's backer, Charles Levine, wanted to choose a pilot photogenic enough for postflight press coverage and movie offers. Aviator Chamberlain, although at the very bottom of Levine's list, got the job due to a web of politics, legal problems, and public pressure. The position of copilot was open until less than a minute prior to takeoff, when Levine himself suddenly jumped into the cockpit—leaving his stunned wife on the runway to pass out. Levine thus became the first transatlantic passenger. The *Columbia* went on to set a distance record of 3,911 mi. and became the first plane to make a mail delivery via an aerial crossing of the Atlantic. While refueling in Germany, the men were mistaken for members of a band of kidnappers. Later, they were billed $1,500 by Vienna sausage venders for wieners wasted when the fliers failed to make a promised visit. And a famous W.W. I draft dodger offered to buy the *Columbia* so that he could use it to return to the U.S., feeling that this heroic effort would redeem him.

10. *AMERICA* (Fokker trimotor monoplane)

Richard E. Byrd and a crew of three
New York, N.Y., to Ver-sur-Mer, France
June 29–July 1, 1927

The *America* took off prematurely when cables holding the plane snapped as the engines were revving up. Due to heavy fog, the Fokker landed in the sea, just 100 mi. short of its Paris destination. Postmaster General New had promised Commander Byrd that the *America* would carry the first official airmail, but a local postmaster (Sealy of Hempstead, N.Y.) exceeded his own authority and bypassed New, allowing the *Columbia* to make the first such delivery.

—D.B.

15 SAFEST AIRLINES

In their book *Destination Disaster*, Paul Eddy, Elaine Potter, and Bruce Page used fatality statistics to determine the safest and most dangerous airlines in the world. Both lists are based on fatality rates per passenger and per kilometers flown.

1. Transportes Aèroes Portuguêses (TAP)
2. Qantas
3. Delta
4. American
5. Scandinavian Airlines (SAS)
6. Trans-Australian
7. Japan Air Lines
8. Continental
9. United
10. Ansett (Australian)
11. National
12. Lufthansa
13. Eastern
14. Iran Air
15. Braniff

SOURCE: Paul Eddy, Elaine Potter, and Bruce Page, *Destination Disaster* (New York: Quadrangle, 1976).

15 MOST DANGEROUS AIRLINES

1. ALIA (Royal Jordanian)
2. VIASA (Venezuelan)
3. Egyptair
4. TAROM (Romanian)
5. Turkish Airlines
6. Middle East Airlines
7. Nigeria
8. AVIACO (Spanish)
9. Air India
10. Philippine
11. CSA (Czechoslovak)
12. Aéro Argentinas
13. Garuda (Indonesian)
14. LOT (Polish)
15. Air Algérie

SOURCE: Paul Eddy, Elaine Potter, and Bruce Page, *Destination Disaster* (New York: Quadrangle, 1976).

9 AUTOMOBILES THAT MADE HISTORY

1. CZAR ALEXANDER II'S LENOIR

A Belgian engineer, J. J. Étienne Lenoir, is said to have built the first automobile with an internal-combustion engine in Paris during May, 1862. The car, which resembled a handsome three-wheeled wagon, ran on hydrocarbon fuel. In 1864, Czar Alexander II of Russia bought one of these pioneer autos and had it shipped by train from Vincennes to St. Petersburg. Czar Alexander was probably the first national leader in history to own an automobile. In 1881, the czar was assassinated by a bomb thrown by terrorists. In 1905, an intensive search was made for the historic car, but it was never found.

2. FERDINAND'S GRAF UND STIFT

Three brothers, Carl, Heinrich, and Franz Graf, formed a partnership with Josef Hans Stift to produce Austria's first automobile in 1897. It was a brand-new, large Graf und Stift phaeton, with a four-cylinder engine and the first front-wheel drive—and Austria's heir to the throne, Archduke Franz Ferdinand, rode in it during a visit to Sarajevo, Bosnia. While in this car, Ferdinand was assassinated by Gavrilo Princip on June 28, 1914, a tragedy that precipitated W.W. I. In the next dozen years, this same car was owned by 15 private parties, and was involved in six major accidents that cost the lives of 13 people. After its last crack-up, in Romania in 1926, the Graf und Stift was retired to Vienna's Museum of War History, where it may still be seen.

3. CZAR NICHOLAS II'S ROLLS-ROYCE

Czar Nicholas II purchased two 1913 Rolls landaulets in Paris and had them shipped to Moscow. Interiors were thickly carpeted, upholstery was pure silk, paneling and fittings were the finest money could buy. The cars were a symbol of everything Bolsheviks hated. Yet, after the revolution, a Soviet comrade also bought a luxurious Rolls-Royce, and had it equipped with skis and half-tracks for travel on Russian snows. The car is still on display in Moscow. Its owner was Vladimir Ilich Ulyanov—better known as Lenin.

4. COL. T. E. LAWRENCE'S ROLLS-ROYCE

Between 1916 and 1918, when Gen. Edmund Allenby was leading his British forces against a Turkish army in Syria, Lawrence of Arabia was assigned to lead a force of Arabian nationalist guerrillas in a combined offensive. Lawrence requested a loan of nine Rolls-Royces to be used as his mobile unit, reserving one Rolls for himself. The request was granted. In a single day, riding his own Rolls, accompanied by two others, Lawrence blew up two enemy bridges, captured two Turkish outposts, and then attacked and crushed a Kurdish cavalry regiment. After the war, when Lowell Thomas asked him what one material object on earth he most desired, Lawrence replied, "Perhaps it is childish, but I should like my own Rolls-Royce car with enough tires and petrol to last me all my life."

5. BONNIE AND CLYDE'S FORD V-8

A roof contractor in Topeka, Kans., Jesse Warren, bought a new Ford V-8—with bumper guards and a hot-water heater—for $785 in March, 1934. On April 29, 1934, the gray Ford was stolen from Warren's driveway by a pair of outlaws, Bonnie Parker and Clyde Barrow. The fleeing pair drove the Ford 7,500 mi. in 23 days before being ambushed by Texas Rangers in Louisiana. Bonnie was hit by 50 bullets, and Clyde by 27. The Ford became famous overnight.

6-7. ADOLF HITLER'S PAIR OF MERCEDES-BENZES

Adolf Hitler had two duplicate 770-K Mercedes-Benz cars in 1941, when he was at his peak as dictator of Germany. Each Mercedes was 20 ft. long and weighed 10,000 lbs. Each was also protected by 1¼-in. armor plate and bulletproof glass ½ in. thick. The gas tanks held 51 gals., and the cars got 3 mi. to the gallon. Hitler used the cars in his victory parades, and on inspections of conquered countries in Europe. After his downfall, the cars came to the U.S. Recently, one of these 770-K Mercedes-Benz autos was auctioned off to a Wisconsin car dealer for $141,000.

Hitler, at the height of his power, in his custom-made
770-K Mercedes-Benz, somewhere in Germany.

8. IBN SAUD'S ROLLS-ROYCE

During W.W. II, a dazzling, handmade Rolls-Royce was a pawn in a game of international one-upmanship between Winston Churchill and Franklin D. Roosevelt. When Roosevelt offered King Ibn Saud of Saudi Arabia the magnificent gift of a C-47 airplane, British pride was at stake. Churchill yanked veteran Rolls-Royce experts from the company's warplane engine plant, then ordered a chariot fit for a king. Ibn Saud's limousine was furnished with a throne in the rear, wide enough for the king to sit cross-legged, Arabian style. The car was outfitted with siren, searchlights, and extra-wide running boards for bodyguards. The body was a shimmering green, with metallic green leather upholstery and cabinetwork. For the king's ritual Muslim ablutions, the passenger compartment was equipped with a copper water tank and a sterling silver basin which tipped back to empty its contents through a drain in the floor. Other royal accoutrements included a powerful radio, alabaster thermos flasks, and a built-in cabinet for brushes and combs. The brushes were made with nylon bristles rather than hog bristles in deference to Ibn Saud's Muslim beliefs.

9. PRESIDENT KENNEDY'S 1961 LINCOLN CONTINENTAL

The car was a custom-built limousine designed to hold seven passengers—a chauffeur and Secret Service agent in the front seat, two people in the rear jump seats, and three people in the back leather-covered seat. A lever could make the back seat raise 10½ in. A bar at the back of the chauffeur's seat could be gripped by the president if he wished to stand up and wave to crowds. On the rear trunk there were metal handles, and stirrups at the back bumper, for Secret Service men to use when the limousine sped up. An accessory was a bubbletop which came in four parts and could cover the Lincoln from the windshield to the rear seat. The bubbletop was not used in Dallas on November 22, 1963. Seated in the back seat, President John F. Kennedy was exposed. As his car passed through Dealey Plaza, shots rang out. The right side of his head was blown off and the interior of the Lincoln Continental was splattered with his brain. The president of the U.S. had been assassinated in his car. The 1961 Lincoln has since been fully equipped with bulletproof glass, protective armor, the latest communication devices, and is part of the U.S. Secret Service's fleet of vehicles.

—I.W. & W.H.

8
IN A WORD
—COMMUNICATIONS

WILFRED J. FUNK'S
10 MOST BEAUTIFUL WORDS
IN THE ENGLISH LANGUAGE

Meanings

1.	*Chimes*	A set of bells or of slabs of metal, stone, wood, etc., producing musical tones when struck
2.	*Dawn*	To begin to grow light as the sun rises
3.	*Golden*	Consisting of, relating to, or containing gold
4.	*Hush*	Calm, quiet
5.	*Lullaby*	A song to quiet children or lull them to sleep
6.	*Luminous*	Emitting light; shining
7.	*Melody*	A sweet or agreeable succession of arrangements of sounds
8.	*Mist*	Water in the form of particles floating or falling in the atmosphere at or near the surface of the earth and approaching the form of rain
9.	*Murmuring*	A soft or gentle utterance
10.	*Tranquil*	Free from agitation; serene

—Definitions selected by The Eds.

THE 10 WORST-SOUNDING
ENGLISH WORDS

Based on a poll taken in August, 1946, by the National Association of Teachers of Speech.

Meanings

1.	*Cacophony*	Harsh or discordant sound
2.	*Crunch*	To chew, grind, or press with a crushing noise
3.	*Flatulent*	Affected with gas in the stomach or intestines
4.	*Gripe*	To complain with sustained grumbling

5. *Jazz*	Popular dance music
6. *Phlegmatic*	Having a sluggish or stolid temperament
7. *Plump*	Somewhat fat
8. *Plutocrat*	One who exercises power by virtue of his wealth
9. *Sap*	The fluid part of a plant
10. *Treachery*	Violation of allegiance, confidence, or faith

—Definitions selected by The Eds.

10 WORDS YOU CAN'T PRONOUNCE CORRECTLY

Can you pronounce all 10 correctly? Robert L. Ripley (of "Believe It or Not" fame), said only one person in 100,000 can get all of them right. Can you?

1. *Data*
2. *Gratis*
3. *Culinary*
4. *Cocaine*
5. *Gondola*

6. *Version*
7. *Impious*
8. *Chic*
9. *Caribbean*
10. *Viking*

Want to check yourself out? OK. Here are the exact pronunciations according to *Webster's Eighth New Collegiate Dictionary*.

1. \'dāt-ə\
2. \'grat-əs\
3. \'kəl-ə-,ner-ē\
4. \kō-'kān\
5. \'gän-də-lə\

6. \'vər-zhən\
7. \'im-pē-əs\
8. \shēk\
9. \,kar-ə-'bē-ən\
10. \'vī-kiŋ\

SOURCE: Robert L. Ripley, *The New Believe It or Not* (New York: Simon and Schuster, 1931).

THE 13 LONGEST WORDS IN THE ENGLISH LANGUAGE

13. *HONORIFICABILITUDINITATIBUS* (27 letters)

The word occurs in Shakespeare's play *Love's Labour's Lost*, and means "with honorablenesses." It can also be viewed as a rearrangement of the Latin sentence "Hi ludi F. Baconis nati tuiti

158

orbi," meaning: "These plays, F. Bacon's offspring, are preserved for the world." This twist has been used to support the "Baconian theory" that Francis Bacon wrote Shakespeare's plays. However, in *The Shakespearean Ciphers Examined* (Cambridge, England: Cambridge University Press, 1957), William F. and Elizebeth S. Friedman have similar anagrams that "prove" Theodore Roosevelt, Lewis Carroll, and Gertrude Stein also wrote Shakespeare.

12. *ANTIDISESTABLISHMENTARIANISM* (28 letters)

The word means, according to Funk & Wagnalls New Standard Dictionary of the English Language, "a doctrine of opposition to disestablishment (withdrawal of state patronage, support, or exclusive recognition from a church)." It is said to have been used once by British Prime Minister William Ewart Gladstone (1809–1898).

11. *FLOCCINAUCINIHILIPIPIFICATION* (29 letters)

This is found in the Oxford English Dictionary, and means "the action or habit of estimating something as worthless."

10. *SUPERCALIFRAGILISTICEXPIALIDOCIOUS* (34 letters)

From the movie *Mary Poppins*. It means "good."

9. *PRAETERTRANSSUBSTANTIATIONALISTICALLY* (37 letters)

Used by Mark McShane in his novel *Untimely Ripped* (1963). It means the act of surpassing the act of transubstantiation, which refers specifically to the transformation of the bread and wine into the body and blood of Christ during the Roman Catholic mass.

8. *HEPATICOCHOLECYSTOSTCHOLECYSTENTEROSTOMY* (40 letters)

Found in Gould's Medical Dictionary. It is defined as "the surgical formation of a passage between the gall bladder and hepatic duct, on the one hand, and between the intestine and the gall bladder, on the other."

7. *PNEUMONOULTRAMICROSCOPICSILICOVOLCANOCONIOSIS* (45 letters)

Found in *Webster's New Collegiate Dictionary*, 8th edition. It is "a pneumoconiosis caused by the inhalation of very fine silicate or quartz dust." It occurs especially in miners.

6. *ANTIPERICATAMETAANAPARCIRCUMVOLUTIORECTUMGUSTPOOPS OF THE COPROFIED* (50 letters)

The title of a book on a shelf in a library in the classic ribald work *Gargantua and Pantagruel*, by François Rabelais.

5. *OSSEOCARNISANGUINEOVISCERICARTILAGININERVOMEDULLARY* (51 letters)

A term that describes the structure of the human body; it occurs in *Headlong Hall* (1816), a novel by Thomas Love Peacock.

4. *AEQUEOSALINOCALCALINOCERACEOALUMINOSOCU-*
   PREOVITRIOLIC (52 letters)

Describes the composition of the spa waters at Bristol, in Gloucestershire, England. The word was coined by an English medical writer, Dr. Edward Strother (1675–1737).

3. *BABABADALGHARAGHTAKAMMINARRONNKONN-*
   BRONNTONNERRONNTUONNTHUNNTROVARR-
   HOUNAWNSKAWNTOOHOOHOORDENENTHURNUK
   (100 letters)

This word is on the first page of *Finnegans Wake* by James Joyce, and is a symbolic thunderclap representing the fall of Adam and Eve. (Other 100-letter words appear throughout the book.)

2. *LOPADOTEMACHOSELACHOGALEOKRANIOLEIPSAN-*
   ODRIMHYPOTRIMMATOSILPHIOPARAOMELITOKATA-
   KECHYMENOKICHLEPIKOSSYPHOPHATTOPERISTER-
   ALEKTRYONOPTEKEPHALLIOKIGKLOPELEIOLAGOIO-
   SIRAIOBAPHETRAGANOPTERYGON (182 letters)

The English transliteration of a Greek word that occurs in Aristophanes' play *The Ecclesiazusae*. The word is defined as "a goulash composed of all the leftovers from the meals of the last two weeks," or "hash." A more detailed translation is "plattero-filleto-mulleti-turboto-cranio-morselo-pickleo-acido-silphio-honeyo-poured on the top of the ouzelo-throstleo-cushato-culvero-cutleto-roastingo-marrowo-dippero-levereto-syrupo-gibleto-wings."

1. (3,600 letters)

A chemical name describing bovine NADP-specific glutamate dehydrogenase, which contains 500 amino acids.

—A.W.

12 MOST COMMONLY USED
WORDS IN WRITTEN ENGLISH

1. *The*
2. *Of*
3. *And*
4. *A*
5. *To*
6. *In*
7. *Is*
8. *You*
9. *That*
10. *It*
11. *He*
12. *For*

SOURCE: *American Heritage Word Frequency Book* (New York: American Heritage, 1971).

TEN TOUGH TONGUE TWISTERS
OTHER THAN PETER PIPER PICKED
A PECK OF PICKLED PEPPERS

1. The sixth sick sheik's sixth sheep's sick.
2. Rubber baby buggy bumpers.
3. She sells seashells by the seashore.
4. The sinking steamer sunk.
5. Toy boat or troy boat. (Repeat six times.)
6. If a three-month truce is a truce in truth,
   Is the truth of a truce in truth a three-month truce? (Willard Espy, author of *An Almanac of Words at Play*.)
7. If you stick a stock of liquor in your locker,
   It is slick to stick a lock upon your stock,
   Or some joker who is slicker's going to trick you of
      your liquor,
   If you fail to lock your liquor with a lock.
8. The skunk sat on a stump; the skunk thunk the stump stunk, but the stump thunk the skunk stunk.
9. How much wood would a woodchuck chuck, if a woodchuck would chuck wood?
10. Iqaqa laziqikaqika kwaze kwaqhawaka uqhoqhoqha. (Xhosa—from Transkei, South Africa—for "The skunk rolled down and ruptured its larynx.")

—A.W.

15 SEMORDNILAP PALINDROMES

A palindrome is a word or sentence that reads the same backward as forward.

1. Lewd did I live, & evil I did dwel. (The first palindrome recorded in the English language.)
2. Madam, I'm Adam.
3. A man, a plan, a canal—Panama.
4. He goddam mad dog, eh?
5. Able was I ere I saw Elba. (Napoleon's lament.)
6. "Naomi, sex at noon taxes," I moan.
7. Doc, note, I dissent. A fast never prevents a fatness. I diet on cod.
8. Step on no pets.
9. Never odd or even.
10. "Rise, sir lapdog! Revolt, lover! God, pal, rise, sir!" (Slogan for opponents of the women's liberation movement.)
11. May a moody baby doom a yam?

12. Sit on a potato pan, Otis.
13. Anna: "Did Otto peep?" Otto: "Did Anna?" (Each word is a palindrome.)
14. Do good? I? No! Evil anon I deliver: I maim nine more hero-men in Saginaw; sanitary sword a-tuck, Carol, I—lo!—rack, cut a drowsy rat in Aswan; I gas nine more hero-men in Miami; reviled I (Nona) live on. I do, O God!"
15. Dennis, Nell, Edna, Leon, Nedra, Anita, Rolf, Nora, Alice, Carol, Leo, Jane, Reed, Dena, Dale, Basil, Rae, Penny, Lana, Dave, Denny, Lena, Ida, Bernadette, Ben, Ray, Lila, Nina, Jo, Ira, Mara, Sara, Mario, Jan, Ina, Lily, Arne, Bette, Dan, Reba, Diane, Lynn, Ed, Eva, Dana, Lynne, Pearl, Isabel, Ada, Ned, Dee, Rena, Joel, Lora, Cecil, Aaron, Flora, Tina, Arden, Noel, and Ellen sinned.

—A.W.

16 NAMES OF THINGS YOU NEVER KNEW HAD NAMES

1. AGLET

The plain or ornamental covering on the end of a shoelace.

2. BIBCOCK

A faucet with a bent-down nozzle.

3. BRASSARD

A cloth band worn around the upper arm. It often bears an identifying mark—like the one with a swastika that Hitler wore.

4. BRETELLES

A pair of ornamental suspenderlike straps that go from the belt on the front of a dress over the shoulders to the belt in the back.

5. DUFF

The decaying organic matter found on a forest floor.

6. HARP

The small metal hoop that supports a lampshade.

7. HEMIDEMISEMIQUAVER

A 64th note. (A 32nd note is a demisemiquaver, and a 16th note is a semiquaver.)

8. KICK or PUNT

The indentation at the bottom of some wine bottles. It gives added strength to the bottle but lessens its holding capacity.

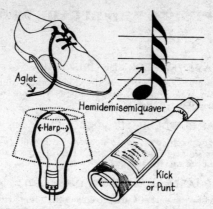

Aglet

Hemidemisemiquaver

←Harp→

Kick or Punt

9. PHOSPHENES

The lights you see when you close your eyes hard. Technically, the luminous impressions are due to the excitation of the retina caused by pressure on the eyeball.

10. PIGGIN

A small wooden pail with one long stave used as the handle.

11. QUARREL

A small, diamond-shaped pane of glass, like that used in lattice windows.

12. SAM BROWNE BELT

A leather belt for a dress uniform. It is supported by a light strap that passes over the right shoulder. The Royal Canadian Mounted Police wear them.

13. SOLIDUS

The oblique stroke (/) used between words, or in fractions, as 7/8. It is also called a diagonal, separatrix, virgule, shilling, slant, or slash.

14. TANG

The projecting prong on a tool or instrument.

15. TOBIES

The small pottery jugs, mugs, and pitchers that are used for ale. A toby is shaped like a stout man with a cocked hat, a corner of which serves as the pourer.

16. ZARF

A holder for a handleless coffee cup.

—S.B.

15 PEOPLE WHO BECAME WORDS

1. AMELIA JENKS BLOOMER (1818–1894)

Bloomers were created by Mrs. Elizabeth S. Miller in 1850. Mrs. Bloomer, a feminist in Seneca Falls, N.Y., wore them in July, 1851, and popularized them.

2. THOMAS BOWDLER (1754–1825)

A self-appointed censor in London, Dr. Bowdler published his own *Family Shakespeare* and Gibbon's *Decline and Fall:* He *bowdlerized* all of the racier passages.

3. CAPT. CHARLES C. BOYCOTT (1832–1897)

Hired by the earl of Earne to collect high rents from impoverished Irish tenant farmers, the captain was silently ignored, or *boycotted,* by the workers.

4. LOUIS BRAILLE (1809–1852)

Blinded in an accident at the age of 3, he learned to read in Paris from the large embossed lettering in three cumbersome books. At 15, he invented his system of raised dots, called *braille.*

5. NICOLAS CHAUVIN

A soldier under Napoleon, Chauvin was wounded 17 times. He was retired on a pension of $40 a year. Instead of being bitter, he was loyal to Napoleon and praised him incessantly. By extension, *chauvinism* has come to mean blind attachment to a group, especially to a country.

6. RUDOLF DIESEL (1858–1913)

A German engineer who worked at the Krupp factory, he invented an internal-combustion engine based on compression ignition that would run on cheap crude oil. It is called a *diesel* engine.

7. JOSEPH I. GUILLOTIN (1738–1814)

A prominent Parisian physician and member of the French National Assembly, Dr. Guillotin spoke out in favor of a more humane method of capital punishment. Decapitation by sword and hanging were soon replaced by a quick and efficient *guillotine* (designed by Dr. Antoine Louis and constructed by Tobias Smith).

8. CAPT. WILLIAM LYNCH (1742–1820)

Organizing a group of Pittsylvania County men to aid him, Virginian Lynch took the law into his own hands in an effort to catch and punish (*lynch*) an elusive band of thugs. Most reference books erroneously trace the derivation of the word to Col. Charles Lynch of the Virginia House of Burgesses. However, this Lynch lynched no one.

Every time you stuff something between two pieces of bread,
think of this man, John Montagu, fourth earl of Sandwich.

9. JOHN MONTAGU (1718–1792)

Montagu, the fourth earl of Sandwich, led a public life laced with political corruption and a private one tainted by questionable mores. A compulsive gambler, Lord Sandwich would refuse to leave the card table for a meal during a game and, instead, would have a servant bring him a slice of meat between two pieces of bread—a *sandwich*.

10. JEAN NICOT (1530?–1600)

During a mission in Portugal, French Ambassador Nicot was given a Florida tobacco plant. He brought it back to France with him and went into business for himself when he discovered a growing interest in the "American powder" and the *nicotine* it contains.

11. MAJ. VIDKUN QUISLING (1887–1945)

Fascist leader of Norway's unpopular National Unity party, Quisling was put in charge of the country by Adolf Hitler during the Nazi occupation of Norway. A traitor who collaborates with invaders is a *quisling*.

12. LEOPOLD VON SACHER-MASOCH (1836–1895)

Due in part to a childhood of bloody horror stories told to him by his nurse Handscha, the prolific Austrian novelist Sacher-Masoch found that he could derive pleasure only from being physically abused and tortured—that is, from *masochism*.

13. MARQUIS DE SADE (1740–1814)

A member of the French aristocracy, the marquis spent many years in jail for committing scandalous crimes of sexual perversion. It was in prison that he wrote novels and plays that depicted countless acts of sexual cruelty (*sadism*).

14. ANTOINE JOSEPH SAX (1814–1894)

While working for his father in a Brussels musical instrument workshop, Sax invented a number of new brass wind instruments, the most popular of which was the *saxophone*.

15. ÉTIENNE DE SILHOUETTE (1709–1767)

In an attempt to restore the postwar French economy, Controller General Silhouette instituted a wave of new taxes—most of which burdened the rich. After eight months, he was forced to resign amid a deteriorating economy. His name soon became associated with cheap and "empty" commodities, such as pocketless trousers and shadow portraits (*silhouettes*).

—I.W. & D.B.

Drawing silhouettes became the rage in 1759.

166

THE MOST COMMON
LAST NAMES IN 10 COUNTRIES

CHINA
1. Chang
2. Wang
3. Li

FRANCE
1. Martin
2. Lefebvre/Lefèvre
3. Bernard
4. Petit
5. Dubois
6. Laurent
7. Moreau
8. Durand
9. Fournier
10. Leroy

GERMANY
1. Schultz/Schulz
2. Müller
3. Schmidt
4. Krüger
5. Hoffmann
6. Fischer
7. Krause
8. Meyer
9. Neumann
10. Richter
11. Schneider
12. Schröder
13. Wolf/Wolff

GREAT BRITAIN
1. Smith
2. Jones
3. Williams
4. Brown
5. Taylor
6. Davies
7. Evans
8. Thomas
9. Roberts
10. Johnson

KOREA
1. Kim
2. Pak
3. Yi

NETHERLANDS
1. De Vries
2. De Jong
3. Boer/De Boer
4. Bakker
5. Meijer/Meyer
6. Smit
7. Visser
8. Bos
9. Mulder
10. Vos

SPAIN
1. García
2. Fernández
3. González
4. López
5. Sánchez
6. Rodríguez
7. Martínez
8. Martín
9. Pérez
10. Gómez

SWEDEN
1. Johansson
2. Andersson
3. Carlsson/Karlsson
4. Eriksson
5. Neilsson
6. Larsson
7. Petersson
8. Olsson
9. Jansson
10. Svensson

U.S.S.R.
1. Ivanov
2. Vasiliev
3. Petrov
4. Smirnov
5. Mikhailov
6. Fedorov
7. Sokolov
8. Yakovlev
9. Popov
10. Andreev

U.S.

1. Smith
2. Johnson
3. Williams
4. Brown
5. Jones
6. Miller
7. Davis
8. Wilson
9. Anderson
10. Taylor

—M.E.C.

39 NON-INDO-EUROPEAN LANGUAGES WHICH HAVE CONTRIBUTED WORDS TO THE ENGLISH LANGUAGE

1.	Algonquin	*Skunk, pecan, squaw, chipmunk*
2.	Arabic	*Almanac, mattress, admiral, sheikh, hashish, fakir, harem*
3.	Araucanian	*Poncho*
4.	Australian Aborigine	*Kangaroo, boomerang, koala*
5.	Basque	*Bizarre, jai alai*
6.	Carib	*Canoe*
7.	Chinese	*Silk, kowtow, tea, catsup, tycoon*
8.	Choctaw	*Bayou*
9.	Cree	*Eskimo, woodchuck*
10.	Dakota	*Tepee*
11.	Eskimo	*Kayak, igloo*
12.	Ewe	*Voodoo*
13.	Finnish	*Sauna*
14.	Guarani	*Jaguar*
15.	Hawaiian	*Hula, lei, muumuu, ukulele, luau*
16.	Hebrew	*Amen, hallelujah, kosher, sabbath*
17.	Hungarian	*Coach, goulash, paprika*
18.	Japanese	*Hara-kiri, kimono, samurai, haiku, karate, geisha*
19.	Javanese	*Batik*
20.	Kikongo	*Zebra*
21.	Lappish	*Tundra*
22.	Malay	*Orangutan, sarong, bamboo, gingham*
23.	Malayalam	*Teak*
24.	Maldivian	*Atoll*
25.	Micmac	*Toboggan*

26. Nahuatl	*Tomato, chocolate, avocado, chili*
27. Narragansett	*Moose, papoose*
28. Ojibwa	*Totem*
29. Powhatan	*Raccoon, persimmon*
30. Quechua	*Coca, quinine, vicuña, condor*
31. Tagalog	*Boondocks*
32. Tahitian	*Tattoo*
33. Taino	*Hammock, hurricane*
34. Tamil	*Catamaran, pariah, curry*
35. Tibetan	*Lama, yeti, yak*
36. Tongan	*Taboo*
37. Tungus	*Shaman*
38. Tupi	*Petunia, tapioca*
39. Turkish	*Yogurt, shish kebab*

—D.W.

THE 10 LANGUAGES OF THE WORLD WITH THE MOST SPEAKERS

	No. of Speakers
1. Mandarin	650,000,000
2. English	358,000,000
3. Russian	233,000,000
4. Spanish	213,000,000
5. Hindi	209,000,000
6. Arabic	125,000,000
7. Portuguese	124,000,000
8. Bengali	123,000,000
9. German	120,000,000
10. Japanese	110,000,000

7 REMARKABLE MESSAGES IN BOTTLES

1. DELIVER US THIS DAY

In 1825, one Major MacGregor bottled a message and dropped it into the Bay of Biscayne: "Ship on fire. Elizabeth, Joanna, and myself commit our spirits into the hands of our Redeemer Whose grace enables us to be quite composed in the awful prospect of entering eternity." The note was found 1½ years later, but the major and his party had already been rescued.

2. DOUBLE JEOPARDY

In the 19th century, a British sailor, perhaps in an attempt to found a lonely hearts club, threw a bottled marriage proposal into Southampton waters as his ship left port for India. At Port Said, on the return journey, he was walking along the quay and saw a bottle bobbing in the water. He retrieved it, opened it, and read his own proposal for marriage!

3. THE LAST MESSAGE FROM THE *LUSITANIA*

In 1916, a British seaman saw a bottle bobbing in the north Atlantic. He fished it from the water, opened it, and read the final message sent from the *Lusitania* before it sank, taking with it some 1,198 passengers: "Still on deck with a few people. The last boats have left. We are sinking fast. Some men near me are praying with a priest. The end is near. Maybe this note will . . ." And there it ended.

4. BETTER LATE THAN NEVER

In 1714, Japanese seaman Chunosuke Matsuyama embarked on a treasure hunt in the Pacific. His ship was caught in a gale and sank, but he and 44 shipmates managed to swim to a deserted coral reef. Matsuyama and his companions eventually died of starvation and exposure, but before they did, Matsuyama attempted to send word home. He wrote the story on chips of wood, sealed them in a bottle, and tossed it into the sea. The bottle washed ashore 150 years later on the beach where Matsuyama grew up.

5. THE FAST MESSAGE

"A bottle thrown overboard into the Pacific to aid the U.S. Navy's Hydrographic Office drifted 1,250 miles in 53 days!" oddity hunter John Hix reported in 1941. "It was picked up in the New Hebrides, southwest Pacific, by a native who could not read any of the eight languages on the papers it contained!"

6. CONSPIRACY IN A BOTTLE

Another chapter in the saga of Adolf Hitler transpired when a note, probably a hoax, was found in a bottle on the Danish coast in 1946. It was written on a page torn from the logbook of the German U-boat *Naueclus* and was dated one year earlier. The note claimed that Hitler did not die in the Berlin bunker, as was widely believed, but aboard the *Naueclus*, which sank on November 15, 1945, while en route from Finland to Spain.

7. A MESSAGE FROM THE NORTH POLE

In 1948, a Russian fisherman found a bottle in the sand bordering Vilkilski Strait in the arctic. A message was inside, written in both Norwegian and English. It was incomprehensible even when translated: "Five ponies and 150 dogs remaining. Desire hay, fish, and 30 sledges. Must return early in August. Baldwin." The bizarre message became clear when it was learned that polar explorer Evelyn

Baldwin had sealed the note and sent it in 1902. He managed to survive the arctic without ever receiving the hay, fish, or 30 sledges. Whether or not he made it back by August is unknown.

—J.B.M.

CHARLES HAMILTON'S 10 RAREST AUTOGRAPHS IN THE WORLD TODAY—AND THE VALUE OF EACH IF AUCTIONED

In 1963, one of the world's leading appraisers of autographs, Charles Hamilton, organized the first American auction house devoted solely to autographs. He is also the author of *Collecting Autographs and Manuscripts* and *The Robot That Helped to Make a President*.

		Value
1.	Julius Caesar	$2,000,000
2.	William Shakespeare	1,500,000
3.	Christopher Columbus	500,000
4.	Button Gwinnett, signer of the Declaration of Independence (letter)	250,000
5.	Abe Lincoln (letter to Mrs. Bixby—mother of five Union Army soldiers killed in action)	150,000
6.	Joan of Arc	125,000
7.	Richard Nixon (letter of resignation)	100,000
7.	Thomas Lynch, signer of the Declaration of Independence (letter)	100,000
9.	William the Conqueror	75,000
9.	Charlemagne	75,000

—Exclusive for The Book of Lists

One of the six known signatures of William Shakespeare in existence.

CAREY McWILLIAMS'S
10 GREATEST MUCKRAKERS
IN THE HISTORY OF JOURNALISM

Carey McWilliams has devoted a lifetime to exposing social injustice. As an author and attorney, he first came to public attention with his best-seller *Factories in the Field*. In 1955, he became editor of *The Nation*, and for nearly a quarter of a century he has maintained the magazine's reputation as the pacesetter for journalistic social criticism.

1. Lincoln Steffens, U.S. journalist
2. Henry Demarest Lloyd, author of *Wealth Against Commonwealth* (1894)
3. Upton Sinclair, author of *The Jungle* (1906)
4. Matthew Josephson, author of *The Robber Barons* (1934)
5. Paul Y. Anderson, correspondent for the *St. Louis Post-Dispatch* and *The Nation*
6. I.F. Stone, U.S. journalist
7. Ralph Nader, U.S. author and lawyer
8. Robert Sherrill, author of *The Last Kennedy* and other books, and Washington correspondent for *The Nation*
9. Fred J. Cook, author of *The FBI Nobody Knows, The Warfare State, The Corrupt Land,* and other books
10. George Seldes, author of *Lords of the Press* (1938)

—Exclusive for *The Book of Lists*

ORIANA FALLACI'S
18 PERSONS IN HISTORY SHE'D
MOST LIKE TO HAVE INTERVIEWED

Considered the best interviewer-journalist in the world today, Italian author Oriana Fallaci began her career writing a crime column in an Italian newspaper. Since then, she has contributed countless headline articles to European magazines. She is the author of many books including *If the Sun Dies, Interview with History,* and *Letter to a Child Unborn*.

1.-2. ADAM and EVE

I had no hesitation in placing Adam and Eve in first place. It all started with those two irresponsible people.

3.-5. JESUS CHRIST, JUDAS and THE VIRGIN MARY

When interviewing Jesus Christ, I wouldn't give up interviewing Judas and the Virgin Mary, too. I'm sure that Judas had a few things to say about the Master. Judas was an intelligent man, a man of culture, and I think that he has been offended a lot by history. And the Virgin Mary? First of all, there is this problem of the virginity which I would like to clear up with her, parthenogenesis and so on. Or was it a handsome Roman soldier, as it seems? Then the poor woman had a few problems because of her son, hadn't she? And finally, she does not know where her son was between the ages of 12 and 30. This has been a puzzle for 2,000 years.

6. ALEXANDER THE GREAT

Why do I list Alexander the Great? But it is so obvious. He was a marvelous fool. He had escaped from some psychiatric clinic. And I would like to ask Alexander the Great how he could have managed it without being caught later. And was Hephaestion, the general, really his great love?

7.-8. HOMER and SHAKESPEARE

I had no hesitation listing these two. They are my beloved ones, along with the authors of the Bible. Someone says that they never existed. The first one, especially. In interviewing them, and asking for their birth certificates and passports, I would finally be sure that they existed. Also, I could ask them a few secrets about writing techniques.

9. SPARTACUS

Of course, I had to name Spartacus. I am on the other side of the barricades, as everyone knows, always on the side of the rebels and disobedient ones, and Spartacus is certainly one of the greatest men who ever existed.

10.-12. MOSES, SOLOMON, and THE QUEEN OF SHEBA

Since disobedience doesn't need to exist when laws do not exist, I had to put in the biggest lawmaker in the world—that is, Moses. Besides, he was quite a leader, indeed. Yet, had I existed in those ages, how could I ignore people like Solomon who wrote the Song of Songs? And that intelligent, adventurous woman called the queen of Sheba?

13-14. HITLER and NAPOLEON

Of course, one cannot ignore Hitler. I can admit that he was no worse than some others in mankind's history, yet there are a few things that puzzle me about him. For instance, homosexuality. What did he do with Eva Braun? But here we go again: Would it be honest to interview Hitler without interviewing Napoleon? In the name of *liberté, égalité, fraternité*, the bloody hypocritical Napoleon was the worst dictator and the most pitiless conqueror. Like Hitler's Goering, Napoleon not only killed and executed resisters, but also stole works of art. Look at all those Etruscan statues he stole from Florence. I would ask the bastard about that.

15. JOAN OF ARC

As a feminist, I feel obliged to mention Joan of Arc. Along with England's Elizabeth I and Catherine the Great of Russia, she is one of the few women we are permitted to mention in order to demonstrate that women aren't stupid. Yet everyone knows that we women write and paint and administer governments as well as men, but nobody seems to recall that we can be very good in the military field, also. And Joan is the demonstration that any illiterate girl from the countryside can be a better general than the American generals in Vietnam. Besides, she was burned at the stake by the Church, and I would like to ask her a few things about that shameful trial that made me recall the Rosenbergs' trial.

16.-17. LENIN and MARX

Of course, I had to put in Lenin. But what interviewer would go to interview Lenin without interviewing Karl Marx?!? Besides, I would like to ask Marx a few things about the way he treated his wife. What about the surplus value theory with her? He treated her as a feudal lord treated his vassals, or a pharaoh, his slaves. Immanuel Kant would have something to say about this inconsistency.

18. A MAN OR A WOMAN FROM ANOTHER PLANET (and A DINOSAUR)

I didn't mention David, Machiavelli, Marco Polo, Helen of Troy, Dante Alighieri, Xerxes, Arthur Rimbaud. My heart bled that I had to ignore them. Yet, in all sincerity, I preferred to close with a man or a woman from another planet. It had nothing to do with the past, apparently, but I am not so sure. Human intelligence is deteriorating, not getting better, and I'm afraid at the time of the dinosaurs men were so intelligent as to be able to get to the other planets without NASA.

—Exclusive for *The Book of Lists*

JOHN C. MERRILL'S 10 TOP WORLD NEWSPAPERS

In 1968, Merrill, a professor at the University of Missouri's School of Journalism, listed "the most qualitative or prestigious" elite newspapers in the world. His listing, he said, was based on a "long-time sampling of opinions of knowledgeable persons from all over the world."

	City	Circulation
1. *The New York Times*	New York City	870,510
2. *Neue Zürcher Zeitung*	Zurich	95,000
3. *Le Monde*	Paris	401,057

4.	*The Guardian*	London	358,895
5.	*The Times*	London	339,594
6.	*Pravda*	Moscow	10,000,000
7.	*Jen-min Jih-pao*	Peking	1,000,000
8.	*Borba*	Belgrade	30,570
9.	*L'Osservatore Romano*	Vatican City	70,000
10.	*ABC*	Madrid	190,220

Пролетарии всех стран, соединяйтесь!

Коммунистическая партия Советского Союза

ПРАВДА

Орган Центрального Комитета КПСС

Газета основана 5 мая 1912 года В. И. ЛЕНИНЫМ · № 363 (21332) · Вторник, 28 декабря 1976 года · Цена 3 коп.

(Translated from Upper Right)
Proletarians of All Countries, Unite!
Communist Party of the Soviet Union
PRAVDA
Organ of the Central Committee of the Communist Party
of the Soviet Union
(Lower Left)
Newspaper founded May 5, 1912, by V. I. Lenin

JOHN TEBBEL'S 11 MOST INFLUENTIAL NEWSPAPERS IN THE WORLD

An educator and writer, John Tebbel taught journalism at Columbia University and New York University. Among the many books he has published are *The Marshall Fields, The Life and Good Times of William Randolph Hearst, Compact History of the American Newspaper,* and *The Media in America.*

		City
1.	*The New York Times*	New York City
2.	*The Washington Post*	Washington, D.C.
3.	*The Wall Street Journal*	New York City
4-5.	*The Times* and *The Sunday Times*	London
6.	*The Guardian*	London
7.	*Le Monde*	Paris
8.	*Die Welt*	Hamburg
9.	*Suddeutsche Zeitung*	Munich
10.	*La Stampa*	Turin
11.	*Journal de Genève*	Geneva

—Exclusive for *The Book of Lists*

RUDY VALLEE'S
10 BEST POPULAR ORCHESTRA
(OR BAND) LEADERS OF ALL TIME

Bandleader-crooner Rudy Vallee, worshiped by teenagers in the 1920s, was master of ceremonies on the first radio variety show, the *Fleischmann Hour*. Among the many tunes he popularized was his song "I'm Just a Vagabond Lover." His most successful acting experience was in the film *How to Succeed in Business Without Really Trying*. His books include *My Time Is Your Time* and *Vagabond Dreams Come True*.

1. Paul Whiteman
2. Lawrence Welk
3. Les Brown
4. Stan Kenton
5. Oriole Terrace Orchestra (1921–1922)
6. Jack Hylton
7. Charles Strick Fadden (1921–1923)
8. Ted Lewis
9. Dixieland Jazz Orchestra
10. Art Hickman

Vallee adds: "These orchestras represent, in my opinion, the finest that were ever enjoyed on records, to dance to, or to just hear."

—Exclusive for *The Book of Lists*

JOHNNY CASH'S
10 GREATEST COUNTRY SONGS
OF ALL TIME

Country singer and songwriter Johnny Cash became an overnight success in 1956 with the release of "I Walk the Line." His talent is appreciated not only by country and western enthusiasts, but by lovers of folk music and popular music as well. Among his many top-selling hits are "Ring of Fire," "Jackson," and "Understand Your Man."

1. "I Walk the Line," Johnny Cash
2. "I Can't Stop Loving You," Don Gibson
3. "Wildwood Flower," Carter Family
4. "Folsom Prison Blues," Johnny Cash

5. "Candy Kisses," George Morgan
6. "I'm Movin' On," Hank Snow
7. "Walking the Floor over You," Ernest Tubb
8. "He'll Have to Go," Joe Allison and Audrey Allison
9. "Great Speckle Bird," Carter Family
10. "Cold, Cold Heart," Hank Williams

—Exclusive for *The Book of Lists*

DAVID EWEN'S
10 BEST AMERICAN
POPULAR SONGS

One of the world's leading experts on songs, David Ewen has published more than 50 books on serious and popular music. Besides authorized biographies of George Gershwin, Jerome Kern, and Richard Rodgers, he has written *The World of Great Composers, Panorama of American Popular Music,* and *The World of 20th-Century Music.* He was writer and coproducer of 56 programs on American popular music that were broadcast on the Voice of America.

1. "Swanee River" (or "Old Folks at Home"), words and music by Stephen Foster
2. "Stormy Weather," words by Ted Koehler, music by Harold Arlen
3. "Stardust," words by Mitchell Parish, music by Hoagy Carmichael
4. "Body and Soul," words by Edward Heyman, Robert Sour, and Frank Eyton, music by John Green
5. "The Man I Love," words by Ira Gershwin, music by George Gershwin
6. "All the Things You Are," words by Oscar Hammerstein II, music by Jerome Kern
7. "Hello, Young Lovers," words by Oscar Hammerstein II, music by Richard Rodgers
8. "Begin the Beguine," words and music by Cole Porter
9. "Cheek to Cheek," words and music by Irving Berlin
10. "Thine Alone," words by Henry Blossom, music by Victor Herbert

—Exclusive for *The Book of Lists*

DR. DEMENTO'S
10 WORST SONG TITLES
OF ALL TIME

Disc jockey Dr. Demento was educated at UCLA, where he received his master's degree in music. His radio program, *The Dr. Demento Show,* is syndicated to over 600 stations throughout the world. His personal collection of 85,000 records is said to be one of the largest private collections in the world.

1. "I Scream, You Scream, We All Scream for Ice Cream"
2. "They Needed a Songbird in Heaven, So God Took Caruso Away"
3. "Plant a Watermelon on My Grave, and Let the Juice Soak Through"
4. "If the Man in the Moon Were a Coon"
5. "Where Did Robinson Crusoe Go with Friday on Saturday Night"
6. "Come After Breakfast, Bring Your Lunch, and Leave Before Suppertime"
7. "How Could You Believe Me When I Said I Love You When You Know I've Been a Liar All My Life"
8. "I've Got Those Wake Up Seven Thirty, Wash Your Ears They're Dirty, Eat Your Eggs and Oatmeal Rush to School Blues"
9. "Would You Rather Be a Colonel with an Eagle on Your Shoulder or a Private with a Chicken on Your Knee?"
10. "A Woman Is Only a Woman, But a Good Cigar Is a Smoke"

—Exclusive for *The Book of Lists*

BING CROSBY'S
10 FAVORITE PERFORMERS
OF ALL TIME

One of the world's most popular performers, the legendary Bing Crosby began his career as a singer in dance bands. Soon he was turning out million-seller records and starring in motion-picture musicals. He was awarded an Oscar for his starring role in *Going My Way.* Other highlights in his long film career include *Pennies from Heaven, White Christmas, Road to Rio,* and *Holiday Inn.*

1. Al Jolson
2. Ethel Waters
3. James Barton
4. Frank Sinatra
5. Lena Horne
6. Louis Armstrong
7. Nat Cole
8. Mel Torme
9. Judy Garland
10. Victor Borge

Crosby adds: "These are not listed in order of preference, and include no actors, only performers. I could, of course, list hundreds more."

—Exclusive for *The Book of Lists*

15 RECORDING ARTISTS WITH MORE THAN 10 ALBUMS THAT HAVE SOLD A MILLION COPIES

		No. of Albums
1.	Elvis Presley	21
2.	The Beatles	20
3.	The Rolling Stones	20
4.	Andy Williams	17
5.	Bob Dylan	15
6.	Frank Sinatra	14
7.	Barbra Streisand	14
8.	Herb Alpert and The Tijuana Brass	13
9.	The Beach Boys	12
10.	Dean Martin	12
11.	Three Dog Night	12
12.	Grand Funk Railroad	11
13.	Elton John	11
14.	Mitch Miller	11
15.	Charlie Pride	11

SOURCE: *Cashbox*, 34th anniversary ed., 1976–1977.

Former truck driver Elvis Presley has recorded more million-seller record albums than any other performer in history—21 in all.

10 RARE ROCK-AND-ROLL
45S FROM THE 1950S

Record and Artist	Label	Value
1. "Blue Moon of Kentucky" (Elvis Presley)	Sun 209	$200
2. "Sleepy Time Blues" (Jess Hooper)	Meteor 5025	100
3. "Movie Magg" (Carl Perkins)	Flip 501	80
4. "Rock and Roll in the Groove" (Cleadus Harrison)	Natural (no number)	75
5. "High Steppin'" (Dale Vaughn)	Von 480	75
6. "Skinny Jim" (Eddie Cochran)	Crest 1026	60
7. "Jitterbug Baby" (David Roy)	Kliff 105	50
8. "Spin the Bottle" (Benny Joy)	Dixie 2001	40
9. "Rock It" (Thumper Jones)	Starday 240	40
10. "Cool Off Baby" (Billy Barrix)	Chess 1662	40

—D.M.S. & J.L.S.

12 RARE 45S BY
RHYTHM AND BLUES VOCAL GROUPS

Record and Group	Label	Value
1. "Stormy Weather" (The Five Sharps)	Jubilee 5104	$1,500
2. "Can't Help Loving That Girl of Mine" (The Hideaways)	Ronnie 1000	500
3. "When I Look at You" (The Encores)	Checker 760	500
4. "There Is Love in You" (The Prisonaires)	Sun 207	450
5. "Tell Me You're Mine" (The Velveteens)	Spitfire 15	400
6. "Count Every Star" (The Ravens)	National 9111	350
7. "Baby It's You" (The Spaniels)	Vee Jay 101	300
8. "The Stars Will Remember" (The Buccaneers)	Rama 21	300
9. "I Couldn't Sleep a Wink" (The Mellomoods)	Red Robin 104	300
10. "Aurelia" (The Pelicans)	Parrot 793	300
11. "Believe" (The Nutones)	Hollywood Star 798	300
12. "Since You've Been Away" (The Swallows)	King 4466	300

—J.L.S.

10 RARE RECORDS BY BLUES ARTISTS

Most of these records are available as both 78 rpm and 45 rpm. However, the value of a 45 is at least four times that of a 78.

Record and Artist	Label	Value (45 rpm)
1. "Sugar Cane Highway" (Playboy Fuller)	Fuller 181	$250
2. "Lonesome Ol' Jail" (D. A. Hunt)	Sun 183	250
3. "Rockin' Chair Daddy" (Harmonica Frank)	Sun 205	200
4. "Nervous Wreck" (Willie Nix)	Chance 1163	150
5. "Dim Lights" (J. B. Hutto)	Chance 1165	135
6. "Kissing in the Dark" (Memphis Minnie)	J.O.B. 1101	125
7. "Dorothy Mae" (Joe Hill Louis)	Checker 763	100
8. "Maggie Campbell" (Robert Nighthawk)	States 131	75
9. "Blow My Baby Back Home" (Mule Thomas)	Hollywood 1091	50
10. "Eisenhower Blues" (J. B. Lenoir; flip side is "I'm in Korea")	Parrot 802	35

—D.M.S. & J.L.S.

DICK CLARK'S 14 MUSIC IDOLS WORSHIPED BY TEENAGERS THROUGH THE YEARS

(L to R) Elton John in wax, Elton John in the flesh.

As host of TV's *American Bandstand*, Dick Clark has offered teenagers since the 1950s a chance to learn the latest dances—the Stroll, the Watusi, the Twist—rate the latest records, and perhaps win a date with their favorite rock-and-roll star. He was responsible for launching the careers of such superstars as Fabian, Bobby Darin, and Connie Francis. He is currently the host of a TV game show, *$20,000 Pyramid*. The idols are listed in reverse chronological order.

1. Elton John
2. Donny Osmond
3. David Cassidy
4. Bobby Sherman
5. The Beatles
6. Fabian
7. Frankie Avalon
8. Ricky Nelson
9. Elvis Presley
10. Johnny Ray
11. Eddie Fisher
12. Frank Sinatra
13. Rudy Vallee
14. Wolfgang Amadeus Mozart

—Exclusive for *The Book of Lists*

ROBERT MERRILL'S 10 GREATEST MALE OPERA SINGERS OF THE PAST

Celebrated worldwide for his appearances in concert, opera, television, and radio, Robert Merrill has performed in the Metropolitan Opera House in New York, the Royal Opera House in London, and elsewhere. A baritone, he has had leading roles in *Carmen, La Traviata, Faust,* and numerous other operas. He has made special appearances before Presidents Franklin D. Roosevelt, Truman, Eisenhower, Kennedy, and Lyndon B. Johnson.

1. Enrico Caruso
2. Feodor Chaliapin
3. Titta Ruffo
4. Jussi Björling
5. Richard Tucker
6. Beniamino Gigli
7. Giovanni Martinelli
8. Leonard Warren
9. Ezio Pinza
10. Giuseppe De Luca

Robert Merrill adds: "As I began to assemble a list of my favorites it grew increasingly difficult to limit the number to just 10. Therefore, what I have done in hopes of not offending any of my colleagues who are still active and for whom I still have great admiration, is to submit a list of 10 male opera singers who are no longer with us but who made unforgettable contributions to the world of opera. I had no intention of slighting the many glorious females, but if they were to be included, we'd need another long list."

—Exclusive for *The Book of Lists*

REGINA RESNIK'S
10 FAVORITE OPERAS

Opera star Regina Resnik has won plaudits in the most prestigious opera houses throughout the world. The famed mezzo-soprano has sung the whole range of operatic repertory, but she is best known for her portrayal of the lead in *Carmen*. Her favorite roles as a mezzo-soprano are Amneris in *Aida* and Carmen in *Carmen*, and her favorite roles as a soprano are Leonora in *Fidelio* and Santuzza in *Cavalleria Rusticana*.

1. *La Bohème*, Giacomo Puccini
2. *Boris Godunov*, Modest Musorgski
3. *Don Carlos*, Giuseppe Verdi
4. *Elektra*, Richard Strauss
5. *Fidelio*, Ludwig van Beethoven
6. *The Makropolous Case*, Leoš Janáček
7. *The Marriage of Figaro*, Wolfgang Amadeus Mozart
8. *Peter Grimes*, Benjamin Britten
9. *Tristan and Isolde*, Richard Wagner
10. *Werther*, Jules Massenet

—Exclusive for *The Book of Lists*

SIR RUDOLF BING'S
2 FAVORITE OPERAS

General manager of the Metropolitan Opera Association (New York, N.Y.) from 1950 to 1972, Bing was also a professor in theater management and opera at New York University. He is the author of 5,000 *Nights at the Opera*.

1. *The Magic Flute*, Wolfgang Amadeus Mozart
2. *Otello*, Giuseppe Verdi

—Exclusive for *The Book of Lists*

SIR RUDOLF BING'S CHOICE OF THE 3 MOST POPULAR OPERAS

1. *Aïda,* Giuseppe Verdi
2. *La Bohème,* Giacomo Puccini
3. *Carmen,* Georges Bizet

—Exclusive for *The Book of Lists*

THE 5 ALL-TIME FAVORITE PERSONS IN THE ARTS

On a yearly basis from 1972 to 1976, Mme. Tussaud's Waxwork Museum in London handed out questionnaires to 3,500 international visitors attending their exhibition. The visitors were asked to choose their all-time favorite persons involved in the arts. The results were tabulated, and the following lists show the five most popular artists for each year.

THE 1976 POLL

1. Pablo Picasso
2. Rembrandt
3. Salvador Dali
3. Margot Fonteyn
3. Leonardo da Vinci

THE 1975 POLL

1. Pablo Picasso
2. Margot Fonteyn
3. Salvador Dali
3. Rudolph Nureyev
5. Vincent van Gogh

THE 1974 POLL

1. Pablo Picasso
2. Rudolph Nureyev
3. Vincent van Gogh
3. Salvador Dali
3. Margot Fonteyn

THE 1973 POLL

1. Pablo Picasso
2. Rudolph Nureyev
3. Leonard Bernstein
3. Salvador Dali
5. Rembrandt

THE 1972 POLL

1. Pablo Picasso
2. Margot Fonteyn
2. William Shakespeare
4. Salvador Dali
5. André Previn

GENE KELLY'S
11 GREATEST DANCERS
OF THE PAST

One of the most famous dancers in film history, Gene Kelly came off the Broadway stage at 30 to star in such musical hits as *Anchors Aweigh, The Pirate, Singin' in the Rain, An American in Paris,* and *Brigadoon.* He also directed numerous films, among them *Gigot* and *Hello, Dolly!* He received a special Academy Award for his innovative contributions to the dance in movies.

1. Salome
2. Master Juba (19th century), minstrel dancer, born William Henry Lane
3. Isadora Duncan
4. Nijinsky
5. Carlotta Grisi (19th century), Italian ballerina
6. Maria Taglioni (19th century), Italian ballerina
7. Fanny Cerito (19th century), Italian ballerina
8-9. Doris Humphrey and Charles Weidman (20th century), U.S. dancing duo
10. John Bubbles (1940s), U.S. tap dancer
11. Bill Robinson

—Exclusive for *The Book of Lists*

Bill "Bojangles" Robinson (1878–1949), U.S. tap dancer and entertainer, held the world's record for running 100 yds. backward.

JOSHUA LOGAN'S
10 BEST STAGE PLAYS
OF ALL TIME

Educated at Princeton and the Moscow Art Theater, Texas-born Joshua Logan is considered one of the top directors in the legitimate theater, as well as a leading producer and writer. Among his great Broadway stage successes are *South Pacific* (for which he received a Pulitzer prize as coauthor), *Mister Roberts*, *Charley's Aunt*, *Picnic*, and *Fanny*. His film credits include such memorable ones as *Bus Stop*, *Picnic*, *Camelot*, and *Paint Your Wagon*.

1. *Oedipus Rex*, Sophocles
2. *Hamlet*, Shakespeare
3. *Hedda Gabler*, Ibsen
4. *Miss Julie*, Strindberg
5. *Playboy of the Western World*, Synge
6. *Charley's Aunt*, Brandon Thomas
7. *Le Malade Imaginaire*, Molière
8. *Faust*, Goethe
9. *Carmen*, Henri Meilhac and Ludovic Halévy (set to music by Bizet)
10. *Long Day's Journey into Night*, O'Neill

—Exclusive for *The Book of Lists*

JOSHUA LOGAN'S
12 BEST STAGE ACTORS
OF ALL TIME

1. David Garrick
2. Edwin Booth
3. Tommaso Salvini
4. Coquelin
5. Eleonora Duse
6. Ivan Moskvin
7. Sokolov
8. Alexander Moissi
9. Laurence Olivier
10. William Gillette
11. Rex Harrison
12. Marlon Brando

—Exclusive for *The Book of Lists*

SIR JOHN GIELGUD'S 6 GREATEST HAMLETS OF ALL TIME

Regarded by many as the foremost Shakespearean actor of the 20th century, Sir John Gielgud became internationally famous for his performance as Hamlet in England during 1930 and 1934, and in the U.S. during 1936. His production of *Much Ado About Nothing* in 1950 was considered a theatrical landmark. He directed Richard Burton in *Hamlet* in 1964. He has appeared in such films as *Julius Caesar, Shoes of the Fisherman,* and *Lost Horizon.* Two volumes of his autobiography, *Early Stages* and *Stage Directions,* have been published.

1. Richard Burbage (1567?–1619)
2. Thomas Betterton (1635?–1710)
3. Edwin Booth (1833–1893)
4. Sir Henry Irving (1838–1905)
5. Sir Johnston Forbes-Robertson (1853–1937)
6. John Barrymore (1882–1942)

—Exclusive for *The Book of Lists*

20 LONGEST-RUNNING BROADWAY SHOWS
(as of January 1, 1977)

(M) denotes musical.

	No. of Performances
1. *Fiddler on the Roof* (M)	3,242
2. *Life with Father*	3,224
3. *Tobacco Road*	3,182
4. *Hello, Dolly!* (M)	2,844
5. *My Fair Lady* (M)	2,717
6. *Man of La Mancha* (M)	2,329
7. *Abie's Irish Rose*	2,327
8. *Oklahoma!* (M)	2,314
9. *Grease* (M)	2,004
10. *Harvey*	1,775
11. *Hair* (M)	1,742
12. *South Pacific* (M)	1,694
13. *Born Yesterday*	1,642
14. *Mary, Mary*	1,572
15. *The Voice of the Turtle*	1,557

16.	*Barefoot in the Park*	1,532
17.	*Mame* (M)	1,508
18.	*Arsenic and Old Lace*	1,444
19.	*The Sound of Music* (M)	1,443
20.	*How to Succeed in Business Without Really Trying* (M)	1,417

SOURCE: *Weekly Variety*, New York.

SAMUEL FRENCH, INC.'S
15 MOST POPULAR PLAYS
PERFORMED BY AMATEUR GROUPS

1. *Ah, Wilderness!*, Eugene O'Neill
2. *Barefoot in the Park*, Neil Simon
3. *Blithe Spirit*, Noël Coward
4. *Charley's Aunt*, Brandon Thomas
5. *Don't Drink the Water*, Woody Allen
6. *The Matchmaker*, Thornton Wilder
7. *The Miracle Worker*, William Gibson
8. *The Odd Couple*, Neil Simon
9. *One Flew Over the Cuckoo's Nest,* Dale Wasserman (adapted from the novel by Ken Kesey)
10. *Our Town*, Thornton Wilder
11. *Play It Again, Sam,* Woody Allen
12. *See How They Run*, Philip King
13. *The Skin of Our Teeth*, Thornton Wilder
14. *Spoon River Anthology,* Charles Aidman (based on the book by Edgar Lee Masters)
15. *Ten Little Indians*, Agatha Christie

Exclusive for *The Book of Lists*

PEGGY GUGGENHEIM'S
10 GREATEST PAINTERS
OF THE PAST

John Davis, biographer of the Bouviers and Guggenheims, writes us:

"Marguerite (Peggy) Guggenheim, daughter of Benjamin Guggenheim, one of the seven famous Guggenheim brothers, founders of the greatest private fortune ever made from mining and metallurgy in history. Niece of Solomon R. Guggenheim, donor of The Solomon R. Guggenheim Museum, designed by Frank Lloyd Wright, in New York, N.Y.

"Peggy founded the Guggenheim Gallery in London, and 'Art of This Century' in New York City. Patroness of Marcel Duchamp,

Max Ernst (whom she married), and Jackson Pollock. Foremost private collector of modern art in the world today."

1. Titian
2. Tintoretto
3. Giorgione
4. Carpaccio
5. Velázquez

6. Rembrandt
7. Giotto
8. Botticelli
9. Dürer
10. Michelangelo

—Exclusive for *The Book of Lists*

A detail of the self-portrait by Titian, "chief master of the Venetian School" of Renaissance painting.

PEGGY GUGGENHEIM'S
10 GREATEST MODERN PAINTERS

1. Picasso
2. Miró
3. Kandinski
4. Klee
5. Duchamp

6. Braque
7. Ernst
8. Matisse
9. Pollock
10. Magritte

Exclusive for *The Book of Lists*

8 FASCINATING
MODELS AND ARTISTS

1. SIMONETTA

Simonetta Catteano and Sandro Botticelli were the odd couple of 15th-century Florentine art. Botticelli was a homosexual and Simonetta was the sweet 16-year-old child bride of highborn Marco Vespucci. Yet a brief encounter between artist and girl was to inspire Botticelli's greatest work. Simonetta's beauty was extraordinary. She was golden-haired, had a delicate pointed chin and high cheekbones, and radiated purity. Poets, musicians, and artists all paid her tribute in their fashion. Lorenzo the Magnificent met her and was content merely to gaze. It was Lorenzo's cousin, Giuliano Medici, who fell in love with Simonetta and who requested Botticelli to paint her portrait on a banner to be carried into a joust. Her beauty was Simonetta's only gift. There is no evidence that she ever said, thought, or did anything noteworthy. Indeed, she did not have the time. In 1476, at the age of 20, she died as she had lived—quietly. Botticelli could not forget her. Three years after her death he began to paint Madonnas with Simonetta's face. Ten years later, when Lorenzo asked Botticelli to create a painting for his villa, Botticelli, again summoning Simonetta from memory, produced her as a shimmery Venus rising from a seashell and entitled the picture *Birth of Venus*. She is said to have haunted him the rest of his life, solely as an object of beauty. In 1502, aged 57, Botticelli, still following his natural sexual proclivities, was arrested for sodomy. Happily for him, the charges were dropped.

2. MONA LISA

The enduring question more than 4½ centuries after Leonardo da Vinci painted the *Mona Lisa* is: What is the meaning of her wispy, close-lipped smile? It has been said she was mourning the death of a baby girl, that she was contemplating taking a lover, even that she was suffering pain after having teeth pulled. Whatever troubled or gladdened her, she must have been inordinately single-minded, for Leonardo spent four years (1503–1507) capturing Lisa del Gioconda's smile with his brush. The most famous of all models was born into a large, impoverished Neopolitan family. In 1495, she became the third wife of Francesco Gioconda, a Florentine merchant 19 years her senior. Fancying himself an art patron, Gioconda engaged Leonardo to produce a portrait of his wife suitable for hanging in his dining hall. Leonardo, a man of immeasurable genius (he was also a sculptor, an engineer, and an architect), presided over a huge studio in which he indulged his various interests. It is possible that he strayed from Lisa and his easel to consider astronomy, construct an airplane mock-up, gaze into a periscope, or disappear with one of his boy pupils about whom a critic sniffed: "None of them was much good, but oh, they had long eyelashes." In time, Francesco Gioconda grew impatient. He terminated his wife's sittings, refused to pay for the unfinished portrait, and probably made other plans for his dining-room wall. Undismayed, Leonardo took his portrait of

Mona Lisa to Paris. King Francis I paid $50,000 for the portrait and hung it in the Louvre where it has been constantly on display except for two years, 1911–1913, when it was stolen. Before the stolen portrait was recovered, six Americans, each convinced he had the original *Mona Lisa,* paid $300,000 apiece for forgeries.

3. HÉLÈNA FOURMENT

The story of Peter Paul Rubens and Hélèna Fourment may be unique in the annals of art, for their marriage appears to have been one of undiluted joy. At 53, Rubens was wealthy, widowed, handsome, virile, and eager to take a new wife. In Antwerp, he met Meer Fourment, a prosperous merchant, who introduced him to his seven overweight, available daughters. Rubens chose the cushiony 16-year-old Hélèna, charmed by her double chin, heavy thighs, fleshy waist and stomach, and 54-in. hips. In 1630, he installed his new bride in a château on a vast estate and built studios and galleries, and a private zoo where he kept wolves, apes, and lions. That done, he put Hélèna to work as his model. Since Rubens's studios were a veritable factory, teeming with apprentices and assistants, carpenters and colorists, it was not unusual for Hélèna to pose in the nude for hours while male workers looked on. Healthy-minded Hélèna was delightfully uninhibited. Her voluptuous body accommodated willingly to any acrobatic position her husband's art required. She can be seen tumbling off a rock in *Fall of the Angels,* ripped from a snorting horse by bandits in *Rape of the Daughters of Leucippus,* and drowning in *Angers of Neptune.* Rubens and Hélèna lived together exuberantly until a heart attack took him from her in 1640, leaving Hélèna, at 26, the widowed mother of two children.

4. HENDRICKJE STOFFELS

Double misfortune befell Rembrandt van Rijn in 1642. His masterpiece, *The Night Watch,* was disappointingly received, sending his career into decline, and his young wife, Saskia, died, leaving him with an infant son, Titus. By the terms of Saskia's will, Rembrandt would have forfeited the income from her estate had he remarried. He chose not to do so. Beset by debts and with a small child to care for, Rembrandt endured three difficult years before "the old widow man," as he called himself, was rescued by Hendrickje Stoffels. Hendrickje, a plain, thickly built, illiterate 23-year-old, came to him as a servant in 1645. Under Rembrandt's roof, she filled a variety of roles. She was housekeeper, nurse to the frail Titus, worshipful mistress to her employer, mother of his daughter Cornelia, manager of his business affairs, and, most memorably, model for such glorious paintings as *A Woman Bathing, Girl in the Window,* and *Bathsheba.* There is no evidence Rembrandt ever married Hendrickje. She remained with him until her death in 1667, a victim—as Saskia had been—of tuberculosis.

5. LA MORPHISE

Louise O'Murphy was only 13 when Casanova discovered her in a squalid Paris attic, the fifth daughter of a shoemaker father who had transported his family from Ireland to France before expiring in Rouen. Casanova's enthusiasm for the beauty he detected beneath Louise's rags and filth led artist-decorator François Boucher to seek her out. She became Boucher's favorite model and before she was 15 her likeness on canvas hung in aristocratic homes all over Paris. Along the way Louise O'Murphy became La Morphise and attracted the notice of Mme. de Pompadour, mistress of Louis XV. Pompadour, sexually weary of the king and aware that he needed a new love, engaged Boucher to decorate Versailles and conspired with the artist to have the merry face and ripe, dimpled body of La Morphise look out at the king from every painting on every wall and ceiling. Enchanted, Louis sent for the girl. He immediately took her to his bed where, in time, he fathered her two children. One night, after lovemaking, La Morphise stupidly asked the king if she still slept with Pompadour. Furious, Louis dismissed her from his chambers, replacing her with one of her sisters. An arranged marriage with a major in the infantry ended when her husband was killed in action. She had two more husbands, the last a deputy 30 years her junior. She died in Paris in the winter of 1814 at the age of 77.

6. THE DUCHESS OF ALBA

Today she would be one of the beautiful people—wealthy, brittle, outrageous—the possessor of numerous estates, a glamorous social life, and a docile, titled husband who looked away whenever she took a new lover. She would have faded into history had she not bedded with, and posed nude for, Francisco Goya, the greatest painter of the 18th century. Goya's *Naked Maja* and *Clothed Maja*, hanging side by side in Madrid's Prado Museum, immortalized Cayetana, the duchess of Alba. Goya was middle-aged, fat, deaf, married, and the father of 20 children when they met. He was also court painter to Spain's royal family, who admired him although he painted them as they were: stupid, mean, ugly. Reputedly, Queen Luisa was jealous of the duchess's four-year affair with Goya and, to separate the pair, twice banished the duchess from Madrid, only to have Goya follow his mistress into exile. The duchess, said to have poisoned her husband, and in turn to have been poisoned by order of the queen, died in 1802. Goya lived another 26 years. He died, aged 82, in Bordeaux, France.

7. SUZANNE VALADON

Suzanne Valadon, born in 1869, was an illegitimate country girl who came to Paris and within a few years managed to become a circus acrobat, a model-protegée to Renoir and Degas, the mother of Maurice Utrillo (she never knew which artist was his father), and a successful artist in her own right. Her adult life was inevitably and inextricably linked to Utrillo's. Although she was usually a neglectful mother (she is said to have introduced Maurice to cognac when he was 6 so that he would sleep through the night while she caroused in Montmartre), she did have periods of intense maternal devotion and concern. Had she considered it, which she did not, she might have found a connection between her own behavior and her son's desperate lifelong addiction to drink. For five years Suzanne was the mistress of Paul Mousis, a lawyer. When Mousis married her, he refused to give Maurice his name and sent the 10-year-old boy out of Paris to live with his grandmother. Aroused, Suzanne determined her son *would* have a name and persuaded a Spanish journalist, Miguel Utrillo, to adopt the boy legally—a gesture Maurice resented. (As a

A Suzanne Valadon drawing of a nude.

grown man, he signed his earliest paintings Maurice Utrillo, V.)
When Suzanne grew bored with Mousis, she drank too much and
threw herself into new affairs. She divorced Mousis and moved in
with Maurice and his roommate, André Utter, a would-be artist 3
years younger than Maurice, and 21 years younger than Suzanne
herself. She had an affair with Utter and then, as a theatrical gesture, married him before he marched off to W.W. I. Utter returned
safely and the trio resumed housekeeping. Although Suzanne was
never as gifted as Maurice, the paintings of mother and son, exhibited together in 1923, brought dazzling sums of money to
Suzanne. She acquired a big car and a liveried chauffeur, fed her dog
filet mignon, and entertained lavishly. Her pleasure was short-lived.
Utter, disgusted with the ménage, drank heavily, sold her car,
flaunted his affairs, and beat her regularly before they parted. Despite her own troubles, Suzanne worried about Maurice. This time it
was his disinterest in women. She found him prostitutes and eventually a wife. In 1938, she died. Every year for the rest of his life,
Maurice Utrillo observed the anniversary of her death by spending
the day in his private chapel, praying for her soul. Today paintings by
mother and son can be seen in the Valadon-Utrillo room of the
Museum of Modern Art in Paris.

8. KIKI OF MONTPARNASSE

She came to Paris at 16, a lusty, generous farm girl named
Marie Prin. It was 1924 and, as she sat alone in a café, her country
freshness attracted Moise Kisling, who made her his model. During
her career she posed for Utrillo, Soutine, Toulouse-Lautrec, Foujita,

Cocteau, and the artist-photographer Man Ray, whose mistress she was for six years. She often posed nude but with some embarrassment because she had no pubic hair. To supplement her modeling fees she sang ribald songs in nightclubs and once, in pursuit of stardom, made a brief, futile trip to New York City. With time, she grew fat and coarse. In her days of glory, she was toasted as the Venus of Montparnasse, but she died alone in 1953, lost to absinthe and cocaine. Stacked beneath the bed in her garret room were valuable paintings and drawings of Kiki of Montparnasse, all gifts of the famous artists who had adored her in her youth.

—S.W.

RUBÉN DE SAAVEDRA'S
8 FAMOUS INTERIOR DESIGNERS

Rubén De Saavedra, of New York., N.Y., is one of today's foremost interior designers, noted both for his personalized traditional and bold contemporary decors. De Saavedra lectures at the New York School of Interior Design—subject, Versatile Design—paints, is working on settings for a Broadway production, and is preparing a book on decoration.

1. CRO-MAGNON MAN (c. 15,000 B.C.)

The artistry of this early example of *Homo sapiens* is vividly demonstrated by the cave paintings discovered in 1879 at Altamira, Spain.

2. ANDREA PALLADIO (1518–1580)

Palladio, an Italian, was one of the great architects of all time. He did not personally take charge of the interior decoration of the villas he constructed, but he did supervise the selection of those who did the work. His Teatro Olimpico in Vicenza is one of the masterpieces of complete architecture and decoration.

3. DIEGO RODRIGUEZ DE SILVA Y VELÁZQUEZ (1599–1660)

One of the greatest painters of all time, Velázquez was a favorite of King Philip IV and was responsible for the decor of the royal palace in Madrid.

4. ROBERT ADAM (1728–1792)

A Scottish architect, Adam designed both the exteriors and interiors—including furniture—of many beautiful English homes. Among the "Adam style" country houses are Luton Hoo, Croome Court, and Kenwood.

5. THOMAS JEFFERSON (1743–1826)

Third president of the U.S., Jefferson was also an architect, interior designer, and furniture maker. He designed Monticello, his home in Virginia.

6. JOHN NASH (1752–1835)

Born in London, Nash was the favorite architect of King George IV. He designed Regent's Park and the Haymarket Theatre. He also remodeled the Royal Brighton Pavilion, which is a masterpiece of the English Regency period.

7. ANTONIO GAUDÍ (1852–1926)

Great Spanish architect, interior designer, and sculptor of forms. His bizarre imagination created some of the most exciting and *complete* buildings ever. The Güell Palace in Barcelona is a perfect example.

8. CARLOS DE BEISTEGUI (1895–1970)

He can only be called a magician. His decorating had an opulence that was unique, a style that defied description. Both his French château and the Palazzo Labia in Venice are monuments to his superb taste.

De Saavedra adds: "The inclusion of designers known primarily as architects may come as a surprise, but upon closer examination, they did create and were responsible for the entire 'package,' which is something we rarely encounter today."

—Exclusive for *The Book of Lists*

9 FAMOUS MAGICIANS AND A FEAT FOR WHICH EACH WAS RENOWNED

1. GIOVANNI BARTOLOMEO BOSCO (b. Italy, 1793)

After beheading two pigeons—one black, the other white—Bosco would put each body in a container with the head of the opposite bird. A moment later he would remove from each box a bird with a mismatched head. Bosco was also known as Italy's greatest cup-and-ball conjurer of the 19th century.

2. JOHN HENRY ANDERSON (b. Scotland, 1814)

Anderson would put 10 dead canaries in a pan and bake them. He would then lift the lid to reveal 2 live birds. "The Great Wizard of the North," as he billed himself, was also one of the first magicians ever to pull a rabbit out of a hat.

3. CARL HERRMANN (b. Germany, 1816)

Although members of the performing Herrmann family drew crowds for 80 years, Carl was the first to achieve international acclaim. Once, while entertaining at an Austrian mansion, Carl borrowed a diamond ring and hurled it out a window. When servants rushed out to search for the jewel, Carl whistled and a parrot flew in—clutching not only the ring, but the servants' powdered wigs.

4. JOHN NEVILL MASKELYNE (b. England, 1839)

Maskelyne was the first magician ever to levitate a person. Without any visible means of support, he caused a woman to rise directly upward and remain suspended off the ground.

5. DAVID DEVANT (b. England, 1868)

Devant would have an assistant—clad as a soldier—march to martial music atop a suspended platform partly surrounded by columns of lights. Three British flags would then be raised to enclose the subject. Upon a command from the magician, the flags would drop to reveal a shrunken, doll-sized marching soldier. Devant (whose real name was David Wighton) performed this feat in a private show for Queen Mary and King George V.

6. HOWARD THURSTON (b. U.S., 1869)

During a performance at the White House, Thurston destroyed President Calvin Coolidge's gold pocket watch and caused the broken parts to vanish. He then had a butler bring in a loaf of bread, which Mrs. Coolidge was instructed to cut in half. The mended watch was found inside.

7. CHARLES JOSEPH CARTER (b. U.S., 1874)

Carter's wife, Corinne, would be shackled and locked in a canopy-covered cage by members of the audience. Within 30 seconds, Corinne would show up at the entrance of the theater. In her place, inside the cage, sat a sad-looking fellow wearing prison stripes.

8. HARRY HOUDINI (Ehrich Weiss; b. Hungary, 1874)

After an unusual "sea monster" was found on a beach near Boston, a handcuffed Houdini forced himself through an opening in the embalmed creature. Although the carcass was sealed with heavy chains, Houdini escaped within 15 minutes. The day of the magician's death (October 31, 1926) is National Magic Day in the U.S.

9. HENRI BOUTON (b. U.S., 1885)

Bouton would be tied to the barrel of a cannon and disintegrate when the weapon was fired. He would then appear from the wings, completely unharmed. Bouton was billed as "Frederick the Great" until W.W. I, when his bookers urged him to change the "German" name. He followed their suggestion and became "Blackstone."

—H. SI. & D.B.

10
COMING ATTRACTIONS
—MOVIES AND TV

THE 25 ALL-TIME
BOX-OFFICE CHAMPION FILMS

(as compiled by *Weekly Variety*, 1976)

Figures as given below signify the rentals received by the distributors from the U.S.-Canada market only, and omit foreign market rentals. The latter, in recent years, sometimes equal—or slightly surpass—the domestic play-off. Film title is followed by total rentals received to date.

		Year Released	Rentals Received
1.	*Jaws*	1975	$118,727,000
2.	*The Godfather*	1972	85,747,184
3.	*The Exorcist*	1973	82,015,000
4.	*The Sound of Music*	1965	78,400,000
5.	*Gone With the Wind*	1939	76,700,000
6.	*The Sting*	1973	72,160,000
7.	*One Flew over the Cuckoo's Nest*	1975	56,500,000
8.	*The Towering Inferno*	1975	55,000,000
9.	*Love Story*	1970	50,000,000
10.	*The Graduate*	1968	49,978,000
11.	*American Graffiti*	1973	47,308,000
12.	*Doctor Zhivago*	1965	46,550,000
13.	*Butch Cassidy and the Sundance Kid*	1969	45,830,000
14.	*Airport*	1970	45,300,000
15.	*The Ten Commandments*	1956	43,000,000
16.	*The Poseidon Adventure*	1972	42,500,000
17.	*Mary Poppins*	1964	42,250,000
18.	*M*A*S*H*	1970	40,850,000
19.	*Ben Hur*	1959	36,650,000
20.	*Earthquake*	1974	36,094,000
21.	*Blazing Saddles*	1974	35,183,000
22.	*Fiddler on the Roof*	1971	34,010,000
23.	*Billy Jack*	1971	32,500,000
24.	*Young Frankenstein*	1975	30,000,000
25.	*All the President's Men*	1976	29,000,000

20 FAMOUS WRITERS
WHO WORKED FOR THE MOVIES

1. MAXWELL ANDERSON (U.S. playwright; 1888–1959)

Movies worked on include: *All Quiet on the Western Front* (1930); *Washington Merry-Go-Round* (1932); *Death Takes a Holiday* (1934); *Joan of Arc* (1948); *The Wrong Man* (1957).

2. RAYMOND CHANDLER (U.S. detective story writer; 1888–1959)

And Now Tomorrow (1944); *Double Indemnity* (1944); *The Unseen* (1945); *The Blue Dahlia* (1946); *Strangers on a Train* (1951).

3. THEODORE DREISER (U.S. novelist; 1871–1945)

An American Tragedy (1931); *Tobacco and Men* (1935); *My Gal Sal* (1942).

4. WILLIAM FAULKNER (U.S. novelist; 1897–1962)

Today We Live (1933); *Road to Glory* (1936); *To Have and Have Not* (1945); *The Big Sleep* (1946); *Land of the Pharaohs* (1955).

5. F. SCOTT FITZGERALD (U.S. novelist; 1896–1940)

A Yank at Oxford (1938); *Three Comrades* (1938); *Gone with the Wind* (1939); *The Women* (1939); *Madame Curie* (1943).

F. Scott Fitzgerald's only screen credit was *Three Comrades*, starring (L to R) Franchot Tone, Robert Taylor, Margaret Sullavan, Robert Young.

6. DASHIELL HAMMETT (U.S. detective story writer; 1894–1961)

City Streets (1931); *Mister Dynamite* (1935); *After the Thin Man* (1937); *Another Thin Man* (1939); *Watch on the Rhine* (1943).

7. BEN HECHT (U.S. writer; 1894–1964)

The Front Page (1931); *Scarface* (1932); *Design for Living* (1933); *Wuthering Heights* (1939); *A Farewell to Arms* (1957).

8. LILLIAN HELLMAN (U.S. playwright; b. 1905)

The Dark Angel (1935); *Dead End* (1937); *The Little Foxes* (1941); *The Children's Hour* (1961); *The Chase* (1966).

9. ERNEST HEMINGWAY (U.S. novelist; 1899–1961)

The Spanish Earth (1937); *The Old Man and the Sea* (1956).

10. JAMES HILTON (English novelist; 1900–1954)

Camille (1936); *We Are Not Alone* (1939); *The Tuttles of Tahiti* (1942); *Mrs. Miniver* (1942); *Forever and a Day* (1944).

11. ALDOUS HUXLEY (English novelist; 1894–1963)

Pride and Prejudice (1940); *Jane Eyre* (1944); *A Woman's Vengeance* (1947).

12. CHRISTOPHER ISHERWOOD (English writer; b. 1904)

Rage in Heaven (1941); *Forever and a Day* (1944); *The Loved One* (1965); *Frankenstein, the True Story* (1973).

13. CLIFFORD ODETS (U.S. playwright; 1906–1963)

The General Died at Dawn (1936); *None But the Lonely Heart* (1944); *Sweet Smell of Success* (1957); *The Story on Page One* (1960); *Wild in the Country* (1961).

14. DOROTHY PARKER (U.S. short-story writer, 1893–1967)

Suzy (1936); *A Star Is Born* (1937); *Weekend for Three* (1941); *Saboteur* (1942); *The Fan* (1949).

15. S. J. PERELMAN (U.S. humorist, b. 1904)

Horse Feathers (1932); *Sitting Pretty* (1933); *Florida Special* (1936); *Boy Trouble* (1939); *Around the World in 80 Days* (1956).

16. AYN RAND (U.S. novelist; b. 1905)

Love Letters (1945); *You Came Along* (1945); *The Fountainhead* (1949).

17. GEORGE BERNARD SHAW (British playwright; 1856–1950)

Pygmalion (1938); *Major Barbara* (1941); *Caesar and Cleopatra* (1946).

18. JOHN STEINBECK (U.S. novelist; 1902–1968)

The Forgotten Village (1941); *The Pearl* (1948); *The Red Pony* (1949); *Viva Zapata* (1952)

19. NATHANAEL WEST (U.S. novelist; 1903–1940)

Ticket to Paradise (1936); *It Could Happen to You* (1937); *Five Came Back* (1939); *I Stole a Million* (1939); *Let's Make Music* (1940).

20. THORNTON WILDER (U.S. novelist and playwright; (1897–1975)

The Dark Angel (1935); *Our Town* (1940); *Shadow of a Doubt* (1943).

—F.B.F.

10 ACTORS AND ACTRESSES MOST OFTEN NOMINATED FOR AN ACADEMY AWARD

(capital letters indicate an Oscar winner)

1. KATHARINE HEPBURN (11)

MORNING GLORY, 1933; *Alice Adams*, 1935; *The Philadelphia Story*, 1940; *Woman of the Year*, 1942; *The African Queen*, 1951; *Summertime*, 1955; *The Rainmaker*, 1956; *Suddenly Last Summer*, 1959; *Long Day's Journey into Night*, 1962; GUESS WHO'S COMING TO DINNER? 1967; THE LION IN WINTER, 1968.

Katharine Hepburn in her first and her latest
Academy Award-winning performances.
(L to R) *Morning Glory* and *The Lion in Winter*.

2. BETTE DAVIS (10)

DANGEROUS, 1935; JEZEBEL, 1938; *Dark Victory*, 1939; *The Letter*, 1940; *The Little Foxes*, 1941; *Now, Voyager*, 1942; *Mr. Skeffington*, 1944; *All About Eve*, 1950; *The Star*, 1952; *Whatever Happened to Baby Jane?* 1962.

3. SPENCER TRACY (9)

San Francisco, 1936; CAPTAINS COURAGEOUS, 1937; BOYS' TOWN, 1938; *Father of the Bride*, 1950; *Bad Day at Black Rock*, 1955; *The Old Man and the Sea*, 1958; *Inherit the Wind*, 1960; *Judgment at Nuremberg*, 1961; *Guess Who's Coming to Dinner?* 1967.

4. LAURENCE OLIVIER (8)

Wuthering Heights, 1939; *Rebecca*, 1940; *Henry V*, 1946; HAMLET, 1948; *Richard III*, 1956; *The Entertainer*, 1960; *Othello*, 1965; *Sleuth*, 1972.

5. MARLON BRANDO (7)

A Streetcar Named Desire, 1951; *Viva Zapata*, 1952; *Julius Caesar*, 1953; ON THE WATERFRONT, 1954; *Sayonara*, 1957; THE GODFATHER, 1972; *Last Tango in Paris*, 1973.

5. GREER GARSON (7)

Good-bye Mr. Chips, 1939; *Blossoms in the Dust*, 1941; MRS. MINIVER, 1942; *Madame Curie*, 1943; *Mrs. Parkington*, 1944; *The Valley of Decision*, 1945; *Sunrise at Campobello*, 1960.

7. INGRID BERGMAN (6)

For Whom the Bell Tolls, 1943; GASLIGHT, 1944; *The Bells of St. Mary's*, 1945; *Joan of Arc*, 1948; ANASTASIA, 1956; MURDER ON THE ORIENT EXPRESS (best supporting actress), 1974.

7. RICHARD BURTON (6)

My Cousin Rachel (best supporting actor), 1952; *The Robe*, 1953; *Becket*, 1964; *The Spy Who Came in from the Cold*, 1965; *Who's Afraid of Virginia Woolf?* 1966; *Anne of the Thousand Days*, 1969.

7. DEBORAH KERR (6)

Edward, My Son, 1949; *From Here to Eternity*, 1953; *The King and I*, 1956; *Heaven Knows, Mr. Allison*, 1957; *Separate Tables*, 1958; *The Sundowners*, 1960.

7. THELMA RITTER (6—all best supporting actress nominations)

All About Eve, 1950; *The Mating Season*, 1951; *With a Song in My Heart*, 1952; *Pickup on South Street*, 1953; *Pillow Talk*, 1959; *Birdman of Alcatraz*, 1962.

—M.G.R.

OWEN LEE'S
5 LISTS OF MOVIE FAVORITES

Father Owen Lee, a native of Detroit, received his Ph.D. from the University of British Columbia and is currently teaching Latin and Greek at Loyola University in Chicago, Ill. Noted as a linguist, his interests range widely. He is a respected lecturer and writer on opera, and he is a devoted movie fan whose enthusiasm stems from a high-school job as a theater usher. The choices in the categories listed below reflect his personal favorites throughout movie history, from 1915 to 1972.

5 BEST PERFORMANCES BY AN ACTOR

1. Emil Jannings (*Variety*)
2. Charles Chaplin (*The Gold Rush*)
3. Laurence Olivier (*Henry V*)
4. Toshiro Mifune (*Rashomon*)
5. Marlon Brando (*On the Waterfront*)

5 BEST PERFORMANCES BY AN ACTRESS

1. Marie Falconetti (*The Passion of Joan of Arc*)
2. Greta Garbo (*Camille*)
3. Anna Magnani (*Open City*)
4. Giulietta Masina (*La Strada*)
5. Katharine Hepburn (*Summertime*)

5 BEST SUPPORTING ACTORS

1. Charpin (*The Pagnol Trilogy*)
2. Michel Simon (*L'Atalante*)
3. Pierre Brasseur (*Les Enfants du Paradis*)
4. Walter Huston (*The Treasure of the Sierra Madre*)
5. George C. Scott (*The Hustler*)

5 BEST SUPPORTING ACTRESSES

1. Mae Marsh (*The Birth of a Nation*)
2. Marie Dressler (*Anna Christie*)
3. Jane Darwell (*The Grapes of Wrath*)
4. Agnes Moorehead (*The Magnificent Ambersons*)
5. Karuna Banerji (*The Apu Trilogy*)

5 BEST SONGS WRITTEN FOR FILM MUSICALS

1. "The Way You Look Tonight" (*Swing Time*), Jerome Kern and Dorothy Fields
2. "In the Still of the Night" (*Rosalie*), Cole Porter
3. "Love Walked In" (*The Goldwyn Follies*), George and Ira Gershwin

4. "Over the Rainbow" (*The Wizard of Oz*), Harold Arlen and E. H. Harburg
5. "It Might as Well Be Spring" (*State Fair*), Richard Rodgers and Oscar Hammerstein II

SOURCE: Owen Lee, *Top Ten: A Personal Approach to the Movies* (New York: Vantage, 1973).

ARTHUR SCHLESINGER, JR.'S
10 BEST POLITICAL MOVIES
OF ALL TIME

Author, historian, and educator, Arthur Schlesinger, Jr., served as special assistant to Presidents Kennedy and Lyndon B. Johnson. His book *A Thousand Days: John F. Kennedy in the White House* won the 1965 Pulitzer prize for biography. He has reviewed films for *Show* and *Vogue*.

1. *Le Chagrin et la Pitié* (The Sorrow and the Pity)
2. *La Guerre Est Finie* (The War Is Over)
3. *The Great Dictator*
4. *Z*
5. *Nashville*
6. *The Conformist*
7. *The Informer*
8. *All the King's Men*
9. *The Great McGinty*
10. *All the President's Men*

—Exclusive for *The Book of Lists*

ORSON WELLES'S
12 BEST MOVIES OF ALL TIME
(and their directors)

1. *City Lights* (Charles Chaplin)
2. *Greed* (Erich Von Stroheim)
3. *Intolerance* (D. W. Griffith)
4. *Nanook of the North* (Robert Flaherty)
5. *Shoeshine* (Vittorio De Sica)
6. *The Battleship Potemkin* (Sergei Eisenstein)
7. *The Baker's Wife* (Marcel Pagnol)
8. *Grand Illusion* (Jean Renoir)
9. *Stagecoach* (John Ford)
10. *Ninotchka* (Ernst Lubitsch)

11. *The Best Years of Our Lives* (William Wyler)
12. *The Bicycle Thief* (Vittorio De Sica)

Source: 1952 Brussels Film Festival Poll.

Charlie Chaplin in *City Lights*.

LUIS BUÑUEL'S
9 BEST MOVIES OF ALL TIME

(and their directors)

1. *Underworld* (Josef von Sternberg)
2. *The Gold Rush* (Charles Chaplin)
3. *The Bicycle Thief* (Vittorio De Sica)
4. *The Battleship Potemkin* (Sergei Eisenstein)
5. *A Portrait of Jennie* (William Dieterle)
6. *Cavalcade* (Frank Lloyd)

7. *White Shadows in the South Seas* (Robert Flaherty and W. S. Van Dyke)
8. *L'Âge d'Or* (Luis Buñuel)
9. *I Am a Fugitive from a Chain Gang* (Mervyn Le Roy)

SOURCE: 1952 Brussels Film Festival Poll.

ARTHUR KNIGHT'S
10 BEST MOVIES OF ALL TIME

Well-known author and educator in the field of filmmaking, Arthur Knight was on the faculty of Columbia University and is now a professor of cinema at the University of Southern California. His books on film include *The Liveliest Art* and *History of Sex in the Movies*.

1. *À Nous la Liberté*
2. *Apu Trilogy*
3. *Bicycle Thief*
4. *Citizen Kane*
5. *Dr. Strangelove*
6. *Modern Times*
7. *The Passion of Joan of Arc*
8. *The Battleship Potemkin*
9. *Singin' in the Rain*
10. *Sullivan's Travels*

—Exclusive for *The Book of Lists*

SIGHT AND SOUND
MAGAZINE'S 1952 POLL:
10-PLUS BEST MOVIES
OF ALL TIME

(and their directors)

1. *The Bicycle Thief* (Vittorio De Sica), 25 votes
2. *City Lights* (Charles Chaplin), 19
2. *The Gold Rush* (Charles Chaplin), 19
4. *The Battleship Potemkin* (Sergei Eisenstein), 16
5. *Intolerance* (D. W. Griffith), 12
5. *Louisiana Story* (Robert Flaherty), 12
7. *Greed* (Erich Von Stroheim), 11
7. *Le Jour se Lève* (Marcel Carné), 11
7. *The Passion of Joan of Arc* (Carl Dreyer), 11
10. *Brief Encounter* (David Lean), 10
10. *Le Million* (René Clair), 10
10. *The Rules of the Game* (Jean Renoir), 10

SIGHT AND SOUND
MAGAZINE'S 1962 POLL

1. *Citizen Kane* (Orson Welles), 22 votes
2. *L'Avventura* (Michelangelo Antonioni), 20
3. *The Rules of the Game* (Jean Renoir), 19
4. *Greed* (Erich Von Stroheim), 17
4. *Ugetsu* (Kenji Mizoguchi), 17
6. *The Bicycle Thief* (Vittorio De Sica), 16
6. *The Battleship Potemkin* (Sergei Eisenstein), 16
6. *Ivan the Terrible* (Sergei Eisenstein), 16
9. *La Terra Trema* (Luchino Visconti), 14
10. *L'Atalante* (Jean Vigo), 13

SIGHT AND SOUND
MAGAZINE'S 1972 POLL

1. *Citizen Kane* (Orson Welles), 32 votes
2. *The Rules of the Game* (Jean Renoir), 28
3. *The Battleship Potemkin* (Sergei Eisenstein), 16
4. *8½* (Federico Fellini), 15
5. *L'Avventura* (Michelangelo Antonioni), 12
5. *Persona* (Ingmar Bergman), 12
7. *The Passion of Joan of Arc* (Carl Dreyer), 11
8. *The General* (Buster Keaton), 10
8. *The Magnificent Ambersons* (Orson Welles), 10
10. *Ugetsu* (Kenji Mizoguchi), 9
10. *Wild Strawberries* (Ingmar Bergman), 9

WILLIAM WYLER'S
10 GREATEST FILMS OF ALL TIME

Director William Wyler's film career has spanned over half a century. He began his career with low-budgeted two-reel westerns and graduated into million-dollar epics. He has been nominated for a dozen Motion Picture Academy Awards. His Oscar-winning films are *Mrs. Miniver, The Best Years of Our Lives,* and *Ben Hur.* Other highly acclaimed films by this outstanding director include *The Little Foxes, The Children's Hour,* and *Funny Girl.*

1. *The Cabinet of Dr. Caligari*
2. *The Battleship Potemkin*
3. *All Quiet on the Western Front*
4. Several Charlie Chaplin films
5. *The Bridge on the River Kwai*
6. Marcel Pagnol's *Fanny* (not the musical)
7. *La Dolce Vita*
8. *The Treasure of the Sierra Madre*
9. *Dr. Strangelove*
10. and (with apologies) *The Best Years of Our Lives*

—Exclusive for *The Book of Lists*

JACK LEMMON'S 10 "SECOND-GREATEST" FILMS OF ALL TIME

Actor and comedian Jack Lemmon has starred in such movie greats as *The Odd Couple, Days of Wine and Roses,* and *The Prisoner of Second Avenue.* He has twice been awarded the Motion Picture Academy Oscar—first as best supporting actor in *Mister Roberts,* and more recently as best actor in *Save the Tiger.* He made his directing debut in 1971 with *Kotch.*

1. *Rashomon*
2. *Safety Last*
3. *A Taste of Honey*
4. *Some Like It Hot*
5. *Closely Watched Trains*
6. *The Gold Rush*
7. *The Best Years of Our Lives*
8. *No Love for Johnny*
9. *One Flew over the Cuckoo's Nest*
10. *Lawrence of Arabia*

Jack Lemmon explains: "Can't think of the top 10."

—Exclusive for *The Book of Lists*

THE 10 WORST FILMS OF ALL TIME

Harry Medved and Randy Dreyfuss, authors of *The 50 Worst Films of All Time,* have selected what they feel are the 10 *very* worst films for *The Book of Lists.* Their choices are presented in alphabetical order.

1. *CHE!* (1969)

A cardboard, pseudo-historical drama with Omar Sharif as Che Guevara and Jack Palance as Fidel Castro. Poor Sharif is forced to deliver such lines as "The peasant is like a wild flower in the forest, and the revolutionary like a bee. Neither can survive or propagate without the other." As critic Steven Scheuer has aptly summarized this film, "Everyone connected with it deserves censure."

2. *THE CONQUEROR* (1956)

A Howard Hughes production starring John Wayne as Genghis Khan. The film is an old-fashioned horse opera with a Mongolian setting. In one of the film's most memorable moments, Genghis Wayne lusts after the Princess Bortai, portrayed by Susan Hayward, and pants, "I feel this Tartar woman is for me, and my blood says, take her!"

Genghis Khan (John Wayne) and Princess Bortai
(Susan Hayward) in Howard Hughes's $6 million epic,
The Conqueror, produced and directed by Dick Powell.

3. *THE HORROR OF PARTY BEACH* (1964)

A ghastly monster musical with a grade Z cast, it manages to combine the worst elements of low-grade science fiction fare with the most irritating conventions of the beach party movies. As cosmic relief it features Eulabelle Moore, playing an Aunt Jemima-style stereotyped black maid. As the "atomic monsters" ravage the town, this good lady insists, "It's the voodoo, I tells ya!"

4. *LOST HORIZON* (1973)

A Ross Hunter remake of the 1937 film classic, based on the novel about Shangri-La by James Hilton. It features such stars as Peter Finch, Sally Kellerman, George Kennedy, Charles Boyer, Sir John Gielgud, and Liv Ullmann in her most embarrassing role. Today this version of *Lost Horizon* is known in the motion-picture industry as "Lost Investment." The backers dropped nearly half of their $6 million ante.

5. *MYRA BRECKINRIDGE* (1970)

The notorious X-rated high-camp disaster features Raquel Welch as the result of a sex-change operation. There is something in this film to offend absolutely everyone. Critic Leonard Maltin called *Myra Breckinridge* "as bad as any movie ever made."

6. *ROBOT MONSTER* (1953)

The ultimate in sci-fi insanity, this one features robot invaders in gorilla suits and diving helmets. The producers of the film were not even sure where the strange creatures came from, as the movie appeared under the alternate titles of *Monsters from the Moon* and *Monster from Mars*. The reaction to this film was so negative that young director Phil Tucker attempted suicide shortly after its release.

7. *SANTA CLAUS CONQUERS THE MARTIANS* (1964)

The children of Mars don't know how to have fun, so the Martians kidnap Santa Claus from the north pole and take him to the red planet. Their evil plot is foiled with the help of two earth children, Billy and Betty, and a lovable Martian named Dropo.

8. *SOLOMON AND SHEBA* (1959)

Would you believe Yul Brynner as King Solomon and Gina Lollobrigida as the queen of Sheba? That's only the beginning of the absurdity in this biblical spectacle that was advertised with the catchy line: "Behold! The love story of the ages!" In the climax of the film, Solomon's badly outnumbered Israelites destroy an entire Egyptian army by polishing their shields and blinding the enemy with reflected sunlight.

9. *THE TERROR OF TINY TOWN* (1938)

This was the first (and last) film in Hollywood history with an all-midget cast. What's more, the little people were given the chance to display their talents in a musical western—galloping over the sagebrush aboard a herd of Shetland ponies.

10. *THAT HAGEN GIRL* (1947)

A cockamamy soap opera about the devastating effect of small-town gossip on 19-year-old Mary Hagen (Shirley Temple). The local biddies whisper that poor Shirl is actually the illegitimate daughter of local lawyer Tom Bates—who is played by none other than Ronald Reagan. After they find out that they are not related, Shirley and Ron decide to get married. Reagan has said several times that this is one part he wishes he had never touched.

9 SHORTEST-RUNNING
NATIONAL TV SERIES

1. *TURN ON* (ABC)
   Feb. 5, 1969 (1 day)

   A fast-paced comedy with computerized music and stop-action photography. The program was canceled immediately when it was discovered that it contained too many double entendres and hidden meanings. In his excellent compendium *The Complete Encyclopedia of Television Programs 1947–1976*, Vincent Terrace cites the following example: "A beautiful woman is about to be executed by a firing squad. The squad leader, instead of saying the usual 'Do you have a last request?' remarks, 'I know this may seem a little unusual, miss, but in this case the firing squad has one last request.'"

2. *PENTHOUSE SONATA* (ABC)
   June 19–26, 1949 (8 days)

   Classical music hosted by June Browne and performed by the Fine Arts Quartet.

2. *SUMMER IN THE CITY* (CBS)
   Aug. 18–25, 1951 (8 days)

   A variety show that starred Bob Sweeny, Hal March, and Nancy Kelly.

2. *THE PROJECTION ROOM* (ABC)
   Mar. 19–26, 1952 (8 days)

   Mystery presentations hosted by Ruth Gilbert.

2. *MEET YOUR MATCH* (NBC)
   Aug. 25–Sept. 1, 1952 (8 days)

   A question-and-answer game show with audience participation, hosted by Jan Murray.

2. *ADAMS OF EAGLE LAKE* (ABC)
   Aug. 23–30, 1975 (8 days)

   A crime drama that took place in a small, peaceful resort town. Starred Andy Griffith as Sheriff Sam Adams and Abby Dalton as his assistant.

7. *BON VOYAGE* (*TREASURE QUEST*) (ABC)
   Apr. 24–May 8, 1949 (15 days)

   Two contestants tried to identify geographical locations by using photographic stills and rhyming clues.

7. *ONE HUNDRED GRAND* (ABC)
   Sept. 15–29, 1963 (15 days)

A quiz show in which contestants were grilled by professional authorities in a quest for $100,000.

9. *JACK CARTER AND COMPANY* (ABC)
Apr. 5–21, 1949 (17 days)

Music and comedy program hosted by Jack Carter.

—D.W.

SOURCE: Vincent Terrace, *The Complete Encyclopedia of Television Programs 1947–1976* (Cranbury, N.J.: A. S. Barnes, 1976).

20 LONGEST-RUNNING NATIONAL TV SERIES

(as of May, 1977)

1. *MEET THE PRESS* (NBC)
Nov. 20, 1947–present (29 years 6 months)

Interviews with contemporary political and social figures.

Meet the Press panelists prepare to interrogate Sen. Joseph McCarthy in 1951.

2. *SEARCH FOR TOMORROW* (CBS)
Sept. 3, 1951–present (25 years 8 months)

The dramatic story of Joanne Barron Vincente of the town of Henderson.

3. *LOVE OF LIFE* (CBS)
Sept. 9, 1951–present (25 years 8 months)

Dramatic incidents in the lives of Vanessa and Bruce Sterling and others.

4. *THE TODAY SHOW* (NBC)
   Jan. 14, 1952–present (25 years 4 months)

   Two hours of early morning news and entertainment. Hosts have included Dave Garroway for nine years and Hugh Downs for nine years.

5. *THE GUIDING LIGHT* (CBS)
   June 30, 1952–present (24 years 11 months)

   The dramatic story of the Bauer family.

6. *THE ED SULLIVAN SHOW (TOAST OF THE TOWN)* (CBS)
   June 20, 1948–June 6, 1971 (22 years 11½ months)

   Variety show that spotlighted popular entertainment acts. The first show featured Dean Martin and Jerry Lewis, and Richard Rodgers and Oscar Hammerstein II. Closing-show performers included Sid Caesar, Carol Channing, and Gladys Knight and the Pips.

7. *THE TONIGHT SHOW* (NBC)
   Sept. 27, 1954–present (22 years 8 months)

   Late night talk and entertainment, hosted since October 1, 1962, by Johnny Carson—except when he is on vacation.

8. *WALT DISNEY'S WONDERFUL WORLD OF COLOR* (NBC)
   Oct. 27, 1954 (on ABC under various titles through Sept. 10, 1961)–present (22 years 7 months)

   Entertainment and education for children and young people.

9. *CAPTAIN KANGAROO* (CBS)
   Oct. 3, 1955–present (21 years 7 months)

   The adult world explained to children in an entertaining manner.

10. *AS THE WORLD TURNS* (CBS)
    Apr. 2, 1956–present (21 years 1 month)

    Dramatic incidents in the lives of the Hughes and Lowell families of Oakdale.

10. *EDGE OF NIGHT* (CBS)
    Apr. 2, 1956–present (21 years 1 month)

    Crime, drama, justice, and emotional crises in Monticello.

12. *TED MACK AND THE ORIGINAL AMATEUR HOUR*
    (CBS, NBC, and ABC)
    Oct. 4, 1949–Sept. 11, 1954 (NBC); Oct. 30, 1955–June 23, 1957 (ABC); Sept., 1957–Oct. 4, 1958 (NBC); Oct., 1958–Sept., 1971 (CBS) (20 years 7 months)

    Variety show that featured performances by undiscovered talent.

13. *THE SECRET STORM* (CBS)
    Feb. 1, 1954–Feb. 15, 1974 (20 years ½ month)

    Incidents in the lives of the Ames family of Woodridge.

14. *GUNSMOKE* (CBS)
    Sept. 10, 1955–Sept. 1, 1975 (19 years 11¾ months)

    The lives of Marshal Dillon, Kitty, Doc, and others in the 1880s in Dodge City, Kans.

15. *AMERICAN BANDSTAND* (ABC)
    Oct. 7, 1957–present (19 years 7 months)

    Music and entertainment for teenagers, hosted by Dick Clark, who began the show locally in Philadelphia in 1952.

16. *THE RED SKELTON SHOW* (CBS and NBC)
    Sept. 22, 1953–June, 1970 (CBS); Sept. 14, 1970–Aug. 29, 1971 (NBC) (17 years 8 months)

    Comedy, music, and dancing hosted by and starring Red Skelton.

17. *WHAT'S MY LINE?* (CBS)
    Feb. 2, 1950–Sept. 3, 1967 (17 years 7 months)

    A celebrity panel tried to guess the occupations of three guests and the identity of a mystery guest. Hosted by John Daly.

18. *ART LINKLETTER HOUSE PARTY*
    (THE LINKLETTER SHOW) (CBS)
    Sept. 1, 1952–Sept. 5, 1969 (17 years)

    Daytime variety show that featured audience participation and interviews with children.

18. *LASSIE* (CBS)
    Sept., 1954–Sept., 1971 (17 years)

    The story of a dog and her masters—first Jeff, then Timmy, then Corey.

20. *THE LAWRENCE WELK SHOW* (ABC)
    July 2, 1955–Sept. 3, 1971 (16 years 2 months)

    Music, singing, dancing, and champagne. Originally *The Dodge Dancing Party*.

—D.W.

SOURCE: Vincent Terrace, *The Complete Encyclopedia of Television Programs 1947–1976* (Cranbury, N.J.: A. S. Barnes, 1976).

13 HIGHEST-RATED EPISODES OF THE MOST POPULAR U.S. TV SERIES SINCE 1960

(in chronological order)

1. *WAGON TRAIN* (Jan. 20, 1960)

A widow, played by Jean Hagen, joins the wagon train. She is beautiful, but filled with bitterness. She distrusts all men and has raised her young son to look down on those who are weak. A fellow passenger seeks to discover the cause of her anger. Average audience: 43.7.

2. *GUNSMOKE* (Feb. 13, 1960).

Two cattle drives are racing toward Dodge, both trying to be the first to reach the town that season. Their paths are blocked by a rain-widened river. The two trail bosses meet there, and find a ragged old cow which could guide one of the herds across. The bosses, however, can't agree which herd it will be. Average audience: 43.9.

3. *THE BEVERLY HILLBILLIES* (Jan. 8, 1964)

The Clampetts decide to have their dinner prepared for them. They call the Beverly Caterers, mistakenly believing that "Beverly" is a friendly widow who will happily prepare the "vittles" they want. Average audience: 44.0.

The Clampett family at home in Beverly Hills, Calif.

214

4. *BONANZA* (Mar. 8, 1964)

Working as an acting deputy, Hoss is sent to a town to pick up a prisoner. Unfortunately, he travels to the wrong town and finds himself charged with bank robbery. Average audience: 41.6.

5. *GOMER PYLE, USMC* (Jan. 29, 1965)

Sergeant Carter is assigned to guard duty and needs someone to substitute for him on a date. Naturally, he picks Gomer, thinking that he'll be the one man who won't take advantage of the situation. Average audience: 35.4.

6. *THE RED SKELTON SHOW* (Feb. 1, 1966)

George Gobel and the British rock group The Hollies were the guests. In the featured skit, Red, as Sheriff Deadeye, hopes to enhance the value of one of his paintings by going to Paris to get the noted artist Toulouse-Lautrec—played by Gobel—to sign it. Average audience: 33.3.

7. *THE LUCY SHOW* (Jan. 15, 1968)

Lucy tries to pick up extra money by working as a waitress in a drive-in restaurant. Not surprisingly, chaos results, and things aren't improved when she attempts to help a young motorcyclist suspected of being a car thief. Average audience: 34.3.

8. *THE ANDY GRIFFITH SHOW* (Jan. 29, 1968)

Former costar Don Knotts returned to the show for a guest appearance. He comes to Mayberry to pick a location for an East-West summit meeting. Unfortunately, he performs with the same efficiency he brought to his old job as deputy sheriff, and Andy has to rescue him. Average audience: 33.4.

9. *ROWAN AND MARTIN'S LAUGH-IN* (Mar. 24, 1969)

Tony Curtis was the guest star, appearing in various skits as Hamlet, an old-time entertainer, and the chairman of a Senate rat control hearing. A new feature was introduced: cast members reading, and responding to, the public's mail. Mod, Mod World conducted a tour of beautiful downtown Burbank, Calif. Average audience: 35.5.

10. *MARCUS WELBY, M.D.* (Jan. 5, 1971)

A young and vital rancher, played by Glen Corbett, is emotionally devastated when he experiences kidney failure. He feels that life on a dialysis machine will mean the end of both his work and his marriage. Average audience: 37.7.

11. *ALL IN THE FAMILY* (Jan. 8, 1972)

This episode dealt with a previously taboo subject. Edith, Archie's wife, goes through menopause with some interesting personality changes. Average audience: 40.7.

12. *THE WALTONS* (Feb. 7, 1974)

An angry young orphan, played by Tiger Williams, influences the lives of a couple who have just learned they're not able to have children. Average audience: 34.5.

13. *SANFORD AND SON* (Dec. 27, 1974)

One of the episodes in which Redd Foxx did not appear because of a contract dispute. Grady, played by Whitman Mayo, is the star of this episode. He allows a former convict friend of Lamont's to stay at the house if he'll agree to some conditions. He is to be watched every second and to empty his pockets on demand. Average audience: 34.3.

—E.F.

10 OUTRAGEOUS MOMENTS OF U.S. TV CENSORSHIP

1. *THE ED SULLIVAN SHOW* (1956)

When Elvis Presley guested, he was shown only from the waist up. CBS censored the singer's hips so his gyrations wouldn't offend viewers.

2. *I DREAM OF JEANNIE* (1965–1970)

During the entire run of the popular series, NBC censors never permitted Barbara Eden to display her navel.

3. *THE SMOTHERS BROTHERS COMEDY HOUR* (1967)

Pete Seeger, blacklisted from network TV for 17 years because of his political beliefs, finally appeared on the CBS show. But one of his songs, "Waist Deep in the Big Muddy," was deleted from the show because CBS construed it as an insult to President Lyndon B. Johnson. The song is about a soldier who drowned in 1942 when his commanding officer forced him to walk in water without knowing how deep it was.

4. *WIDE WORLD OF SPORTS* (1969)

In a last-minute decision, ABC cut out a bikini contest that had been scheduled. When questioned about the reason for this decision, network executives tersely said that the film was of "poor quality."

5. *THE MERV GRIFFIN SHOW* (1969)

Carol Burnett appeared on Christmas Day, and asked viewers to write letters appealing for peace to Mrs. Martin Luther King, Jr. Her request was cut by CBS censors.

6. *THE TONIGHT SHOW* (1969)

Dick Cavett, substituting for Johnny Carson as host, was blipped when he kiddingly mentioned a rumor that Johnny was out with "Portnoy's complaint" instead of the flu. On the same show, the word "diarrhea" was deleted by NBC censors.

7. *STICKS AND BONES* (1973)

Ninety-four of CBS's 186 affiliate stations refused to telecast the Tony award-winning drama when it was aired on August 17. The play, written by David Rabe and directed by Joseph Papp, was about a blind, embittered Vietnam veteran's homecoming. The defection of the affiliates, which was the largest in the history of network TV, made it virtually impossible for CBS to sell commercial spots for the telecast. Thus, the 100-minute program was telecast in many cities that aired it without advertisements. The reason given by the affiliates for the rebellion: The play might offend relatives of POWs in N. Vietnam.

8. *FAY* (1975)

NBC censors deleted the words "stretch marks" from an episode of the short-lived comedy series, starring Lee Grant. The network deemed the words inappropriate for the family hour.

9. *WIDE WORLD OF ENTERTAINMENT* (1975)

When episodes of *Monty Python's Flying Circus* were telecast on this program, ABC blipped two words from a sketch showing two men taking a bath. The voice-over of the sketch originally said, "They washed their arms, their legs, and then they washed their naughty bits." The last two words were deleted even though the show aired at 11:30 P.M.

10. *SATURDAY NIGHT LIVE* (1975)

Saturday Night Live wasn't live at all on its December 13 airing. Richard Pryor hosted the show that night, and fearing that he might speak some obscene words, NBC placed the show on a five-second electronic delay. Two deletions were made during Pryor's monologue. NBC described the deleted words as unacceptable TV vocabulary.

—R.T.

THE 15 MOST BORING CLASSICS

The title page of *Pilgrim's Progress*, John Bunyan's religious allegory of man's passage through life to heaven or hell.

Based on a 1950 survey of readers taken by the Columbia University Press bulletin, *The Pleasures of Publishing.*

1. *Pilgrim's Progress* (1678) by John Bunyan
2. *Moby Dick* (1851) by Herman Melville
3. *Paradise Lost* (1667) by John Milton
4. *Faerie Queene* (1590) by Edmund Spenser
5. *Life of Samuel Johnson* (1791) by James Boswell
6. *Pamela* (1740) by Samuel Richardson
7. *Silas Marner* (1861) by George Eliot
8. *Ivanhoe* (1819) by Sir Walter Scott
9. *Don Quixote* (1605; 1615) by Miguel de Cervantes
10. *Faust* (1808; 1832) by Johann Wolfgang von Goethe
11. *War and Peace* (1866) by Leo Tolstoy
12. *Remembrance of Things Past* (1913–1928) by Marcel Proust
13. *Das Kapital* (1867; 1885; 1895) by Karl Marx
14. *Vanity Fair* (1847–1848) by William Makepeace Thackeray
15. *The Mill on the Floss* (1860) by George Eliot

In this list of tedious tomes, the "winner" was written by John Bunyan, an English tinker-preacher, while he languished in jail for defying a royal edict. The least soporific of the 15 was written by George Eliot, an early feminist who nevertheless hid her authorship behind a masculine pen name. She is also the only writer to make the list twice.

—THE EDS.

THE CATHOLIC INDEX OF FORBIDDEN BOOKS: 37 CENSORED WRITERS

The oldest and most powerful censorship force in world history is the Vatican City's *Index Librorum Prohibitorum.* In 1557, a century after the invention of movable type made mass printings of books possible, the Catholic Church drew up its first list of censored authors and books. At one time the *Index,* a paperback book, contained 550 pages which listed 5,000 banned books. In 1966 the Sacred Congregation for the Doctrine of the Faith ceased publication of the *Index* but claimed that it still served as a "moral guide insofar as it reminds the conscience of the faithful they must avoid writings which can be dangerous to faith and morals." Today, the Church may issue an "Admonitum," a warning to the faithful, that a book might be dangerous. It is only a moral guide, however, without the force of ecclesiastical law. The following have been condemned in the *Index* for being immoral or heretical or both.

12 FAMOUS NOVELISTS IN THE *INDEX*

	Country	Year Banned	Work Banned
1. Samuel Richardson	England	1744	*Pamela*
2. Laurence Sterne	England	1819	*A Sentimental Journey Through France and Italy*
3. Stendhal	France	1828	All his love stories
4. Victor Hugo	France	1834–1869	*Les Misérables; Notre Dame de Paris*
5. George Sand	France	1840	All her love stories
6. Honoré de Balzac	France	1841–1864	All his love stories
7. Eugène Sue	France	1852	All his love stories
8. Alexandre Dumas père	France	1863	All his love stories
9. Alexandre Dumas fils	France	1863	All his love stories
10. Gustave Flaubert	France	1864	*Madame Bovary; Salammbô*
11. Gabriele D'Annunzio	Italy	1911	All his love stories
12. Alberto Moravia	Italy	1952	*The Woman of Rome*

The only English-language novels in the entire *Index* are Samuel Richardson's *Pamela* and Lawrence Sterne's *A Sentimental Journey*. No American novelist is in the *Index*.

25 FAMOUS NONFICTION WRITERS IN THE *INDEX*

	Country	Year Banned	Work Banned
13. Thomas Hobbes	England	1649–1703	All works
14. René Descartes	France	1663	All philosophical works
15. Francis Bacon	England	1668	*The Arrangement and General Survey of Knowledge*
16. Michel de Montaigne	France	1676	*Les Essais*
17. Benedict Spinoza	Netherlands	1690	All posthumous works
18. John Milton	England	1694	*The State Papers*

19.	Joseph Addison	England	1729	*Remarks on Several Parts of Italy*
20.	Richard Steele	England	Unknown	*An Account of the State of the Roman Catholic Religion*
21.	John Locke	England	1734–1737	*An Essay Concerning Human Understanding, etc.*
22.	Emanuel Swedenborg	Sweden	1738	*The Principia*
23.	Daniel Defoe	England	1743	*History of the Devil*
24.	David Hume	Scotland	1761–1827	*All works*
25.	Jean-Jacques Rousseau	France	1762–1806	*The Social Contract, Émile*
26.	Edward Gibbon	England	1783	*Decline and Fall of the Roman Empire*
27.	Blaise Pascal	France	1789	*The Provincial Letters*
28.	Oliver Goldsmith	England	1823	*An Abridged History of England*
29.	Immanuel Kant	Germany	1827	*Critique of Pure Reason*
30.	Giovanni Giacomo Casanova	France	1834	*Memoirs*
31.	John Stuart Mill	England	1856	*Principles of Political Economy*
32.	Ernest Renan	France	1889–1892	*Life of Jesus, etc.*
33.	Émile Zola	France	1894–1898	*All works*
34.	Andrew Lang	England	1896	*Myths, Ritual, and Religion*
35.	Henri Bergson	France	1914	*Creative Evolution*
36.	Benedetto Croce	Italy	1934	*Philosophy/history*
37.	Jean-Paul Sartre	France	1948	*All works*

Not to be found in the *Index* are: Aristophanes, Juvenal, Geoffrey Chaucer, François Rabelais, Marquis de Sade, Leopold von Sacher-Masoch, Henry Miller, John Cleland, James Joyce, and D. H. Lawrence. This is because, in most cases, it took more than pornographic or immoral writing to be condemned. It also took blasphemy, anticlericalism, heresy. Case in point: Boccaccio and *The Decameron* were placed on the *Index* for obscenity as well as an attack on the clergy. When Boccaccio reissued the book changing all the sinning monks and nuns to gentlemen and ladies, the Council of Trent forgave him and removed his name and the book from the *Index*. Galileo was also in the *Index*, but later removed.

The last American writer to be listed in the *Index* was William L. Sullivan, in 1912, for an antireligious nonfiction work entitled *Letter to His Holiness, Pope Pius X.*

—I.W.

12 ALL-TIME BEST-SELLING OR -DISTRIBUTED BOOKS

		Copies
1.	The Bible (1816–1975)*	2,458,000,000
2.	*Quotations from the Works of Mao Tse-tung*	800,000,000
3.	*American Spelling Book,* by Noah Webster	50,000,000–100,000,000
4.	*The Truth That Leads to Eternal Life* (Jehovah's Witnesses)	74,000,000
5.	*A Message to Garcia,* by Elbert Hubbard	50,000,000
6.	*The World Almanac* (1868–)	36,000,000
7.	*In His Steps,* by C. M. Sheldon	28,500,000
7.	*Guinness Book of World Records* (1955–)	28,500,000
9.	*The Common Sense Book of Baby and Child Care,* by Dr. Benjamin Spock	24,000,000
10.	*Valley of the Dolls,* by Jacqueline Susann (1966)	19,300,000
11.	*American Red Cross First Aid Book*	16,000,000
12.	*Infant Care* (U.S. government, 1914)	15,000,000

* This is probably the most complete figure for sales or distribution of the Bible or portions of the Bible ever assembled, but it is still far from complete. Included are figures from the United Bible Societies worldwide. Unavailable are figures from commercial Bible publishers before 1973. Most likely the actual total figure for Bible sales and distribution in all history would be in the area of 3 billion copies.

ROBERT B. DOWNS'S 16 BOOKS THAT CHANGED THE WORLD

1. *THE PRINCE* (1517) by NICCOLÒ MACHIAVELLI

In its 26 chapters, this political treatise studies power—how to get it and how to keep it. Rulers of the past are used as examples, and Cesare Borgia is cited as a model prince. A realist, Machiavelli tells his reader that it is more important to retain power than to be loved, that virtue is commendable but it may not be practical. In sum, the end justifies the means.

2. *DE REVOLUTIONIBUS ORBIUM COELESTIUM* (1530, 1543) by NICOLAUS COPERNICUS

The Polish astronomer laid the groundwork for modern astronomy when he upset the Ptolemaic teachings. *On the Revolution of Heavenly Bodies*—finished in 1530, but not published until 1543—theorized that the earth was *not* the center of the universe. In fact, the earth and all the other planets revolved around the sun in separate orbits, meanwhile rotating on their axes, said Copernicus. Theologic opposition to this theory was immediate and violent since man could then no longer be viewed as the ultimate creation.

3. *DE MOTU CORDIS* (1628) by WILLIAM HARVEY

Published in 1628, this treatise explained a discovery that Harvey had made in 1616: that the blood in animals circulates. This was a major step forward in the study of physiology and anatomy.

4. *PRINCIPIA* (1687) by SIR ISAAC NEWTON

Newton divided his work into three parts: "The Motion of Bodies," "The Motion of Bodies in Resisting Media," and "The System of the World." He advocated reasoning by use of physical events, and he also proposed a new law of gravitation. Hence the book marked the start of the age of scientific exploration and experimentation.

5. *COMMON SENSE* (1776) by THOMAS PAINE

This outspoken pamphlet—bought by over 100,000 colonists in the first few months following its publication—advocated separation from England and helped set the scene for the Declaration of Independence. Tried in absentia for treason by the English, made an honorary citizen by the republican government of France, British-born Paine died in the newly formed U.S. in poverty and obscurity.

6. *WEALTH OF NATIONS* (1776) by ADAM SMITH

In this important work on economics, Smith proposed the laissez-faire system, one embracing a totally free economy, for modern governments.

7. *ESSAY ON THE PRINCIPLE OF POPULATION* (1798) by THOMAS ROBERT MALTHUS

The same year that he became a curate of the Church of England, Malthus put forth his now famous doctrine that population increases in a geometric ratio while food supplies, etc., increase arithmetically. Also he suggested that the evils of society—crime, pestilence, war—are needed to hold down the increase in population. In 1803, as an afterthought, Malthus proposed moral restraint as an additional check for population growth.

8. *CIVIL DISOBEDIENCE* (1849) by HENRY DAVID THOREAU

This essay is the source of the familiar statement: "That government is best which governs least." Thoreau also put being true to oneself above being loyal to a man-made government. Among his famous followers was Mohandas K. Gandhi, whose version of civil disobedience became known as "passive resistance" and was re-imported into the U.S. as "sit-ins."

International revolutionary Thomas Paine.

9. *UNCLE TOM'S CABIN* (1852) by HARRIET BEECHER STOWE

Subtitled *Life Among the Lowly,* the book is remembered today for the Yankee overseer Simon Legree, the death of Little Eva, and the flight of Eliza over the ice. Actually, the book was a fairly balanced treatment of the southern slave problem. Mrs. Stowe expressed admiration in it for the humane slaveholder, and her villain is a displaced northerner from Vermont. Although the book was *not* written by God—despite Mrs. Stowe's claim—it contributed substantially to the abolitionist movement.

10. *ORIGIN OF SPECIES* (1859) by CHARLES DARWIN

A revolutionary theory in its day, the theory of evolution is now accepted by most people. Darwin proposed that species evolve from earlier species, and that evolution is controlled or determined by natural selection. That is, the plant or animal that adapts through positive mutation to its surroundings is the one most likely to survive and reproduce its kind.

11. *DAS KAPITAL* (1867–1895) by KARL MARX

Written in London, Volume I of *Das Kapital* was Marx's major work. (Volumes II and III were completed by Friedrich Engels from Marx's notes.) A study of capitalistic society, the book went on to espouse dialectical materialism. Marx believed in class struggle as the basic force in shaping history, and that the world's increasing industrialization—controlled by the capitalists—would inevitably lead to overt revolution of the proletariat and a classless society.

12. *THE INFLUENCE OF SEA POWER UPON HISTORY* (1890) by ALFRED THAYER MAHAN

Written by an American naval officer/historian, this book sought to prove the importance of naval power in a nation's defenses. Mahan was a lecturer in naval tactics at Newport War College. His ideas were influential in shaping naval policy in the U.S., England, and Germany.

13. *THE INTERPRETATION OF DREAMS* (1900) by SIGMUND FREUD

An early report on Freud's findings, after his long study of the subconscious. Dream interpretation was one of the tools Freud used in analysis. A patient recounted his dreams and they were explored for their symbolic meanings. Freud thought that these dreams reflected repressed emotions, which in turn caused neuroses.

14. "THE GEOGRAPHICAL PIVOT OF HISTORY" (1904) by HALFORD J. MACKINDER

Mackinder, a geopolitician in later life, encouraged the revival of interest in geographical learning in Britain while he was still at Oxford. After establishing geography as an academic subject when he taught at the University of London, he became director of the London School of Economics. "The Geographical Pivot of History" was a 24-page paper later developed into a book, *Democratic Ideals and Reality* (1919), which viewed Eurasia as the "geographical pivot" and the "heartland" of history. The U.S. and Great Britain ignored this theory before W.W. II, but Germany used it to support Nazi geopolitics.

15. *RELATIVITY: THE SPECIAL AND GENERAL THEORIES* (1905, 1916) by ALBERT EINSTEIN

A German-Swiss-U.S. physicist, Einstein proposed his special theory of relativity in 1905, his general theory of relativity in 1916. While these complicated theories made possible the splitting of the atom and the atomic bomb, they did not win a Nobel prize for Einstein.

16. *MEIN KAMPF* (1925) by ADOLF HITLER

This autobiography was dictated to Rudolf Hess while Hitler and Hess were imprisoned following the Beer Hall Putsch in 1923. The unsuccessful uprising in Munich had sought to overthrow the Bavarian government. In addition to being an autobiography, *Mein Kampf* (My Struggle) outlined Hitler's plan to achieve political control of Germany.

—Annotated by E.K.

NORRIS McWHIRTER'S 12 BEST REFERENCE BOOKS IN THE WORLD

Identical twins Norris and Ross McWhirter are responsible for the internationally popular *Guinness Book of World Records*. When Ross called for funds that would help in the capture of those responsible for bombings in England, he was assassinated by terrorists in 1975. In preparing his list of great reference books, Norris was too modest to include two of the greatest reference books in the world—*Guinness Book of World Records* and *Guinness Book of Answers*. They should be included. They are superb.

1. *Encyclopaedia Britannica*
2. *Guide to Reference Books* (American Library Association)
3. *The World Almanac* (1868–)
4. *Yearbook of International Organizations*
5. *Oxford English Dictionary* (13 vols. and supplements)
6. *National Geographic Society Atlas*
7. *Ulrich's International Periodical Directory*
8. *World of Learning* (Europa, 2 vols.)
9. *U.N. Statistical Yearbook*
10. *1,000,000 de Décimales de Pi* (Guilloud et Bouyer)
11. *Dictionary of National Biography* (and supplements)
12. *Halsbury's Laws of England* (43 vols.)

—Exclusive for *The Book of Lists*

HENRY MILLER'S
10 GREATEST WRITERS
OF ALL TIME

One of the most controversial, innovative, realistic writers of modern times, Henry Miller spent the 1930s as an American expatriate in Paris. Two of his major books, *Tropic of Capricorn* and *Tropic of Cancer,* were banned for years in English-speaking countries, and published only after a landmark trial. Among Miller's other books are *The Colossus of Maroussi, Nexus, Plexus,* and *Book of Friends.* Miller lives in Pacific Palisades, Calif.

1. Lao-tzu
2. François Rabelais
3. Friedrich Nietzsche
4. Rabindranath Tagore
5. Walt Whitman
6. Marcel Proust
7. Élie Faure
8. Marie Corelli
9. Fëdor Dostoevski
10. Isaac Bashevis Singer

Élie Faure (1873–1937) was a French art historian who published a five-volume *History of Art* between 1909 and 1921. He had studied medicine, and brought a scientific approach to his examinations of art history. London-born Marie Corelli (1855–1924), whose real name was Mary Mackay, wrote 28 books, most of them lurid romances, many dealing with psychic or religious events, and all enormously popular. Critics held her in disdain (once, in retaliation, she refused to send them review copies), but Queen Victoria adored her work. Among Corelli's most widely read books are *The Sorrows of Satan* and *The Murder of Delicia.*

—Exclusive for *The Book of Lists*

Marie Corelli wrote popular romances that were favorites of Queen Victoria.

MALCOLM COWLEY'S
10 GREATEST NOVELISTS
OF ALL TIME

A graduate of Harvard and chancellor of the American Academy of Arts and Letters, Malcolm Cowley is the compleat man of letters. He has translated Paul Valéry and André Gide from French, has edited collections of writings by Hawthorne, Whitman, Faulkner, and Fitzgerald, and is himself the author of *Exile's Return, After the Genteel Tradition, The Literary Situation,* and *The Faulkner-Cowley File.*

1. Leo Tolstoy
2. Fëdor Dostoevsky
3. Charles Dickens
4. Miguel de Cervantes
5. Marcel Proust
6. Herman Melville
7. Stendhal
8. Thomas Mann
9. James Joyce
10. Lady Murasaki

Cowley adds: "It's easy to list Great Novelists. The hard and painful thing was the great names I had to omit: Balzac, Fielding, Flaubert, Faulkner, Jane Austen, George Eliot, Henry James, Turgenev, Trollope, Conrad—those and how many others. I included Lady Murasaki, who died early in the 11th century, because she wrote the first true novel, *The Tale of Genji,* and also to show that we Americans and Europeans aren't the only ones with a great tradition in fiction."

—Exclusive for *The Book of Lists*

W. SOMERSET MAUGHAM'S
10 BEST NOVELS OF THE WORLD

1. *War and Peace* (1866) by Leo Tolstoy
2. *Père Goriot* (1834) by Honoré de Balzac
3. *Tom Jones* (1749) by Henry Fielding
4. *Pride and Prejudice* (1813) by Jane Austen
5. *The Red and the Black* (1831) by Stendhal
6. *Wuthering Heights* (1848) by Emily Brontë
7. *Madame Bovary* (1857) by Gustave Flaubert
8. *David Copperfield* (1849–1850) by Charles Dickens
9. *The Brothers Karamazov* (1880) by Fëdor Dostoevsky
10. *Moby Dick* (1851) by Herman Melville

SOURCE: W. Somerset Maugham, *Great Novelists and Their Novels* (Philadelphia: Winston, 1948).

CLIFTON FADIMAN'S
10 BEST BOOKS OF FICTION

Versatile and brilliant, Clifton Fadiman, onetime book editor of *The New Yorker,* became a household name on the radio program *Information Please.* He is presently on the selecting committee of the Book-of-the-Month Club and on the board of editors of the Encyclopaedia Britannica. He is the author of many books, among them *Party of One* and *Enter Conversing,* as well as editor of *Reading I've Liked* and *Fantasia Mathematica.*

1. *Tom Jones* by Henry Fielding
2. *Ulysses* by James Joyce
3. *The Magic Mountain* by Thomas Mann
4. *Gargantua and Pantagruel* by François Rabelais
5. *Remembrance of Things Past* by Marcel Proust
6. *Moby Dick* by Herman Melville
7. *Huckleberry Finn* by Mark Twain
8. *Don Quixote* by Miguel de Cervantes
9. *The Brothers Karamazov* by Fëdor Dostoevsky
10. *War and Peace* by Leo Tolstoy

—Exclusive for *The Book of Lists*

L. SPRAGUE DE CAMP'S
10 GREATEST
SCIENCE FICTION WRITERS

Onetime engineer, editor, teacher, surveyor, L. Sprague de Camp turned to science fiction and fantasy writing in 1936 and has since become one of the leading authors in the field. Known for the humor and action he injects into his short stories and novels, de Camp has written, among other books, *Lest Darkness Fall, Genus Homo* (with P. Schuyler Miller), *Lost Continents,* and *Lands Beyond* (with Willy Ley).

1. Jules Verne
2. H. G. Wells
3. Robert A. Heinlein
4. Isaac Asimov
5. Poul Anderson
6. Edgar Rice Burroughs
7. A. E. van Vogt
8. Arthur C. Clarke
9. Fritz Leiber
10. Henry Kuttner and C. L. Moore (collaborators)

—Exclusive for *The Book of Lists*

ELLERY QUEEN'S
17 GREATEST FICTIONAL
DETECTIVES OF ALL TIME

(in alphabetical order)

"Ellery Queen" is the pseudonym adopted by a writing team of two cousins, Frederic Dannay and Manfred B. Lee. Together they have collaborated on over 30 mystery books, numerous radio shows, and *Ellery Queen's Mystery Magazine*.

Fictional Detectives	*Authors Who Created Them*
1. Uncle Abner	Melville Post
2. Lew Archer	Ross Macdonald
3. Father Brown	G. K. Chesterton
4. Albert Campion	Margery Allingham
5. Charlie Chan	Earl Derr Biggers
6. C. Auguste Dupin	Edgar Allan Poe
7. Dr. Gideon Fell	John Dickson Carr
8. Sherlock Holmes	A. Conan Doyle
9. Inspector Maigret	Georges Simenon
10. Philip Marlowe	Raymond Chandler
11. Miss Marple	Agatha Christie
12. Perry Mason	Erle Stanley Gardner
13. Hercule Poirot	Agatha Christie
14. Ellery Queen	Ellery Queen (Frederic Dannay and Manfred B. Lee)
15. Sam Spade	Dashiell Hammett
16. Lord Peter Wimsey	Dorothy Sayers
17. Nero Wolfe	Rex Stout

—Exclusive for *The Book of Lists*

12 BEST DETECTIVE
STORIES EVER WRITTEN

Ellery Queen took a vote of 11 experts, among them Vincent Starrett, Charles Honce, and Lew D. Feldman. There were 83 detective stories nominated.

1. "The Hands of Mr. Ottermole" by Thomas Burke
2. "The Purloined Letter" by Edgar Allan Poe
3. "The Red-Headed League" by A. Conan Doyle
4. "The Avenging Chance" by Anthony Berkeley
5. "The Absent-Minded Coterie" by Robert Barr

6. "The Problem of Cell 13" by Jacques Futrelle
7. "The Invisible Man" by G. K. Chesterton
8. "Naboth's Vineyard" by Melville D. Post
9. "The Gioconda Smile" by Aldous Huxley
10. "The Yellow Slugs" by H. C. Bailey
11. "The Genuine Tabard" by E. C. Bentley
12. "Suspicion" by Dorothy Sayers

SOURCE: *Ellery Queen's Mystery Magazine,* July, 1950.

REX STOUT'S
10 FAVORITE DETECTIVE STORIES

1. *The Moonstone* by Wilkie Collins
2. *The Maltese Falcon* by Dashiell Hammett
3. *The Benson Murder Case* by S. S. Van Dine
4. *The Documents in the Case* by Dorothy L. Sayers and Robert Eustace
5. *The Innocence of Father Brown* by G. K. Chesterton
6. *Call Mr. Fortune* by H. C. Bailey
7. *The Bellamy Trial* by Frances Noyes Hart
8. *The Cask* by Freeman Wills Crofts
9. *The Murder of Roger Ackroyd* by Agatha Christie
10. *Lament for a Maker* by Michael Innes

SOURCE: Vincent Starrett, *Books and Bipeds* (New York: Argus, 1947).

ROBERT L. RIPLEY'S
5 BOOKS HE WOULD TAKE
TO A DESERT ISLAND

Robert L. Ripley was the greatest oddity hunter of all time. In his heyday his "Believe It or Not" cartoon became a byword in the U.S., known to millions through newspaper syndication, best-selling books, lectures, radio, and television. The cartoon also appeared in 300 newspapers in 33 foreign countries with 25 million readers. Although Ripley died in 1949, his successors continue to publish new editions of his *Believe It or Not* books to this day. Some years before Ripley died, one of the authors of *The Book of Lists* asked him, "What five books would you take along if you were obliged to spend five years in exile on a desert island?" Ripley's reply is published for the first time.

1. The Bible
2. *The Good Earth* by Pearl Buck
3. *Les Misérables* by Victor Hugo
4. *Outline of History* by H. G. Wells
5. *Believe It or Not* by Robert L. Ripley

—Exclusive for *The Book of Lists*

CHILDREN'S LITERATURE ASSOCIATION'S 11 BEST AMERICAN CHILDREN'S BOOKS OF THE PAST 200 YEARS

These choices are the result of a 1975–1976 survey of members of the Children's Literature Association, an international group of librarians, teachers, authors, and publishers. The list also includes the suggested readers' age range for each book.

1. *Charlotte's Web* (1952; all ages) by E. B. White
2. *Where the Wild Things Are* (1963; 4–8) by Maurice Sendak
3. *The Adventures of Tom Sawyer* (1876; 10 and up) by Mark Twain
4. *Little Women* (1868; 10 and up) by Louisa May Alcott
5. *Adventures of Huckleberry Finn* (1885; 10 and up) by Mark Twain
6. *Little House in the Big Woods* (1932; 6–10) by Laura Ingalls Wilder
7. *Johnny Tremain* (1943; 10–12 and up) by Ester Forbes
8. *The Wonderful Wizard of Oz* (1900; 8 and up) by Frank Baum
9. *Little House on the Prairie* (1935; 6–10) by Laura Ingalls Wilder
10. *Island of the Blue Dolphins* (1960; 12 and up) by Scott O'Dell
11. *Julie of the Wolves* (1972; 12 and up) by Jean Craighead George

CHARLES M. SCHULZ'S 10 GREATEST CARTOON CHARACTERS OF ALL TIME

Creator of *Peanuts*, the most widely read comic strip in the world, Charles M. Schulz has been the recipient of numerous awards including two Reubens, an Emmy, and the Peabody award. His cast of characters, led by Charlie Brown, Linus, Lucy, and, of course,

Snoopy, have inspired a vast array of spin-offs including TV specials, T-shirts, toys, and even an off-Broadway play.

1. CHARLIE BROWN and SNOOPY

Charlie Brown is the wishy-washy but likable star of *Peanuts*. His dog Snoopy often steals the show by parading as a W.W. I flying ace, baseball player, or novelist.

2. BLONDIE and DAGWOOD

Chic Young's comic strip deals with the domestic misadventures of this happily but crazily married couple.

3. POPEYE and WIMPY

Popeye, the spinach-eating sailor, and Wimpy, his hamburger-eating buddy, are the prime characters of the popular *Popeye* cartoon created by Elzie Segar.

4. KRAZY KAT

The playful romance between the lovesick Krazy Kat and Ignatz Mouse, who throws bricks at Krazy, is the subject of this universally acclaimed comic strip created by George Herriman.

5. WASH TUBBS and CAPTAIN EASY

Wash Tubbs, a funny little guy who liked big women, and his sidekick, a soldier of fortune named Captain Easy, were developed by Roy Crane.

6. SUPERMAN

Faster than a speeding bullet and blessed with X-ray vision, Superman was the brainchild of two teenagers, Jerry Siegel and Joe Shuster.

7. SKIPPY

Skippy, a misanthropic 10-year-old developed by Percy Crosby, starred in one of the first comics in which children adopted adult reactions to the world around them.

8. SKEEZIX

The prime character of Frank King's *Gasoline Alley* was the first character to grow from infancy to adulthood in a comic strip in the same number of years it would take a real person to grow up.

9. LITTLE ORPHAN ANNIE

Created by Harold Grey, this curly-haired, redheaded orphan with blank eyes crept into the hearts of millions.

10. DICK TRACY

Developed by Chester Gould, *Dick Tracy* was the first realistic detective comic strip.

—Exclusive for *The Book of Lists*
with annotations by The Eds.

10 RAREST U.S. COMIC BOOKS

Since prices vary and the number of copies extant is unknown, the rarity of these comics is not judged by dollar value, but how sought-after they are by comic-book collectors. The following 10 comics are listed in descending order of rarity, from the rarest to the least rare.

1. *ACTION COMICS*, #1 (June, 1938; value, $4,200)

Superman first appeared in this comic book. His powers, as described in 1938, differed substantially from those he gained in later years. Initially, he could "leap an eighth of a mile, run faster than an express train, and nothing less than a bursting shell could penetrate his skin!" Later comic books showed that he had the power to fly, was able to withstand the power of 10 atom bombs, and had X-ray vision. Other stories published in this issue concerned Chuck Dawson, a hero of the West; Zatara the Master Magician, who pronounced his sacred spells backward; and Scoop Scanlon, five-star reporter, who broke up a ring of international jewel thieves.

Superman arrives on earth in *Action Comics, #1*, June, 1938.

2. *MARVEL COMICS,* #1 (Nov., 1939; value, $5,000)

This is considered one of the most prized comics because it contained the original stories about the Human Torch and the Sub-Mariner. By the early 1940s both characters graduated into comics of their own. They shared an unresolved sibling rivalry and clashed repeatedly in their separate books. Other heroes who were introduced in this issue: Kazar the Great, the Angel, and the Masked Rider.

3. *DETECTIVE COMICS,* #27 (May, 1939; value, $350)

Batman, whose real name was Bruce N. Wayne, made his first appearance. In those days his ears were much larger and his shadow much bigger than the Batman of the 1960s. When he was 10, Wayne's parents were brutally murdered by a thief—a fact that was not mentioned in #27. He vowed to avenge them by upholding justice and fair play in the world. Upon reaching adulthood, Wayne donned the Batman costume and began his crusade to "strike terror into the hearts of the underworld."

4. *WHIZ COMICS,* #2 (Feb., 1940; value, $3,500)

The first issue of *Whiz Comics* to hit the stands was labeled #2. An earlier issue, titled *Thrill Comics,* had been developed and featured a hero named Captain Thunder. *Thrill Comics,* however, was written solely to secure a copyright and was never issued to the public. Instead, *Whiz Comics* #2 appeared—and Captain Thunder was renamed Captain Marvel. Other heroes who starred in this issue were Golden Arrow, Ibis the Invincible, and Spy Smasher.

5. *WALT DISNEY COMICS & STORIES,* #1 (Oct., 1940; value, $1,200)

A continuation of *Mickey Mouse Magazine* (first published in 1935), this comic book starred Donald Duck, whose popularity, in 1940, was as great as Mickey's. The mouse did appear in the comic, but only as a minor character.

6. *MORE FUN,* #1 (Feb., 1935; value, $350)

This issue is valued not because of its contents, but because of the heroes it introduced, including the Masked Ranger, Dr. Occult, and the Spectre. The latter, who was a policeman named Jim Corrigan, was accosted by a pack of criminals and thrown into the sea. Fortunately, he was resurrected from the dead and from that time on pursued his career in semisubstantial form—as the Spectre.

7. *ADVENTURE,* #1 (Dec., 1935; value, $250)

At first, this was an all-purpose comic with no special feature. It gave the readers only what its title promised: adventure. Then it began introducing characters that grew into some of the most popular heroes of the day. They included the Sandman, the Shining Knight, Starman, and a group of heroes who fought crime in the future: the Legion of Super-Heroes. This group was often joined in its crime-fighting efforts by Superboy, who had the power to break the time barrier. This feat was represented in the comics by a picture of Superboy flying at superspeed and the dates "1942 . . . 1952 . . .

1962 . . ." all the way to the 21st century when the legion's adventures took place.

8. *CAPTAIN AMERICA*, #1 (Mar., 1941; value, $1,500)

This issue introduced the title's hero, Captain America, and his sidekick Bucky. The story unfolded thus: In the midst of W.W. II a noted scientist had developed a serum for making men stronger. The serum was to be used to develop an army of super-Americans. But, as luck would have it, the scientist was murdered by a German infiltrator just seconds after administering the experimental dose to volunteer Steve Rogers. Steve killed the German with one punch of his mighty fist and the serum's formula remained forever a secret. Steve then proceeded to make a name for himself by foiling criminals from one end of the country to the other. One night Bucky inadvertently saw Steve changing into his red, white, and blue costume and Steve's secret identity was exposed. From then on, Captain America fought crime and the Germans with his new partner, Bucky.

9. *SUPERMAN*, #1 (Summer, 1939; value, $2,000)

Reprinted in this premier issue were the first four *Action Comics* stories, including the original Superman adventure. Subsequent stories included the introduction of cub reporter Jimmy Olsen and the first appearance of Mr. Mxyztplk, a creature from the fifth dimension.

10. *DONALD DUCK*, #1 (June, 1938; value, $500)

This issue did not appear under its own title but was in a series of books called *Color Comics*. The series starred a different character each month, and from the beginning Donald was enormously popular. The duck's adventures were fanciful little tales about his searches for gems and gold and his long journeys to the Land of the Aztecs and the Home of the Incas. Donald was continually put in his place by his nephews, Huey, Dewey, and Louie, who accompanied Donald on his trips and provided him with nuggets of wisdom taken from the pages of the *Junior Woodchuck Manual*.

—D.F.

10 MEMORABLE BOOKS
THAT NEVER EXISTED

1. *THE CURIOUS EXPERIENCE OF THE PATTERSON FAMILY ON THE ISLAND OF UFFA,* by JOHN H. WATSON, M.D. (late of the British Army Medical Department)

A Sherlock Holmes exploit mentioned by Dr. Watson but never set down on paper.

2. *HANSARD'S GUIDE TO REFRESHING SLEEP* (19 vols.)

One of the dummy works which seemed to be displayed on bookshelves in the home of Charles Dickens at Gad's Hill. The spines of these make-believe books were used to mask some woodwork that the great novelist chose to cover up.

3. *MAD TRIST*, by SIR LAUNCELOT CANNING

One of the nonexistent books mentioned to build up the atmosphere of mystery and menace in the story "Fall of the House of Usher," by Edgar Allan Poe, who died in 1849.

4. *MEMOIRS*, by THE HON. GALAHAD THREEPWOOD

The title of a nonexistent autobiography to be found in the numerous novels of P. G. Wodehouse.

5. *MODERN WARFARE*, by GENERAL TOM THUMB

Another nonbook that looked like a real book and was used to decorate a portion of Charles Dickens's personal library.

6. *NECRONOMICON*, by ABDUL ALHAZRED (the mad Arab)

A "blasphemous" and "forbidden" work referred to several times in the fantasy and horror tales of H. P. Lovecraft, who died in 1937. This nonexistent book was described as "the ghastly soul symbol of the forbidden corpse-eating cult of inaccessible Leng in Central Asia."

7. *ON POLISHING OFF THE CANONICAL HOURS* (40 vols.), by MASTER GREEDYGUTS

A satire on the clergy who slighted their rituals and observances. One of many imaginary works found in the library of the Abbey of St. Victor by Pantagruel, the fictional character created by François Rabelais, who died in 1553.

8. *PRACTICAL HANDBOOK OF BEE CULTURE*, by SHERLOCK HOLMES

An invaluable, if nonexistent, contribution to human knowledge by the master detective.

9. *THE SEVEN MINUTES*, by J J JADWAY (Paris: Étoile Press)

This 171-page most-banned novel in history was a figment of novelist Irving Wallace's imagination in his real book, also called *The Seven Minutes*. The contents of the nonexistent book, according to Wallace, consisted of "the thoughts in one woman's head during seven minutes of copulation with an unnamed man."

10. *UPON THE DISTINCTION BETWEEN THE ASHES OF THE VARIOUS TOBACCOS*, by SHERLOCK HOLMES

This distinctive monograph by the distinguished detective was probably published between 1880 and 1890. It was Holmes's faithful companion, Dr. John H. Watson, who first spoke of it. The nonexistent monograph and its author, as well as his companion, were created by A. Conan Doyle, who died in 1930.

—H.A.K.

10 REAL PEOPLE
WHO INSPIRED GREAT
CHARACTERS IN FICTION

1. ALEXANDER SELKIRK (inspiration for ROBINSON CRUSOE)

Selkirk (1676–1721), born in Largo, Scotland, became a seaman under Capt. William Dampier. In 1704, objecting to the condition of the ship he was on, Selkirk asked to be put ashore on Más a Tierra, a tiny desert island in the Pacific Ocean off South America. He lived alone on this island for four years and four months before being returned to England. A free-lance writer, Daniel Defoe, read about him, may have met him, and in 1719 published a book based on Selkirk entitled *The Life and Strange Surprising Adventures of Robinson Crusoe, of York, Mariner.*

2. WILLIAM BRODIE (inspiration for DR. HENRY JEKYLL and EDWARD HYDE)

Brodie (1741–1788), cabinetmaker, head of his union, member of the Edinburgh town council, was a respected businessman by day and a masked thief and leader of a gang of robbers by night. He was finally caught and hung. Knowing of Brodie, fascinated by "man's double being," Robert Louis Stevenson created *The Strange Case of Dr. Jekyll and Mr. Hyde* (1886).

In 18th-century Edinburgh deacon, William Brodie was a respected businessman by day and the leader of a gang of thieves at night.

238

3. LEIGH HUNT (inspiration for HAROLD SKIMPOLE)

Hunt (1784–1859), a newspaper editor and publisher—as well as a professional barnacle—was the friend of both Percy Bysshe Shelley and Lord Byron. Charles Dickens also knew him and cruelly caricatured him as the sponger Skimpole in *Bleak House* (1852–1853).

4. JOSIAH HENSON (inspiration for UNCLE TOM)

Henson (1789–1883), born into slavery on a Maryland farm, became overseer of his master's estate and a Methodist preacher. Learning he was to be sold to a southern planter, he escaped to Canada, taking with him his wife and large family. He traveled three times to England, propagandizing for the emancipation of blacks. While there, he was received by Queen Victoria. In Boston, he was interviewed by Harriet Beecher Stowe, who then used Henson as the prototype for Uncle Tom in her 1852 best-seller, *Uncle Tom's Cabin*.

5. CLAIRE CLAIRMONT (inspiration for JULIANA BORDEREAU)

Clairmont (1798–1879), stepdaughter of William Godwin, became Lord Byron's mistress and had a child by him. When Henry James, visiting Florence in 1887, learned that Clairmont had recently been alive in the city, he was inspired to create the character of Bordereau for his novella *The Aspern Papers*.

6. MARY CECILIA ROGERS (inspiration for MARIE ROGET)

Rogers (1820–1841), a beautiful clerk in a tobacco shop in New York, N.Y., where Edgar Allan Poe was a customer, was murdered and found floating in the Hudson River. Her slayer was never apprehended. Poe based "The Mystery of Marie Roget" on her case.

7. DELPHINE DELAMARE (inspiration for EMMA BOVARY)

Delamare (1822–1848), daughter of a prosperous farmer and educated in a finishing school, married a plodding country doctor in Ry, France. She dreamed of a more exciting life, spent money extravagantly, took many lovers, and at last committed suicide by swallowing arsenic. Hearing the story from a close friend, Gustave Flaubert based his *Madame Bovary* (1857) on it.

8. MARIE DUPLESSIS (inspiration for MARGUERITE GAUTIER)

Duplessis (1824–1847) worked for a corsetmaker, then for a hat shop, before she became a prostitute in Paris. She moved up into high society, and was kept by a series of wealthy aristocratic lovers. Her trademark was the white camellia. When she died of tuberculosis, one of her lovers, Alexander Dumas fils, enshrined her in a novel (1848) that became famous on stage and screen as *Camille*.

9. DR. JOSEPH BELL (inspiration for SHERLOCK HOLMES)

Dr. Bell (1837–1911), a surgeon and medical instructor in the Royal Infirmary at Edinburgh, after merely looking at a stranger could deduce much of his life and many of his habits. This impressed a student of his, A. Conan Doyle, who admitted years later, "I used and amplified his methods when I tried to build up a scientific detective who solved cases on his own merits."

10. CHESTER GILLETTE (inspiration for CLYDE GRIFFITHS)

Gillette (1883–1908), who worked in the shirt factory owned by his wealthy uncle, had become the lover of a factory employee, Grace Brown, who thought he was going to marry her. Meanwhile, he was meeting young ladies who were more prominent socially. In 1906, learning that Grace was pregnant, and realizing that he might be trapped into marriage, Gillette took her to Big Moose Lake in New York, rowed her out to the middle of the lake, smashed her on the head with a tennis racket, and dumped her overboard. She drowned. Gillette was caught, tried, electrocuted. Theodore Dreiser followed the case, and from it wrote *An American Tragedy* (1925).

—I.W.

20 FAMOUS PEN NAMES

	Pen Name	Real Name
1.	Nellie Bly	Elizabeth Cochrane Seaman
2.	Boz	Charles Dickens
3.	Lewis Carroll	Charles Lutwidge Dodgson
4.	Elia	Charles Lamb
5.	George Eliot	Mary Ann Evans
6.	Maksim Gorki	Aleksei Maksimovich Peshkov
7.	Knut Hamsun	Knut Pedersen
8.	André Maurois	Émile Herzog
9.	O. Henry	William Sydney Porter
10.	George Orwell	Eric Arthur Blair
11.	Poor Richard	Benjamin Franklin
12.	Ellery Queen	Frederic Dannay and Manfred B. Lee
13.	Sax Rohmer	Arthur Sarsfield Ward
14.	Saki	Hector Hugh Munro
15.	George Sand	Amandine Aurore Dupin Lucie (later the Baronne Dudevant)
16.	Burt L. Standish	Gilbert Patten
17.	Stendhal	Marie-Henri Beyle
18.	Mark Twain	Samuel Langhorne Clemens
19.	Voltaire	François-Marie Arouet
20.	Artemus Ward	Charles Farrar Browne

15 AUTHORS WHO WROTE BEST-SELLERS IN PRISON

1. FRANÇOIS-MARIE AROUET (Voltaire)

Jailed in May, 1717, for writing poems against the regent. Spent 11 months in the Bastille, Paris, where he began his epic poem *Henriade*.

2. JOHN BUNYAN

Imprisoned for holding Puritan services that were not in accordance with the Church of England. In Bedford County Jail for 11 years. Wrote most of *Pilgrim's Progress* while incarcerated. Book published in London, 1678.

3. MIGUEL DE CERVANTES

Jailed in 1597 in royal prison of Seville, Spain, for deficits as naval quartermaster. Released after three months. While in prison he began *Don Quixote*.

4. JOHN CLELAND

Jailed in Newgate Prison, London, for debts. To get him out of debtor's prison, a publisher, Drybutter, offered him 20 guineas to write a pornographic novel. While in prison he wrote *Fanny Hill, or the Memoirs of a Woman of Pleasure* (1750).

5. DANIEL DEFOE

Judged guilty of seditious libel. Jailed indefinitely in May, 1703, in Newgate Prison, London. Wrote *Hymn to the Pillory* while in jail. Released November, 1703.

6. ADOLF HITLER

Found guilty of organizing the unsuccessful Beer Hall Putsch. In 1923, he was sentenced to five years, but was released after nine months. During his confinement in the prison at the fortress of Landsberg, he wrote part of *Mein Kampf*.

7. LEIGH HUNT

Friend of Byron, Shelley, Keats, he was jailed in 1813 for libel when he wrote in his brother's London newspaper, *The Examiner*, that the future King George IV was a "fat Adonis of 50." Spent two years in the prison at Horsemonger Lane, London. Published "Feast of the Poets" and edited *The Examiner* in jail.

8. RICHARD LOVELACE

A Cavalier adventurer, he was jailed in 1642 for presenting a royalist petition to the English Parliament. He served seven weeks in the Gatehouse at Westminster. In jail he wrote "To Althea from Prison," which contains the lines: "Stone walls do not a prison make/

Nor iron bars a cage;/Minds innocent and quiet take/That for an hermitage."

9. KARL MAY

This popular writer was jailed in Germany for fraud. He served two terms in the period 1865-1874. He wrote successfully in prison. His novels about the American West—which he had never visited—were best-sellers in Germany.

10. JAWAHARLAL NEHRU

Arrested by the British as a leader of India's fight for independence. Served altogether 10 years in jail from 1921 to 1945. In prison he wrote *Glimpses of World History,* an erudite and widely read book.

11. MARCO POLO

After returning from China, the Venetian became commander of a galley in a war between Venice and Genoa in 1298. Captured by the enemy and imprisoned for less than a year, he dictated *The Travels of Marco Polo* to a fellow prisoner and scribe from Pisa named Rusticiano.

12. O. HENRY (William Sydney Porter)

In 1898, sentenced to five years in a federal prison—in Columbus, O.—for embezzlement of funds from a First National Bank in Austin, Tex., where he had been a teller. A model prisoner, he was released in three years three months for good behavior. Some of his best short stories—those that made up his widely read collections, including *The Gentle Grafter*—were written in his cell.

O. Henry, one of many famed authors who wrote in jail.

13. SIR WALTER RALEIGH

Thrown into the Tower of London, perhaps unjustly, for high treason in 1603, he was confined for 13 years. During his jail term, he wrote the only volume of his *History of the World*.

14. FRANÇOIS VILLON

Guilty of housebreaking, manslaughter, satirical verse. Sentenced to death and confined to the dungeons of the bishop of Orléans in Meung, France. Wrote *Grand Testament* while in dungeon. Released on general amnesty proclaimed on the state entry of King Louis XI. In Paris, again arrested for manslaughter. Sentenced to hang, but sentence commuted to banishment from Paris. Vanished in 1463.

15. OSCAR WILDE

Convicted on charges of homosexuality and imprisoned in Reading Jail. Served two terrible years during which he wrote *De Profundis* and *Apologia*. The following year he wrote *Ballad of Reading Gaol,* the latter signed C.3.3, meaning the prisoner of Cell 3, third landing. He was released in May, 1897, broken and disgraced.

Other literary prisoners include Roger Bacon, Caryl Chessman, Eldridge Cleaver, William Cobbett, Denis Diderot, Hugo Grotius, King James I of Scotland, Comte de Mirabeau, Richard Savage, and John Selden. According to Vincent Starrett, who wrote *Books Alive,* which relates various anecdotes about books and their authors, most writers who have been jailed were charged with political crimes. Very few were ever imprisoned for theft or murder. And "no writer ever has been charged with arson or kidnapping."

—I.W.

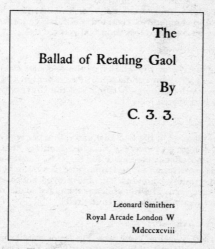

The

Ballad of Reading Gaol

By

C. 3. 3.

Leonard Smithers
Royal Arcade London W
Mdcccxcviii

The title page of Oscar Wilde's classic.

12 WRITERS WHO RAN
(UNSUCCESSFULLY)
FOR PUBLIC OFFICE

1. JOHN GREENLEAF WHITTIER

In 1842, the Quaker poet was disappointed in his bid for a seat in the U.S. Congress. He went on to play a major role in the antislavery movement and the organization of the Republican party in Massachusetts. He had sat in the Massachusetts legislature in 1835.

2. VICTOR HUGO

In 1848, the flamboyant French novelist confidently announced his candidacy for president of the French Republic, but he garnered very few votes. In 1871 he ran for a seat in the National Assembly and won, but soon resigned in frustration.

3. HENRY GEORGE

The brilliant economist and author of *Progress and Poverty* ran for mayor of New York, N.Y., on a radical labor ticket in 1886. His platform called for the abolition of private landownership, among other things. George made a respectable showing and finished second in a tight three-man race. In last place was another writer-politician: Theodore Roosevelt.

4. JACK LONDON

At the age of 18, after serving a brief jail term for vagrancy, Jack London became a committed socialist. In 1905, the sailor-adventurer found time to campaign on the Socialist ticket for the mayoralty of his hometown, Oakland, Calif. His candidacy attracted wide notice, but received less than 500 votes.

5. H. G. WELLS

Long active in the affairs of the socialist Fabian Society, Wells stood as a Labour candidate for Parliament in 1921 and 1922. Though his district principally comprised the University of London, he was easily defeated.

6. UPTON SINCLAIR

As a member of the Socialist party, Sinclair was twice a candidate for Congress, twice the Socialist nominee for governor of California, and once a candidate for the U.S. Senate. In 1934, he changed his registration to the Democratic party, ran in the primary for the gubernatorial nomination, and proved successful in a remarkable campaign. The Republicans managed to discredit and defeat him in the general election in the fall.

7. GORE VIDAL

In 1960, novelist Vidal won the Democratic nomination for Congress in a solidly Republican upstate New York district. He ran a vigorous campaign and received more votes than any Democrat since 1910, finishing 20,000 votes ahead of presidential candidate John F. Kennedy in that district—but he still lost to his Republican opponent.

8. JAMES MICHENER

As a Democratic candidate for Congress in Bucks County, Pa., in 1962, Michener was given a good chance of staging an upset, but his campaign wasn't strong enough to overcome his Republican opponent. After his defeat, he continued to play an active role in Democratic affairs in his district.

9. WILLIAM F. BUCKLEY

In 1965, the columnist, novelist, and TV personality ran as the Conservative party nominee for mayor of New York. Most of Buckley's energy was focused on attacking his old Yale classmate and electoral rival John Lindsay. With his nonchalant attitude and sparkling wit, Buckley attracted wide support. During a televised debate he once declined the opportunity to use his allotted rebuttal period, declaring: "I am satisfied to sit back in silence and contemplate my own former eloquence." In 1971, Buckley's older brother James (a nonwriter) was elected U.S. senator from New York for one term.

10. NORMAN MAILER

In 1969, Mailer sought the Democratic nomination for mayor of New York, N.Y., with an original campaign slogan: "No More Bullshit." His highly imaginative platform called for the city emerging as the 51st state and complete decentralization of all public services down to the neighborhood level. Mailer attracted strong support from the intellectual community and Democratic reform elements, but ran only fourth in a field of five.

11. JIMMY BRESLIN

In 1969, the novelist-columnist ran for Council president of New York, N.Y., as Norman Mailer's running mate in what may have been the most literary ticket in history. Breslin campaigned widely, and received more votes than Mailer.

12. HUNTER S. THOMPSON

Self-described as a "foul-mouthed outlaw journalist," Thompson became a farcical candidate for sheriff of Pitkin County, Colo., then turned serious when his radical platform began to draw popular support. Aspen residents were upset over widespread land exploitation, and the Freak Power candidate's proposals included harassment of real estate exploiters, replacement of streets with plant sod, and renaming Aspen "Fat City." Although he made a good showing in the 1970 race, Thompson was defeated by Carrol Whitmire, the Democratic incumbent.

—M.S.M.

28 WRITERS WHO COULD HAVE WON THE NOBEL PRIZE IN LITERATURE—BUT DIDN'T

All of these writers were officially nominated for the Nobel prize in literature, and each and every one was voted down by the Swedish Academy. Instead, between 1901 and 1976, the prize was given to such geniuses as Sully Prudhomme, Björnson, Echegaray, Carducci, Eucken, Heidenstam, Spitteler, Reymont, Karlfeldt, Bunin, Sillanpää, Jensen, Laxness, Quasimodo, Seferis, E. Johnson, and H. E. Martinson.

Meanwhile, the losers included:

1. Leo Tolstoy
2. Herbert Spencer
3. Anton Chekhov
4. Henrik Ibsen
5. Thomas Hardy
6. Joseph Conrad
7. Mark Twain
8. Rainer Maria Rilke
9. George Meredith
10. Henry James
11. Algernon Swinburne
12. Georg Brandes
13. August Strindberg
14. Maksim Gorky
15. Bertolt Brecht
16. Paul Valéry
17. Sean O'Casey
18. Marcel Proust
19. Gabriele D'Annunzio
20. Theodore Dreiser
21. Benedetto Croce
22. Sigmund Freud
23. Virginia Woolf
24. F. Scott Fitzgerald
25. H. G. Wells
26. Willa Cather
27. W. Somerset Maugham
28. Mao Tse-tung

—I. W.

17 POETS LAUREATE OF ENGLAND

The office of poet laureate is one of great honor, conferred on a poet of distinction. In 1616, James I granted a pension to the poet Ben Jonson, but it was not until 1668 that the laureateship was created as a royal office. When the position of poet laureate falls vacant, the prime minister is responsible for putting forth names for a new laureate, to be chosen by the sovereign. The sovereign then commands the lord chamberlain to appoint the poet laureate, and he does so by issuing a warrant to the laureate-elect. The lord chamberlain also arranges for the appointment—for life—to be announced in the *London Gazette*. Among those who rejected the laureateship are

Thomas Gray in 1757, Sir Walter Scott in 1813, and William Morris in 1894. The following men have filled the office of poet laureate:

1. JOHN DRYDEN (1631–1700; laureate, 1668–1688)

Dryden was the laureate appointed by Charles II. Dryden received a yearly pension of £300 and a tierce of canary wine. William and Mary stripped him of the laureateship in 1688 because he became a Catholic and a supporter of James II.

2. THOMAS SHADWELL (1642?–1692; laureate, 1688–1692)

He began the custom of annual birthday and New Year's odes. Until near the end of George II's reign, the laureate was expected to create commemorative poems for the sovereign's birthday and for national victories.

3. NAHUM TATE (1652–1715; laureate, 1692–1715)

The annuity was reduced to £100 plus the tierce of wine.

4. NICHOLAS ROWE (1674–1718; laureate, 1715–1718)

5. LAURENCE EUSDEN (1688–1730; laureate, 1718–1730)

6. COLLEY CIBBER (1671–1757; laureate, 1730–1757)

7. WILLIAM WHITEHEAD (1715–1785; laureate, 1757–1785)

Appointed after Thomas Gray declined the offer.

8. THOMAS WARTON (1728–1790; laureate, 1785–1790)

9. HENRY JAMES PYE (1745–1813; laureate, 1790–1813)

Appointed after William Hayley declined the offer. Notorious for his bad poetry, he managed to become poet laureate by writing ingratiating poems in honor of George III. The first poem he wrote for the king was so bad and so full of allusions to birds ("feathered songsters"), it inspired George Stevens to write the following famous punning rhyme: "When the Pye was opened/The birds began to sing./Wasn't that a dainty dish to set before the king." During Pye's laureateship, a sum of £27 was substituted for the tierce of canary wine. This was in addition to a payment of £70 per annum.

10. ROBERT SOUTHEY (1774–1843; laureate, 1813–1843)

11. WILLIAM WORDSWORTH (1770–1850; laureate, 1843–1850)

When he accepted the position young poets of the day—who considered him their mentor—were dismayed. One of these poets, Robert Browning, wrote a poem entitled "The Lost Leader," whose opening lines read: "Just for a handful of silver he left us,/Just for a riband to stick in his coat." Wordsworth refused to accept the obligation to write for state occasions, and in fact did not produce any poetry during the seven years he filled the office.

12. ALFRED, LORD TENNYSON (1809–1892; laureate, 1850–1892)

Appointed after Samuel Russell declined the offer. When Wordsworth was made poet laureate, he borrowed a suit from a friend, Samuel Rogers, to wear to the palace. Tennyson was also faced with the problem of not having suitable attire for the palace, and he borrowed the same suit from Rogers.

13. ALFRED AUSTIN (1835–1913; laureate, 1896–1913)

14. ROBERT BRIDGES (1844–1930; laureate, 1913–1930)

15. JOHN MASEFIELD (1878–1967; laureate, 1930–1967)

16. CECIL DAY-LEWIS (1904–1972; laureate, 1968–1972)

17. SIR JOHN BETJEMAN (b. 1906; laureate, 1972–   )

Instead of the £27 compensation, Betjeman chose to receive bottles of wine of equal value from the queen's wine merchant.

—F.B.F. & J.BE.

12
LO AND BEHOLD!
—SCIENCE AND TECHNOLOGY

MAJOR MISTAKES BY
12 GREAT MEN OF SCIENCE

1. ARISTOTLE (384–322 B.C.)

He was regarded for nearly 1,800 years as the last word in physical and biological science. Yet he taught that flying objects—arrows and thrown stones—were partly moved by the atmosphere. He claimed that the heart, not the brain, was the seat of sensation and intelligence. He also believed that heavy objects fell faster than lighter ones. In addition to these errors, he proposed that living creatures could be spontaneously generated without ancestors—such as maggots from decaying meat or insects from mud. Edmund Whittaker (1873–1956), a distinguished mathematician, said that Aristotle's "natural philosophy was worthless and misleading from beginning to end."

2. LEONARDO DA VINCI (1452–1519)

A brilliant pioneer in scientific observation and speculation, as well as a masterful artist, he tried—in his private notebooks—to describe how a heavy object fell toward the earth. He stated, rightly, that its speed constantly increases. But he added, wrongly, that the speed increases in proportion to the *distance* it has dropped. (In fact, it increases in proportion to the elapsed *time* it has been dropping.)

3. GALILEO GALILEI (1564–1642)

Although he finally solved the motion problems of objects thrown, fired, or dropped, in 1604 Galileo wrote to a friend and repeated Leonardo da Vinci's error by stating, "The naturally moving body increases its velocity in the proportion that it is distant from the origin of its motion." Nearly 30 years later, in 1633, he got it right—and earned eternal fame.

4. JOHANN WOLFGANG VON GOETHE (1749–1832)

The greatest German man of letters believed his fame rested more securely on his scientific rather than his literary works. However, his lengthy tome on light and color, the *Farbenlehre* (1810), runs counter to most of the scientific findings and interpretations of his time and the present. Goethe also supported a geological theory called neptunism, which held that the rocks of the earth had been deposited in seas that once covered most of the world. He scoffed at the rival theory, called vulcanism, which credited the earth's internal heat with significant rock formation. Neptunism remains a rejected curiosity of geology, and the ideas of the vulcanists have triumphed.

5. DR. DIONYSIUS LARDNER (1793–1859)

In the 1830s, Irish-born Dr. Lardner, a professor of natural philosophy and astronomy at University College in London, warned that no large steamship would ever be able to cross the Atlantic, because it would need more coal than it could carry. However in 1838, the *Great Western* made such a voyage. Earlier, Lardner had warned that if railway trains attained high speeds, such as 120 mph, the passengers would be unable to breathe and would die of asphyxiation.

6. WILLIAM THOMSON (1824–1907)

Known as Lord Kelvin, he was one of Britain's most famous and versatile scientists. He made enormous contributions to thermodynamics and applied electricity. Yet, in 1897, he stated that the earth could not have been inhabited for more than 20 million years, despite geological evidence of life dating back much further. He was unaware of the facts and effects of radioactivity. When they were called to his attention during his last years, he rejected them. He also rejected the theory, now universally held, that light is equivalent to very rapid electromagnetic vibrations, and that light exerts pressure on bodies that absorb it. Kelvin called these hypotheses "curious and ingenious, but not wholly tenable."

7. SIMON NEWCOMB (1835–1909)

He stood preeminent among American astronomers during the latter part of his life. His calculations of the motions of heavenly bodies were superb. But around the turn of the century he wrote a number of articles flatly stating that flight by heavier-than-air machines was impossible. Even after the first short flights of the Wright brothers (1903–1905), he clung to the position that airplanes were impractical and insignificant, if not utterly impossible.

8. ERNST MACH (1838–1916)

He attained great fame as a physicist at the University of Prague and the University of Vienna. The famous Mach number reflects but one of his contributions to science, and his work in mechanics and on inertia won the admiration of Albert Einstein. Yet to the end of his life he rejected—as a "mental artifice"—the view that matter is made up of atomic structures. Also, he stated, "I can accept the theory of relativity as little as I can accept the existence of atoms and other such dogma."

9. PERCIVAL LOWELL (1855–1916)

He established his own astronomical observatory in Arizona about 1894 and conducted extensive studies of the planet Mars. He claimed that it was netted with a multitude of long straight "canals," and that he had mapped over 500 of them. They do not exist, as the latest space probes have amply proved. Yet Lowell made valid contributions in other areas of astronomy.

10. WILLIAM PICKERING (1855–1938)

A noted astronomer, he opposed Lowell's contentions regarding the "canals" on Mars. But, in 1924, he offered an even more bizarre theory to account for a number of dark spots observed in the lunar crater Eratosthenes. They were due, he argued, to enormous swarms of insects on the moon. He suggested that a lunar astronomer might have seen spots on the great prairie regions of North America, caused by the huge buffalo herds that roamed there in the early 19th century.

11. NIKOLA TESLA (1856–1943)

A brilliant physicist and inventor of electrical devices, he made enormous contributions in the field of generation and distribution of power. Yet, in the 1930s and early 1940s, he asserted that atomic power was an illusion. The energies in atomic nuclei, he insisted, could not be unlocked by humans.

12. ERNEST RUTHERFORD (1871–1937)

He was the pioneer and trailblazer in nuclear physics. His Cambridge laboratory led the world in discovering, interpreting, and teaching nuclear science. However, in 1933, he scoffed at the notion that the vast energies in the atomic nucleus ever could be unlocked. And he was reluctant to accept Einstein's theory of relativity, basic to an understanding of how those energies are produced. Rutherford even applied the term "moonshine" to speculations that humans might someday learn how to use nuclear energy.

—H.A.K.

ISAAC ASIMOV'S 10 MOST IMPORTANT SCIENTISTS IN HISTORY

(alphabetically arranged)

Isaac Asimov began his writing career as a biochemistry professor at Columbia University. He has since published over 140 books, including *Fantastic Voyage* and *Asimov's Biographical Encyclopedia of Science and Technology*.

1. Archimedes
2. Charles Darwin
3. Albert Einstein
4. Michael Faraday
5. Galileo
6. Antoine Lavoisier
7. James Clerk Maxwell
8. Sir Isaac Newton
9. Louis Pasteur
10. Ernest Rutherford

—Exclusive for *The Book of Lists*

Louis Pasteur, who proved the existence of airborne bacteria,
also discovered vaccines for anthrax and rabies.

14 MEN WHO BECAME
UNITS OF MEASUREMENT AND
THE UNITS NAMED AFTER THEM

1. AMPERE

After André-Marie Ampère, French (1775–1836). The ampere is a unit of electrical current, or the flow of electricity.

2. COULOMB

After Charles Augustin de Coulomb, French (1736–1806). The coulomb is a unit of electrical charge.

3. FARAD

After Michael Faraday, English (1791–1867). The farad is a unit of electrical capacitance.

4. HENRY

After Joseph Henry, U.S. (1797–1878). The henry is a unit of electrical inductance.

5. HERTZ

After Heinrich Rudolf Hertz, German (1857–1894). The hertz is a unit of frequency: 1 hertz = 1 cycle per second. Thus, 1 kilocycle and 1 kilohertz both equal 1,000 cycles per second.

6. JOULE

After James Prescott Joule, English (1818–1889). The joule is a unit of energy.

7. KELVIN

After William Thomson Lord Kelvin, British (1824–1907). The kelvin is the unit of absolute temperature. Thus, absolute zero is zero kelvin, symbolized by 0 K. And water, which boils at 212°F. or 100°C., boils also at 373.15 K.

8. NEWTON

After Sir Isaac Newton, English (1642–1727). The newton is a unit of force. Thus, 1 newton equals the force with which a mass of 101.97 grams presses downward under standard gravitational conditions on earth. And a mass of 1 kilogram presses down with a force of 9.80665 newtons.

9. OHM

After Georg Simon Ohm, German (1787–1854). The ohm is a unit of electrical resistance.

10. PASCAL

After Blaise Pascal, French (1623–1662). The pascal, like the pound per square inch, or the kilogram of force per square meter, is a unit of pressure.

11. TESLA

After Nikola Tesla, a Croatian born in what was then part of Austria-Hungary and is now in Yugoslavia. He came to the U.S. at the age of 27, became an American citizen, and lived in the U.S. the rest of his life (1856–1943). The tesla is a unit of magnetic flux density, also called magnetic induction.

12. VOLT

After Alessandro Volta, Italian (1745–1827). The volt is a unit of electrical potential difference, or electromotive force.

13. WATT

After James Watt, Scottish (1736–1819). The watt is a unit of power, also described as the time rate of energy delivery or conversion.

14. WEBER

After Wilhelm Eduard Weber, German (1804–1891). The weber is a unit of magnetic flux.

—H.A.K.

10 MEDICAL BREAKTHROUGHS BY NONDOCTORS

1. ACUPUNCTURE (c. 2700 B.C.)

Its discovery is attributed to the legendary Emperor Shen Nung of China, who also compiled the first known list of effective herbal remedies.

2. ANATOMICAL DRAWINGS (c. 1500)

The first accurate and detailed anatomical drawings were made by the artist and inventor Leonardo da Vinci, who dissected cadavers for the purpose. His intricate drawings of the heart showed the true function of its valves, and he gave medicine a precise picture of the cavities of the brain.

3. BACTERIAL IDENTIFICATION (1683)

The Dutch merchant and amateur microscopist Anton van Leeuwenhoek made his own microscopes—200 or more—and through them became the discoverer of bacteria, protozoa, and spermatozoa. He had no medical or scientific training of any kind. His finest microscope achieved a magnification of up to 250 diameters.

4. OXYGEN THERAPY (1771)

An English clergyman and chemist, Joseph Priestley, through his new methods of "pneumatic chemistry" (the collection of gases over water or mercury), discovered and isolated oxygen, which he called "dephlogisticated air." He isolated 10 other gases, among which were nitrous oxide, carbon monoxide, and ammonia.

5. ANESTHESIA (1842)

Ether was first used by an American dentist for tooth extraction. The method was suggested by a young chemistry student, William E. Clarke, who had seen the effects of ether at several "ether frolics," parties where young people sniffed the exhilarating gas for pleasure. Clarke administered the gas during a dental operation.

6. AIRBORNE BACTERIA (1861)

Louis Pasteur, a French chemist and bacteriologist, exploded the theory of spontaneous germ generation and proved the existence of airborne bacteria. Pasteurization of milk to free it of harmful bacteria was a result of his discovery. He also discovered vaccines for anthrax and rabies.

7. X RAYS (1895)

Wilhelm Roentgen, a doctor of philosophy and professor of mathematics and physics, discovered X rays during an investigation of cathode rays. He called them "X" rays because the radiation that caused them was unknown. Roentgen received many awards for his discoveries, including the first Nobel prize for physics in 1901.

8. SYPHILIS (1905)

A German protozoologist, Fritz Schaudinn, discovered the tiny corkscrew organisms (*Spirochaeta pallida*) that carry syphilis, while working in the Imperial Health Office in Berlin. The discovery was made despite official orders that he spend his time in administrative work and do no research.

9. CRYOGENICS (1908)

Heike Kamerlingh Onnes, a Dutch physicist, first produced the liquid helium that led to the use of the "cold knife" in cryosurgery, quick-freezing of blood plasma, and new techniques in the treatment of Parkinson's disease.

10. RADIUM (1910)

Marie Curie, a chemist and physicist, and her husband, Pierre Curie, a physicist, discovered the elements polonium and radium in pitchblende. Their researches into the nature and uses of radium led to the development of radiotherapy and other advances in the treatment and diagnosis of disease.

—J.B.

THE 7 WONDERS OF THE ANCIENT WORLD

Who created one of the earliest and most enduring of all lists, a list that arbitrarily named the seven most spectacular sights existing in the world 150 years before the birth of Jesus Christ? The list was created by a most respected Byzantine mathematician and traveler named Philon. In a series of arduous trips, Philon saw all of the western civilized world there was to see in his time, and then he sat down and wrote a short but widely circulated paper entitled *De Septem Orbis Spectaculis* (The Seven Wonders of the World).

1. THE GREAT PYRAMID OF CHEOPS (Egypt)

Begun as a royal tomb in c. 2600 B.C., standing in splendor 2,000 years before any of the other Seven Wonders were built, this largest of Egypt's 80-odd pyramids is the only Wonder to have survived to this day. Located outside of Cairo, near Giza, the burial tomb of King Cheops was made up of 2.3 million blocks of stone, some of them 2½ tons in weight. The height is 481 ft., the width at the base 755 ft. on each side, large enough to enclose London's Westminster Abbey, Rome's St. Peter's, and Milan's and Florence's main cathedrals.

2. THE HANGING GARDENS OF BABYLON (Iraq)

They were not hanging gardens, but gardens on balconies or terraces. When Nebuchadnezzar brought home his new wife, a princess from Medes, she pined for the mountains and lush growth of her native land. To please her, in 600 B.C. the king started to build a man-made mountain with exotic growths. Actually it was a square building 400 ft. high, containing five terraces supported by arches climbing upward, each densely planted with grass, flowers, and fruit trees, irrigated from below by pumps manned by slaves or oxen. Inside and beneath the gardens, the queen held court amid the vegetation and artificial rain. Due to the erosion of time and influx of conquerors, the Hanging Gardens had been leveled and reduced to wilderness when Pliny the Elder visited them before his death in 79 A.D.

3. THE STATUE OF ZEUS AT OLYMPIA (Greece)

The multicolored Temple of Zeus, in the area where the Greek Olympic Games were held every fifth year, contained the magnificent statue of Zeus, king of the gods. Sculptured by Phidias (who had done Athena for the Parthenon) some time after 432 B.C., the statue was 40 ft. high, made of ivory and gold plates set on wood. Zeus, with jewels for eyes, sat on a golden throne, feet resting on a footstool of gold. Ancients came from afar to worship at the god's feet. A Greek writer, Pausanias, saw the statue intact as late as the second century A.D. After that it disappeared from history, probably the victim of looting armies and fire.

4. THE TEMPLE OF DIANA AT EPHESUS (Turkey)

Summing up his Seven Wonders, Philon chose his favorite: "But when I saw the temple at Ephesus rising to the clouds, all these other wonders were put in the shade." The temple, a religious shrine built after 350 B.C., housed a statue of Diana, goddess of hunting, symbol of fertility. The kings of many Asian states contributed to the construction. The temple, 225 ft. wide and 525 ft. long, was supported by 127 marble columns 60 ft. high. St. Paul, in the New Testament, railed against it, being quoted as saying that "the temple of the great goddess Diana should be despised, and her magnificence should be destroyed, whom all Asia and the world worshippeth." The craftsmen of the temple disagreed: "And when they heard these sayings, they were full of wrath, and cried out saying, Great is Diana of the Ephesians." Ravaged and brought down by invaders, the temple was rebuilt three times before the Goths permanently destroyed it in 262 A.D. In 1874, after 11 years of digging, the English archaeologist J. T. Wood unearthed fragments of the original columns.

5. THE TOMB OF KING MAUSOLUS AT HALICARNASSUS (Turkey)

King Mausolus, conqueror of Rhodes, ruled over the Persian province of Caria. His queen, Artemisia, was also his sister. When he died in 353 B.C., he was cremated and his grieving widow drank his ashes in wine. As a memorial to him, she determined to build the most beautiful tomb in the world at Halicarnassus, now called Bodrum. She sent to Greece for the greatest architects and sculptors, and by 350 B.C. the memorial was completed. There was a rectangular sculptured marble tomb on a platform, then 36 golden-white Ionic columns upon which sat an architrave, which in turn held a pyramid topped by a bronzed chariot with statues of Mausolus and Artemisia.

The monument survived 1,900 years, only to tumble down in an earthquake. What remains of it today is the word "mausoleum."

6. THE COLOSSUS OF RHODES ON THE ISLE OF RHODES (in the Aegean Sea)

To celebrate being saved from a Macedonian siege by Ptolemy I, the Rhodians, between 292 and 280 B.C., erected a mammoth statue to their heavenly protector, the sun-god Apollo. Chares, who had studied under a favorite of Alexander the Great, fashioned the statue. The nude Colossus was 120 ft. tall, with its chest and back 60 ft. around, built of stone blocks and iron and plated with thin bronze. It did not stand astride the harbor, with room for ships to pass between the legs, but stood with feet together on a promontory at the entrance to the harbor. In 224 B.C., it was felled by an earthquake. It lay in ruins almost 900 years. In 667 A.D., the Arabs, who controlled Rhodes, sold the 720,900 lbs. of the broken statue for scrap metal to a Jewish merchant. When the merchant hauled his purchase to Alexandria, he found that it required 900 camel loads.

7. THE LIGHTHOUSE ON THE ISLE OF PHAROS (off Alexandria, Egypt)

On orders of Ptolemy Philadelphus, in 200 B.C., the architect Sostratus of Cnidus constructed a pharos or lighthouse such as the world had not seen before. Built on a small island off Alexandria, the tiers of the marble tower—first square, then round, each with a balcony—rose to a height of 400 ft. At the summit a huge brazier with an eternal flame was amplified by a great glass mirror so that the fire could be seen 300 mi. at sea. Half the lighthouse was torn down by occupying Arabs, who hoped to find gold inside the structure. The rest of the structure crashed to the ground when an earthquake struck in 1375.

—I.W.

THE 7 WONDERS
OF THE MIDDLE AGES

1. The Colosseum of Rome
2. The Catacombs of Alexandria
3. The Great Wall of China
4. Stonehenge
5. The Leaning Tower of Pisa
6. The Porcelain Tower of Nanking
7. The Mosque of St. Sophia, Constantinople

THE GOLDEN BOOK OF FACTS AND FIGURES' 7 WONDERS OF THE MODERN WORLD

1. EMPIRE STATE BUILDING (U.S.)

This skyscraper is 102 stories high, can hold 80,000 people, has 7 mi. of elevator shafts.

Empire State Building and friend.

2. JODRELL BANK TELESCOPE (England)

A radio telescope, not an optical one. Has a curved reflecting surface 250 ft. wide. Receives signals sent by stars and other bodies.

3. GOLDEN GATE BRIDGE (U.S.)

Joins San Francisco and Marin County. Its suspension span is 4,200 ft. Its two main cables hold 80,000 mi. of wire.

4. PANAMA CANAL (Panama)

Over 200 million tons of dirt and rock were dug up to create this 50-mi. ditch that bisects the Isthmus of Panama and connects the Atlantic and Pacific oceans.

5. *SPUTNIK 1* (U.S.S.R.)

The first artificial satellite rocketed into space. It weighed 23 lbs., circled the earth every 96 mins. until it burned up in the atmosphere.

6. HOOVER DAM (U.S.)

Located between Nevada and Arizona, it is 1,244 ft. long, 726 ft. high, and its 247-sq.-mi. reservoir holds 10 trillion gallons of water.

7. *NAUTILUS* (U.S.)

First submarine driven by atomic power, it crossed under the north pole in 1958.

SOURCE: Bertha Morris Parker, *The Golden Book of Facts and Figures* (New York: Golden Press, 1962).

WILLY LEY'S 7 FUTURE WONDERS OF THE WORLD

1. THE CHANNEL TUNNEL

The construction of a tunnel under the English Channel to link England and continental Europe at the Strait of Dover was originally proposed in 1802. Beyond some test work done in 1880, the project has not yet been realized; military and economic considerations have continually blocked progress.

2. THE AEROGENERATOR

Construction of a wind-powered generator was proposed in 1925 but became a reality for only a brief period in 1941 in the U.S., and on a small scale in Salach, Germany. Although the U.S. Federal Power Commission later funded a study of aerogenerators from which construction plans were proposed, the basic idea was viewed as too risky due to the power source's inherent unreliability.

3. THE TAMED VOLCANO

By 55 B.C., a hot spring of Tuscany, Italy, had become a source of superstition. By 1930 A.D., it had become a source of power. It was found that the well's steam could be tapped and used as a major source of energy for local towns. Later, it was theorized that the deeper one digs—anywhere in the earth—the hotter it gets, thus suggesting the existence of an enormous reservoir of untapped power.

4. VALLEY OF THE JORDAN

Plans for supplying Palestine with irrigation and electric power were drawn up in 1925 and again in 1943, entailing the construction of a dam, a reservoir, a canal, and a power plant. Political and economic obstacles have prevented its realization.

5. AFRICA'S CENTRAL LAKE

In 1935, German architect Herman Sörgel found a way to create two large freshwater lakes in central Africa, but political considerations put a damper on the idea.

6. ATLANTROPA

Herman Sörgel in 1928 proposed the reclamation of land beneath the Mediterranean Sea to join together the continents of Europe and Africa and to provide the means for producing electric power. Although the plan drew much support, technical and political difficulties blocked any action.

7. SOLAR ENERGY

In 1615, the sun was first used to power toys, and in 1864, the first sun-heated steam engine was built. "Solar-boiler" plants have since been modified and used on a limited scale. While solar "fuel" is virtually without cost, operational efficiency is low due to the intermittence of supply and the high cost of energy storage.

—Annotated by D.B.

SOURCE: Willy Ley, *Engineers' Dreams* (New York: Viking Press, 1954).

25 PRODUCTS: THE INTERVAL BETWEEN THEIR CONCEPTION AND THEIR REALIZATION

	Conception	Realization	Interval (years)
1. Antibiotics	1910	1940	30
2. Automatic transmission	1930	1946	16
3. Ballpoint pen	1938	1945	7
4. Filter cigarettes	1953	1955	2
5. Fluorescent lighting	1901	1934	33
6. Frozen foods	1908	1923	15
7. Heart pacemaker	1928	1960	32
8. Helicopter	1904	1941	37
9. Instant coffee	1934	1956	22
10. Long-playing records	1945	1948	3
11. Minute rice	1931	1949	18
12. Nuclear energy	1919	1965	46
13. Nylon	1927	1939	12
14. Photography	1782	1838	56
15. Radar	1904	1939	35

16.	Radio	1890	1914	24
17.	Roll-on deodorant	1948	1955	7
18.	Silicone	1904	1942	38
19.	Stainless steel	1904	1920	16
20.	Telegraph	1820	1838	18
21.	Television	1884	1947	63
22.	Transistor	1940	1956	16
23.	Videotape recorder	1950	1956	6
24.	Xerox copying	1935	1950	15
25.	Zipper	1883	1913	30

SOURCE: Stephen Rosen, *The New York Times,* June 18, 1976.

TIME OUT FOR 18 EVENTS AND THEIR DURATIONS

We experience only a narrow range (from about 0.1 sec. to the years in a lifetime) of the spectrum of time taken by events in the universe. The following 18 events and their durations will provide a sense of the vastness of that spectrum.

Duration (secs.)

1. Recoil of atomic nucleus   0.000 000 000 000 000 001

When a subatomic particle crashes into an atomic nucleus, as in an atomic reactor, the nucleus is stretched way out of shape. It either springs back to shape (recoils), or it explodes. Either of these events occurs within a quintillionth of a second—an *attosecond.*

2. Compression of deuterium   0.000 000 001
pellet by laser light

In a system now being developed, small pellets of deuterium and other materials are simultaneously heated and compressed by powerful laser beams. The process takes a billionth of a second—a *nanosecond.* Temperatures within the pellets reach several million degrees, and the atoms of the pellet fuse into larger atoms, releasing tremendous energy. This is the same process that powers the sun—fusion.

3. Bullet cap explodes 0.000 001

   This takes a millionth of a second—
   a *microsecond*.

4-5. Nerve impulse crosses 0.001
   synapse; *or,* a soap bubble explodes

   Duration: a thousandth of a second—a
   millisecond.

6. Bee's wing beat 0.03

7. Human heartbeat 1

8. Time it takes sunlight to 492
   travel from the sun to earth

   That's a little over 8 mins.

9. Average time between high 21,600
   and low tides on earth

   It's 6 hrs. between high and
   low tides.

10. The earth rotates once 86,164.1
   on its axis

   23 hrs. 56 mins. 4.1 secs. =
   1 day.

11. The earth completes an orbit 31,472,329
   around the sun

   365 days 6 hrs. 13 mins. 53 secs.
   = 1 year.

12. Greatest authenticated age 3,575,000,000
   to which a person has lived

   Mrs. Delina Filkins of Herkimer County,
   N.Y., lived 113 years 214 days.

13. Age of the oldest living   145,000,000,000
    thing on earth

    A bristlecone pine, which has been named
    Methuselah, has grown for 4,600 years
    in the White Mountains of California.

14. Half-life of carbon 14   179,000,000,000

    In 179 billion seconds, or 5,700 years,
    half of a mass of this radioactive
    isotope has broken down. This
    fact is used in carbon dating.

15. The time since Creation,   180,525,000,000
    according to the Jewish calendar

    This was at the end of the year 5736
    (September 24, 1976 A.D.) Rabbis
    have kept count of the passage of
    years for millennia. The first calendar
    was introduced by Hillel II in 358–359
    A.D. The Jewish calendar's present
    form was determined after 1000 A.D.

16. Time it takes the solar   7,080,000,000,000,000
    system to complete one orbit
    around the center of our galaxy

    Our sun's year, called a cosmic year,
    takes 225,000,000 earth years.

17. Estimated time since   70,800,000,000,000,000
    life appeared on earth

    About 10 cosmic years.

18. Estimated age of the universe   320,000,000,000,000,000

    The latest estimate is 10,125,000,000
    years—about 45 cosmic years. We have
    traveled from a quintillionth of a second to
    320 quadrillion seconds—the spectrum of time.

—J.BER.

DR. WILLARD LIBBY'S
7 RICHEST CARBON-DATED
OBJECTS ON EARTH

Author, educator, and chemist, Dr. Willard Libby invented the first reliable method for measuring the age of ancient objects: the carbon 14 dating process. This discovery won him the 1960 Nobel prize for chemistry. He was also the recipient of the gold medal from the American Institute of Chemists and the Albert Einstein award. His books include *Radiocarbon Dating* and *Environmental Geology*.

Index No.	Object	Years Old
1. C-1	Acacia, from Zoser at Sakkara (first carbon-dated object)	4,000
2. C-576	Dead Sea scrolls: Isaiah manuscript	2,000
3. C-406	Lascaux, the cave paintings	15,500
4. C-353	Wooden platform near Starr Carr, England	9,500
5. C-308	Fossilized wood of spruce trees at Two Creeks, Wis.—last ice advance	11,400
6. C-159	Redwood—date matches tree-ring count	2,700
7. C-917	Zimbabwe—the fabulous walled city in Rhodesia	1,500

Dr. Libby adds that by "richest" he means that these are the carbon-dated objects from which we have learned the most.

—Exclusive for *The Book of Lists*

On September 12, 1940, five boys in Lascaux, southwest France, discovered the vivid Stone Age paintings on the walls of a cave. The paintings were later proved to be 15,500 years old.

21 ENERGETIC EVENTS AND THEIR ERGS

From the splitting of a single atom to the explosion of a star, every event in the universe represents the release of energy. Here are the energies represented by 21 events, in ergs (a metric unit). Remember, an erg is quite small on the human scale—a foot-pound equals almost 14 million ergs.

Energy (ergs)

1. Splitting of a uranium atom
   0.000 1

   This takes only a ten-thousandth of an erg.

2. Pronouncing an average syllable of a word
   200

3. Moonlight on your face for 1 sec.
   300

4-5. Cricket's chirp; *or,* bee's wing beat
   9,000

6-7. A 50¢ piece falling from the hand to the ground; *or,* a typewriter key being pressed down
   1,000,000

8. Using a 10-watt flashlight for 1 min.
   6,000,000,000

9. Lethal X-ray dose
   9,000,000,000

10-11. Shooting an elephant gun; *or,* striking a match
   12,000,000,000

12. Accelerating a 4-ton truck to freeway speed
   9,000,000,000,000

   We are already up to 9 trillion ergs.

13. A day's hard labor (ditchdigging, chopping wood)
   100,000,000,000,000

14. Atlas rocket blasting off
   9,000,000,000,000,000,000

   And that's 9 *quintillion* ergs.

15. First atom bomb   1,000,000,000,000,000,000,000

16. Hurricane   50,000,000,000,000,000,000,000

17. A 100-megaton H-bomb   10,000,000,000,000,000,000,000,000

18. Major earthquake (8-9   60,000,000,000,000,000,000,000,000
    points on the Richter scale)

    The 1906 San Francisco earthquake was
    one of these.

19. Energy the earth receives from the sun in 1 year
                100,000,000,000,000,000,000,000,000,000,000

20. The sun's annual production of energy
            80,000,000,000,000,000,000,000,000,000,000,000

21. Supernova—seen when a star explodes
        10,000,000,000,000,000,000,000,000,000,000,000,000,-
        000,000,000

    One supernova, in 1054, was thought by
    many to herald the biblical Day of
    Judgment. We have reached an energy
    level of 10 quindecillion ergs,
    or 10^{49} ergs.

                                            —J.BER.

25 TEMPERATURE READINGS

| | Temperature | |
	(°C.)	(°F.)
1. Water boils.	100	212
2. Best temperature for brewing coffee—water dissolves the flavor-bearing oils at this temperature, yet leaves the bitter alkaloids in the grounds.	82.2	180
3. A few varieties of bacteria thrive in hot-spring waters, an indication that bacteria are very hardy organisms.	70	158

4. Milk heated for 30 mins. will be pasteurized without curdling or clotting, but most of the vitamin C and D will be destroyed.	62.8	145
5. World's record shade temperature, recorded by the National Geographic Society at El Azizia, Libya (Sept. 13, 1922).	58	136.4
6. A hot bath.	43.3	110
7. Most people die if their fever reaches this temperature.	41.7	107
8. Ideal temperature for baby's bath.	37.8	100
9. Normal human body temperature; ideal temperature for baby's bottle.	37	98.6
10. Warmest sea on earth, the Red Sea, is maintained at this unusually high temperature by hot-water seepages along its floor.	35	95
11. Butter melts.	30.6	88
12. During winter in cold climates, drunks have been found collapsed in a stupor with body temperatures in the range of 80°–85°F. At first glance, these people appear dead; their skin has a gray pallor, and their muscles are rigid, as if they are in rigor mortis. But when they warm up, they "come to life."	29.4	85
13. A temperate bath.	26.7	80
14. A cool bath.	22.2	71
15. Lowest internal human body temperature survived—by a young patient.	20.5	69
16. Room temperature.	20	68
17. A cold bath.	10	50
18. Best temperature for storing milk, or for refrigeration of food in general.	4.4	40
19. Pure water freezes.	0	32
20. Frigid arctic waters (they have a lower freezing point because of their salt content). A person who falls in water this cold has no more than 2 mins. to get out before he becomes unconscious—one reason so many died when the *Titanic* sank in icy north Atlantic waters.	−1.1	30
21. Typical daytime temperature recorded on Martian surface by *Viking 1*.	−30	−22
22. Mercury freezes.	−38.87	−38.0
23. Carbon dioxide gas freezes, becoming a dry ice without passing through a liquid phase.	−78	−108.4
24. Typical dawn temperature recorded on Martian surface by *Viking 1*.	−86	−122.8
25. Earth's coldest temperature recorded, at Vostok, Antarctica (Aug. 24, 1960).	−88.3	−126.9

—J. BER.

HOW TO GET FROM
THE ATOM TO THE ULTIMATE
HORIZON—26 DISTANCES

The range in size we experience in a lifetime, from a speck of dust to a massive mountain, encompasses but a fraction of the vast scale of spatial dimensions in the universe, as the following 26 points on the distance spectrum demonstrate. We use the metric millimeter as the basic unit—it takes about 25 of them to make an inch.

Length or Dimension (millimeters)

1. Hydrogen atom   0.000 000 03

2. Glucose (sugar) molecule   0.000 000 7

3. Hemoglobin molecule   0.000 006 8

4. DNA molecule   0.000 002

   DNA is the substance in the chromosomes of a cell that carries genetic information.

5. Width of tobacco mosaic virus   0.000 04

   The length of this rod-shaped virus, 0.017 mm. is longer than that of the next two entries.

6. Wavelength of red light   0.000 7

   This length sets the limit to the magnification a light microscope can achieve.

7. Chloroplast   0.008

   Chloroplasts are the bodies in plant cells in which photosynthesis occurs.

8. Average body cell (from the liver)   0.05

The Good Earth—7,927 mi. in diameter—as photographed on October 25, 1975, by the Geostationary Operational Environmental Satellite-1 (GOES-1).

Length or Dimension (millimeters)

9–10. Dust particle; *or,* thickness of a coat of paint   0.1

11. Head of a pin   1

12. Flea   1.5

13. Width of a fingernail   10

14. Average human foot   299

15. Average length of human digestive tract   10,000

16. Tallest tree known   109,860

    This is the Howard Libbey redwood in
    Redwood Grove, Calif. (366.2 ft.).

17. Diameter of the earth   12,750,000,000

    The distance through the earth to
    the other side is 7,927 mi.

18. Distance light travels   300,000,000,000
    in 1 sec. in a vacuum

    This is 186,300 mi., or 300,000
    kilometers.

19. Average distance from   384,300,000,000
    the earth to the moon

    The distance to the moon (238,840 mi.)
    is about 30 times the diameter of the
    earth.

20. Average distance from   149,500,000,000,000
    the earth to the sun

    This *astronomical unit* (A.U.) equals
    92,957,200 mi.—389 distances
    from the earth to the moon.

21. Distance light travels   9,460,000,000,000,000,000
    in 1 year

    This distance, which equals about 63,000
    A.U., is called a *light-year*.

22. Distance to nearest star,   40,200,000,000,000,000,000
    Proxima Centauri

    It took the astronauts about 3 days to get
    to the moon; at the same speed, it
    would take them about 878,000 years
    to get to Proxima Centauri, which is
    4.25 light-years away.

23. Diameter of our galaxy (100,000 light-years)

946,000,000,000,000,000,000,000

24. Distance across the local group of galaxies of which our galaxy is a member

49,200,000,000,000,
000,000,000,000

There are 27 known galaxies in this group, including Andromeda, Triangulum Spiral, and the Clouds of Magellan, and it takes a beam of light 5,200,000 years to cross the group.

25. Distance to the most distant observable object: OQ172

94,600,000,000,000,000,
000,000,000,000

It's 10 billion light-years away.

26. Distance to the ultimate horizon

189,200,000,000,000,000,000,000,000,000

According to Hubble's law, the ultimate horizon is 20 billion light-years away.

—J.BER.

13
AT HOME AND GROWING UP

15 FAMOUS EVENTS THAT HAPPENED IN THE BATHTUB

1. POISONING OF PELIAS

According to Greek mythology, Medea murdered Jason's uncle (Pelias, king of Thessaly) by giving him a bath in a vat of deadly poison which she falsely claimed would restore his lost youth.

2. MURDER OF AGAMEMNON

Shortly after his return from the Trojan War, the Greek hero Agamemnon was murdered by his wife, Clytemnestra, who struck him twice with an ax while he was relaxing in the tub.

3. ARCHIMEDES' DISCOVERY

While soaking in the bathtub, the Greek scientist Archimedes formulated the law of physics—known as the Archimedean principle —that a body immersed in fluid loses weight equal to the weight of the fluid it displaces. He became so excited about his discovery that he rushed out stark naked into the streets of Syracuse, Sicily, shouting "Eureka!" ("I have found it!").

4. BURNING OF ALEXANDRIA

When the Arabs conquered Alexandria, they were alleged to have burned the 700,000 books in the library to keep up the fires in the city's 4,000 public baths.

5. QUEEN ANNE'S BURNING BATH

Anne, queen of Denmark, was the wife of James I of England. In 1615, gases from her mineral bath momentarily ignited, causing Her Majesty great consternation.

6. FRANKLIN'S PASTIME

Benjamin Franklin is reputed to have imported the first bath-tub into America. He improved upon its design, and contemporary reports indicate that he carried on much of his reading and correspondence while soaking in the tub.

7. MARAT'S ASSASSINATION

Jean-Paul Marat played an active part in the French Revolution. As editor of the journal *L'Ami du peuple,* he became known

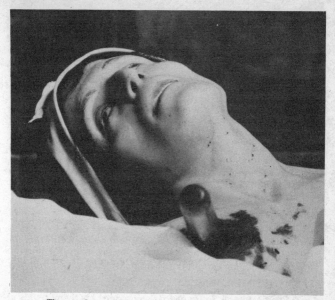

The wax figure of Marat is based on an actual plaster cast
taken of the dead man by Mme. Marie Tussaud herself.

as an advocate of extreme violence. The moderate Girondists were
driven out of Paris and took refuge in Normandy. There, some of
them met and influenced a young woman named Charlotte Corday.
Convinced that Marat must die, she went to Paris and bought a
butcher knife. When she arrived at Marat's house on July 13, 1793,
he was taking a bath. (He spent many hours in the tub because of
a painful skin condition.) Overhearing Corday, he asked to see her.
They discussed politics for a few minutes; then Corday drew her
knife and stabbed Marat to death in the bathtub.

8. THE BONAPARTES' ARGUMENT

While Napoleon was taking a bath one morning in 1803, his
brothers Joseph and Lucien rushed in, seething with rage because
they had just heard of his plan to sell Louisiana to the Americans.
They were furious because he refused to consult the legislature about
it. Lucien had worked hard to make Spain return the colony to
France, and now his work would be for naught. Joseph warned
Napoleon that he might end up in exile if he carried out his plan.
At this, Napoleon fell back angrily in the tub, splashing water all
over Joseph. Napoleon's valet, who was standing by with hot towels
over his arm, crashed to the floor in a dead faint.

9. WAGNER'S INSPIRATION

Composer Richard Wagner soaked in a tub scented with vast
quantities of Milk of Iris perfume for several hours every day while

working on his final opera, *Parsifal* (1882). He insisted that the water be kept hot and heavily perfumed so that he could smell it as he sat at his desk, clad in outlandish silk and fur dressing gowns and surrounded by vials and sachets of exotic scents.

10. MORPHY'S DEATH

Paul Morphy of New Orleans defeated famous chess players when he was still a child. As an adult, he could play eight games simultaneously while blindfolded. Some people consider him the greatest chess player who ever lived, but from the age of 22 until his death on July 10, 1884, at 47, he played no more chess. Believing that people were trying to poison him or burn his clothes, Morphy became a virtual recluse. On one oppressively hot day he returned from a walk and took a cold bath. In the tub he died from what doctors described as "congestion of the brain or apoplexy, which was evidently brought on by the effects of the cold water on his overheated body."

11. ROSTAND'S WRITING

Edmond Rostand, French poet and playwright, hated to be interrupted while he was working, but he did not like to turn his friends away. Therefore, he took refuge in the bathtub and wrote there all day, creating such successes as *Cyrano de Bergerac* (1898).

12. SMITH'S MURDERS

George Joseph Smith of England earned his living by his almost hypnotic power over women. In 1910, he met Bessie Mundy, married her (without mentioning that he already had a wife), and disappeared with her cash and clothes. Two years later they met by chance and began living together again. After Smith persuaded Bessie to write a will in his favor, he took her to a doctor on the pretense that she suffered from fits. (Both she and the doctor took his word for it.) A few days later she was found dead in the bathtub, a cake of soap clutched in her hand. Everyone assumed she had drowned during an epileptic seizure. Smith married two more women—Alice Burnham and Margaret Lofty—took out insurance policies on their lives, and described mysterious ailments to their doctors. They, too, were found dead in their bathtubs. When Alice Burnham's father read of Margaret Lofty's death, he was struck by its similarity to his daughter's untimely end. The police were notified, and Smith was tried for murder and sentenced to be executed. His legal wife, Edith, testified at the trial that she could remember only one occasion when Smith himself took a bath.

13. CARROLL'S ORGY

America was shocked by reports of an orgy on February 22, 1926, at the Earl Carroll Theatre, New York, N.Y., after a performance of his *Vanities*. To climax a midnight party onstage, a bathtub was filled with champagne and a nude model climbed in, while the men lined up and filled their glasses from the tub. This was during the Prohibition era, so a federal grand jury immediately began an inquiry into whether or not the tub really did contain liquor and, if so, who had supplied it. Earl Carroll, the producer who staged the party, was convicted of perjury for telling the grand jury that no wine had been in the bathtub. He was sentenced to a year and a day in prison, plus a $2,000 fine. After he suffered a nervous breakdown on the way to the penitentiary, his fellow prisoners were ordered never to mention bathtubs in his presence.

14. KING HAAKON'S FALL

On June 29, 1955, the reign of King Haakon VII, who had ruled Norway from the time of its independence in 1905, effectively came to an end when the beloved monarch fell in the royal bathtub at his palace in Oslo. The elderly king lingered on for over two years before succumbing on September 21, 1957, to complications resulting from his fall.

15. GLENN'S CAREER

The momentum of what contemporary experts considered to be an unstoppable political career was interrupted in 1964 when astronaut hero John Glenn fell in the bathtub and had to withdraw from his race for senator from Ohio. He was finally elected to the Senate in 1974.

—P.S.H., L.B., & J.BE.

RATING THE CLEANLINESS OF 6 EUROPEAN PEOPLES

Here is the consumption of soap, in ounces of soap per person per year:

1.	British Isles	40
2.	Switzerland	37
3.	Germany	34
4.	Sweden	33
5.	France	22.6
6.	Netherlands	22.2

SOURCE: Swiss Union of Soap and Detergent Manufacturers, 1974.

15 FAMOUS PEOPLE WHO NEVER GRADUATED FROM GRADE SCHOOL

1. Andrew Carnegie, U.S. industrialist and philanthropist
2. Charles Chaplin, British actor and film director

3. William "Buffalo Bill" Cody, American scout and showman
4. Noel Coward, British actor, playwright, and composer
5. Charles Dickens, British novelist
6. Isadora Duncan, U.S. dancer
7. Thomas Edison, U.S. inventor
8. Samuel Gompers, U.S. labor leader
9. Maksim Gorky, Russian writer
10. Claude Monet, French painter
11. Sean O'Casey, Irish playwright
12. Alfred E. Smith, U.S. politician
13. John Philip Sousa, U.S. bandleader and composer
14. Henry M. Stanley, British explorer
15. Mark Twain, U.S. humorist and writer

20 FAMOUS HIGH-SCHOOL
OR SECONDARY-SCHOOL DROPOUTS

1. Harry Belafonte, U.S. singer
2. Cher, U.S. singer and comedienne
3. Mary Baker Eddy, U.S. founder of Christian Science
4. Henry Ford, U.S. automobile manufacturer
5. George Gershwin, U.S. composer
6. D. W. Griffith, U.S. motion-picture pioneer
7. Adolf Hitler, German führer
8. Jack London, U.S. writer
9. Dean Martin, U.S. entertainer
10. Bill Mauldin, U.S. cartoonist
11. Rod McKuen, U.S. poet
12. Steve McQueen, U.S. actor
13. Amedeo Modigliani, Italian painter and sculptor
14. Al Pacino, U.S. actor
15. Will Rogers, U.S. humorist
16. William Saroyan, U.S. writer
17. Frank Sinatra, U.S. singer
18. Marshal Tito, Yugoslav prime minister
19. Orville Wright, U.S. aviation pioneer
20. Wilbur Wright, U.S. aviation pioneer

11 WOMEN WHO WERE
CHEERLEADERS IN HIGH SCHOOL

1. Ann-Margret
2. Dyan Cannon
3. Eydie Gorme
4. Patty Hearst
5. Vicki Lawrence
6. Eleanor McGovern
7. Cybill Shepherd
8. Dinah Shore
9. Carly Simon
10. Lily Tomlin
11. Raquel Welch

SOURCE: Ralph Keyes, *Is There Life After High School?* (Boston: Little, Brown, 1976). Copyright © 1976 by Ralph Keyes.

20 FAMOUS PEOPLE
WHO NEVER ATTENDED COLLEGE

1. Joseph Chamberlain, British statesman
2. Grover Cleveland, U.S. president
3. Joseph Conrad, British author
4. Aaron Copland, U.S. composer
5. Hart Crane, U.S. poet
6. Eugene Debs, U.S. socialist leader
7. Amelia Earhart, U.S. aviator
8. Paul Gauguin, French painter
9. Kahlil Gibran, Syrian author and painter
10. Ernest Hemingway, U.S. author
11. Rudyard Kipling, British author
12. Abraham Lincoln, U.S. president
13. H. L. Mencken, U.S. editor and journalist
14. John D. Rockefeller, U.S. oil magnate
15. Eleanor Roosevelt, U.S. lecturer, author, and humanitarian
16. George Bernard Shaw, British playwright and critic
17. Dylan Thomas, British poet
18. Harry S Truman, U.S. president
19. George Washington, U.S. president
20. Virginia Woolf, British author

24 NOTED PEOPLE
WHO NEVER MARRIED

1. Jane Addams, U.S. social settlement worker
2. Susan B. Anthony, U.S. women's rights leader
3. Jane Austen, English novelist
4. Ludwig van Beethoven, German composer
5. Elizabeth Blackwell, U.S. physician
6. James Buchanan, U.S. president
7. Frédéric Chopin, Polish composer and pianist
8. Emily Dickinson, U.S. poet
9. Elizabeth I, queen of England and Ireland
10. J. Edgar Hoover, U.S. director of the FBI
11. Henry James, English novelist
12. Joan of Arc, French heroine and saint
13. Charles Lamb, English essayist
14. Maria Montessori, Italian physician and educator
15. Ralph Nader, U.S. consumer advocate
16. Sir Isaac Newton, English physicist and mathematician
17. Florence Nightingale, English nurse and hospital reformer
18. Alexander Pope, English satiric poet
19. Cecil Rhodes, South African administrator and financier
20. Arthur Schopenhauer, German philosopher
21. Adam Smith, English economist
22. Henry David Thoreau, U.S. author
23. Henri de Toulouse-Lautrec, French painter
24. Voltaire, French author

Maria Montessori, who revolutionized teaching,
in 1913, bore a son out of wedlock.

21 OF THE MOST MARRIED PEOPLE IN HISTORY

1. King Mongut, Siam; the king in *The King and I* — 9,000 wives and concubines*
2. King Mutesa, Uganda — 7,000 wives*
3. King Solomon, Israel — 700 wives*
4. Queen Kahena, Barbary — 400 husbands*
5. Augustus the Strong, Saxony — 365 wives*
6. Fon of Bikom, Cameroon — 100 wives*
7. Theresa Vaughn, England — 61 husbands*
8. Joseph Smith, U.S. — 49 wives*
9. Ibn-Saud, Saudi Arabia — 35 wives*
10. Brigham Young, U.S. — 27 wives*
11. Hieronymus, Rome — 21 wives
12. Glynn de Moss Wolfe, U.S. — 19 wives
13. Beverly N. Avery, U.S. — 16 husbands
14. Ike Ward, U.S. — 16 wives
15. Edward Teach, England; "Blackbeard" — 14 wives
16. Martha Jane Burke, U.S.; "Calamity Jane" — 12 husbands
17. Tommy Manville, U.S. — 11 wives
18. Kid McCoy, U.S. — 10 wives
19. Pancho Villa, Mexico — 9 wives
20. Marie McDonald, U.S. — 8 husbands
21. Artie Shaw, U.S. — 8 wives

* Polygamist.

25 WEDDING ANNIVERSARIES —AND THE GIFT TO GIVE ON EACH ONE

1st Paper	13th Lace
2nd Cotton (or calico)	14th Ivory
3rd Leather	15th Crystal (or glass)
4th Linen (or silk)	20th China
5th Wood	25th Silver
6th Iron (or candy)	30th Pearls
7th Wool (or copper)	35th Coral (or jade)
8th Bronze (or small electrical appliances)	40th Rubies
	45th Sapphires
9th Willow (or pottery)	50th Gold
10th Tin (or aluminum)	55th Emeralds
11th Steel	60th Diamonds
12th Silk (or linen)	75th Diamonds again

MARABEL MORGAN'S
10 WAYS WOMEN PLEASE MEN

Author and lecturer Marabel Morgan is the leading spokesperson in the U.S. for the antifeminist movement. Her controversial best-seller *The Total Woman* is a handbook on how women might most successfully please their men. Mrs. Morgan advises members of her sex to be devoted and submissive to the males in their lives. Her most recent book is *Total Joy*.

1. Provide excitement and high adventure at his own address.
2. Ask questions about his favorite pastime.
3. Listen as he talks about his favorite pastime.
4. Admire the same tiger he sees in the mirror. Tact is the ability to see another person as he sees himself.
5. Tell him what's bothering you. Then don't remind him. Assume he heard you. If he doesn't move after two hours, take his pulse.
6. One Saturday morning, serve him breakfast and you in bed (not necessarily in that order).
7. Be available.
8. Pray for him.
9. Understand his problems. A man must know how much you care before he cares how much you know.
10. Appreciation comes in two flavors—thanks and compliments.

—Exclusive for *The Book of Lists*

10 MEN WHO WERE
SUPPORTED BY THEIR WIVES

1. SOCRATES

Although Socrates was trained as a stonecutter, he never worked at his trade as an adult and he never charged for the lessons that he gave the Athenian young. In his play *Barefoot in Athens*, Maxwell Anderson suggests that Socrates' wife took in washing to support the family. Although this may not be true, she certainly provided and maintained a home for Socrates and at least three children.

2. CHRISTIAN DAVIES'S HUSBAND

Christian Davies (1667–1739) was a woman who disguised herself as a man and fought as a private in various European armies during her lifetime. She was granted a pension for her military service by George I of Great Britain and used the money to open various beer shops. She did so well that she was able to purchase her husband's release from the army, but he drank up her money so quickly that she had to sell several of her business establishments. She recouped her resources, however, when she was granted a monopoly on selling beer in Dublin's Phoenix Park on review days. Later she succeeded in getting both herself and her husband additional pensions.

3. DAVID DOUGLAS

David Douglas married the widow of Lewis Hallam in Jamaica sometime between 1754 and 1758. Mrs. Douglas brought with her Hallam's theater company of which she was the star. Douglas became the manager of the company, but it was the talents of his wife—who was probably the leading actress in colonial America—that supported them.

4. WILLIAM CARTER

The wedding announcement of William Carter and Sarah Ellyson appeared in the *Virginia Gazette* on March 15, 1771. It was clear that Carter intended to live off his wife. The *Gazette* wrote: "Yesterday was married, in Henrico, Mr. William Carter, third son of Mr. John Carter, aged 23, to Mrs. Sarah Ellyson, relict of Mr. Gerard Ellyson, deceased, aged 85, a sprightly old tit, with £3,000 fortune."

5. BEN DUNIWAY

After her husband became an invalid in an accident, Abigail Duniway taught school and then opened up a millinery shop to support him and their six children. She was also an ardent feminist and the founder of a woman's newspaper, the *New Northwest,* in Portland, Ore., in 1871. Circulation boomed when Susan B. Anthony came to town, and Abigail managed her lecture tour of the Northwest. Abigail spent much of the rest of her life advocating women's suffrage in the West.

6. ISAAC PINKHAM

After 30 years of struggling to make ends meet on the income from her husband's real estate speculations, Mrs. Lydia E. Pinkham went into her cellar and mixed up a batch of her "vegetable compound" for commercial distribution. The compound's main ingredients were "unicorn root" and "pleurisy root," but it was also 18% alcohol, or 36 proof. The first batch was sold in 1875. By the time of her death in 1883, the company formed by Lydia and her sons was grossing almost $300,000 a year. The vegetable compound was intended mainly for disorders of the female reproductive system, but it was also advertised as being effective for kidney problems in the male.

7. OSCAR WILDE

Although he had published a book of poetry and a melodrama, *Vera, or the Nihilists,* before he was married, Wilde lived mainly on his wife's fortune, which enabled him to move around in English high society and gain a reputation as a wit. His most successful play, *The Importance of Being Earnest,* closed the same year that it opened because of a sexual scandal that involved Wilde and another man. The scandal ruined both his marriage and his career.

8. HENRI MATISSE

Matisse was supported by his wife for a time, after his father cut off his allowance because the elder Matisse was displeased with the direction his son's art was taking. Mme. Matisse opened a milliner's shop on the rue de Châteaudun in Paris and supported her husband. However, two of their three children had to be put in the care of their grandparents.

9. PAUL LAFARGUE

Laura Lafargue was the daughter of Karl Marx. At one time her husband, Paul Lafargue, author of *The Right to Be Lazy,* had a medical practice, but he abandoned it to open a photographer's studio. His new business brought in some money, but not enough to support the couple. Their real means of subsistence was a legacy left to Laura by Friedrich Engels. When that money ran out in 1911, the Lafargues committed double suicide by injecting overdoses of morphine.

10. JACK GEE

The blues singer Bessie Smith supported her husband Jack Gee throughout their six-year marriage, which broke up when Bessie found out that he had used her money to finance another woman's show. Before they were married, the illiterate Gee was a night watchman who had been rejected by the Philadelphia police department when he applied for a job. Gee did do something for Bessie—he found out that Clarence Williams, with whom she had a contract in the early days of her career, was ripping her off—but it was Bessie who beat up Williams when she and Gee went to Williams's office to demand a release from her contract.

—M.W.J.

19 WIVES OLDER THAN THEIR HUSBANDS

		Age Difference (years)
1. Catherine of Aragon (b. 1485)	King Henry VIII of England (b. 1491)	6
2. Mary I ("Bloody Mary"; 1516)	King Philip II of Spain (1527)	11
3. Mary, Queen of Scots (1542)	King Francis II of France (1544)	2

4. Anne Hathaway (1557)	William Shakespeare (1564)	7
5. Joséphine de Beauharnais (1763)	Napoleon (1769)	6
6. Mary Anne Wyndham Lewis (1792)	Benjamin Disraeli (1804)	12
7. Abigail Powers (1798)	Millard Fillmore (1800)	2
8. Elizabeth Barrett (1806)	Robert Browning (1812)	6
9. Jenny von Westphalen (1814)	Karl Marx (1818)	4
10. Jenny Lind (1820)	Otto Goldschmidt (1829)	9
11. Caroline Lavinia Scott (1832)	Benjamin Harrison (1833)	1
12. Jennie Jerome Churchill (1854)	George Cornwallis-West (1874)	20
	Montagu Porch (1877)	23
13. Florence Kling De Wolfe (1860)	Warren G. Harding (1865)	5
14. Pearl Cecily Bowen (1871)	Raymond Chandler (1888)	17
15. Isadora Duncan (1878)	Sergei Esenin (1895)	17
16. Frieda von Richthofen (1879)	D. H. Lawrence (1885)	6
17. Ruth Gordon (1896)	Garson Kanin (1912)	16
18. Irène Curie (1897)	Frédéric Joliot (1900)	3
19. Thelma Catherine Patricia Ryan (1912)	Richard M. Nixon (1913)	1

Isadora Duncan, dancer and uninhibited soul, and her Russian husband, poet Sergei Esenin. She was 17 years older than Sergei.

10 MOTHERS OF
INFAMOUS CHILDREN

1. AGRIPPINA, THE YOUNGER (mother of NERO, monstrous Roman emperor)

Raised by her grandmother, Agrippina was accused of having had incestuous relations with her brother Caligula. Lucius Domitius Ahenobarbus (later called Nero) was the product of her first marriage. She was believed to have poisoned her second husband before embarking upon a third marriage, which was to her uncle, Emperor Claudius I. She held such sway over Claudius that she convinced him to set aside his own son and make her son Nero heir to the throne. When Nero was 16 she poisoned Claudius, thus setting the scene for Nero to be proclaimed emperor. Resentful of his mother's continuing interference, Nero later arranged to have her assassinated.

2. HANNAH WATERMAN ARNOLD (mother of BENEDICT ARNOLD, American traitor in Revolutionary War)

Hannah belonged to a prominent family and when, as a young widow, she married Benedict Arnold III she brought with her considerable wealth inherited from her first husband. Unfortunately, her new husband squandered this fortune, and as his ineptitude increased, Hannah assumed a dominant position in the household. She achieved a reputation as a long-suffering, pious woman, and she was pitied by her neighbors. When her young son, Benedict Arnold IV, was sent away to school, she wrote him long letters advising him as to proper Christian behavior. Hannah lost five of her seven children in a yellow-fever epidemic, and thereafter she was obsessed by fears of death. She continually exhorted young Benedict and his sister to submit to God's will and urged them to be prepared to die at any moment. Hannah herself died when her son Benedict was 18.

3. MARY ANN HOLMES BOOTH (mother of JOHN WILKES BOOTH, assassin of Abraham Lincoln)

Eighteen-year-old Mary Ann was a London flower girl when she first met Junius Brutus Booth, a talented but dissolute tragedian. Already legally married, Junius fell madly in love with the gentle, warmhearted Mary Ann. In 1821, he accompanied her to the U.S. Eventually she bore Junius 10 children, and John Wilkes was her ninth and favorite child. Although she was acknowledged as his wife in America, Mary Ann's existence was kept secret from Junius's legal wife in England. However, in 1846 his double life was exposed, and in 1851 he obtained a divorce and at last wed Mary Ann. John Wilkes was devoted to his mother, and it is reputed that his dying words after he had assassinated Abraham Lincoln were "Tell Mother . . . tell Mother . . . I died for my country."

4. TERESA CAPONE (mother of AL CAPONE, U.S. gangster)

Born in Italy, Teresa immigrated with her husband to New York, N.Y., in 1893, where she worked as a seamstress to help support her family in Brooklyn's Italian colony. Alfonso, Teresa's fourth son, was forced to take over as head of the household when his father died in 1920. By that time, Al had already begun to establish his underworld connections. Later, during the periods when he was imprisoned, Teresa visited him regularly and she always maintained, "Al's a good boy."

5. MARIE ÉLÉNORE MAILLÉ DE CARMAN (mother of the MARQUIS DE SADE, noted debauchee and author)

Marie Élénore, lady-in-waiting in a royal family related to the de Sades, married the Count de Sade in 1733 and gave birth to a son, the future Marquis de Sade, in 1740. By 1750, the count had become increasingly difficult to live with, and as a result Marie Élénore removed herself to a Carmelite convent in Paris, where she remained until her death in 1777. Despite her pleas to the king, her son was imprisoned numerous times for his debauchery. Upon hearing of his mother's impending death, he escaped from prison and hurried to Paris. Unfortunately, he arrived too late and was rearrested through the efforts of his mother-in-law. During his subsequent 13 years in prison the marquis wrote books which made him infamous.

6. VANNOZZA DEI CATTANEI (mother of CESARE BORGIA, ruthless Renaissance politician)

Vannozza was the mistress of Cardinal Rodrigo Borgia (who later became Pope Alexander VI), and bore him at least four children, of whom Cesare was reputedly the first. During the course of her life Vannozza also had four husbands, the last one hand-picked by the pope. Always known for her piety, by the time of her death in 1518 she had left so much money to the church where she was buried that Augustine monks were still saying masses for her soul 200 years later.

7. EKATERINA GHELADZE DZHUGASHVILI (mother of JOSEPH STALIN, dictator of U.S.S.R.)

Born in 1856 in a Georgian village, Ekaterina was the daughter of serfs. After her marriage to Beso Dzhugashvili she supported her new family by working as a washerwoman and seamstress. When her son Joseph was born she hoped he would become a priest, and throughout her life she was disappointed at his choice of a different career. Ekaterina never learned to speak Russian, and even after her son's rise to power, she had no desire to leave her home in the Caucasus.

8. KLARA PÖLZL HITLER (mother of ADOLF HITLER, Nazi dictator)

A simple, uneducated Bavarian girl, 18-year-old Klara joined the household of her second cousin, "Uncle" Alois Hitler, whose mistress she became and whom she eventually married. Three of her children died in infancy prior to the birth of Adolf, and Klara was always fearful of his death as well. Disappointed in her marriage,

Klara Pölzl Hitler, Adolf's mother.

she pinned all her hopes on her surviving son. When she died of breast cancer in 1908, Hitler was overcome with grief.

9. ZERELDA COLE JAMES (mother of JESSE JAMES, U.S. bandit)

Married at the age of 17, Zerelda went west with her husband Robert to homestead in Missouri in the early 1840s. Jesse was their second son. The elder James died while Jesse was still a boy, and Zerelda then married a man named Simms. The marriage failed, but Zerelda was determined that her sons should have a father and so she embarked upon a third marriage, this one to Dr. Reuben Samuels. Throughout the bank-robbing careers of Jesse and his younger brother Frank, Zerelda remained loyal to her sons. A very pious woman, Zerelda would often attend church in Jesse's company. Zerelda was described by a newspaper reporter who interviewed her in later years as "graceful in carriage and gesture, calm and quiet in demeanor, with a ripple of fire now and then breaking through the placid surface." Perhaps it was this fire which she had imparted to her sons.

10. ROSA MALTONI MUSSOLINI (mother of BENITO
    MUSSOLINI, Italian dictator)

Born in a small Italian village in 1858, Rosa Maltoni was known for her retiring and gentle disposition. While employed as a schoolteacher in the village of Dovia, she met and married the village blacksmith, Alessandro Mussolini. Benito, their first child, was constantly in trouble and the source of much anxiety to Rosa. She was worn out and disheartened when she died of meningitis in 1905.

Recommendation: If you are turned on to mothers, by all means read *Mothers: 100 Mothers of the Famous and Infamous,* edited by Richard Ehrlich (New York: Paddington Press, 1976).

—F.B.F.

20 CHILDREN OF
UNMARRIED PARENTS

1. Joséphine de Beauharnais, French wife of Napoleon
2. Giovanni Boccaccio, Italian author
3. Cesare Borgia, Italian cardinal
4. Willy Brandt, German statesman
5. Paul Cézanne, French painter
6. Leonardo da Vinci, Italian artist
7. Alexandre Dumas fils, French playwright and novelist
8. Desiderius Erasmus, Dutch scholar and author
9. Alexander Hamilton, U.S. secretary of the treasury
10. T. E. Lawrence, English W.W. I hero and author
11. Jack London, U.S. author
12. Sophia Loren, Italian actress
13. Ramsay MacDonald, English prime minister
14. Juan Perón, Argentine political leader
15. Francisco Pizarro, Spanish conqueror of Peru
16. Henry M. Stanley, British journalist and explorer
17. August Strindberg, Swedish playwright
18. Richard Wagner, German composer
19. Booker T. Washington, U.S. educator
20. William the Conqueror, king of England

F. SCOTT FITZGERALD'S
21 PIECES OF ADVICE
TO HIS DAUGHTER ON LIVING

1. Worry about courage.
2. Worry about cleanliness.
3. Worry about efficiency.
4. Worry about horsemanship.
5. Don't worry about popular opinion.
6. Don't worry about dolls.
7. Don't worry about the past.
8. Don't worry about the future.
9. Don't worry about growing up.
10. Don't worry about anyone getting ahead of you.
11. Don't worry about triumph.
12. Don't worry about failure unless it comes through your own fault.
13. Don't worry about mosquitoes.
14. Don't worry about flies.
15. Don't worry about insects in general.
16. Don't worry about parents.
17. Don't worry about boys.
18. Don't worry about disappointments.
19. Don't worry about pleasures.
20. Don't worry about satisfactions.
21. Think about: What am I really aiming at?

SOURCE: F. Scott Fitzgerald, *Letters to His Daughter*, ed. Andrew Turnbull (New York: Scribner, 1965).

Scott to Scottie: "Don't worry about anyone getting ahead of you."

14
FROM HEAD TO TOE

REMAINS TO BE SEEN
—14 PRESERVED ANATOMICAL
PARTS OF RENOWNED PEOPLE

1. SIR THOMAS MORE'S HEAD

After the English statesman (1478–1535) was beheaded, his head was parboiled, stuck on a pole, and exhibited on London Bridge. A month later his daughter, Margaret Roper, bribed the bridge keepers to knock the head down (which she then caught) and allow her to smuggle it home. She had it placed in a lead box and preserved in sweet-smelling spices. Spies betrayed her, and she was arrested. Margaret supported her claim to the head by saying, "My father's head should not be food for fishes." She was imprisoned but soon released. She died in 1544 and the head was buried with her. In June, 1824, her vault was opened and the head placed on public view in St. Dunstans Church in Canterbury. It has only recently been removed.

2. ANNE BOLEYN'S HEART

After the English queen (1507–1536), the second wife of King Henry VIII, had been beheaded, her heart was stolen and secretly hidden in a church near Thetford in Suffolk. It was rediscovered in 1836 and reburied under the church organ.

3. HENRY GREY'S HEAD

The duke of Suffolk, father of England's nine-day queen, Lady Jane Grey, was beheaded in 1554. His mummified head can be seen in a glass-topped box in the vestry of St. Botolph Aldgate in London.

4. SIR WALTER RALEIGH'S HEAD

After the English courtier (1552?–1618) was beheaded, his wife, Elizabeth Throgmorton, had his body buried but his head embalmed and placed in a red leather bag which she kept by her side for the remaining 29 years of her life. Their son, Carew, took great care of the head until he died in 1666, when it was buried with him in his father's grave. In 1680, Raleigh's head was again parted from his body when Carew was exhumed and reburied—with his father's head—in West Horsley, Surrey.

5. BEN JONSON'S HEEL BONE

The English dramatist (1573?–1637) was buried standing up in Westminster Abbey. His grave was disturbed in 1849 during a nearby interment. The ubiquitous dean of Westminster, William Buckland, seized the opportunity and stole Jonson's heel bone. It later disappeared but was found in 1938 in an old furniture shop.

6. OLIVER CROMWELL'S HEAD

The English statesman (1599–1658) was given one of the most lavish funerals in English history and buried in Westminster Abbey. Little more than two years later his body was savagely disinterred, dragged to Tyburn on a sledge, and there hung until sundown. The public executioner cut down the body and threw it onto the block (bending Cromwell's embalmed nose in the process); he took eight strikes to sever the head. The body was flung into a pit and the head impaled on a 25-ft. wooden pole tipped with an iron spike, then lashed to the roof of Westminster Hall. There it remained for 24 years until 1685 when a violent storm blew it off its perch. A captain of the guard took it home and hid it in his chimney. Meanwhile the whole of London was looking for the purloiner of Cromwell's head. The captain told no one, but on his deathbed he bequeathed the relic to his only daughter. By 1710, the head had appeared in a freak show. Described as "The Monster's Head," it was valued at 60 guineas. In 1775, actor Samuel Russell had possession of the head. He offered it to Sydney Sussex College (where Cromwell had studied), but they refused the offer. Russell had been paying his rent by showing it to sensation seekers for half a crown. In 1787, Russell sold it for £118 to a jeweler named James Fox. A decade later, Fox sold the head for £230 to a syndicate of three entrepreneurs who exhibited it in London's fashionable Bond Street. The show was a failure. In 1814, after all three members of the syndicate had died under mysterious circumstances, a surviving daughter, who didn't want the relic "about the house," sold it to a Dr. Wilkinson. In 1960, the Wilkinson family, who kept it in a large oak box wrapped in red and black silk, offered it again to Sydney Sussex College. This time the college gratefully accepted the relic and gave it a dignified but secret burial in the college grounds.

7. CHARLES I'S FOURTH CERVICAL VERTEBRA

The English king (1600–1649) was beheaded, then buried at Windsor Castle in the same vault as Henry VIII. For many years the coffins were lost, but in 1813 they were rediscovered and an autopsy was performed by the royal surgeon, Sir Henry Halford. He secretly stole Charles's fourth cervical vertebra, which had been cleanly sliced by the ax. For the next 30 years he loved to shock friends at dinner parties by using the vertebra as a salt holder. The bone was returned to Charles's coffin, at Queen Victoria's command.

8. NICOLAS VAUBRUN'S HEART

Lieutenant General Vaubrun, a Frenchman, was killed in the battle of Altenheim (1675). His widow had his heart embalmed and placed in a glass case. For the remaining 29 years of her life, she sat for seven hours a day looking at the heart. After her death in

1704, the heart was removed from the Castle of Serrant. However, everything else in the castle remains as she left it.

9. LOUIS XIV'S HEART

During the French Revolution, rebels wrecked and plundered the tomb of the French king (1638–1715). His heart was stolen and sold to Lord Harcourt, who later resold it to the dean of Westminster, the Very Rev. William Buckland. At dinner one night, the dean (who experimented with foods) ate the embalmed heart.

10. PETER I'S MISTRESS'S HEAD

A Mrs. Hamilton was the beloved mistress of the powerful Russian czar Peter the Great (1672–1725). When she was unfaithful to the czar, he had her head removed. Still, he loved her and wanted her near. So he preserved her head in a jar of alcohol and set it in his bedroom as a remembrance—and as a warning to his other mistresses.

11. CATHERINE I'S LOVER'S HEAD

The Russian empress (1684?–1727), a predecessor of Catherine the Great, had an affair with William Mons (appropriately, her Gentleman of the Bedchamber). When her husband, Peter the Great, learned of the affair, he had Mons executed, his head preserved in a glass jar and placed by Catherine's bed.

12. NAPOLEON'S HAIR, WISDOM TOOTH, HEART, STOMACH, INTESTINES, AND PENIS

After the death of the French emperor (1769–1821), his head was completely shaved, giving hundreds of people precious souvenirs. In 1817, a painful wisdom tooth had been removed. This was later found among the effects of Dr. O'Meara, and sold for 7½ guineas. Napoleon's heart was put into a silver vase and his stomach into a silver pepper pot. A portion of his intestines, which ended up in the Royal College of Surgeons, was destroyed in a 1940 air raid. On his deathbed, he commanded his heart be preserved in spirits of wine and given to "dear Marie Louise." In 1972, his 1-in.-long penis, looking "like a sea horse" and listed as "a small dried-up object," was offered for sale at Christie's but failed to reach the reserve price. It is claimed the penis was obtained by Napoleon's confessor-priest.

13. PERCY BYSSHE SHELLEY'S HEART AND A LOCK OF HIS HAIR

The English poet (1792–1822) died of drowning. Attended by Lord Byron, Leigh Hunt, and Edward Trelawny, Shelley's body was cremated on the Italian beach where it had been washed up. During the burning, Byron asked Trelawny for the skull, but remembering Byron's famous drinking cup, Trelawny refused. They were all surprised that the heart didn't burn and so, despite the heat, Trelawny thrust his hand into the virtual furnace and snatched out the relic. (His hand was racked by continual pain for many years thereafter.) Trelawny gave the heart to Hunt who eventually gave it to the poet's wife, Mary Shelley. For the remainder of her widowhood, she preserved it in a silken shroud and carried it with her everywhere. When their son Percy died, the heart was placed in a silver case and buried

with him. Claire Clairmont, a close friend and possible mistress of
Shelley, always kept a lock of his hair in a red box in her Florence
apartment.

14. JOAQUIN MURRIETA'S HEAD

This Mexican bandit (1832?–1853), operating in California,
became a legend. He and his sidekick—known as Three-Fingered
Jack—intercepted stagecoaches to rob passengers and swept down
on mining encampments to steal gold bullion. A $1,000 reward
was placed on his head by the California governor. Capt. Harry Love,
a Texas Ranger, promised to get Murrieta. After several unsuccessful
hunts, Captain Love returned from a successful one—carrying the
head of a man he claimed was Murrieta and the severed hand of
Three-Fingered Jack pickled in alcohol. Authorities auctioned off the
preserved head and hand for $36, and the buyer exhibited them to
paying customers in Stockton, Calif., and elsewhere.

—J.BE.

7 FAMOUS BODILY PARTS

1. ACHILLES' HEEL

A famous metaphor for human vulnerability, Achilles' heel
proved to be the undoing of the otherwise invulnerable Greek warrior.
His mother Thetis held the infant Achilles by the heel as she immersed him in the River Styx to render him unassailable. Many years
later in battle, the poisoned arrow of Paris found that one unprotected
spot and slew Achilles, the bravest of Greek heroes.

2. CAPT. JEAN DANJOU'S WOODEN HAND

The wooden hand of this French legionnaire has been enshrined as a symbol of the Foreign Legion's legendary heroism and
self-sacrifice. During the Mexican campaign of 1863, Danjou volunteered to lead a company of 64 men to probe the strength of Mexican
forces threatening an important legion convoy. Danjou and his men
were searching a ruined hacienda at Camerone when they were
ambushed by 2,000 Mexican soldiers. Hopelessly outnumbered, the
French were given the opportunity to surrender, but the captain
refused and instead had each of his men swear to die rather than
give up. The men fought bravely against the Mexican charge, but in
the end all were killed. The captain's wooden hand, later rescued
by comrades from the litter of bodies, was kept in the legion mausoleum in Algeria. In 1962 it was moved to the legion's new headquarters near Marseilles and still figures prominently in the legion's
annual observance of Camerone Day on April 30.

The wooden hand of Captain Danjou.

3. VINCENT VAN GOGH'S EAR

Van Gogh, a leading postimpressionist painter, worked with the great Paul Gauguin for two months until their relationship, strained from the beginning, was brought to a gory conclusion. On Christmas Eve, 1888, the distraught van Gogh came at Gauguin with a knife and ended up cutting off part of his own left ear. This mutilation was later to figure in his *Self-Portrait with Bandaged Ear*.

4. THE HAARLEM HERO'S FINGER

The legend of the 8-year-old Dutch boy who saved Holland from a catastrophic flood was immortalized in Mary Elizabeth Dodge's *Hans Brinker, or the Silver Skates* (1865). On his way home from another good deed, the boy heard water spilling through the dike, Holland's only defense against the flood tides. Realizing there wasn't a moment to lose, he plugged his finger in the hole and held it there through the dark, freezing night. The teacher who related the story summed up its impact on the Dutch people: "Not a leak can show itself anywhere, either in politics, honor, or public safety, that a million fingers are not ready to stop it at any cost."

5. CORNELIS KETEL'S FINGERS AND TOES

The Dutch painter Ketel specialized in royal portraits, including one of Elizabeth I. Bored with the conventional idiom of the brush, Ketel began painting with his fingertips and later with his toes.

6. MAJOR KOVATZOV'S NOSE

In Nikolai Gogol's bizarre short story "The Nose," Major Kovatzov's nose detaches itself and is later discovered in a slice of bread by Ivan Yakovlevich, who throws the offending object in the Neva River. However, it reappears on the streets where it is spotted by the frantic Kovatzov, whose social status is threatened by the loss of his nose. He trails it into a church, but it manages to give him the slip. At one point Kovatzov catches his nose, but it will not stay attached to his face. Finally, the nose simply reappears on the major's face. He is "whole" once again and regains his social eminence.

7. NICCOLÒ PAGANINI'S HANDS

An ardent musician and showman, Paganini was celebrated throughout Europe for his virtuosity on the violin and his almost satanic command over audiences. His incessant practice of difficult, almost impossible techniques on the violin resulted in some remarkable physical features, most notably a hand span of 18 in. He sometimes played with frayed strings on his violin, hoping one or more might break, so that he could show his ability to play on those that were left.

—L.C.

18 FAMOUS BRAINS
—AND WHAT THEY WEIGHED

The brain is really an enlarged end of the spinal cord. The ratio of the weight of the brain to that of the spinal cord is a fair criterion of an animal's intelligence. In fish, this ratio is about 1:1; in people, 55:1—the brain weighs 55 times as much as the spinal cord. The human brain isn't the largest (the elephant's is four times as heavy) nor the most convoluted (a dolphin's is even more wrinkled), but it's the best one around. The average man's brain weighs 49 oz. The average woman's brain weighs 44 oz. Apparently the weight of the brain has nothing to do with the degree of intelligence. The weights of the following were determined after death (when the brain weighs a little less).

	Oz.
1. George Gordon, Lord Byron, English poet	82.25
2. Oliver Cromwell, lord protector of England	82.25
3. Ivan Turgenev, Russian novelist	74
4. Georges Cuvier, French naturalist	64
5. William Makepeace Thackeray, English novelist	58

Lord Byron possessed a five pound brain.

6.	James Fisk, U.S. financier	58
7.	Leon Trotsky, Russian leader	56
8.	George Francis Train, U.S. millionaire eccentric	53.8
9.	Daniel Webster, U.S. politician	53
10.	Abigail Folger, U.S. coffee heiress (Manson Family victim)	52.91
11.	Robert F. Kennedy, U.S. presidential candidate	51.15
12.	Janis Joplin, U.S. singer	51.15
13.	Marilyn Monroe, U.S. actress	50.79
14.	Howard Hughes, U.S. billionaire recluse	49
15.	Walt Whitman, U.S. poet	44.87
16.	Donald DeFreeze, U.S. abductor of Patricia Hearst	42.33
17.	Léon Gambetta, French statesman	39
18.	Anatole France, French author	35

—I.W. & J.BER.

ABIGAIL VAN BUREN'S READERS' 10 MOST COMMON PROBLEMS

Columnist Abigail Van Buren, better known as "Dear Abby," is the twin sister of her biggest rival—Ann Landers. Both began writing columns of advice for their readers in 1955, with Dear Abby's column appearing a few months after that of her sister's. Dear Abby is now syndicated in over 800 newspapers throughout the world. She is the hostess of her own radio program and the author of several books including *Dear Teenager* and *Dear Abby on Marriage*.

1. "My wife doesn't understand me."
2. "My husband never gives me any money."
3. "My parents don't trust me."
4. "My grandchildren never come to visit me."
5. "We never hear from our married kids unless they want something."
6. "My boyfriend keeps wanting me to 'prove my love.' "
7. "My girlfriend wants to get married and I'm not ready."
8. "My neighbor keeps dropping in uninvited."
9. "How does a nice woman meet a nice man?"
10. "How does a nice man meet a nice woman?"

—Exclusive for *The Book of Lists*

ANN LANDERS' READERS' 10 MOST COMMON PROBLEMS

Once voted among the 10 most important women in the U.S. by United Press International, Ann Landers (née Esther Pauline Friedman) continues as one of the most popular syndicated columnists in America. She has been giving advice to the lovelorn since 1955.

1. *Sexual problems between husband and wife:* "I'm not getting enough" or "I'm getting too much" or "He's impotent" or "She's frigid."
2. *Cheating spouses:* Men used to be the cheaters nine times out of ten. Now it's almost 50–50.
3. *Problems with in-laws:* "They are too demanding of our time." "They interfere." "They spoil our children."
4. *Teenagers complaining about parents who don't understand them:* "They're living in the olden days" or "They never talk to us about anything that matters."
5. *Teenage love:* "How can I be sure it's the real thing?" or "He likes someone else" or "He never takes me anyplace, he just wants to park and make out" or "Where can I get the pill?"
6. *Loneliness:* "How can a respectable girl" (or guy) "meet people?"
7. *Physical appearance problems:* These include weight, birthmarks, crooked teeth, baldness, acne, and being flat-chested, too short, or too tall.
8. *Pregnant girls:* "Should I have an abortion?" "Should I marry him?" "Should I keep my baby?" "How do I tell my parents?"
9. *Problems at work:* "My boss is on the make, I don't want to lose my job—but I can't stand him." Or "Someone in this store" (or

office) "is stealing. Should I tell?" Or "A woman I work next to has terrible body odor. What can I do?"

10. *Drug, tobacco, and alcohol addiction:* "My parents smoke. I hate it. How can I get them to stop?" "How do I get my husband," (or wife, or friend) "off the booze?" Or "My parents are drunk all the time. I'm ashamed to have any friends in." Or "My best friend is on LSD or heroin." Or "Is marijuana harmful?"

—Exclusive for *The Book of Lists*

ABIGAIL VAN BUREN'S READERS' 7 MOST UNUSUAL PROBLEMS

1. "I'm a bus driver and want some information on how to become a shepherd."
2. "I want to have a child but don't even have a boyfriend. Can you line me up with somebody?"
3. "I hear there is life after death. If that is true, can you put me in touch with my Uncle LeRoy Albert from Victoria, Tex.?"
4. "Will you please send me all the information you have on the rhythm method? I'm learning how to dance."
5. "I'm a 50-year-old widow and my doctor says I need a husband or the equivalent. Would it be all right if I borrowed my sister's husband? It's all right with them."
6. "My husband burns the hair out of his nose with a lighted match. And he thinks I'm crazy because I voted for Goldwater."
7. "I can't trust my husband. He cheats so much I'm not even sure my last baby is HIS."

—Exclusive for *The Book of Lists*

ANN LANDERS' READERS' 10 MOST UNUSUAL PROBLEMS

1. The man who hid his wife's dentures so she couldn't go out and vote for a Democrat.
2. The bride who phoned her mother on her honeymoon to say she was on. her way home. Her husband was a mortician and confessed that he could enjoy sex only with women who were dead or pretended to be. He instructed her to lie in a bathtub filled with very cold water for at least 20 minutes, then come to bed and pretend she was dead.
3. The man who wanted to be buried in his 1939 Dodge.

4. The man who was unable to urinate in public bathrooms.
5. The girl who had a leg crippled by polio and wanted to have it amputated and replaced by an artificial limb so she wouldn't limp at her wedding.
6. The woman who wrote to inquire about who owned the walnuts from the tree which grew on her property but very close to the neighbor's property. Most of the nuts were falling on the neighbor's property and she felt that since it was her tree which produced the nuts, she was entitled to them. (Answer: The neighbor could use the nuts that fell on her property, but couldn't sell them).
7. The woman whose husband was going to have a transsexual operation. She wanted to know what the children should call their father after the operation. "Daddy" didn't seem appropriate for a "woman." (Answer: They can call him "Bob" or "Bill" or whatever he changes his name to—probably "Mary" or "Sue').
8. The totally bald woman who used to remove her wig at poker games and place it on her chips for luck.
9. The man who kept a pig in his apartment and insisted the pig was a wonderful "watchdog." The neighbors complained.
10. The woman who did her housework in the nude and enjoyed it thoroughly until one day she went to the basement to do her laundry and was surprised by the meter reader.

—Exclusive for *The Book of Lists*

20 FAMOUS INSOMNIACS

1. NAPOLEON BONAPARTE

He simply learned to get along on three or four hours of sleep each night.

2. CATHERINE THE GREAT

In hope of falling asleep, she would have her hair brushed every night while she relaxed in bed.

3. REP. SHIRLEY CHISHOLM

To unwind before bedtime, she takes a hot bubble bath.

4. WINSTON CHURCHILL

He had twin beds, and when he couldn't fall asleep in one, he would move to the other.

5. CHARLES DICKENS

He believed that his own position, and the location of the bed, were all-important in overcoming insomnia. He checked to be sure that the head of the bed was pointing due north. Then he would place himself exactly in the center of the bed, measuring the distance to both edges with his outstretched arms as he reclined.

Alexandre Dumas père had little time to sleep—he produced enough words to fill 1,200 volumes and claimed to have fathered 500 children.

6. ALEXANDRE DUMAS (PÈRE)

Under doctor's orders, he ate an apple every day at 7:00 A.M. under the Arc de Triomphe. The physician hoped this would force Dumas into a regular schedule of rising and retiring.

7. THOMAS EDISON

Although constitutionally able to survive on very little sleep, he would take a catnap of 30 minutes to an hour after a particularly strenuous period of work.

8. BENJAMIN FRANKLIN

He would get out of bed when bothered by sleeplessness, and let the bed air out. Once the bed was cool, he would return to it and try to fall asleep again.

9. CARY GRANT

The movie star watches old movies on TV until he finally dozes off.

10. FRANZ KAFKA

He felt that his insomnia was triggered by his creative pattern—when a piece of writing was growing within him, he was unable to sleep. In his diary, he mentions a favorite sleeping technique: "To make myself as heavy as possible, which I consider good for falling asleep, I had crossed my arms and laid my hands on my shoulders, so that I lay there like a soldier with his pack."

11. DOROTHY KILGALLEN

She regularly took sleeping pills to battle her insomnia. In 1965, she died of a combination of sleeping pills and alcohol.

12. RUDYARD KIPLING

When unable to sleep, he wandered through his house and garden. He wrote, "Pity us! Oh pity us! We wakeful . . ."

13. OSCAR LEVANT

Every night, the pianist would take a 1-oz. bottle of paraldehyde. Then he would get into bed, set his head at one end of the pillow, and begin counting silently in hope of inducing sleep.

14. MARILYN MONROE

She took 20 tablets of phenobarbital a day to calm her nerves and help her sleep.

15. MARCEL PROUST

He took Veronal for his sleeplessness. When he was writing *Remembrance of Things Past,* he lined his room with cork to keep out the noises that prevented him from sleeping—as well as dust that might provoke an asthma attack.

16. EARL OF ROSEBERY

This gentleman was forced to resign as prime minister of England because of his chronic insomnia. Eight years later, he wrote, "I cannot forget 1895. To lie, night after night, staring wide awake, hopeless of sleep, tormented in nerves . . . is an experience which no sane man with a conscience would repeat."

17. JACQUELINE SUSANN

She took sleeping pills, and then edited her day's writing until she could finally doze off.

18. JAMES THURBER

He was "a three o'clock waker," who wooed sleep by "tinkering with words and letters of the alphabet and spelling words backward." One of his favorite sleeping aids was rewriting Poe's "The Raven" from the viewpoint of the bird.

19. VINCENT VAN GOGH

He treated his insomnia with a very strong dose of camphor applied to his pillow and mattress.

20. EVELYN WAUGH

He was a heavy user of sleep medications containing bromides, which often caused hallucinations instead of inducing sleep.

—R.T., A.W., & J.M.

10 WELL-KNOWN ONE-EYED PERSONS IN HISTORY

The one-eyed star—Rex Harrison.

1. JOHN MILTON (1608–1674)

   English poet, champion of the freedom and dignity of man.

2. HORATIO NELSON (1758–1805)

   British naval wizard and national hero, victor at the fateful battle of Trafalgar against the French fleet.

3. GUGLIELMO MARCONI (1874–1937)

Irish-Italian inventor, father of radio.

4. ARCHIBALD PERCIVAL WAVELL (1883–1950)

Soldier, administrator, poet, commander in chief (Middle East, W.W. II), British viceroy of India.

5. HERBERT MORRISON (1888–1965)

British Labour party statesman, home secretary, foreign secretary, deputy prime minister.

6. JOHN FORD (Sean O'Feeney) (1895–1973)

Irish-American film director, famous for his westerns.

7. JOE DAVIS (b. 1901)

World snooker-break record holder, top scorer, and champion.

8. REX HARRISON (b. 1908)

Distinguished stage and screen actor, the acknowledged star of many productions, unforgettable as Professor Higgins in *My Fair Lady*.

9. ERIC J. HOSKING (b. 1909)

International bird photographer, ornithologist, pioneer of new techniques for flash work and cinematography of wild birds.

10. MOSHE DAYAN (b. 1915)

Israeli soldier and statesman, former chief of staff and minister of defense, supreme military commander, architect of Israel's victories in the Middle East.

—D.G.

10 FAMOUS SNORERS

1. Beau Brummell, English dandy and gambler
2. Cato the Elder, Roman statesman
3. Lord Chesterfield, English statesman
4. George II, king of England
5. Abraham Lincoln, U.S. president
6. Benito Mussolini, Fascist dictator of Italy
7. Marcus Otho, Roman emperor
8. Plutarch, Greek biographer
9. Theodore Roosevelt, U.S. president
10. George Washington, U.S. president

SOURCE: Marcus H. Boulware, *Snoring* (Rockaway, N.J.: American Faculty Press, 1974).

10 HEAVIEST HUMANS

Most ancient tales of heavy people have been weighed in the balance and found wanting. There were, however, at least three kings who were called "the Fat" or "le Gros": Alfonso II of Portugal, Charles II of France, and Louis VI of France. The following 10 individuals are all reputed to have weighed in excess of 800 lbs.

1. JOHN LANG, alias Michael Walker* (U.S.; b. 1934)

Top weight: 1,187 lbs.; 6 ft. 2 in. tall. His top weight was claimed by a spokesman for Christian Farms of Killeen, Tex., an antidrug religious organization with which Lang is affiliated. Lang was released from a Houston hospital in 1971 after treatment for extreme obesity and drug-induced bulimia—a morbid desire to overeat.

2. ROBERT EARL HUGHES (U.S.; 1926–1958)

Weight at death: 1,069 lbs., the heaviest human whose weight has been verified. When he died, his coffin—the size of a piano case—had to be lowered into the ground by a crane.

3. MILLS DARDEN (U.S.; 1798–1857)

Top weight: 1,020 lbs. His wife weighed only 98 lbs., but she bore him three children before her death in North Carolina in 1837.

4. IDA MAITLAND* (U.S.; 1898–1932)

Top weight: 911 lbs.; bust measurement of 152 in. Mrs. Maitland reputedly died trying to pick a four-leaf clover.

5. JOHN HANSON CRAIG (U.S.; 1856–1894)

Top weight: 907 lbs.; 6 ft. 5 in. tall. At the age of 2, he won $1,000 in a New York, N.Y., beautiful baby contest.

6. ARTHUR KNORR (U.S.; 1914–1960)

Top weight: 900 lbs.; 6 ft. 1 in. tall. During the last six months before his death, he gained 300 lbs.

7. PERCY PEARL WASHINGTON (U.S.; 1926–1972)

Weight at death: approximately 880 lbs., the heaviest medically verified weight for a woman. However, since hospital scales only went up to 800 lbs., doctors estimated the additional 80 lbs.

8. TOUBI (Cameroon; b. 1946)

Present weight: 857½ lbs., the world's heaviest verified weight for a person alive today.

9. FLORA MAE KING JACKSON (U.S.; 1930–1965)

Weight at death: 840 lbs.; 5 ft. 9 in. tall. Known in show business as "Baby Flo."

10. **WILLIAM J. COBB** (U.S.; b. 1926)

Top weight: 802 lbs.; 6 ft. tall. From his top weight in 1962 this wrestler reduced to 232 lbs. by 1965 (the world's greatest slimming feat), but was back up to 650 lbs. by 1973.

* Indicates a medically unsubstantiated weight.

—R.H.

11 FAMOUS 300-POUNDERS

Each of the following persons weighs or *has weighed* at least 300 lbs.

1. James Beard, gastronome
2. "Diamond Jim" Brady, 19th-century millionaire
3. Oliver Hardy, screen comedian
4. Al Hirt, trumpeter
5. Herman Kahn, economist, futurist
6. Malama, 19th-century queen of Hawaii
7. Luciano Pavarotti, operatic tenor
8. William Howard Taft, president of the U.S.
9. Tupou IV, king of Tonga
10. Orson Welles, actor, producer, director
11. Paul Whiteman, bandleader

—B.F.

Four workers lounging in the bathtub which was specially built to accommodate U.S. President William Howard Taft.

2 FAMOUS HEMORRHOID SUFFERERS

1. NAPOLEON (French emperor; 1769–1821)

Because of hemorrhoidal pain during the battle of Waterloo, Napoleon was unable to mount his horse to survey the battlefield. This hampered his ability to gain a clear picture of the situation and was one factor which worked against him in his ill-fated attempt to resurrect his empire.

2. FUMIMARO KONOYE (Japanese prime minister; 1891–1945)

Konoye suffered intensely from hemorrhoids. In April, 1939, the pain he experienced when sitting down was at least partly responsible for his refusal to ride with Minister of Foreign Affairs Yosuke Matsuoka to an important cabinet meeting. This lost opportunity to clear up a misunderstanding with Matsuoka about a U.S. peace proposal may very well have contributed to Japan's entry into W.W. II.

—R.J.F.

20 PROMINENT VICTIMS OF SYPHILIS

French poet Charles Baudelaire was a victim of VD.

1. Charles Baudelaire, French poet
2. Ludwig van Beethoven, German composer
3. Al Capone, U.S. gangster
4. Lord Randolph Churchill, English statesman
5. Christopher Columbus, Italian discoverer of America
6. Capt. James Cook, English mariner and explorer
7. George Armstrong Custer, U.S. army officer
8. Paul Gauguin, French artist
9. Johann Wolfgang von Goethe, German poet and scientist
10. Henry VIII, king of England
11. "Wild Bill" Hickok, U.S. frontier marshal
12. John Keats, English poet
13. Louis XIV, king of France
14. Ferdinand Magellan, Portuguese navigator
15. Mary I ("Bloody Mary"), queen of England
16. Napoleon, French emperor
17. Friedrich Nietzsche, German philosopher
18. Peter the Great, czar of Russia
19. Marquis de Sade, French writer of erotica
20. Robert Schumann, German composer

SHOE SIZES OF 20 FAMOUS MEN

		Shoe Size
1.	Bing Crosby	7½
2.	Edward G. Robinson	8½
3.	Jack Benny	9
4.	Al Jolson	9
5.	Neil Armstrong	9½
6.	Humphrey Bogart	10
7.	Fred Astaire	10½
8.	Douglas Fairbanks	11
9.	Cecil B. De Mille	11
10.	Frank Sinatra	11
11.	Dean Martin	11½
12.	Cary Grant	12
13.	John Barrymore	12½
14.	Clark Gable	12½
15.	Thomas Jefferson	12½
16.	Woodrow Wilson	12½
17.	Bob Hope	13
18.	George Washington	13
19.	Gary Cooper	14
20.	Warren G. Harding	14

Gary Cooper's size 14 shoeprints at Grauman's Chinese Theater in Hollywood.

Sizes are based on the measurement of the length of the shoe or the length of the footprint. Variation in the height of the heel might throw an estimate of shoe size off, but probably not more than half a size. Neil Armstrong's 9½ is the actual size of the boot he wore when he became the first human to step on the moon. It is impossible to estimate the shoe size of a woman from the length of her footprint without examining her foot in person or knowing the exact height of her heel. However, it is known that Greta Garbo wears a size 7AA shoe.

—P.S.H.

15 GIANTS

All persons except the two women on this list are reputed to have stood 8 ft. or taller. No woman has ever achieved a scientifically verified height of 8 ft. Currently, the tallest living woman is the "still growing" Sandy Allen (b. 1955) of Shelbyville, Ind., who measures 7 ft. 5⁵⁄₁₆ in.

1. GOLIATH OF GOTH* (c. 1060 B.C.)

Philistine giant killed by David with a sling. The Bible puts his height at "six cubits and a span" (9 ft. 6½ in.), but some early historians claim he was only 6 ft. 10 in.

2. JAN VAN ALBERT* (c. 1920)

Dutch giant, 9 ft. 5 in., whose photograph appeared in *The New York Times* in June, 1920.

3. MACHNOW* (c. 1905)

Russian giant, 9 ft. 3 in., who appeared at the London Hippodrome in 1905.

4. JOHN MIDDLETON* (c. 1610)

A giant in the reign of England's James I. He is said to have measured 9 ft. 3 in.

5. ROBERT PERSHING WADLOW (1919–1940)

An American giant born in Alton, Ill., who, at 8 ft. 11.1 in., attained the greatest scientifically verified height for a human being.

Robert Wadlow (C) with his Alton, Ill., high-school French class.

6. JOHN F. CARROLL (1932–1969)

Born in Buffalo, N.Y., Carroll measured 8 ft. 7¾ in.

7. GAIUS JULIUS MAXIMINUS* (173–238)

A Thracian of unusual size and strength who was emperor of Rome (235–238). He is reputed to have been 8 ft. 6 in. in height.

8. JAMES TOLLER* (1795–1819)

Born on August 28, 1795, James Toller, known as "the Young English giant," stood 8 ft. 1½ in. at age 18 and is reported to have been 8 ft. 6 in. when he died. He was exhibited in London in 1815–1816 and was presented at court to the czar of Russia and the king of Prussia.

9. JOHN WILLIAM ROGAN (1871–1905)

Born in Gallatin, Tenn., he measured 8 ft. 6 in.

10. DON KOEHLER (b. 1925)

A resident of Chicago, Ill., Koehler is the world's tallest living person at 8 ft. 2 in.

11. VÄINÖ MYLLYRINNE (1909–1963)

Born in Helsinki, Finland, Myllyrinne measured 8 ft. 1.2 in.

12. SULAIMAN ALI NASHNUSH (b. 1943)

A Libyan giant who stands 8 ft. 0.4 in. tall after having undergone a successful operation to halt abnormal growth.

13. CHARLEMAGNE* (742–814)

King of the Franks and founder of the Holy Roman Empire, Charlemagne is said to have been 8 ft. tall.

14. JANE BUNFORD (1895–1922)

Born at Bartley Green, England, Jane Bunford stood 7 ft. 7 in., though she would have measured 7 ft. 11 in. had it not been for a curvature in her spine. She attained the greatest scientifically verified height for a woman, and she grew her hair to a record length of 8 ft.

15. ANNA SWAN* (c. 1865)

A Nova Scotian giantess 7 ft. 5½ in. in height who became a member of P. T. Barnum's Museum at age 17. She nearly burned to death in 1865 when the museum caught fire and rescue attempts were hampered because of her size. She was at last lifted to safety by means of a tackle and derrick. Anna Swan was presented to Queen Victoria in 1869, and later married Capt. Martin Van Buren Bates, a Kentucky giant approximately 7 ft. 2½ in.

*Indicates a medically unsubstantiated height.

—R.H.

15 VERY SMALL PEOPLE

1. THE FAIRY QUEEN* (c. 1850)

A young dwarf exhibited in London who reputedly measured 1 ft. 4 in. and weighed 4 lbs. Her feet were said to be 2 in. long.

2. LUCIA ZARATE* (1863–1889)

The shorter of two sisters who formed a circus act, "The Mexican Midgets," Lucia measured 1 ft. 8 in. She weighed 4.7 lbs. at age 17.

"The Mexican Midget" Lucia Zarate, shown here at 15, when she was 20 in. high and weighed 5 lbs.

3. CAROLINE CRACHAMI (1814–1824)

Born in Sicily, Caroline Crachami, at 1 ft. 8.2 in., was the shortest human of whom there is accurate record. She was taken to London at the age of 9 and, under the guardianship of a man named Gilligan, was publicly exhibited until her death a year later in June, 1824. Much to the horror of her father, Gilligan disappeared with her body, hoping to sell it at a high price for anatomical research. He eventually left it in the care of Sir Everard Home, who agreed to present it to the Royal College of Surgeons. Her father learned of Caroline's whereabouts too late to stop the dissection of her body.

4. PAULINE MUSTERS (1876–1895)

A Dutch midget who measured 1 ft. 9.65 in. at the time of her death at age 19. She is the shortest human *adult* of whom there is accurate record.

5. M. RICHEBOURG* (c. 1768–1858)

Reputedly only 1 ft. 11 in. tall, Richebourg served as a spy in the French Revolution. He was given secret dispatches and was carried through enemy lines—disguised as a baby nursing on a bottle.

6. CALVIN PHILLIPS (1791–1812)

Bridgewater, Mass., dwarf who measured 2 ft. 2.5 in. at the time of his death and weighed 11 lbs. He is the shortest male of whom there is accurate record.

7. NRUTURAM (b. 1929)

A dwarf of Naydwar, India, Nruturam measures 2 ft. 4 in. He is the world's shortest human alive today.

8. A. L. SAWYER* (c. 1883)

Editor of the *Florida Democrat*, Sawyer stood 2 ft. 6½ in.

9. LAVINIA WARREN (1841–1919)

Lavinia married "General Tom Thumb" in 1863 when she was 22 years old and 2 ft. 8 in. tall. After Tom Thumb's death, she married Count Primo Magi (2 ft. 8 in.).

10. GEORGE TROUT (c. 1830)

Barely 3 ft. tall, Trout served as a messenger in the service of the British Houses of Parliament from 1830 to 1850. It has been reported that he once made an agreement with Anthony White, chief surgeon of Westminster Hospital, to allow White to dissect his body upon his death. He got the better of the bargain, however, by demanding a £10 payment immediately, and then managing to outlive White.

11. "GENERAL TOM THUMB" (Charles Sherwood Stratton, 1838–1883)

The most famous American midget, Tom Thumb measured 2 ft. 6.5 in. at age 12, 3 ft. 4 in. at the time of his death. He joined P. T. Barnum's organization in 1842 and was on exhibition in New York, England, and continental Europe from 1844 to 1847.

12. JEFFERY HUDSON* (1619–1682)

An English dwarf of Charles I's court. Measured 18 in. at age 30, later growing to 3 ft. 6 in. He was involved in many adventures, including capture by Flemish pirates in 1630 and by Barbary pirates in 1649. In 1679 he was imprisoned briefly for conspiracy. Hudson's portrait was painted by Vandyke.

13. EDDIE GAEDEL (1925–1961)

An American midget 3 ft. 7 in. small, Gaedel is renowned as the only midget ever to take part in a major-league baseball game. He appeared as a pinch hitter (and walked) for the St. Louis Browns against the Detroit Tigers on August 19, 1951.

14. RICHARD GIBSON* (1615–1690)

English portrait painter. Both he and his wife stood 3 ft. 10 in.

15. ATTILA THE HUN* (c. 406–453)

King of the Huns. Attila was thought to have been a dwarf, although his exact height is not recorded.

*Indicates a medically unsubstantiated height.

—R.H. & W.K.

EXTRA! EXTRA!
READ ALL ABOUT IT:
10 PEOPLE WITH EXTRA
LIMBS OR DIGITS (AND 2
VERY SPECIAL CASES)

1. FRANK BENTENIA

By coincidence there were two Franks with three legs, both from Sicily. This Frank supported his parents and four brothers and sisters in Middletown, Conn., by traveling with the Ringling Brothers circus at the turn of the century. "This is a matter of business with me," he told a New York newspaper in 1905. "You pay your money and I eat my meals."

2. ANNE BOLEYN

Anne Boleyn is proof that having an extra finger on one hand (and three breasts) is no handicap. She became a queen, the second wife of King Henry VIII. But when she failed to give him a male heir (producing only Elizabeth I), he got rid of her. He charged her with adultery—with her own brother among others—and had her beheaded in 1536, three years after the marriage. Her uncle and father concurred in the sentence. If the king's charges against her of adultery and incest had failed, he had intended to use the sixth finger and third breast to accuse her of being a witch.

3. MYRTLE CORBIN

"The woman from Texas with four legs" was the only freak who could challenge the "King of Freaks" Frank Lentini as a box-office attraction. ("Freak" expresses dramatic physical deviation from the norm and was not offensive to those in the sideshows.) The body of a twin grew from between Myrtle's legs, well developed from the waist down and completely functional. Myrtle was married and, according to her billing, had five children—three from her own body and two from her twin's.

4. FOLDI FAMILY

Written up in a book called *Anomalies and Curiosities of Medicine* in 1896, the Foldi family was described as living in the tribe of Hyabites in "Arabia" for many generations. Each member of the large family had 24 digits. They confined their marriages to other members of the tribe, so the trait was usually inherited. In fact, if a baby was born with only 10 fingers and 10 toes, it was sacrificed as the product of adultery.

5. LALOO

Laloo was a Hindu, born in India in 1874. He had an extra set of arms, legs, and sex organs from a headless twin attached to his body at the neck. He, too, traveled with carnivals and circuses in the U.S. and Europe and was written up in many medical textbooks. He married in Philadelphia in 1894 and his wife traveled with him. His "parasitic twin" was, of course, male, but the circuses liked to advertise it as female to add to Laloo's strangeness.

6. FRANK LENTINI

For years acknowledged as the "King of Freaks," Frank Lentini was the result of nonseparating triplets. He had three legs, two sets of genital organs, four feet, and 16 toes. He could use the third leg, which grew out of the base of his spine, as a stool; in his circus act he used it to kick a football the length of the sideshow tent. Born in Sicily in 1889, he came to the U.S. at the age of 9. He married and raised four children.

7. JEAN LIBBERA

"The Man with Two Bodies" was born in Rome in 1884. He traveled with several circuses displaying his miniature "twin," named "Jacques." Jacques had hips, thighs, arms, legs . . . a German doctor using X rays found a rudimentary structure resembling a head inside Jean's body. Jean covered Jacques with a cape when he went out. Walking with his wife and four children he looked just like any other family man.

8. LOUISE L.

Known as "La Dame à Quatre Jambes" ("the lady with four legs"), Louise was born in France in 1869. Attached to her pelvis was a second, rudimentary pelvis from which grew two atrophied legs. There were two rudimentary breasts where the legs joined her body. In spite of this handicap, Louise not only married but gave birth to two healthy children.

9. JEAN BAPTISTA DOS SANTOS

Born in Cuba in 1843, Jean was a good-looking, well-proportioned boy who happened to have two penises and scrotums and an extra pair of legs behind and between his own, united along their length. His mental and physical capacities were considered above normal and so, according to one report, was his "animal passion" and sexual functioning. He was exhibited in Havana in 1865 and later in Paris.

10. BETTY LOU WILLIAMS

Betty Lou Williams was the daughter of poor black share-croppers. She looked very pretty and shapely in her two-piece bathing suit on the sideshow stage—but growing out of her left side was the bottom half of a body, with two legs and one misplaced arm. Betty, who died at the age of 21, made a lot of money during the depression. Her friends say she died of a broken heart, jilted by a man she loved.

2 VERY SPECIAL CASES

1. EDWARD MORDAKE

An heir to a peerage, handsome, gifted as a scholar and musi-cian, Mordake was also gifted with something else which made him very unhappy. On the back of his head he had another face. It was said to be a girl's. Although it couldn't eat or speak, the face's eyes moved; it could also laugh and cry. Edward begged to have his "devil twin" removed, even if the surgery killed him, but no doctor would attempt it. He committed suicide at the age of 23.

2. PASQUAL PIÑON

A Mexican with an extra head growing out of his forehead was reported in 1917. The extra head could move its eyes and see, but the mouth, which also moved, could not speak. This must have been a relief to Pasqual. Eventually, say the reports, the extra head lost even these abilities and became simply a lifeless growth.

—P.F.

15
PRIVATE PARTS

6 POSITIONS FOR
SEXUAL INTERCOURSE
—IN ORDER OF PREFERENCE

Gershon Legman, an American who writes about sex, calculates that there are more than 4 million possible ways for men and women to have sexual intercourse with each other. Most of these "postures," as he calls them, are probably variations on the six main positions which Alfred C. Kinsey used as categories in the questionnaires on sexual habits which were the basis for his Kinsey Reports in 1948 and 1953.

The *Kama Sutra,* a Hindu love manual written somewhere between 100 and 400 A.D., lists many imaginative and acrobatic variations on these positions—for example, the Bamboo Cleft, the Crab, the Wild Boar; some *Kama Sutra* experts suggest that people try out difficult positions in the water first. Chinese pillow books, written more than 400 years ago, show more feasible positions with titles like "Two Dragons Exhausted by Battle" and name the parts of the body equally poetically—the penis is called the "Jade Stem" and the clitoris, the "Pearl on the Jade Step."

According to these sources, interpretations of ancient art, and anthropological studies, humans have changed their preference rankings of sexual positions—the "missionary" (man-on-top) position, overwhelmingly the number one choice of the Americans Kinsey studied, was not that high on the lists of ancient Greeks and Romans, primitive tribes, or many other groups.

In the following list, the statistical references concerning preference are from *Kinsey's Sexual Behavior in the Human Female.* (Males, in his earlier study, ranked the positions in the same order, and the statistics were similar.) The advantages and disadvantages of each position are taken from Albert Ellis's *The Art and Science of Love* and from *Human Sexual Inadequacy* by William H. Masters and Virginia E. Johnson.

1. MAN ON TOP

Most frequently used by 100% of married females in Kinsey's survey, and the *only* position ever used by 9% of married females. To many Americans this is the only position considered biologically "natural," though other primates use the rear-entry position almost exclusively. Called the "missionary" position because it was introduced to native converts—who liked to make fun of it—by Christian missionaries who regarded other positions as sinful.

Advantages: Allows face-to-face intimacy, deep thrusting by male, pace setting by male. *Disadvantages:* Does not allow good control for the premature ejaculator, or freedom of movement for the woman. *Chances for conception:* Good.

2. WOMAN ON TOP

Frequently used by 45% of married females. Shown in ancient art as most common position in Ur, Greece, Rome, Peru, India, China, and Japan. Roman poet Martial portrayed Hector and Andromache in this position. Generally avoided by those at lower educational levels, according to Kinsey, because it *seems* to make the man less masculine, the woman less feminine.

Advantages: Allows freedom of movement for women, control for premature ejaculators, caressing of female by male. Most often results in orgasm for women. Good when the man is tired. *Disadvantage:* Too acrobatic for some women. *Chances for conception:* Not good.

3. SIDE BY SIDE

Frequently used by 31% of married women. From Ovid, a poet of ancient Rome: "Of love's thousand ways, a simple way and with least labor, this is: to lie on the right side, and half supine withal."

Advantages: Allows manipulation of clitoris, freedom of movement for man and woman. Good for tired or convalescent people, and premature ejaculators, as well as pregnant women. *Disadvantages:* Does not allow easy entry. *Chances for conception:* OK.

4. REAR ENTRANCE (or "dog fashion")

Frequently used by 15% of married women. Favored by primates and early Greeks. Rejected by many Americans because of its "animal origins" and lack of face-to-face intimacy.

Advantages: Allows manual stimulation of clitoris. Exciting for men who are turned on by female buttocks. Good for pregnant women, males with small penises, women with large vaginas. *Disadvantages:* Does not allow easy entry or face-to-face intimacy. Penis tends to fall out. *Chances for conception:* Good.

5. SITTING

Frequently used by 9% of married women. According to Kinsey, learned by many while "making out" in back seats of cars.

Advantages: Allows clitoral contact with male body, free movement, intimacy. Good for male who wants to hold off orgasm, pregnant women. *Disadvantages:* Does not allow vigorous thrusting. Sometimes tiring. Penetration may be too deep. *Chances for conception:* Poor.

6. STANDING

Frequently used by 4% of married women. Has echoes of a "quickie" against alley wall with prostitute, therefore exciting. Indian lotus position: each stands on one leg, wraps other around partner.

Advantages: Allows caressing. Exciting, can flow from dancing, taking shower. *Disadvantages:* Does not allow much thrusting. Entry difficult, particularly when one partner is taller than the other. Tiring. Not good for pregnant women. *Chances for conception:* Poor.

—A.E.

15 WELL-KNOWN LOVE OFFERINGS

1. PEARLS IN WINE

When Mark Antony expressed surprise at the opulence of a banquet Cleopatra had prepared for him, she dropped two pearls of inestimable value in her wine and drank the concoction to his health, insisting that her tribute to him should far surpass the cost of the feast. After they became lovers, he presented her with Cyprus, Phoenicia, Coele-Syria, and parts of Arabia, Cilicia, and Judea.

2. THE HEAD OF JOHN THE BAPTIST

When Herodias, after her husband's death, broke Mosaic law by marrying her brother-in-law, Herod, the marriage was denounced by John the Baptist. Later, the dancing of Salome, the daughter of Herodias, so pleased Herod that he promised to grant her anything she wanted. At her request, John the Baptist was beheaded, his head placed on a silver platter and presented to Salome, who then gave it to her mother.

3. FREEDOM

Suleiman the Magnificent, ruler of the Ottoman Empire, gave the enslaved Roxelana her freedom, as a love offering, and then married her. An observer wrote: "This week there has occurred in this city a most extraordinary event, one absolutely unprecedented in the history of the sultan's period. Suleiman has taken unto himself a slave woman from Russia as his empress."

4. SHAKESPEAREAN SONNETS

Not Shakespeare, but the publisher who pirated the sonnets, wrote the dedication, "To Mr. W.H." The 154 poems are among the greatest love offerings of all time, but it is not known for whom they were written.

5. TAJ MAHAL

When his favorite wife, Mumtaz Mahal, died giving birth to her 14th child in 1631, the grief-stricken Shah Jahan, emperor of the Moguls, ordered the white alabaster mausoleum built. Twenty thousand workmen labored 15 years to erect this most beautiful and costly tomb. Perfectly preserved, it stands on the Jumna River in north India inside a walled garden surrounded by reflecting pools and marble pavements. Shah Jahan intended to duplicate the Taj in black marble for his own tomb, but he was deposed by his son before he could realize this ambition.

6. "A VISIT FROM ST. NICHOLAS"

Clement C. Moore wrote this poem in 1822 as a Christmas gift to his children. The opening words, " 'Twas the night before Christmas," are more commonly—but incorrectly—identified as its title.

7. FAUST'S SOUL

In *Faust,* Goethe's classic poem, Dr. Faust contracted to give his soul to the devil, Mephistopheles, for the love of Margaret, a village maiden.

8. *SONNETS FROM THE PORTUGUESE*

Elizabeth Barrett's sonnets were begun when she first met Robert Browning, and they chronicle her reactions to their developing friendship and love. Browning learned of the sonnets early in 1847 after their son Robert Wiedemann Barrett was born. Elizabeth confessed to her husband, "I had written some poems about you."

9. A $10,000 BICYCLE

"Diamond Jim" Brady presented actress Lillian Russell with a gold-plated bicycle complete with mother-of-pearl handlebars and spokes encrusted with chips of diamonds, emeralds, rubies, and sapphires. When Miss Russell went on tour, the bicycle—kept in a blue plush-lined morocco case—traveled with her.

10. "THE GIFT OF THE MAGI"

O. Henry's famous Christmas story tells of the sacrifices made by two young lovers. Della cut off and sold her luxuriant long hair in order to buy a platinum watch-fob chain for her husband Jim. He in turn sold his precious gold watch to buy expensive tortoiseshell combs for Della.

11. MOTHER'S DAY

The wearing of a white carnation and the observance of special church services every second Sunday in May were proposed by Miss Anna Jarvis, in commemoration of her own mother and other mothers throughout the country. Because of Miss Jarvis's perseverance, the U.S. Congress was finally persuaded in 1914 to give official recognition to Mother's Day.

12. THE CHAGALL WINDOWS

Marc Chagall's 12 stained-glass windows were created for the Synagogue of the Hadassah-Hebrew University Medical Center in Jerusalem. Speaking at the dedication ceremony, Chagall said, "Thoughts of love emboldened me to bring this modest gift to the Jewish people . . ."

13. RED ROSES . . . FOREVER

Since Marilyn Monroe's death in 1962, Joe DiMaggio, her second husband, has had fresh red roses delivered to her grave site three times a week.

14. 69.42-CARAT CARTIER-BURTON DIAMOND

Richard Burton purchased the $1,050,000 gem from Cartier as a gift for Elizabeth Taylor Burton. Other tokens of his devotion to her included the most expensive mink coat in the world ($125,000), the 33.9-carat Krupp diamond ($350,000), the "Ping-Pong" diamond

($38,000), La Peregrina pearl ($37,000), a $93,000 emerald, and a sapphire brooch valued at $65,000.

15. SKORPIOS ISLAND

When Aristotle Onassis married Jackie Kennedy in October, 1968, one of his wedding gifts to her was a share of the Greek island of Skorpios, on which they were married. Before their marriage, he provided her with a gem wardrobe valued at $1.2 million. He is said to have spent $20 million for her pleasure during the first year of their marriage.

—M.A.A.

10 FOODS CLAIMED
TO BE APHRODISIACS

1. ASPARAGUS

Asparagus contains a diuretic that increases the amount of urine excreted and excites the urinary passages. The vegetable is rich in potassium, phosphorus, and calcium—all necessary for maintenance of a high energy level. However, it also contains aspartic acid, which neutralizes excess amounts of ammonia in one's body and may cause apathy and sexual disinterest.

2. CAVIAR

In addition to being nutritious (30% protein), caviar has been considered an aphrodisiac because of its obvious place in the reproductive process. All fish and their by-products have been linked to the myth of Aphrodite, the goddess of love who was born from the foam of the sea. Supposedly, anything that came from the sea would partake of Aphrodite's power.

3. EEL

Eel, like most fish, is rich in phosphorus and has an excitant effect on the bladder. In addition to its general associations with the aphrodisiac effect of fish, it has probably been favored as an aphrodisiac because of its phallic appearance.

4. GARLIC

Both Eastern and Western cultures have long regarded garlic as an aphrodisiac. The Greeks and Romans sang its praises and oriental lovers claimed to be towers of strength because of eating it.

5. GINSENG

The Chinese call ginseng the "elixir of life" and have used it for over 5,000 years. Although medical opinion is sharply divided as to its merits, recent Russian experiments claim that ginseng increases sexual energy and has a general healing and rejuvenating influence on the body.

6. HONEY

Honey is highly nutritious and rich in minerals, amino acids, enzymes, and B-complex vitamins. Galen, Ovid, and Sheikh Nefzawi, author of *The Perfumed Garden,* believed that honey has outstanding aphrodisiac powers.

7. LOBSTER

The lobster has been described as an amatory excitant by many writers, including Henry Fielding in *Tom Jones*. In addition, it shares the Aphrodite-derived power attributed to all seafood.

8. OYSTERS

Oysters are one of the most renowned aphrodisiac foods. Like other seafood, they are rich in phosphorus. Although they are not a high source of energy, oysters are easily digestible. Among the eminent lovers who have vouched for oysters was Casanova, who called them "a spur to the spirit and to love."

9. PEACHES

"Venus owns this tree . . . the fruit provokes lust . . ." wrote herbalist Nicholas Culpeper. The Chinese considered the fruit's sweet juices symbolic of the effluvia of the vagina, and both the Chinese and Arabs regard its deep fur-edged cleft as symbolic of the female genitalia. A "peach house" was once a common English slang term for a house of prostitution, and the term "peach" has been used almost universally to describe a pretty or sexually appealing girl.

10. TRUFFLES

Truffles, the expensive underground fungi, are similar to oysters in that they are composed mostly of water and are rich in protein. Rabelais, Casanova, George Sand, Sade, Napoleon, and Mme. Pompadour are a few of the many notables who have praised the truffle's aphrodisiac powers. An ancient French proverb warns: "Those who wish to lead virtuous lives should abstain from truffles."

—R.H.

7 FAMOUS MEN WHO WERE FULL-TIME OR PART-TIME VIRGINS

1. SIR ISAAC NEWTON (English scientist; 1642–1727)

He died a virgin. It was said his abstinence was the cause of his acute insomnia.

2. IMMANUEL KANT (German philosopher; 1724–1804)

He died a virgin.

3. LOUIS XVI (French king; 1754–1793)

The first seven years of his marriage to Marie Antoinette were entirely sexless. He suffered from phimosis—an abnormal growth of foreskin—that made erection painful and intercourse impossible. He refused an operation on the grounds that this was how God had made him. Eventually persuaded, he underwent the simple surgery and finally consummated his marriage on his 23rd birthday.

4. JOHN RUSKIN (English writer; 1819–1900)

On his wedding night he was shocked into sexual abstinence for the remainder of his life by the sight of his wife's pubic hair. He became an obsessive masturbator—"a suicide committed daily," he called it. Sexual repression drove him mad. He kept a diary of his sex dreams. He died a virgin.

5. GEORGE BERNARD SHAW (British playwright; 1856–1950)

A virgin until the age of 29 when he was seduced by an aging widow. The experience shocked him into 15 years of total abstinence. He was never explicit in writing about sex, using the words "manroot" for penis and "her sex" for vagina.

6. HAVELOCK ELLIS (English sexologist; 1859–1939)

He never masturbated because he feared that he would contract VD from wet dreams. He was a virgin until he was 32. He married a lesbian.

7. ADOLF HITLER (German leader; 1889–1945)

It was thought that he had only one testicle. He loved pornographic films and books. At a Christmas party a woman kissed him under the mistletoe and he literally shook with rage. Despite his last-minute marriage to Eva Braun, many authorities believe that he died a virgin.

—J. BE.

23 OF THE BUSIEST
LOVERS IN HISTORY

Tireless lover Giovanni Giacomo Casanova spent the
last 13 years of his life as a librarian.

1. KING SOLOMON (c. 973–c. 933 B.C.)

The son of David and Bath-sheba became the third king of Israel and reigned some 40 years, during which time he enjoyed 700 wives and from 60 to 300 mistresses. His women were both Israeli and foreign (some taken to further political alliances) and were among the most beautiful in all antiquity. Although polygamy was the matrimonial standard of the time, later rabbis claimed that Solomon's single son was proof of punishment by God for Solomon's violation of monogamy.

2. MNESARETE (c. 4th century B.C.)

Mnesarete was a Greek hetaera and possibly the most beautiful prostitute of all time. The nickname Phryne ("toad"), given to her because of her complexion, has since become synonymous with "courtesan." Her fine body was reputedly the model for Praxiteles' statue of the goddess Aphrodite at Cnidus, and when, during a festival, she let down her hair, took off her clothes and stepped into the sea, she inspired Apelles to paint his great *Aphrodite Anadyomene*. Phryne was later accused of profaning the Eleusinian mysteries and was defended by one of her lovers, the statesman and orator Hyperides. Just when it seemed she would lose her case—and therefore her life—Hyperides ripped open her robe and exposed her breasts to the jury. She was acquitted.

3. CLEOPATRA (69–30 B.C.)

No great beauty, Cleopatra was among the most alluring women of all time and was well-versed in the art of lovemaking. From the time she took her first lover (at the age of 12), the queen of the Nile used sex for power, as well as for pleasure. It is said that she erected a small temple where she kept scores of young male lovers who were fed drugs to increase their lust. It was with these slaves that she practiced the erotic secrets she had learned from courtesans in a bordello in Alexandria. Allegedly she could take on 100 men in a single night. At 38, the Egyptian queen committed suicide.

4. EMPRESS THEODORA (508?–548)

Theodora was an actress during her childhood in Constantinople. A Roman law prohibiting senators from marrying actresses was repealed just prior to her marriage to Roman Emperor Justinian I. Possessed of great beauty, intellect, and will—along with a reputation for severity—Theodora advocated great moral reforms for the city of Rome while constituting herself "the protectress of faithless wives." So as not to break Rome's laws against total nudity, "the most depraved of all courtesans" would appear in public—clothed only with a ribbon. It has also been said that when picnicking outside Rome, Theodora would open her "gates of Venus" to at least 10 young men for an entire evening. The following day, she would take on their 30 servants.

5. QUEEN ZINGUA (early 17th century)

Angola's Queen Zingua was among the cruelest of nymphomaniacs, rivaled only by the legendary Amazons, who were said to make sex slaves of male captives and cripple them because "the lame best perform the act of love." The queen, who kept a large harem of males, enjoyed arranging battles to the death between warriors, then going to bed with the winner. It is said that she would make love with a man all night and have him killed in the morning. The jealous Zingua also had all pregnant females executed. Her bizarre sex life apparently continued until she was converted to Catholicism at the age of 77.

6. WILLIAM DOUGLAS (1724–1810)

The third earl of March and fourth duke of Queensberry, certainly the prototype of the "dirty old man," often leered at beauties passing by from the window of his Piccadilly house and sent his groom out to bring him any girl whose body particularly pleased him. This approach usually worked, for "Old Q" was one of the richest and most influential men of his time. He consorted with women ranging in rank from duchesses to prostitutes, and held "oriental orgies" at his great estates, orgies which were unrivaled since those of Tiberius. During his old age, he hired Louis XV's former private physician, not only to keep him alive, but to arrange his love festivals. When, at the age of 86, the "Piccadilly Ambulator" died of overeating, at least 70 unopened love letters were found in his bed. He willed over £1 million to his lovers and servants.

7. GIOVANNI GIACOMO CASANOVA (1725–1798)

According to his voluminous memoirs, Casanova seduced thousands of women; only 116 of them are actually named in published records. Life for the Italian adventurer was a continual search for new pleasures, and his name equals Don Juan's as a synonym for a promiscuous womanizer. Casanova's specialty was seducing his friends' wives and daughters—often two at a time. He frequently bathed with his companions in a bathtub built for two, and sometimes shared with them the 50 oysters he customarily ate for breakfast. Women, he once said, were his cuisine.

8. CATHERINE THE GREAT (1729–1796)

Sexually insatiable, the empress of Russia advocated sexual relations six times a day. She had 21 official lovers, although her final total would exceed 80. An avid voyeur as well as an insomniac, Catherine claimed that sex was the best sleeping pill. Rogerson, her physician, and Mme. Protas, her procurer, respectively examined and tried out all male prospects before approving them for the empress.

9. MARQUIS DE SADE (1740–1814)

The man who gave us the word *sadism* lived a life of scandalous debauchery marked by habitual infidelity and sexual perversions. Comte Donatien Alphonse François de Sade (he encouraged people to call him "Marquis") was a handsome little Frenchman and a "fanatic of vice." He was involved in the notorious Rosa Keller affair, in which he tortured a Parisian prostitute, and was tried in absentia and sentenced to death for his part in the Marseilles scandal—an orgy in which he was accused of sodomy, torture, and poisoning participants with chocolate-covered bonbons. Eventually reprieved by the king, Sade authored numerous novels and plays, including *100 Days of Sodom*, in which he described 600 variations of the sex instinct. In 1803, he was committed to an insane asylum at Charenton, where he died 11 years later.

10. MLLE. DUBOIS (c. 1770)

"Her greed for gold was equal to her greed for pleasure," a chronicler of the day wrote. The French actress once made a catalog of her lovers over a 20-year period. The final tally: 16,527 individuals, or three per day. This accounting was so well known that even the Marquis de Sade was influenced by the figures. In his fictional *Philosophy in the Boudoir*, his character Mme. de Saint-Ange declares, "In the 12 years I have been married I have been had by perhaps 10,000 or 12,000 individuals."

11. KING LAPETAMAKA II (c. 1778)

It is said that on his third voyage, in 1777, Captain Cook visited the Pacific island kingdom of Tonga, where he met Tonga's King Lapetamaka II. Strong, raven-haired, and in his 80s, the king claimed that it was his duty to deflower every native maiden. He said that he had never been with the same woman twice and was presently performing his appointed task 8-10 times a day, every day.

12. LOLA MONTEZ (1818?-1861)

Whatever Lola wanted, Lola got. By the time she turned 13, the British-Irish dancer and adventuress had discovered she could sell her body for money. She was very particular. She refused to allow the viceroy of Poland to sleep with her because he had false teeth. After taking three husbands and innumerable lovers (including Franz Liszt and Alexandre Dumas père), Lola became the mistress of King Louis I of Bavaria, who made her baroness of Rosenthal and countess of Lansfeld. One writer claims that the king confided she could "perform miracles with the muscles of her private parts" and that he "gave her his kingdom" when she "caused him to achieve 10 orgasms in a 24-hour period." Her influence over Louis precipitated a revolution that forced him to abdicate. Lola fled to England, and later to America—where she lectured, danced, made love, and became the mistress of several wealthy Americans. Toward the end of her life she devoted much of her money and energy to "helping fallen women."

13. SARAH BERNHARDT (1844-1923)

"The divine Sarah," as Oscar Wilde called her, went through more than 1,000 lovers in her colorful life, many of them famous artists and writers like Edmond Rostand. The energetic French actress once observed, "It is by spending oneself that one becomes rich." Sarah often slept in a rosewood coffin lined with letters from her lovers.

14. FRANK HARRIS (1854-1931)

The Irish-born author and "sexpert" had Lloyd's of London insure for $150,000 the card file of 2,000 women he claimed he had seduced in his lifetime. His first job, at age 10, consisted of selling dirty postcards, and later he invented a card game called Dirty Banshee in which the cards depicted satyrs and goddesses engaged in sexual acts. Harris's book *My Life and Loves*, banned for 40 years in the U.S. and England, sold for a long time in Parisian bookstores for $100 and more. He also worked as editor for England's *Saturday Review* magazine.

15. GABRIELE D'ANNUNZIO (1863–1938)

The Italian poet, dramatist, novelist, and adventurer is said to have dominated the Italian literary scene for 40 years. Stating that "a good soldier is prepared for anything," D'Annunzio would carry condoms into battle in Napoleon's snuffbox, which he had won. There are legends that he rode to the hounds in the raw with a naked lady at the front of his saddle, nonchalantly strolled nude into the dining room of an illustrious hotel, slept on a pillow filled with locks of hair from his conquests, served wine from a carafe made from the skull of a virgin who had committed suicide because of him, and used strychnine as an aphrodisiac. D'Annunzio, whose most famous affair was with the actress Eleonora Duse, publicly boasted that he was hated by 1,000 husbands.

16. GRIGORI EFIMOVICH RASPUTIN (1871?–1916)

The name Rasputin, or Rasputnik, was given to him by fellow villagers and meant "libertine." The Russian mystic spent his life living up to it. By diverting his followers' religious fervor into sexual channels, this "savior and healer" seduced hundreds of women, ranging from peasant girls to aristocrats. After he became "a member" of the royal family (he won the confidence of the czar and czarina by assuaging the pain of their hemophiliac son), noble ladies vied for Rasputin's favors. "The Holy Satyr" would accommodate them in his bedroom, which he called "the holy of holies." There were even public charges—probably untrue—that he had affairs with Czarina Alexandra and her young daughters. The "mad monk" with the hypnotic eyes had few equals in history.

17. MATA HARI (1876–1917)

Probably the most notorious spy since Delilah and the most accomplished mistress since La Pompadour, Mata Hari (born Margarete Zelle in Holland) worked as a spy for the Germans while posing as an exotic dancer in Paris. Her lovers included Jules Cambron, chief of the French Ministry, the crown prince of Germany, the Dutch prime minister, and the duke of Brunswick. (It has been estimated that her activities caused the deaths of 50,000 Allied soldiers.) When she did not sleep with men for state secrets, she did so for money. Though Mata Hari probably hated men due to the brutality of her first husband, she did enjoy sex, often relaxing in French brothels after work. When the Germans betrayed her, at least half a dozen former lovers hatched absurd plans to save Mata Hari from the French firing squad that eventually took her life.

18. GENERAL CHANG CHUNG-CH'ANG (c. 1880–c. 1935)

"The general with the three long legs," as Shanghai prostitutes called him, is said to have taken on entire brothels at one time. Because he ate black chow meat (reputedly an aphrodisiac) every day of the year, he became known as "The Dog-Meat General." The Chinese warlord was dubbed "72-Cannon Chang" because his "manhood" supposedly equaled 72 stacked silver dollars in length and diameter.

19. KING IBN-SAUD (1880–1953)

From the age of 11 until his death at 72, the Saudi Arabian monarch had sexual relations with three different women every night—except during battles.

20. MAE WEST (b. 1892)

"I do all of my best work in bed," the legendary lady replied when a reporter asked her how she went about writing her memoirs. It is not known how many lovers Mae West has had, or if she is still sexually active in her 80s. But the star of stage and screen, whose name has become synonymous with the word "vamp," must rank among the world's most sexually active women. In her memoirs she writes of one session of lovemaking with a prodigy named Ted that lasted 15 consecutive hours—possibly the sexual marathon record.

Mae West: "I do all of my best work in bed."

21. KING CAROL II (1893–1953)

Like his mother Queen Marie, the Romanian ruler was a sexual athlete whose affairs numbered in the thousands. It is said that because of the king's "abnormally large sex organ," operations had to be performed on the vaginas of several dozen women so that they could accommodate him. A number of young girls reputedly died "when their perinea were ruptured during intercourse with the king." Eventually, a "court abortionist" was appointed. In 1925, King Carol was forced to abdicate and go into exile—largely at the instigation of the Liberal party—because of a scandal caused by the king's liaison with his mistress Magda Lupescu (née Elena Wolff). Carol returned in 1930, but again he was forced to abdicate because he refused to give up Magda. The two were married in 1947 and lived together in exile until Carol's death.

22. ANONYMOUS (b. c. 1900)

Alfred C. Kinsey, a professor of zoology at Indiana University, noted in his famous 10-year sex study, published in 1948, the case of a man whose frequency of coitus was 33.1 acts per week, over a period of 30 years—apparently with no harm to his health. (This equals almost 52,000 times for the period—nearly five times a day.) Other sex researchers have recorded examples of people who have engaged in sexual intercourse twice a day for periods of 30 years. Kinsey approximated the average (mean) frequency of total sexual outlet for the general male population at 2.3 acts per week, up to the age of 85.

23. BRIGITTE BARDOT (b. 1934)

At the age of 40, the French film star boasted in an interview that she "must have a man every night." Assuming that her need began at age 20, and subtracting an arbitrary 76 days a year for travel, illness, menstruation, or even rest, that would mean that Brigitte (without considering daylight liaisons) had a total of 4,980 nights of sexual activity. Formidable.

—R.H. & D.B.

6 OF THE MOST EXPENSIVE WOMEN IN HISTORY

1. LAMIA (charged 250 talents)

This Greek courtesan demanded the equivalent of $300,000 to service Demetrius Poliorcetes, king of Macedonia. He agreed to the sum—and put a special tax on soap to raise the money.

2. LAIS (charged 10,000 drachmas)

Demosthenes wanted this Sicilian-born Greek courtesan so badly that he offered her 1,000 drachmas for a single night. When she saw him, she upped the figure to 10,000 drachmas. Yet, she gave herself for nothing to the unkempt, ascetic philosopher Diogenes.

3. NINON DE LENCLOS (charged 50,000 crowns)

Cardinal Richelieu, the French statesman, once paid 50,000 crowns for a night with the renowned Ninon, France's greatest sexologist in the 17th century. She took the money, but sent a female friend in her place.

4. LAURA BELL (charged £250,000)

An ex-Belfast shop assistant, she became London's leading prostitute. In 1850, for a single night's sexual encounter, she charged Prince Jung Badahur, wealthy prime minister to the maharaja of Nepal, £250,000. He paid it. Later, she got religion, married the bishop of Norwich's nephew, and became a lay preacher.

5. COUNTESS NICCHIA DE CASTIGLIONE (charged 1 million francs)

The Italian countess, mistress of Napoleon III of France and Prince Jérôme Bonaparte, was the most beautiful woman of her time. However, she was wildly extravagant. When the earl of Yarmouth, son of one of England's richest men, offered her a million francs— $200,000—for her favors, she accepted. He ravished her so vigorously that she had to stay in bed for a week.

6. KITTY FISHER (charged 100 guineas)

She was the highest paid of London prostitutes. When the duke of York gave her a pitiful £50 note, less than half her fee for a night, she threw him out of bed. She then had the note baked in a pie and ate it for breakfast. In 1765, she married a member of parliament.

—J.BE.

BENJAMIN FRANKLIN'S 8 REASONS TO MARRY AN OLDER WOMAN

1. Because they have more Knowledge of the world, and their Minds are better stored with Observations; their Conversation is more improving, and more lastingly agreeable.
2. Because when Women cease to be handsome, they study to be good. To maintain their Influence over Men, they supply the Diminution of Beauty by an Augmentation of Utility. They learn to do a thousand Services, small and great, and are the most tender and useful of all Friends when you are sick. Thus they continue amiable. And hence there is hardly such a thing to be found as an old Woman who is not a good Woman.

3. Because there is no hazard of children, which irregularly produced may be attended with much inconvenience.

4. Because through more Experience they are more prudent and discreet in conducting an Intrigue to prevent Suspicion. The Commerce with them is therefore safer with regard to your reputation; and with regard to theirs, if the Affair should happen to be known, considerate People might be rather inclined to excuse an old Woman, who would kindly take care of a young Man, form his manners by her good Councils, and prevent his ruining his Health and Fortune among mercenary Prostitutes.

5. Because in every Animal that walks upright, the Deficiency of the Fluids that fill the Muscles appears first in the highest Part. The Face first grows lank and wrinkled; then the Neck; then the Breast and Arms; the lower parts continuing to the last as plump as ever; so that covering all above with a Basket, and regarding only what is below the Girdle, it is impossible of two Women to know an old one from a young one. And as in the Dark all Cats are grey, the Pleasure of Corporal Enjoyment with an old Woman is at least equal and frequently superior; every Knack being by Practice capable of improvement.

6. Because the sin is less. The Debauching of a Virgin may be her Ruin, and make her Life unhappy.

7. Because the Compunction is less. The having made a young Girl miserable may give you frequent bitter Reflections; none of which can attend making an old Woman *happy*.

8th & lastly. They are so grateful!!!

SOURCE: *Advice to a Young Man* (Philadelphia, June 25, 1745).

THE SEXUAL ABERRATIONS
AND PECULIARITIES
OF 20 WELL-KNOWN MEN

1 CALIGULA (Roman emperor; 12–41 A.D.)

Raped one sister and made prostitutes out of the others. After committing adultery (whether the women agreed or not), he would forbid his partners ever to have intercourse again, then publicly issue divorce proceedings in their husbands' names. Whenever he kissed his wife's or mistress's neck he would whisper, "Off comes this head whenever I give the word."

2. ST. AUGUSTINE OF CANTERBURY (first archbishop of Canterbury; d. 604)

Abstained from sex because sperm comes from the same organ that produces urine.

3. POPE ALEXANDER VI (1431?–1503)

Enthusiastic orgiast. Once had 50 nude prostitutes servicing guests at a banquet where he offered prizes to the man who could copulate the most times.

4. LEONARDO DA VINCI (Italian artist; 1452–1519)

Drew detailed diagrams of the penis showing canals connecting it to the lungs. These canals presumably supplied the "breath" that produced an erection.

5. SAMUEL PEPYS (English diarist; 1633–1703)

Used to buy pornographic books, wrap them in plain paper, read them at one sitting, masturbating throughout, then burn them. Noted all his masturbations in his diary using a special symbol. He was also surprised at his wife's annoyance with him for fondling her maid's breasts. "I feel myself begin to love too much by handling of her breasts in the morning when she dresses me, they being the finest that ever I saw in my life."

6. LOUIS FRANÇOIS DE BOURBON, PRINCE DE CONDÉ (French politician; 1717–1776)

At the age of 40, he engaged Mme. Deschamps 12 times in a single night. So proud was he of his achievement that he had all his buttons imprinted with the number 12, his shirts marked with the number 12, bought 12 guns and 12 swords, had 12 table settings and 12 courses at each dinner, took 1,200 francs pocket money every day, and always tipped 12 louis.

7. SIR FRANCIS DASHWOOD (English politician; 1708–1781)

Founder of the notorious Hell-Fire Club. Claimed to have seduced Empress Anna of Russia while disguised as King Charles XII of Sweden. Converted to satanism after seeing and hearing the "devil" (in fact it was two cats copulating in the night). Organized elaborate orgies with participants dressed up as monks and nuns (Ben Franklin was a member). His "church" was adorned with obscene carvings.

8. JAMES BOSWELL (Scottish biographer; 1740–1795)

Was very proud of the fact he once made love five times in a row. The girl was named Louise and, as he recorded it, he "was fairly lost in supreme rapture no less than five times and the worthy Louise called me a prodigy."

9. VICTOR EMMANUEL I (Sardinian king; 1759–1824)

The social highlight of one of his official visits to France was the discovery that French women did not wear underpants. He saw a lady-in-waiting tumble over, and said to the French empress, "I am delighted to see, madame, that your ladies do not wear drawers, and that the gates of paradise are always open."

10. DUC DE RICHELIEU (French statesman; 1766–1822)

Not Cardinal Richelieu. Discovered his wife in flagrante delicto and said, "Madame, you really must be more careful. Suppose it had been someone else who had found you like this."

11. DUKE OF WELLINGTON (English soldier; 1769–1852)

A sexual cold fish, he had one well-publicized affair with a notorious whore, Harriette Wilson, who described him, out of all her lovers, as being the "most unentertaining." When she threatened, unless paid off, to publish her memoirs and include their liaison, he wrote back, "Publish and be damned!"

12. NAPOLEON (French emperor; 1769–1821)

Had more mistresses than Louis XV, Francis I, and Henry IV put together. Liked his sex fast and furious—"Like a fireman tackling a fire," said his first wife, Joséphine. On their wedding night Joséphine's dog, believing Napoleon was attacking her, jumped under the sheets and bit him.

13. KARL MARX (German political philosopher; 1818–1883)

Deeply disapproved of Engels's mistress not because having a mistress was middle class but because the one Engels chose was common.

14. LEWIS CARROLL (English writer; 1832–1898)

Hobby was photographing naked prepubescent girls.

15. LEOPOLD VON SACHER-MASOCH (Austrian writer; 1836–1895)

As a child he hid in his aunt's wardrobe and watched her having sex with her lover. He was discovered and beaten. The pleasure/pain association remained and he loved to listen to his mistress having sex with lovers he supplied. He insisted that when women beat him they wear furs.

16. ALGERNON SWINBURNE (English poet; 1837–1909)

Excessive beatings at Eton (where the master made pupils splash eau de cologne on their bodies so as to excite pleasure before inflicting pain) caused him to become a keen flagellant. His one heterosexual affair, with a middle-aged, plump American circus rider, ended in failure. She said, "I can't make him understand that biting's no good."

17. SIR EDMUND GOSSE (English critic; 1849–1928)

Was discovered in Westminster Abbey drooling over pictures of male nudes during Robert Browning's memorial service.

18. LEONARD SMITHERS (English publisher; 1861–1907)

Hobby was deflowering little girls. "He loves first editions," said Oscar Wilde.

19. HENRI DE TOULOUSE-LAUTREC (French painter; 1864–1901)

Lived in a brothel. Stunted by childhood accidents, he suffered from hypertrophy (excessive enlargement) of the penis so that the girls nicknamed him "Teapot."

20. JEAN GENET (French writer; b. 1909)

Addicted to masturbation. Jean-Paul Sartre said that Genet "prefers his own caresses, since the enjoyment received coincides with the enjoyment given."

—J.BE.

SEXUAL CURIOSITIES
ABOUT 9 WELL-KNOWN WOMEN

1. SHAN-YIN (Chinese princess; Sung Dynasty)

Had a special bed made to her personal design so that 30 men could lie on it while she enjoyed them all.

2. EMPRESS MARIA THERESA (Austrian empress; 1717–1780)

She handsomely rewarded her physician, to whom she had complained about her unsatisfactory sex life with her husband, the duke of Lorraine. (She had borne him 16 children.) Her physician had recommended that "Your Most Sacred Majesty's vulva be titillated for a considerable time before coitus."

3. JOSÉPHINE DE BEAUHARNAIS (French empress; 1763–1814)

An extremely vigorous and loud sex technique with Napoleon resulted in her waking the whole household and twice falling out of bed.

4. PAULINE BONAPARTE (Napoleon's sister; 1780–1825)

An incorrigible nymphomaniac, she unfortunately married a man with a tiny penis. She quickly found a lover whose penis was so large that it not only satisfied her but also wounded her. Her doctors insisted that she terminate the affair. Said her gynecologist, "The present condition of the uterus is caused by a constant and habitual excitation of that organ; if this does not cease, an exceedingly dangerous situation may result."

5. THERESA BERKLEY (English brothelkeeper; d. 1836)

Queen of the flagellants. In her establishment clients could be (according to her own advertisements) "birched, whipped, fustigated, scourged, needle-picked, half-hung, holly-brushed, furze-brushed, butcher-brushed, stinging-nettled, curry-combed, phlebotomized." Always kept her whips in water to ensure their suppleness. After particularly severe beatings, she would revive unconscious clients with stinging nettles. Liked being flogged herself and invented an amazing flogging machine known as the Berkley horse. So popular was this ingenious gadget that when she died she left a fortune in excess of £10,000 to her brother who was a missionary. Her brother later found out the source of her wealth and refused his inheritance.

6. LADY JANE ELLENBOROUGH (English adventuress; 1807–1881)

Among her lovers were King Louis I of Bavaria, his son King Otto of Greece, and Honoré de Balzac. She married a bedouin chief and at the age of 73 wrote in her diary, "It is now a month and 20 days since Medjuel last slept with me! What can be the reason?"

Lady Jane Ellenborough, an English beauty whose lovers included King Louis I of Bavaria, his son King Otto of Greece, and Honoré de Balzac.

7. GEORGE ELIOT (English novelist; 1819–1880)

Lived in a very successful ménage à trois situation. Henry James's sister described her as "a fungus of pendulous shape."

8. VICTORIA (English queen; 1819–1901)

She had no idea lesbianism existed until an antihomosexual bill was brought before her. Then she simply refused to recognize its existence and struck out all female references—thus making male homosexuality illegal, but lesbianism legal.

9. PRINCESS ANNE (daughter of Queen Elizabeth II; b. 1950)

Was the only female competitor at the 1976 Montreal Olympics not to be given a sex test.

—J.BE.

3 PEOPLE
WHO DIED DURING SEX

1. ATTILA THE HUN (invader of Europe; 406?–453)

    Died in action.

2. FELIX FAURE (French president; 1841–1899)

    He was sitting on a specially designed sex chair with his mistress performing a sex act when he had a heart attack and expired.

3. LEO VIII (pope d. 963–965)

    Died of a stroke while committing adultery.

—J.BE.

10 WOMEN OFFERED
$1 MILLION EACH
—IF THEY POSE NUDE
FOR A GIRLIE MAGAZINE

In February, 1976, Larry Flynt, editor and publisher of *Hustler* magazine (an overtly sexual imitation of *Playboy*), selected 10 famous American women he'd like to feature as nudes in his periodical. He offered each of these women $1 million to pose "nude in *Hustler* magazine . . . in the same manner as other *Hustler* models." His list of million-dollar nudes:

1. Patty Hearst
2. Raquel Welch
3. Caroline Kennedy
4. Julie Nixon Eisenhower
5. Susan Ford
6. Sally Struthers
7. Mary Tyler Moore
8. Gloria Steinem
9. Barbara Walters
10. Cher

To date not one of Flynt's 10 has agreed to pose nude despite the lavish sum offered.

67 RENOWNED
HOMOSEXUALS AND BISEXUALS

With the assistance of the researchers of the *Advocate*, a national gay periodical published in San Mateo, Calif., two lists have been assembled of the leading female and male homosexuals from past times to the present. Included, also, are celebrated persons who were both homosexual and heterosexual—that is, bisexual. In noting modern-day names we have confined ourselves to those who have announced or publicly discussed their homosexuality.

FEMALE

1. Sappho (flourished c. 600 B.C.), Greek poet
2. Christina (1626–1689), Swedish queen
3. Madame de Staël (1766–1817), French author
4. Charlotte Cushman (1816–1876), U.S. actress
5. Gertrude Stein (1874–1946), U.S. author
6. Alice B. Toklas (1877–1967), U.S. author-cook
7. Virginia Woolf (1882–1941), British author
8. Victoria Sackville-West (1892–1962), British author
9. Bessie Smith (1894–1937), U.S. singer
10. Kate Millett (b. 1934), U.S. author
11. Janis Joplin (1943–1970), U.S. singer

Gertrude Stein (L), innovative U.S. author, and
Alice B. Toklas, inventor of the hashish brownie.

MALE

1. Zeno of Elea (fifth century B.C.), Greek philosopher
2. Sophocles (496?–406 B.C.), Greek playwright
3. Euripides (480?–406? B.C.), Greek dramatist
4. Socrates (470?–399 B.C.), Greek philosopher
5. Aristotle (384–322 B.C.), Greek philosopher
6. Alexander the Great (356–323 B.C.), Macedonian ruler
7. Julius Caesar (100–44 B.C.), Roman emperor
8. Hadrian (76–138 A.D.), Roman emperor
9. Richard the Lion-Hearted (1157–1199), British king
10. Richard II (1367–1400), British king
11. Sandro Botticelli (1444?–1510), Italian painter
12. Leonardo da Vinci (1452–1519), Italian painter-scientist
13. Julius III (1487–1555), Italian pope
14. Benvenuto Cellini (1500–1571), Italian goldsmith
15. Francis Bacon (1561–1626), British philosopher-statesman
16. Christopher Marlowe (1564–1593), British playwright
17. James I (1566–1625), British king
18. John Milton (1608–1674), British author
19. Jean-Baptiste Lully (1632–1687), French composer
20. Peter the Great (1672–1725), Russian czar
21. Frederick the Great (1712–1786), Prussian king
22. Gustavus III (1746–1792), Swedish king
23. Alexander von Humboldt (1769–1859), German naturalist
24. George Gordon, Lord Byron (1788–1824), British poet
25. Hans Christian Andersen (1805–1875), Danish author
26. Walt Whitman (1819–1892), U.S. poet
27. Horatio Alger (1832–1899), U.S. author
28. Samuel Butler (1835–1902), British author
29. Algernon Swinburne (1837–1909), British poet
30. Pëtr Ilich Tchaikovsky (1840–1893), Russian composer
31. Paul Verlaine (1844–1896), French poet
32. Arthur Rimbaud (1854–1891), French poet
33. Oscar Wilde (1854–1900), British playwright
34. Frederick Rolfe (Baron Corvo) (1860–1913), British author
35. André Gide (1869–1951), French author
36. Marcel Proust (1871–1922), French author
37. E. M. Forster (1879–1970), British author
38. John Maynard Keynes (1883–1946), British economist
39. Harold Nicholson (1886–1968), British author-diplomat
40. Ernst Röhm (1887–1934), German Nazi leader
41. T. E. Lawrence (1888–1935), British soldier-author
42. Jean Cocteau (1889–1963), French author
43. Waslaw Nijinsky (1890–1950), Russian ballet dancer
44. Bill Tilden (1893–1953), U.S. tennis player
45. Christopher Isherwood (b. 1904), British author
46. Dag Hammarskjöld (1905–1961), Swedish U.N. secretary-general
47. W. H. Auden (1907–1973), British-U.S. poet
48. Jean Genet (b. 1909), French playwright
49. Tennessee Williams (b. 1911), U.S. playwright
50. Merle Miller (b. 1919), U.S. author

51. Pier Paolo Pasolini (1922–1975), Italian film director
52. Brendan Behan (1923–1964), Irish author
53. Malcolm Boyd (b. 1923), U.S. theologian
54. Allan Ginsberg (b. 1926), U.S. poet
55. David Bowie (b. 1947), British singer
56. Elton John (b. 1947), British singer

Big Bill Tilden, ranked by AP poll as the greatest
male tennis player of the first half of the 20th century.

2 MEN WHO POSED AS WOMEN
AND
9 WOMEN WHO POSED AS MEN

1. THE ABBÉ D'ENTRAGUES

When she was pregnant, the mother of the Abbé d'Entragues—
an ancestor of Balzac—had had her heart set on having a girl, and
when a boy came forth instead, she determined to raise him as a
daughter. Hence the abbé's feminine predisposition. He achieved
fame as an abbé, dressing in proper garb by day, but switching to
wigs and dresses at night. Eventually he left the Church, but after a
brief flirtation with Protestantism, he returned. Although normally in
good health (he lived to be 80) the abbé affected a pale, effeminate
look which he produced by frequent bleedings and sleeping with his
arms locked unnaturally over his head.

2. PHILIP, DUKE OF ORLÉANS

Everyone in the court of Louis XIV of France knew that Philip,
who was the king's brother and duke of Orléans, was biologically a
man, yet the duke persisted inexplicably in dressing and carrying
himself at all times as a woman. The writer Saint-Simon depicted
Philip as "a little potbellied man, mounted on . . . high heels. . . . He

338

always dressed as a woman and was covered with rings, bracelets, and precious stones everywhere. He wore a long wig, black and powdered, and ribbons wherever they could be placed. He was redolent of all kinds of perfumery and . . . wore rouge." And the Princess Palatine, Philip's second wife, reported that he "had the manners of a woman. . . . He delighted to be with women and young girls, to attire them, and dress their hair."

3. CATALINA DE ERANSO

Catalina de Eranso's family had intended for her to be a nun, but when an older nun abused her sexually, she fled the Dominican novitiate and thereafter embarked on a life of male impersonation. As Alonso Díaz Ramírez de Guzmán she served bravely with the Spanish Army in Chile and Peru for many years, concealing her true gender not only from her commanding officers but from her own brother as well. Wounded in 1624, she ended the ruse and returned to Spain, although a special dispensation from Pope Urban VIII allowed her to continue to dress as a man.

4-5. ANNE BONNEY and MARY READ

Anne and Mary served together in the crew of the buccaneer vessel commanded by Capt. "Calico Jack" Rackham. Anne came on board as Rackham's lover, but Mary, who had previously fought in a European army as a man, persuaded her to wear men's clothing and carry both a cutlass and pistols. The two women fought alongside the men and were captured with the rest of the crew when a government vessel from Jamaica caught up with Calico Jack in October, 1720. At their trial both women claimed to be pregnant and thus were not hanged, but Mary died in jail of "prison fever."

6. DEBORAH SAMPSON

Deborah enlisted in the American Army in 1778 as "Robert Shirtliffe," and signed up for the duration of the war for independence from Great Britain. Although she was badly wounded in both the head and the shoulder, she escaped detection until she became ill with "brain fever" in Philadelphia. A doctor who discovered her sex at that time notified General Washington, who gave her a discharge and some money. After the war she married a farmer, Benjamin Gannett of Massachusetts. The American government recognized her services by giving her a land grant and a lifelong pension.

7. DR. JAMES BARRY

Without disclosing her secret even to close friends or associates, this British lady (c. 1793–1865), whose real name is unknown, assumed the role of a man when she was 16 and entering Edinburgh University to study medicine. She served as an army surgeon in posts all over the world, worked with lepers in Africa, and achieved the rank of inspector of the Colonial Medical Board. The first person to detect her true sex was the attending physician who examined her body and signed the death certificate.

8. MARIE-DOROTHÉE

The case of Marie-Dorothée—her surname remains unknown —baffled physicians at the beginning of the 19th century. Although she went by a feminine name and dressed as a woman throughout her early adulthood, five doctors who examined her at age 23 could not agree on her sex: Three felt she was a woman, two that she was a man. Slight of stature and smooth of face, she possessed two birth certificates—one for each sex.

9. ELLEN CRAFT

Ellen engineered both her own and her husband's escape from slavery by disguising herself as a man. Because she was light-skinned and her husband was dark-skinned, she masqueraded as a plantation owner, and he played the part of her servant while the two of them traveled from Macon, Ga., to the North, staying in the best hotels along the way. Afterward, they both traveled on the European continent, speaking in favor of abolition.

10. K'UO CH'UN-CH'ING

K'uo Ch'un-ch'ing—who was on the Long March with Mao—disguised herself as a male so that she could fight. She was wounded and received the army's highest decoration. Some women on the Long March were allowed to fight as female guerrillas, but most of them were confined to support and supply work, in spite of Mao's theoretical commitment to women's liberation.

11. BARBARA ANN MALPASS

In November, 1959, "Charles Richard Williams"—who had recently been released from the Jefferson County, N.Y., jail—was discovered to be a girl. She had run away from home and had succeeded (for four months) in masquerading as a male. She donned her disguise because she found it easier to pass as a male runaway, and was not discovered to be a girl by either her jailers or the other prisoners in spite of the fact that she was frisked when she was arrested.

—B.F. & M.W.J.

DR. WARDELL POMEROY'S 10 MOST IMPORTANT BOOKS ABOUT SEX

Renowned as a sex surveyor and marriage counselor, Dr. Wardell Pomeroy was a leading member of Dr. Alfred C. Kinsey's Institute for Sex Research at Indiana University. He was one of the authors of both *Sexual Behavior in the Human Male* and *Sexual Behavior in the Human Female*. He also authored *Dr. Kinsey and the Institute for Sex Research*.

1. *Studies in the Psychology of Sex* (1897–1928), Havelock Ellis
2. *Three Contributions to the Sexual Theory* (1905; trans, 1910), Sigmund Freud

3. *Ideal Marriage* (1930), T. H. van De Velde
4. *Sexual Behavior in the Human Male* (1948), Alfred C. Kinsey et al.
5. *Patterns of Sexual Behavior* (1951), C. S. Ford and F. A. Beach
6. *Sexual Behavior in the Human Female* (1953), Alfred C. Kinsey et al.
7. *Human Sexual Response* (1966), William H. Masters and Virginia E. Johnson
8. *Human Sexual Inadequacy* (1970), William H. Masters and Virginia E. Johnson
9. *The Joy of Sex* (1972) Alex Comfort
10. *The New Sex Therapy* (1974), Helen Kaplan

Dr. Pomeroy adds: "Books were not included that affected other cultures, such as the *Ananga-Ranga,* the *Kama Sutra,* and the *Chin Ping Mei.* Nor did I include books that had a negative impact, such as *Psychopathia Sexualis* by Krafft-Ebing. Books are listed here chronologically rather than by order of importance."

—Exclusive for *The Book of Lists*

8 CELEBRITIES WHO
HAVE HAD VASECTOMIES

1. Jim Bouton, author, actor, ex-baseball pitcher
2. Billy Eckstine, singer
3. Arthur Godfrey, radio and TV entertainer
4. Abbie Hoffman, political activist
5. Dean Martin, singer, actor, comedian
6. Pat Paulsen, comedian
7. Lord Snowden, photographer, brother-in-law of Elizabeth II
8. Faron Young, singer

—D.S.G.

SOURCE: Association for Voluntary Sterilizations, Inc.

BILL SCHROEDER'S
13 GREAT SPORTS LISTS

If there existed an all-time list of great sports authorities, Willrich R. "Bill" Schroeder would rank among the top five. Born in Texas and educated in California, he has always been involved in athletic activities. He was on the U.S. Olympic Administrative Committee in 1952 and 1956. He was chairman of various Olympic Fund committees in 1952, 1956, 1960, 1968, and 1972. He was president of the Association of Sports Museums and Halls of Fame in 1973, and still serves as an officer. Since 1970, he has been managing director of the Citizen Savings Athletic Foundation Hall of Fame, a sports shrine located in Los Angeles.

10 GREATEST MALE ATHLETES IN U.S. HISTORY

1. Jim Thorpe, track and field, football, baseball
2. Ty Cobb, baseball
3. Babe Ruth, baseball
4. Jackie Robinson, baseball, football, track
5. Jesse Owens, track and field
6. Bob Mathias, track and field, football
7. Rafer Johnson, track and field
8. Ernie Nevers, football, baseball, basketball
9. Gene Tunney, boxing
10. Jack Dempsey, boxing

The greatest all-around athlete in sports history,
Indian Jim Thorpe was a 1912 Olympic hero, all-American football
player, and major league baseball star who once batted .327.

10 GREATEST FEMALE ATHLETES IN WORLD HISTORY

1. Mildred "Babe" Didrikson Zaharias, U.S., golf, track and field
2. Stella Walsh, Poland-U.S., track
3. Fanny Blankers-Koen, Netherlands, track
4. Kornelia Ender, E. Germany, swimming
5. Suzanne Lenglen, France, tennis
6. Tamara Press, U.S.S.R., shotput, discus
7. Wilma Rudolph, U.S., track
8. Patricia McCormick, U.S., diving
9. Irena Szewinska, Poland, track
10. Faina Melnik, U.S.S.R., discus

10 GREATEST ALL-TIME MALE TRACK AND FIELD STARS

1. Jesse Owens, U.S.
2. Emil Zatopek, Czechoslovakia
3. Paavo Nurmi, Finland
4. Peter Snell, New Zealand
5. Kipchoge Keino, Kenya
6. Hannes Kolehmainen, Finland
7. Bob Mathias, U.S.
8. Cornelius Warmerdam, U.S.
9. Rafer Johnson, U.S.
10. Parry O'Brien, U.S.

7 GREATEST ALL-TIME FEMALE TRACK AND FIELD STARS

1. Stella Walsh, Poland-U.S.
2. Wilma Rudolph, U.S.
3. Fanny Blankers-Koen, Netherlands
4. Mildred ("Babe") Zaharias, U.S.
5. Tamara Press, U.S.S.R.
6. Irena Szewinska, Poland
7. Betty Cuthbert, Australia

10 GREATEST ATHLETES IN OLYMPIC HISTORY

1. Paavo Nurmi, Finland, distance running
2. Jesse Owens, U.S., sprints, broad jump
3. Emil Zatopek, Czechoslovakia, distance running
4. Bob Mathias, U.S., decathlon
5. Al Oerter, U.S., discus
6. Peter Snell, New Zealand, distance running
7. Fanny Blankers-Koen, Netherlands, sprints, hurdles
8. Mark Spitz, U.S., swimming
9. Lasse Viren, Finland, distance running
10. Viktor Saneev, U.S.S.R., triple jump

10 ALL-TIME BEST MALE SWIMMERS

1. Mark Spitz, U.S.
2. John Weissmuller, U.S.
3. Murray Rose, Australia
4. Don Schollander, U.S.
5. Duke Kahanamoku, U.S.
6. Roland Matthes, E. Germany
7. John Naber, U.S.
8. Ford Konno, U.S.
9. James McLane, U.S.
10. Mike Burton, U.S.

7 ALL-TIME BEST FEMALE SWIMMERS

1. Kornelia Ender, E. Germany
2. Dawn Fraser, Australia
3. Shane Gould, Australia
4. Debbie Meyer, U.S.
5. Helene Madison, U.S.
6. Ann Curtis, U.S.
7. Shirley Babashoff, U.S.

5 ALL-TIME BEST MALE FIGURE SKATERS

1. Dick Button, U.S.
2. Gillis Grafstrom, Sweden
3. Hayes Alan Jenkins, U.S.
4. David Jenkins, U.S.
5. John Curry, Great Britain

5 ALL-TIME BEST FEMALE FIGURE SKATERS

1. Sonja Henie, Norway
2. Peggy Fleming, U.S.
3. Tenley Albright, U.S.
4. Carol Heiss, U.S.
5. Dorothy Hamill, U.S.

10 GREATEST PRO ICE HOCKEY PLAYERS OF ALL TIME

1. Gordie Howe
2. Bobby Hull
3. Bobby Orr
4. Eddie Shore
5. Max Bentley
6. Phil Esposito
7. Bernie Geoffrion
8. Stan Mikita
9. Elmer Lach
10. Ted Lindsay

10 GREATEST BOWLERS OF ALL TIME

Men	*Women*
1. Don Carter	1. Marion Ladewig
2. Ned Day	2. Dorothy Fothergill
3. Buddy Bomar	3. Marie Warmbier
4. Steve Nagy	4. Helen Duval
5. Billy Hardwick	5. Merle Matthews

10 BEST JOCKEYS IN U.S. HORSE RACING

1. Eddie Arcaro
2. Willie Shoemaker
3. Johnny Longden
4. Bill Hartack
5. Ted Atkinson
6. Earle Sande
7. Johnny Adams
8. Walter Miller
9. Braulio Baeza
10. Laffit Pincay, Jr.

THE 6 MOST DRAMATIC EVENTS IN SPORTS HISTORY

1. THE BANNISTER-LANDY 1-MI. DUEL (1954)

In what was billed as the mile race of the century, England's Roger Bannister, Australia's John Landy, and four others ran before 35,000 people at Empire Stadium, Vancouver, B.C., Canada, as the feature of the British Commonwealth Games. Three months earlier, Bannister had been the first person to break the 4-min. mile. Landy was the only other person to have covered a mile in under 4 mins. and now held the world's record. At the gun, Landy got off to a fast lead with Bannister running third, then second, behind him. As the bell sounded for the last lap, the final 440 yds., Landy was still in front, with Bannister at his heels. Coming into the stretch, Landy looked back over his shoulder. Bannister was not there. Then Landy realized Bannister was in front of him and gaining. Bannister won the historic mile by 5 yds., in 3:58.8 against his rival's 3:59.6.

2. THE DEMPSEY-FIRPO HEAVYWEIGHT TITLE FIGHT (1923)

New York's Polo Grounds was jammed with 88,000 boxing fans who had paid $1,127,882 to see heavyweight champion Jack Dempsey demolish his 6 ft. 3 in., 220-lb. Argentine challenger, Luis Firpo, known as the Wild Bull of the Pampas. What the fans saw were the most savage moments in fighting history. The brawl lasted 3 mins. 57 secs. In the first round, Dempsey knocked Firpo down seven times, and then an infuriated Firpo battered the champion through the ropes, out of the ring into the press section. Friends pushed Dempsey back into the ring and saved him from defeat. In the second round, Dempsey floored Firpo once, then knocked him out to win the most dramatic fight in pugilistic history.

Roger Bannister (L), dueling with John Landy, holder of the mile record, at Vancouver in 1954. As Landy turned to see where his rival was, Bannister passed him to win the race.

3. BOBBY THOMSON'S WINNING HOME RUN (1951)

The race for the National League championship ended in a dead heat between the Brooklyn Dodgers and the New York Giants. The two teams split the first two games of the playoff series, setting up the final tie breaker at the Polo Grounds in New York. In the top of the eighth inning, the Dodgers scored three runs to break a 1-1 tie and move ahead 4-1. The situation looked bleak for the Giants, but in the bottom of the ninth they put together two singles and a double to inch a run closer. With two men on base and one out, Dodger manager Charlie Dressen removed starting pitcher Don Newcombe and replaced him with Ralph Branca. The first batter Branca faced was third baseman Bobby Thomson, who already had a single and a double in the game. With Willie Mays on deck, Dressen chose to pitch to Thomson rather than walk him intentionally. Branca's first pitch was a called strike. The next pitch, a fast ball, high and slightly inside, was just Thomson's style and he slashed a line drive into the left-field stands for a home run. Deliriously shocked, New York fans poured onto the field and mobbed Thomson as he reached home plate. Final score: Giants 5, Dodgers 4.

4. THE U.S.-U.S.S.R. OLYMPIC BASKETBALL FINAL (1972)

The U.S. had won seven Olympic titles and 64 consecutive games in 36 years. At Munich, the U.S. basketball team went up against the U.S.S.R. in the finals. In a hectic finish, as the horn sounded, the U.S. had won 50–49. Then it was ruled that the clock was wrong, and there were still 3 secs. more to play. Protesting, the U.S. was forced to take the court again, and the Russians scored a basket to win 51–50, as the horn sounded a second and last time, and the American winning streak was ended. The U.S. refused to accept its second-place silver medals.

5. THE U.S.C.-WISCONSIN ROSE BOWL FOOTBALL GAME (1963)

In the biggest offensive contest in Rose Bowl history, the University of Southern California took a lead of 42–14, as quarterback Pete Beathard threw four touchdown passes. Then Wisconsin rallied. Its quarterback, Ron VanderKelen, went to the air—completed 33 passes in 48 attempts—while Wisconsin racked up 32 first downs to U.S.C.'s 15. But time was on the side of U.S.C., which barely won, 42–37.

6. DON LARSEN'S PERFECT WORLD SERIES GAME (1956)

The 1956 World Series between the Brooklyn Dodgers and the New York Yankees stood at two games apiece. The fifth game was a must-win proposition for the Yankees because the last two games were to be played in Brooklyn, and the Dodgers were unlikely to lose two straight at Ebbets Field. So the sports world was taken by surprise when Yankee manager Casey Stengel chose Don Larsen as his starting pitcher. Larsen, who had compiled a 3–21 season record two years earlier, had started the second game of the 1956 Series and been knocked out of the box in the second inning when he walked four batters. But Stengel had faith in Larsen and Don didn't let him down. Thanks to a spectacular running catch by Mickey Mantle in the fifth inning, a great throw to first by Gil McDougald in the seventh, and a lunging catch by Andy Carey in the eighth, Larsen entered the ninth inning without having allowed a single batter to reach first base. Carl Furillo led off for the Dodgers. After hitting four foul balls, he flied out to right field. He was followed by Roy Campanella, who grounded out to second. This left one man between Don Larsen and baseball history. Up came pinch hitter Dale Mitchell. Larsen threw one ball wide and then drilled in two strikes, as the crowd roared after each pitch and hushed before the next. Mitchell fouled back the next pitch as the tension in Yankee Stadium built to an almost unbearable level. For his 97th pitch of the day, Don Larsen threw a fast ball, low and outside. It caught the corner and Mitchell, who had checked his swing, was called out on strikes. Don Larsen had pitched the only perfect game in World Series history.

—Annotated by I.W. & D.W.

AP MIDCENTURY POLL (1950) —4 CATEGORIES OF THE GREATEST ATHLETES AND EVENTS

At the halfway mark of the 20th century, the Associated Press polled sports editors throughout the U.S. to learn who they thought were the greatest athletes between 1900 and 1950 in 13 different categories.

15 GREATEST MALE ATHLETES

1. Jim Thorpe, track and field, football, baseball
2. Babe Ruth, baseball
3. Jack Dempsey, boxing
4. Ty Cobb, baseball
5. Bobby Jones, golf
6. Joe Louis, boxing
7. Red Grange, football
8. Jesse Owens, track
9. Lou Gehrig, baseball
10. Bronko Nagurski, football
11. Jackie Robinson, baseball
12. Bob Mathias, track and field
13. Walter Johnson, baseball
14. Glenn Davis, football
15. Bill Tilden, tennis

15 GREATEST FEMALE ATHLETES

1. Mildred Zaharias, golf, track
2. Helen Wills Moody, tennis
3. Stella Walsh, track and field
4. Fanny Blankers-Koen, track
5. Gertrude Ederle, swimming
6. Suzanne Lenglen, tennis
7. Alice Marble, tennis
8. Anne Curtis, swimming
9. Sonja Henie, figure skating
10. Helen Stephens, track and field
11. Eleanor Holm, swimming
12. Patty Berg, golf
13. Helene Madison, swimming
14. Glenna Collett Vare, golf
15. Mary K. Browne, golf, tennis

10 MOST DRAMATIC EVENTS

1. Dempsey-Firpo fight (1923)
2. Babe Ruth "calling" World Series homer (1932)

The 1923 Dempsey-Firpo heavyweight title match. After Dempsey had floored him seven times in the first round, Firpo knocked Dempsey out of the ring, as seen here. Dempsey came back to KO Firpo in the second round.

3. Dempsey-Tunney "long count" fight (1927)
4. Lou Gehrig's farewell appearance (1939)
5. Grover Alexander's strikeout of Tony Lazzeri in the 1926 World Series
6. Notre Dame's 18–13 football victory over Ohio State (1935)
7. Red Grange's feats (he scored 5 touchdowns) against Michigan (1924)
8. Babe Ruth's farewell (1948)
9. Floyd Bevens's near no-hitter in 1947 World Series
10. Joe Louis's first-round knockout of Max Schmeling (1938)

10 GREATEST UPSETS

1. Boston Braves' four-straight World Series victory over Philadelphia Athletics (1914)
2. Gene Tunney's victory over Jack Dempsey in their first heavyweight title fight (1926)
3. Centre College's 6–0 football victory over Harvard (1921)
4. Jim Braddock's victory over Max Baer for world heavyweight title (1935)
5. Upset's victory over Man o' War (1919)
6. Max Schmeling's knockout of Joe Louis (1936)
7. Notre Dame's 35–13 football victory over Army (1913)
8. Jack Dempsey's knockout of Jess Willard (1919)
9. Holy Cross's 55–12 football victory over Boston College (1942)
10. Navy's 21–21 football tie with Army (1948)

SOURCE: Courtesy of the Associated Press.

24 FEATS OF PHYSICAL STRENGTH

1. BYBON (Olympia; 6th century B.C.)

    Threw a 315-lb. block of red sandstone over his head. The feat was reported after archaeologists found a description of Bybon's act inscribed on the rock itself.

2. MILO OF CROTONA (Greece; 540 B.C.)

    Carried a 4-year-old ox (about 1 ton) a distance of 600 ft.

3. KING WILLIAM I OF ENGLAND (England; late 11th century)

    William the Conqueror could vault onto the saddle of a horse while fully clad in armor.

4. THOMAS FISHER (London, England; 1716)

    Held a 10-lb. weight at arm's length for 12 mins.

5. THOMAS TOPHAM (Derby, England; 1736)

    While lying with his head on one chair and his heels on another, Topham had four men stand on his body. Meanwhile, with his teeth, he lifted a 6-ft. table on which sat a 5-lb. weight. He then snapped his fingers as a man danced on each of his outstretched arms.

6. GUSTAV REHARD (Lyons, France; 1793)

    Carried for a distance of 20 ft. a billiard table on which two thugs were dueling with knives.

7. WILLIAM CARR (Blyth, England; 1798)

    Carried a 1,120-lb. anchor ½ mi.

8. GIOVANNI BATTISTA BELZONI (Italy; c. 1800)

    Walked around a stage while supporting on his shoulders an iron frame on which stood 11 men (over 1,700 lbs.).

9. MILLS DARDEN (North Carolina, U.S.; 1798–1857)

    Darden carried with him 1,020 lbs.—his *own* weight. Standing 7½ ft. tall, with a chest measurement of over 80 in., he *had* to be extremely strong even to move. Darden's voice could be heard for miles around during hog-calling sessions due to his powerful set of lungs.

10. LOUIS CYR (Sohmer Park, Montreal, P.Q., Canada; 1891)

    Withstood the pull of four 1,000-lb. horses—two on each arm—in opposite directions. Other feats by Cyr included the lifting into the air of 18 men (4,300 lbs.) seated on a platform atop Cyr's back, the pushing of a loaded freight car up an incline, and the raising of a 535-lb. weight off the floor using a single finger.

11. JOSEPHINE BLATT (Bijou Theater, Hoboken, N.J., U.S.; 1895)

The greatest lift ever made by a woman: 3,564 lbs.

12. EUGENE SANDOW (New York, N.Y., U.S.; 1890s)

Performed the Bent Press—a feat that entailed the lifting with one hand of a hollow-ended barbell that housed two people. In exercising the Roman Column, Sandow would hang downward from a pole and then lift his body to an upright position while holding a man or a weight. He also wrote music, including a waltz, "Sandownia."

13. PAUL VON BOECKMANN (New York, N.Y., U.S.; 1900)

With thumb and forefinger, Boeckmann tore a hole through a deck of cards. Using the middle finger of his right hand, Boeckmann was able to do three consecutive chin-ups.

14. WILLIAM PAGEL (Australia or South Africa; c. 1900)

Carried a 1,000-lb. horse up a set of two 12-ft. ladders.

15. ANTHONY BARKER (New York, N.Y., U.S.; c. 1900)

Barker, lying flat on the floor, had a man jump off a chair (which was on top of a table) and land on Barker's face. He lived to be 103.

16. LIONEL STRONGFORT (Hippodrome, New York, N.Y., U.S.; c. 1902)

Became the "Human Bridge" by supporting a 3,200-lb. carload of people on a platform. Performed the One-Hand Snatch by lifting a 175-lb. weight with his right hand.

17. WARREN L. TRAVIS (Brooklyn, N.Y., U.S.; 1907)

Lifted a 667-lb. weight with one finger and lifted 1,105 lb. with two fingers. Other feats: supported 14 men on a turning carousel; caught a 15-in. projectile hurled from a catapult; supported 26 men with his hands and knees while lying on a revolving platform.

18. RAMA MURTI NAIDU (Madras, India; 1910)

Naidu, "The Indian Hercules," supported the entire weight of a 7,000-lb. elephant. The animal stood on a cushioned plank that had been laid across Naidu's decumbent body. The strong man actually seemed to be flattened under the load, though he completed the feat uninjured.

19. SIEGMUND BREITBART (Essen, Germany; 1923)

With his teeth, Breitbart bit all the way through a 5-n.m-thick steel bar and bit 1½ mm into an 11-mm-thick steel bar. Breitbart also broke chains by expanding his chest, and drove large nails through iron with his bare fist.

20. ALEKSANDR "SAMSON" ZASS (U.S.S.R.; 1924)

A 104-lb. girl would be fired from a cannon, travel a distance of 42 ft. at a speed of 45 mph, and be caught by Samson—creating an impact of 2,150 lbs. With his bare hands, Samson bent a straight iron bar (5 in. long, ⅝ in. square) into a U shape.

21. ARTHUR DANDURAND (Montreal, P.Q., Canada; 1920s)

Carried a 455-lb. automobile engine for a distance of 84 ft. and put it down on a table.

22. FRANK RICHARDS (Los Angeles, Calif., U.S.; 1920s)

Richards accepted into his stomach the close-range firing of a 104-lb. cannonball from a 12-ft. cannon. He developed the act after becoming bored with the numerous attempts other strong men made to best him—including attacks with a 4-by-4-in. timber and with a sledgehammer.

A cannon (R) shooting a 104-lb. cannonball into the stomach of strong man Frank "Cannonball" Richards.

23. ALEX KHATIASHVILI (Tbilisi, U.S.S.R.; 1948)

Using both arms, he jerked a 72-lb. barbell over his head at least 170 times.

24. PAUL ANDERSON (Toccoa, Ga., U.S.; 1957)

Anderson—the 1956 Olympic heavyweight weight-lifting champion—back-lifted off the ground a table on which sat heavy auto parts and a safe full of lead, totaling 6,270 lbs. (the greatest weight ever lifted by a human).

Recommendation: If you want to know more about feats of strength, read *The Super Athletes*, by David Willoughby (New York: A. S. Barnes, 1970

—D.B.

MARIO ANDRETTI'S
9 GREATEST AUTO RACING
DRIVERS OF ALL TIME

Most renowned for his versatility, race-car driver Mario Andretti is equally masterful in a drag race, a grand prix, or a 100-mi. championship test. His victories include international endurance races, the Indianapolis 500, the Daytona 500, and Formula One Grand Prix races.

1. Alberto Ascari
2. Jim Clark
3. Juan Manuel Fangio
4. A. J. Foyt
5. Stirling Moss

6. Tozio Nuvolari
7. Richard Petty
8. "Fireball" Roberts
9. Jackie Stewart

—Exclusive for *The Book of Lists*

PRESIDENT
RICHARD M. NIXON'S
ALL-TIME ALL-STAR
BASEBALL TEAMS

On June 22, 1972, during a news conference in the oval office of the White House, Cliff Evans, of RKO General Broadcasting, asked President Nixon if he would be willing to name his "all-time baseball team." President Nixon agreed to try. Three days later, at Camp David, with the help of his son-in-law, baseball buff David Eisenhower, President Nixon put his superteam together. Actually, superteams. Nixon explained, "We first decided that we would select National League and American League teams for both the post-W.W. II and pre-W.W. II periods. We decided to include only players after 1925 since that was about the time that I began to follow major-league baseball in the sports pages." On July 2, 1972, Nixon's selections were released to the sports world by Tom Seppy, of the Associated Press. (Abbreviations: 1b, first base; 2b, second base; 3b, third base; ss, shortstop; of, outfielder; c, catcher; p, pitcher; if, infielder; rp, relief pitcher; mgr, manager.)

NATIONAL LEAGUE
(1925–1945)

1b, Bill Terry
2b, Rogers Hornsby
3b, Pie Traynor
ss, Arky Vaughan
of, Paul Waner
of, Mel Ott
of, Hack Wilson
c, Ernie Lombardi
c, Gabby Hartnett
p, Carl Hubbell
p, Dizzy Dean
p, Bucky Walters
p, Mort Cooper
p, Burleigh Grimes

Reserves

of, Joe Medwick
of, Chuck Klein
of, Edd Roush
if, Frankie Frisch
if, Marty Marion
rp, Mace Brown
mgr, Branch Rickey

AMERICAN LEAGUE
(1925–1945)

1b, Lou Gehrig
2b, Charlie Gehringer
3b, Red Rolfe
ss, Joe Cronin
of, Babe Ruth
of, Joe DiMaggio
of, Al Simmons
c, Mickey Cochrane
c, Bill Dickey
p, Satchel Paige
p, Herb Pennock
p, Lefty Grove
p, Red Ruffing
p, Bobo Newsom

Reserves

of, Goose Goslin
of, Harry Heilmann
if, Jimmy Foxx
if, Hank Greenberg
if, Luke Appling
rp, Johnny Murphy
mgr, Connie Mack

NATIONAL LEAGUE
(1945–1970)

1b, Stan Musial
2b, Jackie Robinson
3b, Eddie Mathews
ss, Ernie Banks
of, Henry Aaron
of, Willie Mays
of, Roberto Clemente
c, Roy Campanella
c, Johnny Bench
p, Sandy Koufax
p, Warren Spahn
p, Juan Marichal
p, Bob Gibson
p, Robin Roberts

Reserves

if, Maury Wills
if, Dick Groat
if, Willie McCovey
if, Ken Boyer
of, Duke Snider
rp, Roy Face
mgr, Walter Alston

AMERICAN LEAGUE
(1945–1970)

1b, Harmon Killebrew
2b, Nellie Fox
3b, Brooks Robinson
ss, Lou Boudreau
of, Ted Williams
of, Mickey Mantle
of, Frank Robinson
c, Yogi Berra
c, Elston Howard
p, Bob Lemon
p, Bob Feller
p, Early Wynn
p, Whitey Ford
p, Dave McNally

Reserves

if, Bobby Richardson
if, Luis Aparicio
of, Al Kaline
of, Carl Yastrzemski
of, Tony Oliva
rp, Hoyt Wilhelm
mgr, Casey Stengel

PRESIDENT NIXON'S BEST INDIVIDUAL PERFORMERS

Best hitter, Ted Williams
Best outfielder, Joe DiMaggio
Best base runner, Maury Wills
Best pitcher, Sandy Koufax
Best infielder, Brooks Robinson
Best all-around athlete, Jackie Robinson
Most courageous player, Lou Gehrig

A dissent: Four days after President Nixon's selections were announced, Arthur Daley, sports columnist for *The New York Times,* took exception to a number of them. Daley contended that naming "Branch Rickey as the National League manager for the 1925–1945 period" was the worst "clinker" of them all. As a manager, "he was a bad one." Daley felt that John McGraw should have been the choice. Daley thought that Nixon's selection of Hack Wilson as a National League all-time outfielder was "ridiculous," that Joe Medwick or Kiki Cuyler or Chick Hafey would have been a better selection. Daley thought Nixon's choice of Nellie Fox for second base was "unprofessional," and either Joe Gordon or Bobby Doerr would have been superior. Daley called Nixon's choice of Johnny Bench for catcher "premature," and his choice of Satchel Paige "presumptive, because Ol' Satch crossed the color line too late to show his true skills." However, Daley felt that Nixon's pick of Ernie Banks for shortstop showed "perception," because so many fans had long forgotten that Banks had been a brilliant shortstop before switching to first base.

Actually, in the judgment of the authors, President Nixon's selections for his baseball teams were even-handed and judicious compared to the lapses he suffered in picking his White House staff and reelection committee. But, as the saying goes, you can't win them all.

—I.W.

HARRY STEIN'S
ALL-TIME ALL-STAR
ARGUMENT STARTER
(5 ALL-TIME ETHNIC
BASEBALL TEAMS)

(Further abbreviations: rhp, right-handed pitcher; lhp, left-handed pitcher; lf, left fielder; cf, center fielder; rf, right fielder.)

1. THE LATINS

rhp, Juan Marichal (1960–1975; Dominican)
lhp, Mike Cuellar (1959– ; Cuban)
rp, Luis Arroyo (1955–1963; Puerto Rican)
c, Manny Sanguillen (1967– ; Panamanian)
1b, Orlando Cepeda (1958–1974; Puerto Rican)
2b, Bobby Avila (1949–1959; Mexican)

ss, Luis Aparicio (1956–1974; Venezuelan)
3b, Tony Perez (1964– ; Cuban)
lf, Tony Oliva (1962– ; Cuban)
cf, Cesar Cedeno (1970– ; Dominican)
rf, Roberto Clemente (1955–1972; Puerto Rican)

2. THE POLES

rhp, Stan Coveleskie, (1912–1928)
lhp, Harry Coveleskie (1907–1918)
rp, Ron Perranoski (1961–1973)
c, Carl Sawatski (1948–1963)
1b, Ted Kluszewski (1947–1961)
2b, Bill Mazeroski (1956–1972)

ss, Tony Kubek (1957–1965)
3b, Whitey Kurowski (1941–1949)
lf, Carl Yastrzemski (1961–)
cf, Al Simmons (1924–1944)
rf, Stan Musial (1941–1963)

3. THE JEWS

rhp, Ed Reulbach (1905–1917)
lhp, Sandy Koufax (1956–1966)
rp, Larry Sherry (1958–1968)
c, Johnny Kling (1900–1913)
1b, Hank Greenberg (1930–1947)

2b, Rod Carew (1967–)
ss, Buddy Myer (1925–1941)
3b, Al Rosen (1947–1956)
lf, Sid Gordon (1941–1955)
cf, Benny Kauff (1912–1920)
rf, George Stone (1903–1910)

4. THE BLACKS

rhp, Bob Gibson (1959–1975)
lhp, Vida Blue (1969–)
rp, Satchel Paige, (1948–1953)
c, Roy Campanella (1948–1957)
1b, Frank Robinson (1956–)
2b, Joe Morgan (1963–)

ss, Ernie Banks (1953–1971)
3b, Jackie Robinson (1947–1956)
lf, Lou Brock (1961–)
cf, Willie Mays (1951–1973)
rf, Henry Aaron (1954–)

5. THE ITALIANS

rhp, Eddie Cicotte (1905–1920)
lhp, Johnny Antonelli (1948–1961)
rp, Dave Giusti (1962–)
c, Yogi Berra (1946–1963)
1b, Dolph Camilli (1933–1945)

2b, Tony Lazzeri (1926–1939)
ss, Phil Rizzuto (1941–1956)
3b, Joe Torre (1960–)
lf, Dom DiMaggio (1940–1953)
cf, Joe DiMaggio (1936–1951)
rf, Carl Furillo (1946–1960)

Source: Reprinted from *Esquire* magazine (July, 1976).

Leroy "Satchel" Paige, first black pitcher in major league
history and the oldest (59) to hurl in the big leagues.

THE 8 MOST VALUABLE
BASEBALL CARDS

1. HONUS WAGNER (shortstop; $1,500)

This card was issued in 1910 by a tobacco company, Sweet
Caporal, and was inserted in cigarette packs. The card was printed
without Wagner's permission, and Wagner (a nonsmoker) requested
that it be withdrawn from distribution. Only 96 got into circulation;
30 still exist.

2. EDDIE PLANK (pitcher; $1,000)

This card was also issued in 1910 by Sweet Caporal; 30
still exist.

3. NAP LAJOIE (second base; $800)

Issued in 1933 by Goudey Gum Co.; 50 still exist.

4. **GROVER LOWDERMILK** (pitcher; $200)

Issued in 1910 by Broadleaf Tobacco Co.; 100 still exist.

5. **ART HOUTTEMAN** (pitcher; $100)

Issued in 1953 by the Glendale Meat Co.; 20 still exist.

6. **GIL HODGES** (first base; $50)

Issued in the mid-1950s as a postcard by the Dormand Co. The precise year of this card is disputed; only one is known to exist.

6. **ANY PLAYER** ($50)

Issued by a hot-dog manufacturer, Briggs Frankfurters, throughout the mid-1950s; 100 cards still exist.

8. **ANY PLAYER** ($25)

Issued in 1932 by the George Miller Candy Co.; 200 still exist.

—R.T.

JOHN WOODEN'S ALL-TIME ALL-STAR COLLEGE BASKETBALL TEAM

In his college days, John Wooden was a three-time all-American basketball guard at Purdue. In the 27 years he coached the University of California at Los Angeles, Wooden became the greatest mentor in college basketball history. During his tenure, UCLA won 10 national titles in 12 years, won 88 consecutive games between 1970 and 1974, won a total of 620 games against 147 losses, and produced such stars as Kareem Abdul-Jabbar (Lew Alcindor), Bill Walton, and Gail Goodrich.

1. Lewis Alcindor, UCLA
2. Elgin Baylor, Seattle Univ.
3. Wilt Chamberlain, Kansas
4. Tom Gola, La Salle
5. Elvin Hayes, Houston
6. Jerry Lucas, Ohio State
7. Charles Murphy, Purdue
8. Oscar Robertson, Cincinnati
9. Bill Russell, Univ. of San Francisco
10. Bill Walton, UCLA

John Wooden adds: "This list is in alphabetical order and includes only players that I personally saw play collegiate basketball. Professional status or college players whom I did not personally see are not included."

—Exclusive for *The Book of Lists*

NAT FLEISCHER'S
10 ALL-TIME GREATEST WORLD
BOXERS IN EACH DIVISION

The late Nat Fleischer, editor and publisher of *The Ring* magazine and the dean of boxing writers and archivists, ranked his 10 best in each weight division in 1962. While these rankings were made before—for example, in the heavyweight class—the advent of Muhammad Ali, Joe Frazier, and George Foreman, they remain an authoritative and classic series of lists.

HEAVYWEIGHTS

1. Jack Johnson
2. Jim Jeffries
3. Bob Fitzsimmons
4. Jack Dempsey
5. Jim Corbett
6. Joe Louis
7. Sam Langford
8. Gene Tunney
9. Max Schmeling
10. Rocky Marciano

LIGHT HEAVYWEIGHTS

1. Kid McCoy
2. "Philadelphia" Jack O'Brien
3. Jack Dillon
4. Tommy Loughran
5. Jack Root
6. Battling Levinsky
7. Georges Carpentier
8. Tom Gibbons
9. Jack Delaney
10. Paul Berlenbach

MIDDLEWEIGHTS

1. Stanley Ketchel
2. Tommy Ryan
3. Harry Greb
4. Mickey Walker
5. "Sugar" Ray Robinson
6. Frank Klaus
7. Billy Papke
8. Les Darcy
9. Mike Gibbons
10. Jeff Smith

WELTERWEIGHTS

1. Joe Walcott
2. "Mysterious" Billy Smith
3. Jack Britton
4. Ted "Kid" Lewis
5. Dixie Kid
6. Harry Lewis
7. Willie Lewis
8. Henry Armstrong
9. Barney Ross
10. Jimmy McLarnin

LIGHTWEIGHTS

1. Joe Gans
2. Benny Leonard
3. Owen Moran
4. Freddy Welsh
5. Battling Nelson
6. George "Kid" Lavigne
7. Tony Canzoneri
8. Willie Ritchie
9. Lew Tendler
10. Charley White

FEATHERWEIGHTS

1. Terry McGovern
2. Jem Driscoll
3. Abe Attell
4. Johnny Dundee
5. Johnny Kilbane
6. Kid Chocolate
7. Willie Pep
8. Young Griffo
9. George "KO" Chaney
10. Louis "Kid" Kaplan

BANTAMWEIGHTS	FLYWEIGHTS
1. George Dixon	1. Jimmy Wilde
2. Pete Herman	2. Pancho Villa
3. Kid Williams	3. Frankie Genaro
4. Joe Lynch	4. Fidel La Barba
5. Bud Taylor	5. Benny Lynch
6. Johnny Coulon	6. Elky Clark
7. Pal Moore	7. Johnny Buff
8. Frankie Burns	8. Midget Wolgast
9. Eddie Campi	9. Peter Kane
10. "Panama" Al Brown	10. Pascual Perez

SOURCE: *Nat Fleischer's Ring Record Book and Boxing Encyclopedia* (New York: Ring Book Shop, 1962).

THE RING MAGAZINE'S 10 ALL-TIME GREATEST WORLD HEAVYWEIGHT FIGHTERS

Selections made by *The Ring* editors of fighters from 1892, when boxing gloves were first used, to 1975.

1. JOE LOUIS

Fought 1934–1951. Won title from James J. Braddock in 1937 (KO in 8); lost title to Ezzard Charles in 1950 (decision in 15). Fought 71 fights: won 54 by KO, 13 by decision, 1 by foul; lost 2 by KO, 1 by decision.

Joe Louis receiving *The Ring* magazine's Fighter of the Year Award from Nat Fleischer in 1937.

2. JACK DEMPSEY

Fought 1915–1931. Won title from Jess Willard in 1919 (KO in 3); lost title to Gene Tunney in 1926 (decision in 10). Fought 148 fights: won 108 by KO, 25 by decision, 1 by foul; 5 draws, 4 no decision; lost 1 by KO, 4 by decision.

3. JIM JEFFRIES

Fought 1896–1921. Won title from Bob Fitzsimmons in 1899 (KO in 11); retired in 1904, came back to fight Jack Johnson in 1910 (lost by KO in 15), retired again 1921. Fought 23 fights: won 16 by KO, 4 by decision; 2 draws; lost 1 by KO.

4. JACK JOHNSON

Fought 1897–1945. Won title from Tommy Burns in 1908 (KO in 14); lost title to Jess Willard in 1915 (KO in 26). Fought 113 fights: won 44 by KO, 30 by decision, 4 by fouls; 14 draws, 14 no decision; lost 5 by KO, 1 by decision, 1 by foul.

5. ROCKY MARCIANO

Fought 1947–1955. Won title from Joe Walcott in 1952 (KO in 13); retired in 1956. Fought 49 fights: won 43 by KO, 6 by decision.

6. GENE TUNNEY

Fought 1915–1928. Won light-heavyweight title from Battling Levinsky in 1922 (decision in 12); lost title to Harry Greb in 1922 (decision in 15); regained title from Greb in 1923 (decision in 15). Won heavyweight title from Jack Dempsey in 1926 (decision in 10); retired in 1928. Fought 76 fights: won 41 by KO, 14 by decision, 1 by foul; 1 draw, 17 no decision, 1 no contest; lost 1 by decision.

7. BOB FITZSIMMONS

Fought 1882–1914. Won heavyweight title from Jim Corbett in 1897 (KO in 14); lost title to Jim Jeffries in 1899 (KO in 11). Won light-heavyweight title from George Gardner in 1903 (decision in 20); lost title to Jack O'Brien in 1905 (KO in 13). Fought 41 fights: won 23 by KO, 5 by decision; 1 draw, 5 no decision; lost 6 by KO, 1 by foul.

8. JIM CORBETT

Fought 1886–1903. Won title from John L. Sullivan in 1892 (KO in 21); lost title to Bob Fitzsimmons in 1897 (KO in 14). Fought 33 fights: won 9 by KO, 11 by decision; 6 draws, 2 no decision; lost 3 by KO, 1 by decision, 1 by foul.

9. MUHAMMAD ALI

Fought 1960–   . Won title from Sonny Liston in 1964 (KO in 7); stripped of title in 1967; regained title from George Foreman in 1974 (KO in 8). Fought 55 fights: won 37 by KO, 16 by decision; lost 2 by decision.

10. JOE FRAZIER

Fought 1965–   . Won title from Jimmy Ellis in 1970 (KO in

5); lost title to George Foreman in 1973 (KO in 2). Fought 36 fights: won 27 by KO, 5 by decision; lost 3 by KO, 1 by decision.

—Annotated by The Eds.

SOURCE: By permission of *The Ring* magazine.

GLENN DAVIS'S
ALL-TIME ALL-STAR
COLLEGE FOOTBALL TEAM

One of West Point's greatest football heroes, 170-lb. halfback Glenn Davis, known as "Mr. Outside"—paired with 205-lb. fullback Felix "Doc" Blanchard, known as "Mr. Inside"—led the Army Cadets to three undefeated college seasons (1944–1946). While his team rolled up 1,179 points to its opponents' 161, Davis averaged 11.1 yards per carry and scored 59 touchdowns. An all-American, winner of the Heisman trophy, member of the Football Hall of Fame, Davis played pro ball briefly and starred in a film, *The Spirit of West Point*. Today, he is director of special events for the *Los Angeles Times*.

1. Barney Poole
2. Len Ford
3. Don Whitmire
4. Tex Coulter
5. Mel Hein
6. Bill Willis
7. Leo Nomellini
8. Joe Namath
9. Doc Blanchard
10. O. J. Simpson
11. Tom Harmon
12. "Red" Blaik (coach)

—Exclusive for *The Book of Lists*

PRO FOOTBALL DIGEST'S
ALL-TIME ALL-PRO TEAM

Split end	Don Hutson, Green Bay Packers
Tight end	Pete Pihos, Philadelphia Eagles
Flanker	Lance Alworth, San Diego Chargers
Tackle	Forrest Gregg, Green Bay Packers
Tackle	Cal Hubbard, Green Bay Packers
Guard	Lou Creekmur, Detroit Lions
Guard	Jim Parker, Baltimore Colts
Center	Clyde "Bulldog" Turner, Chicago Bears
Quarterback	John Unitas, Baltimore Colts
Halfback	Gale Sayers, Chicago Bears

Halfback	Hugh McElhenny, San Francisco 49ers
Fullback	Jim Brown, Cleveland Browns
Placekicker	George Blanda, Chicago Bears, Houston, Oilers, Oakland Raiders
Defensive end	Gino Marchetti, Baltimore Colts
Defensive end	David "Deacon" Jones, Los Angeles Rams
Defensive tackle	Leo Nomellini, San Francisco 49ers
Defensive tackle	Bob Lilly, Dallas Cowboys
Linebacker	Bobby Bell, Kansas City Chiefs
Linebacker	Chuck Bednarik, Philadelphia Eagles
Middle linebacker	Dick Butkus, Chicago Bears
Cornerback	Jack Butler, Pittsburgh Steelers
Cornerback	Herb Adderley, Green Bay Packers, Dallas Cowboys
Safety	Jack Christiansen, Detroit Lions
Safety	Emlen Tunnell, New York Giants, Green Bay Packers
Punter	Sammy Baugh, Washington Redskins

SOURCE: Permission of Robert Billings, ed., *Pro Football Digest* (Northfield, Ill.: Digest Books, 1973).

PELÉ'S
50 BEST FOOTBALL (SOCCER)
PLAYERS IN HISTORY

Superstar athlete Edson Arantes do Nascimento, better known as Pelé, is the world's greatest soccer player and perhaps the world's greatest athlete. He has been awarded the French Legion of Honor, invited to appear before the queen of England, and granted a private audience with Pope Paul VI. His $4.7 million dollar contract with the New York Cosmos made him the highest-paid team athlete in the world.

Garrincha, Brazil	Neeskens, Netherlands
Zizinho, Brazil	Cruyff, Netherlands
Didi, Brazil	Suarez, Spain
Nilton Santos, Brazil	Gento, Spain
Luis Pereira, Brazil	Eusebio, Portugal
Djalma Santos, Brazil	Coluna, Portugal
Gerson, Brazil	Dzajic, Yugoslavia
Zito, Brazil	Sekularac, Yugoslavia
Coutinho, Brazil	Masopust, Czechoslovakia
Carlos Alberto, Brazil	Kvasnak, Czechoslovakia
Julinho, Brazil	Fachetti, Italy
Altafini, Brazil	Rivera, Italy
Metreveli, U.S.S.R.	Bob Moore, England

Yashin, U.S.S.R.
Beckenbauer, Germany
Uwe Seeler, Germany
Albert, Hungary
Puskas, Hungary
Bene, Hungary
Carrizo, Argentina
Dostefano, Argentina
Sivori, Argentina
Figueiroa, Chile
Reynoso, Chile
Deyna, Poland
Tomaszewski, Poland

Bob Charlton, England
Kamamoto, Japan
Benitez, Peru
Fontaine, France
Kopa, France
Gunnar Green, Sweden
Pedro Rocha, Uruguay
George Best, Northern
   Ireland
Van Hinst, Belgium
Rivelino, Brazil
Carbajal, Mexico

Pelé's manager, Julio Mazzei, adds: "Pelé wants to name the players that he saw during his 20-year career, but he has seen so many that it was almost impossible to name only 10. He does not want, as usual, to be unfair with so many great players that played with or against him. He used another criterion; he chose only players that played in the period 1956–1976. He realizes that there are other great names before his time, but since Pelé has never seen them, he cannot name them. He wants it so they are not listed from 1st to 50th, but just by name."

—Exclusive for *The Book of Lists*

JOHNNY MILLER'S
10 GREATEST GOLFERS
OF ALL TIME

A San Franciscan, a Mormon, a boy wonder, Johnny Miller is the hottest young player to hit the international golf circuit in a decade. After turning pro in 1969, Miller had an incredible year in 1974 when he won eight tournaments and a record $353,201 and was named Professional Golf Association (PGA) player of the year. By 1975, he had won 15 PGA events and earned almost a million dollars.

1. Jack Nicklaus
2. Bobby Jones
3. Walter Hagen
4. Sam Snead
5. Ben Hogan

6. Byron Nelson
7. Arnold Palmer
8. Bobby Locke
9. Gary Player
10. Gene Sarazen

—Exclusive for *The Book of Lists*

SAM SNEAD'S
9 GREATEST GOLFERS
OF ALL TIME

Winner of 134 golf tournaments—84 of them PGA events—Virginian Sam Snead probably has the longest successful career in the game. He was victor in the Masters Tournament three times, the PGA championship three times, the British Open once, and placed second in the U.S. Open four times. He is a member of the PGA Hall of Fame.

1.
2. Jack Nicklaus
3. Ben Hogan
4. Byron Nelson
5. Arnold Palmer

6. Bobby Jones
7. Walter Hagen
8. Gene Sarazen
9. Billy Casper
10. Gary Player

One of Snead's managers wrote us that Snead wanted his first choice left blank—and his list started with second place—"inasmuch as he fears that if he lists someone as the number one greatest golfer of all time, he could make a lot of enemies."

—Exclusive for *The Book of Lists*

Jack Nicklaus, winner of over 60 PGA golf tournaments,
four times PGA's Player of the Year, member of the World Golf Hall of Fame.

HERBERT WARREN WIND'S 12 GREATEST GOLFERS OF ALL TIME

Herbert Warren Wind, one of the world's foremost golf authorities, is a graduate of Yale University and *The New Yorker* magazine. He started playing golf at 10, and has played on every continent except Antarctica and Africa. He is the author of *Thirty Years of Championship Golf, The Greatest Game of All* (with Jack Nicklaus), and *The Story of American Golf*.

1. Young Tom Morris
2. Harry Vardon
3. Walter Hagen
4. Bobby Jones
5. Gene Sarazen
6. Henry Cotton
7. Byron Nelson
8. Sam Snead
9. Ben Hogan
10. Arnold Palmer
11. Jack Nicklaus
12. Gary Player

Wind adds: "You asked for the 10 best, but it would work best, as I view things, if you people would accept a list of the 12 best. I have three main criteria in my selection of the players: tournament record and particularly major championships won; technique, style, and command; and, to a degree, longevity. If I had to drop two of my selections from the list, they would be Young Tom Morris [Tom Morris, Jr.] and Henry Cotton, but if possible, I would like to retain them because Morris's score of 149 for 36 holes in 1870 in winning the British Open is one of the most remarkable golfing achievements of all time—his career record is remarkable, too—and because Cotton, though restricting himself almost totally to European tournaments during his prime, is in my opinion one of the three finest strikers of the ball I have ever seen."

—Exclusive for *The Book of Lists*

AMY ALCOTT'S 11 GREATEST WOMEN GOLFERS OF ALL TIME

At 21, golfer Amy Alcott has already won an impressive array of honors including the 1973 USGA Junior Girls Championship, the 1975 Orange Blossom Classic, and the 1976 Trenton Classic. She is the current women's record holder for the course at Pebble Beach with a score of 70.

1. Lady Heathcoat Amory
2. Mickey Wright
3. Patty Berg
4. Glenna Collett Vare
5. Catherine Lacoste de Prado
6. Alexa Sterling
7. Kathy Whitworth
8. JoAnne Gunderson Carner
9. Betsy Rawls
10. Louise Suggs
11. "Babe" Didrikson Zaharias

Amy Alcott adds: "This list of the 11 greatest women golfers is not in any order of their prominence. To do this, I would have to spend a lengthy amount of time going back into the golf record books. I have listed those whom I feel are the 11 greatest golf stars according to their outstanding accomplishments in the past, whether they be professional or amateur or have gone from amateur to professional standing."

—Exclusive for *The Book of Lists*

ARNOLD PALMER'S 18 BEST GOLF HOLES IN THE U.S.

The most popular and glamorous golfer in modern times, and the first to win over $100,000 in prize money in one year, Arnold Palmer was voted the athlete of the decade in 1969 by Associated Press. Palmer has won four Masters Tournaments, two British Opens, a U.S. Open, and almost every other major contest in the world.

1. 12th hole, Augusta National Golf Club, Augusta, Ga.
2. 15th hole, Oakmont Country Club, Oakmont, Pa.
3. 18th hole, Laurel Valley Golf Club, Ligonier, Pa.
4. 12th hole, Southern Hills Country Club, Tulsa, Okla.
5. 11th hole, Composite Course, The Country Club, Brookline, Mass.
6. 8th hole, Pebble Beach Golf Links, Pebble Beach, Calif.
7. 17th hole, Cypress Point Club, Pebble Beach, Calif.
8. 13th hole, East Course, Merion Golf Club, Ardmore, Pa.
9. 17th hole, Bay Hill Club, Orlando, Fla.
10. 13th hole, Augusta National Golf Club, Augusta, Ga.
11. 2nd hole, no. 3 Course, Medinah Country Club, Medinah, Ill.
12. 16th hole, Oakland Hills Country Club, Birmingham, Mich.
13. 15th hole, Seminole Golf Club, Palm Beach, Fla.
14. 14th hole, Champions Golf Club, Houston, Tex.
15. 4th hole, Lower Course, Baltusrol Golf Club, Springfield, N.J.
16. 16th hole, South Course, Firestone Country Club, Akron, O.
17. 17th hole, Cherry Hills Country Club, Denver, Colo.
18. 16th hole, Lake Course, Olympic Club, San Francisco, Calif.

Arnold Palmer adds: "In no particular order of preference or rating; selected to be geographically representative and to include eight par 4s, five par 3s, and five par 5s."

—Exclusive for *The Book of Lists*

PETER CHEW'S
10 GREATEST RACEHORSES
OF ALL TIME

A staff writer for *The National Observer*, Peter Chew has a knowledge of horse racing that has won him awards from the Thoroughbred Racing Associations. He is author of the book *The Kentucky Derby—The First 100 Years*. For this list, he writes, he conducted a survey among "experts who are friends of mine," and allowed "a few of my own biases to creep in."

1. Eclipse (18th century), England
2. St. Simon (19th century), England
3. Sysonby (20th century), U.S.
4. Colin (20th century), U.S.
5. Man o' War (20th century), U.S.
6. Phar Lap (20th century), New Zealand-Australia
7. Citation (20th century), U.S.
8. Ribot (20th century), Italy
9. Kelso (20th century), U.S.
10. Secretariat (20th century), U.S.

Chew adds: "Although Phar Lap raced for Australia, he was foaled in New Zealand and New Zealand is generally given some credit when he is mentioned. Ribot's dam happened to be in England when he was foaled so technically he is an English horse, but he is, in reality, Italian-bred."

—Exclusive for *The Book of Lists*

JEAN-CLAUDE KILLY'S
12 FAVORITE SKI RUNS

Considered by many experts the greatest skier of all time, French-born Jean-Claude Killy captured all three gold medals in men's alpine skiing at the 1968 Olympics in Grenoble, France. He is also the holder of two World Cup titles. Killy won his first race at the age of 5, and since then he has accumulated over 700 trophies for his competitive efforts.

1. OK (Oreilier-Killy) Piste, Val-d'Isère, France
2. Hannenkham, Kitzbühel, Austria
3. Exhibition, Sun Valley, Ida., U.S.
4. Bugaboos (Helicopter Powder Skiing), Alberta, Canada
5. Kilometro Lanciatro, Cervinia, Italy

6. Ruthie's Run, Aspen, Colo., U.S.
7. Léo Lacroix, Les Menuires, France
8. Gornergrat, Zermatt, Switzerland
9. Nose Dive, Stowe, Vt., U.S.
10. Piste Verte, Chamonix, France
11. Cup Run, Snowshoe, W.Va., U.S.
12. Arrowhead, Shawnee-on-Delaware, Pa., U.S.

—Exclusive for *The Book of Lists*

RICHARD SCHICKEL'S
11 GREATEST MALE TENNIS
PLAYERS IN HISTORY

Author of *The World of Tennis,* Richard Schickel is also well known as a film critic, formerly for *Life* magazine. He has produced and directed several TV documentaries and one TV series, *The Men Who Made the Movies.* His other books include *The Stars* and *His Picture in the Papers.*

1. William T. Tilden
2. Rod Laver
3. Don Budge
4. Fred Perry
5. Ken Rosewall
6. Roy Emerson
7. Ricardo "Pancho" Gonzales
8. Jack Kramer
9. Lew Hoad
10. René Lacoste
11. Henri Cochet

Richard Schickel adds: "My choices are weighted toward the modern era, largely because I believe the game has truly changed and that the tempo of play is now such that the demands placed on champions are so great that only the certified geniuses of earlier years could compete with the bigger, faster people who have risen to the top of late. In drawing the list I have tried to strike a balance (at least among the less obvious choices) between people capable of great, isolated heights (Hoad and Gonzales, for example) and the stayers—those who have demonstrated a capacity to win major titles over long periods of time (Rosewall and Emerson, for example)."

—Exclusive for *The Book of Lists*

PANCHO GONZALES'S
10 GREATEST MALE TENNIS
PLAYERS OF ALL TIME

Noted for his powerful service, Pancho Gonzales won the U.S. championship at Forest Hills in 1948 and 1949, and then turned pro. He retired in 1961 to coach the Davis Cup team, but he has repeatedly returned to tournament play. In 1969, 41-year-old Gonzales won the longest match ever played at Wimbledon, against the 25-year-old Charles Pasarell.

1. Don Budge
2. Lew Hoad
3. Jimmy Connors
4. Rod Laver
5. Jack Kramer

6. Frank Sedgman
7. Ilie Nastase
8. Pancho Segura
9. John Newcombe
10. Bobby Riggs

Pancho Gonzales adds: "These are players I have played against. Not having known Mr. Bill Tilden, for example, I cannot make a true judgment of his ability."

—Exclusive for *The Book of Lists*

RICHARD SCHICKEL'S
10 GREATEST FEMALE TENNIS
PLAYERS IN HISTORY

1. Billie Jean King
2. Suzanne Lenglen
3. Helen Wills Moody
4. Maureen Connolly
5. Chris Evert

6. Margaret Smith Court
7. Evonne Goolagong
8. Alice Marble
9. Helen Jacobs
10. Maria Bueno

—Exclusive for *The Book of Lists*

ALICE MARBLE'S
10 GREATEST WOMEN TENNIS
PLAYERS OF ALL TIME

Alice Marble, who is enshrined in the Tennis Hall of Fame, won all six major women's tennis tournaments, including the U.S.

singles at Forest Hills and the English singles at Wimbledon in 1939, a feat that remains unequaled. In 1940 she turned professional, and later coached Maureen Connolly and Billie Jean King. She is now social director of the Palm Desert Country Club in California.

1. Pauline Betz, U.S.
2. Maria Bueno, Brazil
3. Maureen Connolly, U.S.
4. Helen Jacobs, U.S.
5. Billie Jean King, U.S.
6. Mrs. Lambert Chambers, Great Britain
7. Suzanne Lenglen, France
8. Alice Marble, U.S.
9. Molla Mallory, Finland-U.S.
10. Helen Wills Moody, U.S.

—Exclusive for *The Book of Lists*

Suzanne Lenglen (L) and Helen Wills Moody met only once in singles competition—at Cannes in 1926 when Lenglen triumphed 6-3, 8-6.

SIR ROGER BANNISTER'S 8 GREATEST RUNNERS OF ALL TIME

Sports history was made when Dr. Roger Bannister, English track star, broke the "4-minute mile" on May 6, 1954, at Oxford, where he covered the distance in 3:59.4. Bannister was the British mile champion in 1951, 1953, 1954, and European 1,500-meter title-holder in 1954. He is now a consultant physician at the National Hospital for Nervous Diseases and consultant neurologist at the Western Ophthalmic Hospital in London. He has written a book, *First Four Minutes,* and published numerous medical papers.

1. Paavo Nurmi, Finland
2. Emil Zatopek, Czechoslovakia
3. Jesse Owens, U.S.
4. Kipchoge Keino, Kenya
5. Peter Snell, New Zealand
6. Jim Ryun, U.S.
7. Alberto Juantorena, Cuba
8. Lasse Viren, Finland

—Exclusive for *The Book of Lists*

NAT FLEISCHER'S
6 GREATEST WRESTLERS
OF ALL TIME

1. FRANK GOTCH (U.S.; 205 lbs.)

"The greatest wrestler of modern times," said Fleischer in *The Ring* magazine. Gotch won the U.S. heavyweight championship in 1904, lost and regained it twice. Highlight of his career occurred in 1908 with his first world title match against George Hackenschmidt, which he won (using many unfair tactics) with a toehold after a 2 hr. 3 min. bout. He held the record for the quickest fall. In 1910, he downed Zbyszko in 6¼ secs.

The greatest grappler of the modern era, 205-lb. Frank Gotch.

2. GEORGE HACKENSCHMIDT (Russia; 225 lbs.)

Promoter Jack Curley, who considered him the top wrestler in history, said Hackenschmidt was "the best, most physically perfect mat star who ever came to these shores." Born of a German father and Swedish mother, he grew up to speak seven languages. He was undefeated in his lifetime except for two losses to Gotch.

3. STANISLAUS ZBYSZKO (Poland; 255 lbs.)

His real name was Cyganiewicz. A graduate of the University of Vienna, he knew 12 languages. He came to the U.S. in 1909. A year later, with 944 victories behind him, he suffered his first loss to Gotch. After W.W. I, he made a comeback, and at the age of 40 won his first world title by beating Strangler Lewis. After losing the title, he regained it at the age of 50 by beating Wayne Munn. He died in Missouri in 1967.

4. THE GREAT GAMA (India; 250 lbs.)

Fleischer believed that he was "the only grappler of recent years who could have been the master of both Gotch and Hackenschmidt." A Hindu whose real name was Gulam Mohammed, Gama came out of Punjab to win the championship of India in 1909. Several times he took on and licked 15 opponents in a day. In London, he threw an American, Dr. Benjamin Roller, twice in 7 mins. Then he fought a draw with Zbyszko, because the Pole refused to get off his hands and knees for 2 hrs. 45 mins. In 1928, when Gama was 50 and Zbyszko 48, they had a rematch in a mud pit outside Bombay before 100,000 people. Gama flattened Zbyszko in 10 secs.

5. ED (STRANGLER) LEWIS (U.S.; 225 lbs.)

Fleischer said he was the "past master of every trick." A sports star at the University of Kentucky, he quit school to play professional baseball. He practiced his feared headlock on a dummy head filled with coils and springs. He won the wrestling championship from Joe Stecher in 1920, and later lost and won the title four more times. In his 44-year career, he lost only 33 out of 6,200 matches, and earned $3 million. He died in 1966.

6. JIM LONDOS (Greece; 200 lbs.)

He came to New York at the age of 13. He gave up a strongman vaudeville act to turn to wrestling, and became famous for pinning Stecher and Charlie Cutler. In 1930, he downed Dick Shikat to win the world championship. In 1934, he dared to defend his title against Strangler Lewis, who had earlier beaten him 14 consecutive times. This time Londos won. In 1950, at the age of 53, he came out of retirement to do battle with Primo Carnera in Chicago's Wrigley Field.

—Annotated by i.w.

IRVING CHERNEV'S
12 GREATEST CHESS PLAYERS
OF ALL TIME

1. José R. Capablanca, Cuba
2. Alexander Alekhin, Russia, France
3. Emanuel Lasker, Germany
4. Robert J. Fischer, U.S.
5. Mikhail Botvinnik, U.S.S.R.
6. Tigran Petrosian, U.S.S.R.

7. Mikhail Tal, U.S.S.R.
8. Vasili Smyslov, U.S.S.R.
9. Boris Spassky, U.S.S.R.
10. David Bronstein, U.S.S.R.
11. Akiba Rubinstein, Poland
12. Aron Nimzowitsch, Latvia

SOURCE: Irving Chernev, *The Golden Dozen: The Twelve Greatest Chess Players of All Time* (New York: Oxford University Press, 1976).

15 FANATICAL CARD PLAYERS
AND GROUPS OF PLAYERS

1. JOHN G. BENNETT and MYRTLE BENNETT (bridge)

This Kansas City couple were bridge fiends. In 1929, playing as partners against two friends, Mrs. Bennett castigated Mr. Bennett for his play. He slapped her. She ran into the bedroom, grabbed a revolver, fired twice at her husband and killed him.

2. NAPOLEON BONAPARTE (solitaire)

The French emperor played solitaire constantly while in exile on St. Helena.

3. RICHARD CANFIELD (Canfield solitaire)

He was a gambler and proprietor of a gambling casino at Saratoga in the 1890s. Canfield sponsored a popular form of solitaire which was named after him.

4. DWIGHT D. EISENHOWER (bridge)

Said expert Oswald Jacoby of the U.S. president: "He plays better bridge than golf; he tries to break 90 at golf; at bridge you would say he does break 80." During W.W. II, an unspoken qualification for service on Eisenhower's staff was an officer's ability to play bridge. Eisenhower particularly admired Gen. Alfred Gruenther because Gruenther was the best bridge player in the U.S. Army.

5. GEN. NATHAN B. FORREST (draw poker)

This U.S. Confederate cavalry officer was near bankruptcy.

With almost his last $10 he got into a poker game, won several hundred dollars and was on his way to a comeback.

6. WILD BILL HICKOK (poker)

Famed gunfighter Hickok arrived in Deadwood, Dakota Territory, to play some poker. On August 2, 1876, he was playing poker with three companions at Carl Mann's saloon. Eager to get into the game, he uncharacteristically took a seat with his back to the door because someone else had taken his wall seat. Jack McCall, another gunfighter, came in, walked along the bar until he was behind Hickok, drew a Colt .45, and shot Hickok through the head. Hickok's poker hand that moment was a pair of black aces and a pair of black eights—ever since known as the "dead man's hand."

7. EDMOND HOYLE (whist)

Because he published *A Short Treatise on the Game of Whist* in 1742, we today have the expression "according to Hoyle." This ex-law student also wrote books on piquet, quadrille, backgammon, and chess, but died in 1769, 50 years before poker was invented.

8. J. P. MORGAN (solitaire)

During the 1907 financial panic, bankers hammered at Morgan's door, and found him deliberating over a form of two-deck solitaire known as Miss Milligan. During the game Morgan decided to support the stock market and stop the panic.

9. THE POKER CABINET (poker)

U.S. President Warren G. Harding devoted himself more vigorously to his regular poker game in the White House than to the nation's business. Besides the president, the other players were Secretary of the Interior Albert Fall, Attorney General Harry Daugherty, Jesse Smith, and Veterans Bureau head Charles R. Forbes. After the Teapot Dome scandal, Fall and Forbes went to jail, Daugherty got two hung juries, and Smith committed suicide.

10. FRANKLIN D. ROOSEVELT (poker, whist, solitaire)

The U.S. president once went directly from a poker game, carrying his chips, to the radio to make a fireside chat to the nation. Throughout his speech he absently clicked his chips, obliterating many of his words.

11. ROBERT CUMMING SCHENCK (poker)

He was U.S. minister to Great Britain from 1871 to 1876, and he taught the entire British royal family how to play poker.

12. WILLIAM MAKEPEACE THACKERAY (écarté)

The novelist wrote in detail about his favorite game in *Vanity Fair* and *Barry Lyndon*.

13. THANATOPSIS LITERARY AND INSIDE STRAIGHT CLUB (poker)

A subsidiary of the Algonquin round table, the group met

weekly at New York's Algonquin Hotel to play a marathon game of poker all afternoon and evening. The regulars and occasional guests included the following: columnist Franklin P. Adams, journalist Heywood Broun, actor Harpo Marx, raconteur Alexander Woollcott, playwright George S. Kaufman, playwright Marc Connelly, actors Alfred Lunt and Lynn Fontanne, author Ring Lardner, humorist Robert Benchley, journalist Herbert Bayard Swope, singer Paul Robeson. Chips were $1 each.

14. COUNT LEO TOLSTOY (solitaire)

Whenever the Russian novelist was faced with a problem, he tried to resolve it while playing this lone game.

15. HARRY S TRUMAN (poker)

This U.S. president loved poker because, as Merriman Smith reported, "Poker was his safety valve." Truman liked to introduce unorthodox variations of the game, employing numerous wild cards.

—I.W.

THE 10 MOST LANDED-UPON MONOPOLY™ SPACES

Monopoly™, a Parker Brothers board game, has enjoyed sales of more than 70 million sets since it came on the market in the 1930s. Every *Monopoly*™ player has his own strategy. Now Irvin R. Hertzel has used a computer to determine the overall probability of landing on each square. Hertzel, an assistant professor of mathematics at Iowa State University, fed the computer every conceivable variable, such as what happens when a player goes to jail or draws a card after landing on Community Chest or Chance. Results of his computer analysis are as follows:

1. Illinois Avenue
2. Go
3. B. & O. Railroad
4. Free Parking
5. Tennessee Avenue
6. New York Avenue
7. Reading Railroad
8. St. James Place
9. Water Works
10. Pennsylvania Railroad

—R.T.

17

HERE'S TO YOUR HEALTH

10 FAMOUS GOURMANDS

1. AESOP

Not to be confused with his namesake known for *Aesop's Fables*, this Aesop, a Roman actor, was known for the vulgarity of his gastronomic predilections. One meal cost several thousand dollars and consisted of a pie prepared solely from birds that could imitate the human voice. Aesop's son Clodius was similarly self-indulgent and is said to have insisted that every dish he consumed contain a powdered gem.

2. HONORÉ DE BALZAC

A physically unappealing man given to loud dress and coarse ways, Balzac was as accomplished a trencherman as he was a writer. At one meal he devoured a dozen cutlets, a duck, two partridges, and 110 oysters. He topped it all off with 12 pears and a variety of desserts.

Honoré de Balzac, great 19th-century French novelist and notorious glutton.

3. JACK BIGGERS

Biggers was one of the best-known "feeders" of 18th-century England; his gluttony was his undoing. Having consumed within one hour all but the last morsels of a meal consisting of 6 lbs. of bacon, a huge green salad, 12 suet dumplings, a loaf of bread, and a gallon of beer, Biggers suffered a fatal attack of apoplexy.

4. "DIAMOND JIM" BRADY

Multimillionaire railroad tycoon Brady was at least as well known for his gargantuan appetite as he was for his fiscal successes. A typical day's menu began at breakfast with hominy, eggs, corn bread, muffins, griddle cakes, chops, fried potatoes, a beefsteak, and a gallon of orange juice, his favorite drink. Next came a late morning snack of two to three dozen clams and oysters, followed at 12:30 P.M. by lunch (clams, oysters, boiled lobsters, deviled crabs, a joint of beef, and a variety of pies). At afternoon tea Jim would sit down to a heaping dish of seafood and copious drafts of lemon soda. Dinner, of course, was the major meal of the day, and Jim often supped at Rector's, a posh New York restaurant. The meal included two or three dozen lynnhaven oysters, six crabs, several bowls of green turtle soup, six or seven lobsters, a pair of canvasback ducks, a double serving of terrapin, a sirloin steak, vegetables, and much orange juice. Generally Jim would top off the meal with a piled-high platter of cakes and pies and a 2-lb. box of candy.

5. MATTHEW DAKING

One of the earliest recorded sufferers of bulimia (an irrational compulsion to overeat), 12-year-old Matthew Daking ate 384 lbs. 2 oz. of food in six days in 1743.

6. JOHN MARRIOTT

The public gluttony of John Marriott, lawyer and social figure, was well known in England during the reign of King James I. In a pamphlet entitled *The Great Eater of Graye's Inn, or the Life of Mr. Marriott, the Cormorant*, it was claimed that he once ate a lunch that had been prepared for 20 men, and that he frequently dined on dog and monkey meat.

7. EDWARD ABRAHAM "BOZO" MILLER

Miller has been called "the world's greatest trencherman" by *The Guinness Book of World Records*. Born in 1909, he is 5 ft. 7 in. tall, weighs 280–300 lbs., and consumes as much as 25,000 calories daily. In 1963, at Trader Vic's in San Francisco, Miller ate 27 2-lb. pullets, the world's record for a single sitting.

8. WILLIAM DOUGLAS, DUKE OF QUEENSBERRY

Known popularly as "Old Q," he was surely one of the most voracious eaters in all 18th-century England. A normal day's regimen included two mammoth breakfasts, two lunches, and five full-course dinners eaten at intervals between 5:00 P.M. and 3:00 A.M.

9. WALTER WILLEY

Willey was an obscure brewer's servant living in London in the 18th century, but he achieved fame, of sorts, through his public gluttony. The November, 1765, edition of the *Annual Register* reported that in 1½ hours, at a public house, Willey devoured a 6-lb. roast goose, a quartern loaf (about 4 lbs. of bread), and 3 qts. of porter.

10. NICHOLAS WOOD

Wood's gastronomic excesses inspired songs, poems, and at least one book—John Taylor's *The Great Eater of Kent, or Part of the Admirable Teeth and Stomach Exploits of Nicholas Wood, of Harrison in the County of Kent.* At one historic sitting, Wood consumed an entire sheep, leaving only the bones, wool, skin, and horns. At another, he put away nearly 400 pigeons. His favorite breakfast was 18 yds. of black pudding.

—B.F.

DIETS OF 10 FAMOUS PEOPLE

1. CAROL BURNETT

Influenced by her yoga instructor, the comedienne has changed her dietary habits. She now eats raw or lightly cooked vegetables, fruits, fish, poultry (no red meats), fertile eggs, and raw milk. She also takes vitamins and drinks herb teas instead of coffee. For breakfast she has a protein drink which she concocts for herself. It contains such exotic ingredients as sunflower meal, wheast, chia seeds, date and date-pit powder, and wheat germ, mixed with raw milk and a fertile egg. She admits this tastes like a dog biscuit. For lunch she eats fruit and raw vegetables. (She sometimes cheats on her diet and eats a bite of conventional dessert.)

2. GEORGE GORDON, LORD BYRON

A poet inclined to put on weight, Byron was grimly determined to stay slender. For days, he would live on biscuits and soda water. Or he would diet by having just a cup of tea for breakfast, and some combination of cold potatoes, rice, fish, or vegetables sprinkled heavily with vinegar for supper. Chewing tobacco kept his mind off his hunger.

3. JULIA CHILD

For breakfast, the TV chef likes whole raw fruit (apples, bananas, pears, or grapes), fresh orange juice on occasion, and a different tea (without sugar) each morning. On Sundays only, she has bacon and eggs, but never indulges in toast with butter—too fattening! Depending upon her willpower, she may skip lunch altogether. If she and her husband dine alone, they omit both appetizer and dessert, except perhaps for fruit. They have meat or fish, vegetables, and a salad, and they always leave room in their calorie count for the proper wine. When she's terribly hungry between meals, she eats a dill pickle.

4. GRETA GARBO

The legendary actress prefers simple food: Swedish bread with unsalted butter, cheese, and ham. She also likes tartar steak (raw chopped beef mixed with egg yolk and chopped onion) and huge green salads. She enjoys drinking beer and vodka.

5. ERNEST HEMINGWAY

When writing, he existed on rye crisps, raw green vegetables, and peanut butter sandwiches. He avoided sweets and starches, and obtained his sugar from his daily intake of liquor. When he was active in the mountains or on a boat, he would eat more heartily. At those times he liked grilled fresh fish, a rare steak with the bone left in, or rare lamb. He relished wild game, such as elk, mountain sheep, venison, or antelope. He also enjoyed grouse, quail, or mallard duck served with mashed potatoes. He loved all kinds of fruits, and his favorite vegetables were brussels sprouts, Swiss chard, broccoli, and artichokes served with sauce vinaigrette.

6. BILLIE JEAN KING

Eating balanced meals and counting calories is the key to this tennis champion's diet. She stays away from red meat, which can have twice the calories of fish. If she has a potato, she'll add just a little butter. She avoids food with white flour and white sugar, and instead chooses whole wheat bread or bran muffins. She doesn't drink, with the exception of one or two beers, when she's working out for a tennis match.

7. MICHELANGELO

According to Vasari, Michelangelo's contemporary and biographer, the Renaissance artist was "all intent upon his work" when he was young, and contented himself with a little bread and wine. He continued this practice when he was old, taking his refreshment in the evening when he had finished the day's work. Although he was rich, he lived as frugally as a poor man.

8. JACQUELINE KENNEDY ONASSIS

When dining out at restaurants, the former first lady often orders a favorite meal containing an estimated 500 calories or less. The meal consists of a large baked potato, split and heaped with fresh caviar, accompanied by a glass of champagne.

9. ARTHUR RUBINSTEIN

The ageless pianist enjoys the best of wines each day in addition to two or three cigars with coffee. He maintains a low-fat diet: His wife cuts all the fat off his meat but, if called for in a sauce, she will use a little cream. He loves chicken and she cooks it "a million ways." He eats little red meat.

10. GEORGE BERNARD SHAW

A vegetarian for aesthetic and hygienic reasons, the playwright took light and frugal meals. A tall man, he never weighed more than 9 stone (126 lbs.). He avoided meat, tea, and alcohol. For breakfast he always had grapefruit and also liked a bowl of porridge or, occasionally, shredded wheat. His main meals consisted of dishes prepared with beans, lentils, macaroni, spaghetti, or rice. He also enjoyed sandwiches of chopped raw vegetables with a glass of yogurt. Between lunch and dinner he might have a glass of milk if there were a visitor staying for tea. Other acceptable drinks were apple juice and instant Postum.

—M.B.T.

20 PRESENT-DAY VEGETARIANS

1. Marisa Berenson, actress
2. Candice Bergen, actress
3. David Carradine, actor
4. Cesar Chavez, labor organizer
5. Marty Feldman, actor
6. Dick Gregory, author and political activist

Gloria Swanson, whose last great acting role was in
Sunset Boulevard, was 80 years old in 1977. A long-standing
vegetarian, she maintains a strict diet of organic foods.

380

7. George Harrison, musician
8. Laura Huxley, author
9. Gladys Knight, singer
10. Peter Max, artist
11. Yehudi Menuhin, musician
12. Carlos Santana, musician
13. Peter Sellers, actor
14. Ravi Shankar, musician
15. Isaac Bashevis Singer, author
16. Gloria Swanson, actress
17. Twiggy, model, actress, singer
18. Lasse Viren, long-distance runner
19. Bill Walton, basketball player
20. Dennis Weaver, actor

SOURCE: Courtesy of *Vegetarian World,* a Los Angeles, Calif., newspaper.

22 LEAST CALORIC FOODS

	Calories per 100 Grams
1. Water	—
2. Club soda	—
3. Coffee	1
4. Tea	2
5. Freshly harvested Jerusalem artichoke	7
6. Sour pickle	10
7. Sauerkraut juice	10
8. Dill pickle	11
9. Cooked zucchini	12
10. Raw lettuce	13
11. Cooked New Zealand spinach	13
12. Cooked cabbage	14
13. Cooked celery	14
14. Cooked summer squash	14
15. Cider vinegar	14
16. Raw chicory (Belgian endive)	15
17. Raw cucumbers	15
18. Cooked purslane leaf	15
19. Raw rhubarb	16
20. Raw celery	17
21. Raw radish	17
22. Raw zucchini	17

100 grams is about 3.5 ounces.

SOURCE: U.S. Dept. of Agriculture, *Composition of Food* (1963).

9 MOST CALORIC FOODS

		Calories per 100 Grams
1.	Lard	902
2.	Salad oil	884
3.	Butter, oil, or dehydrated butter	876
4.	Raw pork back fat	841
5.	Raw double-bone sirloin fat (choice grade)	793
6.	Raw pork fat (fat class)	784
7.	Raw salt pork	783
8.	Raw lamb rib fat (prime grade)	779
9.	Raw porterhouse fat (choice grade)	777

100 grams is about 3.5 ounces.

SOURCE: U.S. Dept. of Agriculture, *Composition of Food* (1963).

13 ACTIVITIES AND
THE CALORIES THEY CONSUME

		Calories Expended (per hr.)
1.	Calisthenics	250–820
2.	Bicycling	200–600
3.	Roller skating	200–500
4.	Skipping rope	300
5.	Playing volleyball	300
6.	Dancing	200–400
7.	Throwing a frisbee	200
8.	Making love	150 (per act)
9.	Playing golf (no cart allowed)	133
10.	Walking slowly	115
11.	Playing cards	100
12.	Flying a kite	30
13.	Standing at cocktail parties	20

SOURCE: *New York* magazine (Dec. 8, 1972); other sources.

11 FOOD PRODUCTS
AND THEIR FILTH LEVELS

According to the Public Health Service of the Food and Drug Administration, the following "defect levels" are not to be exceeded if the products are made available for human consumption. Anything at these levels or below is considered *acceptable* for public sale in the U.S.

1. ASPARAGUS (canned or frozen)

Ten percent of spears infested with six asparagus beetle eggs; either 40 thrips or five insects in 100-gram samples.

2. CHOCOLATE; CHOCOLATE LIQUOR

Up to 60 microscopic insect fragments per 100-gram sample or up to 100 fragments in one sample; or an average of 1.5 rodent hairs in each sample or up to 4 hairs in any one sample.

3. COFFEE BEANS

Ten percent insect infested, damaged, or molded.

4. FIG PASTE

Thirteen insect heads in two 100-gram samples.

5. FISH (fresh frozen)

Five percent of fish or fillets with "definite odor of decomposition" over 25% of fish area; or 20% of the fish fillets with "slight odor of decomposition" over 25% of fish area.

6. HOPS

Average of 2,500 aphids per 100 grams.

7. PEPPER

Average of 1% insect infested or mold by weight; or 1 milligram of excreta per pound.

8. POPCORN

In six 10-oz. samples, either one rodent pellet or one rodent hair per sample; two rodent hairs or 20 gnawed grains per pound with hairs in 50% of samples or 5% by weight of field corn in popcorn.

9. SPINACH (canned or frozen)

In 100-gram samples, either 50 aphids, thrips, or mites or eight leaf miners; two spinach worms or 10% decomposition.

10. STRAWBERRIES (frozen, whole, sliced)

Mold count of 55% in half of the samples.

11. TOMATO PASTE (pizza and other sauces)

In 100-gram samples, either 30 fly eggs, 15 eggs and one larvae, or two larvae; or mold count averaging 40% (30% for pizza sauce).

—D.W.

SOURCE: U.S. Food and Drug Administration.

35 FOODS MOST CONSUMED IN THE U.S.

		Lbs. per capita (1975)
1.	Fluid milk and cream	291.2
2.	Potatoes	120.2
3.	Beef	88.9
4.	Refined sugar	87.7
5.	Canned vegetables	53.2
6.	Noncitrus fruits (fresh)	52.4
7.	Pork	41.0
8.	Chicken	40.3
9.	Eggs (35.3 lbs. = 263 eggs)	35.3
10.	Citrus fruits (fresh)	28.6
11.	Oil and edible fats	20.3*
12.	Canned fruit	19.1
13.	Ice cream	18.5
14.	Melons	17.5
15.	Shortening	17.3
16.	Canned juice	14.7
17.	Frozen fruits, juices	12.6
18.	Fish	12.1
19.	Margarine	11.2
20.	Frozen vegetables	9.6
21.	Coffee	9.0
22.	Turkey	8.6
23.	Rice	7.7
24.	Shelled peanuts	6.8
25.	Dry edible beans	6.4
26.	Chilled citrus juice	6.0
27.	Condensed and evaporated milk	5.3
28.	Sweet potatoes	5.0
29.	Butter	4.8
30.	Veal	3.5
31.	Dried fruit	3.3
32.	Lard	2.9
33.	Cocoa	2.4

| 34. Lamb and mutton | 1.8 |
| 35. Tea | 0.8 |

*Does not include butter, margarine, lard, or shortening, which are listed as separate entries.

SOURCE: U.S. Dept. of Agriculture.

—J. BER.

12 MOST POPULAR
MAIN DISHES IN THE U.S.

Not all of eat-out America subsists on the hamburger-and-cola standby served up by the fast-food chains. For those who take the time to sit down and stay a while, the following main-dish orders are the most popular.

1. Fried chicken (far ahead of the pack!)
2. Roast beef
3. Spaghetti
4. Turkey
5. Baked ham
6. Fried shrimp
7. Beef stew
8. Meat loaf
9. Fish (preferred: cod and haddock)
10. Macaroni and cheese
11. Pot roast
12. Swiss steak

HOLD THE PICKLE, HOLD THE RELISH: THE FAST-FOOD WINNERS

1. Hamburger
2. Cheeseburger
3. Ham and grilled cheese (honorable mention)

SOURCE: *Institutions/Volume Feeding* magazine (1976).

—W.K.

Fried-chicken magnate Colonel Sanders and friend
at the Wailing Wall in Jerusalem.

10 BEANS AND
THEIR FLATULENCE LEVELS

Concern about food shortages around the world has caused increased attention to be paid to beans as a source of inexpensive protein. Unfortunately, many people are hesitant to eat beans because of the discomfort that is caused to the eater and his companions approximately four hours after leaving the dinner table. Here is a list of beans in order of their flatulence production: number 1 produces the most gas, number 10 the least. Dr. Louis B. Rockland of the Western Regional Research Laboratory of the U.S. Dept. of Agriculture in Berkeley, Calif., warns that "the state of the art is not very advanced" and that these preliminary results might prove incorrect after the completion of further tests. In essence, Dr. Rockland implies that this list should be taken with a grain of salt.

1. Soybeans
2. Pink beans
3. Black beans
4. Pinto beans
4. California small white beans
6. Great northern beans
7. Lima beans (baby)
7. Garbanzos
9. Lima beans (large)
10. Blackeyes

Although not literally beans, garbanzos and blackeyes were included in the tests since they are also gas producers and are often categorized as beans.

Cooking soybeans with an equal portion of rice eliminates two-thirds of their flatulence as well as increasing the amount of usable protein.

—D.W.

5 RECENT WINNERS OF
THE PILLSBURY BAKE-OFF®

Remember "Nothin' says lovin' like somethin' from the oven?" Remember who says it best? Right! It's the Pillsbury Co. of Minneapolis, Minn. Every year for the past couple of decades, Pillsbury has sponsored a baking/recipe contest known as the Bake-Off®. Eleanor Roosevelt, Margaret Truman, and the duke and duchess of Windsor have been among the event's guests of honor. Although most of the $25,000 grand prizewinners have been housewives, a teenage girl won the 1965 contest with a recipe she developed as a class project in school. No man has ever won the grand price, but the chief steward of the submarine *Catfish* once won best-of-class with a "Sub-Meringue Pie," and other men have also won best-of-class awards. Since 1972, the Bake-Off® has awarded two grand prizes each year.

1. **MRS. GERALD COLLINS** (Elk River, Minn.; 1972)

Chewy Coconut Crescent Bars (3–4 dozen bars)
(refrigerated quick mix division)

8-oz. can Pillsbury Refrigerated Quick Crescent Dinner Rolls
14-oz. can (1⅓ cups) sweetened condensed milk
1 package (9.9 oz.) Pillsbury Coconut Almond Frosting Mix
¼ cup butter or margarine, melted

Preheat oven to 400°F. Unroll crescent dough. Place rectangles in ungreased 15-by-10-in. jelly roll pan. Gently press dough to cover bottom of pan. Seal perforations. Pour condensed milk evenly over dough. Sprinkle with frosting mix. Drizzle with butter. Bake at 400°F. for 12–15 mins. until golden brown. Cool. Cut into bars.

2. **MRS. JEROME FLIELLER, JR.** (Floresville, Tex.; 1973)

Quick Crescent Pecan Pie Bars (2 dozen bars)
(refrigerated quick mix division)

8-oz. can Pillsbury Refrigerated Quick Crescent Dinner Rolls
1 egg, beaten
½ cup chopped pecans
½ cup sugar
½ cup corn syrup
1 tablespoon butter or margarine, melted
½ teaspoon vanilla

Preheat oven to 375°F. Lightly grease 13-by-9-in. pan. Separate crescent dough into 2 large rectangles. Press rectangles over bottom and ½ in. up sides of prepared pan to form crust. Seal perforations. Bake crust at 375°F. for 5 mins. In medium bowl, combine remaining ingredients. Pour over partly baked crust. Bake at 375°F. for 18–22 mins. until golden brown. Cool. Cut into bars.

3. **MRS. EMIL JERZAK** (Porter, Minn.; 1974)

Chocolate Cherry Bars (about 3 dozen bars)

1 package Pillsbury Fudge Cake Mix
21-oz. can cherry fruit filling
1 teaspoon almond extract
2 eggs, beaten

Preheat oven to 350°F. Using solid shortening or margarine (not oil), grease and flour 15-by-10-in. jelly roll or 13-by-9-in. pan. In large bowl, combine all ingredients. Stir well by hand until mixed well. Pour into prepared pan. Bake jelly roll pan 20–30 mins., rectangle pan 25–30 mins. or until toothpick inserted in center comes out clean. Remove, cool, cut into bars.

Frosting:
1 cup sugar
5 tablespoons butter or margarine
⅓ cup milk
6-oz. package (1 cup) semisweet chocolate pieces

In small saucepan combine sugar, butter, and milk. Boil, stirring constantly, 1 min. Remove from heat. Stir in chocolate pieces until smooth. Pour over bars.

4. MRS. LUELLA E. MAKI (Ely, Minn.; 1975)

Sour Cream Apple Squares (12–15 squares)

2 cups Pillsbury's Best All Purpose or Unbleached Flour (when using self-rising flour, omit salt)
2 cups firmly packed brown sugar
½ cup butter or margarine, softened
1 cup chopped nuts
1–2 teaspoons cinnamon
1 teaspoon baking soda
½ teaspoon salt
1 cup dairy sour cream
1 teaspoon vanilla
1 egg
2 cups (2 medium) peeled, finely chopped apples

Preheat oven to 350°F. Lightly spoon flour into measuring cup and level off. In large bowl combine flour, sugar, and butter. Blend at low speed until crumbly. Stir in nuts. Press 2¾ cups crumb mixture into ungreased 13-by-9-in. pan. To remaining mixture, add cinnamon, soda, salt, sour cream, vanilla, and egg. Blend well. Stir in apples. Spoon evenly over base. Bake 25–35 mins. until toothpick inserted in center comes out clean. Cut into squares. Serve with whipped cream, if desired.

Mrs. Luella E. Maki, of Ely, Minn., with her sour cream apple squares. *Right:* Mrs. Isabelle Collins, of Elk River, Minn., displaying her cherry coconut crescent bars.

5. MRS. EDWARD F. SMITH (Harahan, La.; 1976)

Whole Wheat Raisin Loaf (2 loaves)

2 cups milk
¾ cup water
¼ cup oil
3–3¾ cups all-purpose flour
½ cup sugar
3 teaspoons salt
1 teaspoon cinnamon
½ teaspoon nutmeg
2 packages dry yeast
4 cups whole wheat flour
1 cup rolled oats
1 cup raisins

In medium saucepan, heat milk, water, and oil until very warm (120°–130°F.). In large bowl, combine warm liquids, 2 cups all-purpose flour, sugar, salt, cinnamon, nutmeg, and yeast. Beat 4 mins. at medium speed of electric mixer. By hand, stir in whole wheat flour, oats, raisins, and remaining all-purpose flour. On well-floured surface, knead dough until smooth and elastic, about 5 mins. Place in greased bowl. Cover. Let rise in warm place 20–30 mins.

Punch down dough. Divide and shape into two loaves. Place in two greased 9-by-5-in. or 8-by-4-in. loaf pans. Brush with oil or melted margarine. Cover. Let rise in warm place until light and doubled in size, 30–45 mins. Bake at 375°F. 40–45 mins. until loaf is deep golden brown and sounds hollow when lightly tapped. If loaf becomes too brown, loosely cover with foil the last 10 mins. of baking. Immediately remove from pans. If desired, brush with oil or margarine and sprinkle with sugar.

—B.H.

SOURCE: Louis Gelfand and Deborah Ellefson (Pillsbury Co., Minneapolis, Minn.).

11 PROMINENT COFFEE DRINKERS

1. JOHANN SEBASTIAN BACH

Bach wrote the *Coffee Cantata,* a humorous one-act operetta about a stern father's attempt to check his daughter's indulgence in the coffee habit. From the *Cantata:* "Betty: 'Dear father, don't be so strict! If I can't have my little demitasse of coffee three times a day, I'm just like a dried-up piece of roast goat!' "

2. HONORÉ DE BALZAC

Coffee was his mainstay. Balzac went to bed at 6:00 P.M., slept until 12:00, then rose and wrote for 12-hour stretches, drinking coffee all the while. He wrote, "This coffee falls into your stomach, and straightway there is a general commotion. Ideas begin to move like the battalions of the Grand Army on the battlefield, and the battle takes place. Things remembered arrive at full gallop, ensign to the wind. The light cavalry of comparisons deliver a magnificent deploying charge, the artillery of logic hurry up with their train and ammunition, the shafts of wit start up like sharpshooters. Similes arise, the paper is covered with ink; for the struggle commences and is concluded with torrents of black water, just like a battle with powder."

3. NAPOLEON BONAPARTE

He said, "Strong coffee, and plenty, awakens me. It gives me a warmth, an unusual force, a pain that is not without pleasure. I would rather suffer than be senseless."

4. ANTHELME BRILLAT-SAVARIN

Brillat-Savarin, French gastronome (1755–1826), praised coffee highly in his writings. He chose to give it up, however, because he "one day fell too surely beneath its spell." He had drunk a large quantity in order to stay up late at night and work, and did not sleep for 40 hours. He wrote: "It is the duty of all papas and mamas to forbid their children coffee, unless they wish to have little dried-up machines stunted and old at the age of 20."

5. FREDERICK THE GREAT

The Prussian monarch often had his coffee made with champagne instead of water.

6. GEN. ULYSSES S. GRANT

During the Wilderness campaign, General Grant was content to make a meal of a sliced cucumber with vinegar and a cup of strong coffee—one cup being the full ration.

7. IMMANUEL KANT

Kant became extremely fond of coffee in his old age. Thomas De Quincey relates an anecdote which shows Kant's addiction to the after-dinner cup: "At the beginning of the last year of his life, he fell into the custom of taking, immediately after dinner, a cup of coffee . . . Sometimes, in the interest of conversation, the coffee was forgotten, but not for long. He would remember and with the querulousness of old age and infirm health would demand that coffee be brought 'upon the spot.' Arrangements had always been made in advance, however; the coffee was ground, and the water was boiling; and in the very moment the word was given the servant shot like an arrow and plunged the coffee into the water. All that remained, therefore, was to give it time to boil up. But this trifling delay seemed unendurable to Kant. If it were said, 'Dear Professor, the coffee will be up in a moment,' he would say '*Will be!* There's the rub, that it only *will* be.' Then he would quiet himself with a stoical air, and say, 'Well, one can die after all; it is but dying; and in the next world, thank God, there is no drinking of coffee and consequently no waiting for it.' When at length the servant's steps were heard upon the stairs, he would turn round to us, and joyfully call out: 'Land, land! my dear friends, I see land!' "

8. SIR JAMES MACKINTOSH

This Scottish philosopher and statesman claimed that the powers of a man's mind were directly proportional to the quantity of coffee he drank.

9. JEAN-JACQUES ROUSSEAU

Rousseau loved his coffee so much that when he died, "he just missed doing it with a cup of coffee in his hand."

10. TALLEYRAND

Talleyrand, the French diplomat and wit, expounded on the ideal cup of coffee: He said it should be "black as the devil, hot as hell, pure as an angel, sweet as love."

11. VOLTAIRE

Even in his old age, Voltaire was said to have consumed 50 cups daily. He is credited with the famous reply to the remark that coffee was a slow poison: "I think it must be, for I've been drinking it for 65 years and am not dead yet!"

—A.W.

SOURCE: *All About Coffee* by William H. Ukers (Detroit: Gale Research Co., 1976).

Voltaire drank 50 cups of coffee a day.

18 DRINKS NAMED AFTER PEOPLE OR PEOPLES

1. ALEXANDER

Made with crème de cacao, gin, or brandy, and cream, this cocktail was named for Alexander the Great, centuries after his death.

2. BENEDICTINE

One of the oldest liquers in the world, Benedictine is named after the Benedictine monks who first made it at their monastery at Fécamp, France, in 1510, and dedicated it "To God, most good, most great."

3. BLOODY MARY

Ferdinand L. Petiot, bartender at Harry's New York Bar in Paris, mixed vodka and tomato juice in 1920; American entertainer Roy Barton gave it the name "bucket of blood" after the club in Chicago. The drink was renamed "the red snapper" when Petiot spiced it up with salt, pepper, lemon, and Worcestershire sauce. Though it has been said that this "queen among drinks" was named after Mary, Queen of Scots, it was Queen Mary I of England who was known as "Bloody Mary."

4. BOURBON

A Baptist preacher, Rev. Elijah Craig of Bourbon County, Ky., allegedly invented bourbon in 1789. The county itself had been named after the Bourbon kings of France, a dynasty that took power in 1589 and reigned for over 200 years.

5. BRONX COCKTAIL

The drink was labeled in 1919 in honor of a New York City borough—the Bronx—which, in turn, was named after Jonas Bronck, a Dane who first settled the area for the Dutch West India Company in 1641.

6. DOM PÉRIGNON

Moët et Chandon named its most famous vintage after Dom Pierre Pérignon (1638–1715), the blind Benedictine monk who invented the first true sparkling champagne.

7. GIBSON

Toward the beginning of the 20th century, a bartender at the New York Players Club was fixing a martini for artist Charles Dana Gibson. When he discovered that there were no more olives, the bartender substituted a pearl onion and named the drink after his customer.

8. GIMLET

Believing that straight gin harmed the health of naval officers, British naval surgeon Sir T. O. Gimlette created the "healthy cocktail" by diluting gin with lime juice in 1890.

9. GIN RICKEY

According to H. L. Mencken, "a distinguished Washington guzzler" named Colonel Rickey invented the gin rickey—a mixture of gin, carbonated water, and lime juice—around 1895. Other sources say the drink honors Civil War Col. James K. Rickey, who ordered it so often at New York City's St. James Hotel that the bartender named the drink after him.

10. GROG

British Vice Admiral Sir Edward Vernon was called Old Grog because he wore an impressive grogram coat on deck in all kinds of weather. When in 1740 he ordered that all rum rations be diluted with water to curb drunken brawling aboard ships, incensed old sea dogs dubbed the diluted rum "grog," which later came to mean any cheap liquor.

11. HARVEY WALLBANGER

California surfer Tom Harvey (c. 1970) had a great passion for the "Italian screwdriver" (orange juice, vodka, Galliano). After a day of surfing, Harvey still couldn't stay off the waves. He would rush to his favorite bar, overindulge himself—and then walk into a wall when it came time to go home.

12. KICKAPOO JOY JUICE

Early settlers in Pennsylvania and Ohio, along with the resident Algonquin Kickapoo Indians, enjoyed drinking a particular home-brewed liquor. The settlers borrowed the tribe's name when labeling the drink.

13. MANHATTAN COCKTAIL

The concoction of whiskey, sweet vermouth, and bitters was named after the Manhattan Club in New York, N.Y., where it was first mixed in the mid-1870s at a dinner given by Lady Randolph Churchill in honor of Gov. Samuel J. Tilden. The club itself got its name from the Manhattan Indians who had, it was said, sold their New York island to the Dutch for $24 worth of trinkets.

14. MARTINI

American bartender Jerry Thomas claimed to have created the "Martinez" between 1860 and 1862 at San Francisco's Occidental Hotel for an unidentified gentleman who was traveling from San Francisco to Martinez, Calif. Other tales of the drink's origin point to a long forgotten Italian bartender named Martini, and to the Martini & Rossi firm—makers of the popular vermouth.

15. MICKEY FINN

Mickey Finn was apparently the name of a bartender who worked in Chicago around 1896–1906. He served knockout drinks (which probably contained chloral hydrate) to his customers so that they could be robbed.

16. ROB ROY

This concoction of Scotch whiskey, sweet vermouth, and bitters, topped with a maraschino cherry, bears the nickname of the legendary 18th-century Scottish freebooter Robert Macgregor.

17. SCOTCH

This whiskey, made from malted barley, was invented in Scotland—by the Scots, of course. One native sage said of the drink: "If a body could just find oot the exac' proper proportion and quantity that ought to be drunk every day, and keep to that, I verily vow that he might leeve forever, without dying at a', and that doctors and kirkyards would go oot of fashion."

18. TOM COLLINS

This drink was named after a 19th-century bartender at Limmer's Old House in London who was famous for his gin slings —a tall drink that resembles the Collins's mixture of gin, lemon, sugar, and soda water.

—R.H. & D.B.

10 BIGGEST
WINE-DRINKING COUNTRIES

		Liters per Capita (1974)
1.	Italy	110.5
2.	France	103.04
3.	Portugal	80
4.	Argentina	77.2
5.	Spain	75
6.	Switzerland	45
7.	Luxembourg	40.3
8.	Chile	40
9.	Hungary	38
10.	Austria	36.8

A liter is 1.06 quarts.

SOURCE: *1976 Britannica Book of the Year* (Chicago: Encyclopaedia Britannica, 1976).

10 BIGGEST
BEER-DRINKING COUNTRIES

		Liters per Capita (1974)
1.	Czechoslovakia	152.7
2.	W. Germany	147
3.	Australia	141.3
4.	Belgium	140
5.	Luxembourg	135
6.	New Zealand	126.1

7. E. Germany	114.9
8. United Kingdom	114.3
9. Denmark	111.96
10. Austria	106.2

The U.S. ranks 13th. A liter is 1.06 quarts.

SOURCE: *1976 Britannica Book of the Year* (Chicago: Encyclopaedia Britannica, 1976).

RATINGS OF 18 BEERS IN THE WASHINGTONIAN'S FIRST ANNUAL BEER TASTING

A panel of seven—two noted local beer experts, two former professional athletes, and three beer drinkers of some repute—conducted a taste test of 18 popular beers for *Washingtonian* magazine (Washington, D.C.). The beers were served without labels in groups of three, with bread available between tastes to reset the taste buds and a 10-minute break between groups. Panelists were asked to score each beer from 1 (terrible) to 10 (excellent), with 5 considered average. The results are as follows (maximum score 100):

1. Heineken	83.7	11. National Premium	52.2
2. Old Milwaukee	71.5	12. Schmidt's of	
3. Pabst Blue Ribbon	68.6	Philadelphia	48.6
4. Schlitz	68.6	13. Yuengling	47.9
5. Miller High Life	67.2	14. Coors	47.2
6. Tuborg	61.5	15. Rolling Rock	47.2
7. Budweiser	60.8	16. Lowenbrau Light	46.5
8. Michelob	60.8	17. Carlings Black	
9. National Bohemian	57.9	Label	43.6
10. Andeker	54.3	18. Schaefer's	33.6

There was a surprising disparity in ratings for beer no. 16, Lowenbrau Light. The two experts rated this beer superior to all other brands, but the nonexperts placed it at the bottom of the list.

SOURCE: *Washingtonian* magazine (June, 1975).

UPTON SINCLAIR'S
15 LEADING HEAVY DRINKERS
OF THE 20TH CENTURY

1. KING EDWARD VIII OF ENGLAND

Before and during the period of his abdication in December, 1936, he drank brandy and soda—so much, once, that it was necessary to use a stomach pump on him.

2. DOUGLAS FAIRBANKS

The swashbuckling film star of *The Thief of Bagdad* drank more as he grew older. "One does not remain America's leading juvenile forever," wrote Sinclair. "Cocktails may nelp one regain the feeling, but not the fact."

3. EDNA ST. VINCENT MILLAY

Winner of the Pulitzer prize for her lyrical poetry in 1923, when she was 31. According to Sinclair, she was a steady drinker. He once watched her empty a flask of strong stuff.

U.S. poet Edna St. Vincent Millay (1892–1950).

4. JOAQUIN MILLER

On a visit from California to England, where his poetry had been well received, Miller, in sombrero and riding boots, bit the ankles of English debutantes, smoked three cigars at once, and announced that "the source of his inspiration was whiskey."

5. AMBROSE BIERCE

One of America's leading journalists, he disappeared in Mexico in 1913. He called himself "an eminent tankardman."

6. MAXWELL BODENHEIM

His shocking novels brought him passing fame. In 1954, he was murdered in his Bowery apartment. Wrote Sinclair: "He lived in an alcoholic glory."

7. SHERWOOD ANDERSON

His short stories made him a literary giant. In later years, he confessed he could only write "when I am slightly under the influence of strong drink." In 1941—after swallowing a toothpick at a cocktail party—he died of peritonitis on an ocean liner bound for Brazil.

8. THEODORE DREISER

He reached his literary peak in 1925 with *An American Tragedy*. Just before his death he embraced communism. Sinclair did not believe that Dreiser was an alcoholic, but rather a heavy drinker whose "perceptions were sometimes blurred by drink."

9. KLAUS MANN

The son of Thomas Mann, and himself author of a half-dozen books, he had a permanent acquaintance with "champagne, beer, and Scotch."

10. STEPHEN CRANE

With the publication of *The Red Badge of Courage* in 1895, he became famous. He married a Florida brothelkeeper. Wrote Sinclair: "He drank steadily."

11. EUGENE V. DEBS

Founder of the U.S. Socialist party, he ran for president of the U.S. five times, the last time while he was in jail for sedition. "So desperately a captive of alcohol!" Sinclair wrote of him.

12. FINLEY PETER DUNNE

He gained renown in 1898 when he created "Mr. Dooley," an Irish saloonkeeper, in the first of many humorous books. Wrote Sinclair: "Nor was it a mystery that his famous character was a saloonkeeper, for Dunne was a saloonkeeper's victim."

13. ISADORA DUNCAN

Liberated and flamboyant, she promoted expressionism in her modern dance performances. She had her first success in Budapest in 1903, later shocked Boston by dancing in the nude. Wrote Sinclair: "She became a dipsomaniac, struggling in vain against the need to drink."

14. GEORGE STERLING

Leader of an artists' colony in Carmel, Calif., he published 10 volumes of poetry. He committed suicide in 1926. Of Sterling's heavy drinking, H. L. Mencken wrote to Sinclair: "I am sure he got a great deal more fun out of alcohol than woe. It was his friend for many years and made life tolerable."

15. DONALD MACLEAN

A highly regarded member of the British Foreign Service, he was an espionage agent for the U.S.S.R. He was also a homosexual and an alcoholic. When he was suspected of espionage in 1951, he fled to the U.S.S.R., surfaced at a Kremlin press conference in 1956, and died shortly thereafter.

—Annotated by I.W.

SOURCE: Upton Sinclair, *The Cup of Fury* (New York: Channel Press, 1956).

GASTONE DE CAL'S
15 LEADING EUROPEAN BARTENDERS

For weary travelers seeking an oasis, here is a guide. Gastone De Cal, veteran barman at the Hotel Danieli Royal Excelsior in Venice, Italy, and onetime friend of Ernest Hemingway, has selected an all-star list of old world drink mixers. Cheers.

1. Ernst Bardof, Hotel Sacher, Vienna 1, Austria
2. Georges Broucke, Hotel Westbury, Brussels, Belgium
3. Michel Bigot, Bar Anglais, Hotel Plaza Athénée, Paris, France
4. C. A. Tuck, Cavendish Hotel, London, England
5. P. Brennan, Mayfair Hotel, London, England
6. J. G. van Hagen, Hotel Klein-Switzerland, Heelsum, Netherlands
7. Jerry Fitzpatrick, Gresham Hotel, Dublin, Ireland
8. Leif Solbu, Hotel Norum, Oslo 2, Norway
9. Felicio Batista Nogueira, Restaurante Caprilia, Lisbon, Portugal
10. Enrique Batsante, Bar Henry, Basilica 17, Madrid 20, Spain
11. Karl J. E. Davidsson, Hotel Skogshojd, Tppgatan 15-151, 33 Södertälje, Sweden
12. Alain Ostertag, Bar Restaurant Grill Chez Alain, Binninger str. 9, Basel, Switzerland
13. Emil Jankovic, Hotel Slon, Ljubljana, Yugoslavia
14. Osvaldo Lodola, Hotel Ambasciatori, Milan, Italy
15. Lotti Mauor, Grand Hotel, Rome, Italy

—Exclusive for *The Book of Lists*

10 PEOPLE WHO HAVE
TAKEN COCAINE

"It is the best stomachic after a debauch
either in eating or drinking."
—Dr. Sigmund Freud

1. Robert Louis Stevenson (1850–1894), Scottish essayist, novelist, poet
2. Dr. William Stewart Halsted (1852–1922), U.S. surgeon
3. Sigmund Freud (1856–1939), Austrian founder of psychoanalysis
4. A. Conan Doyle (1859–1930), English mystery writer
5. Aleister Crowley (1875–1947), English mystic, writer, eccentric
6. James Joyce (1882–1941), Irish writer
7. Wallace Reid (1892–1923), U.S. actor
8. Hermann Göering (1893–1946), German head of the Nazi air force
9. Mabel Normand (1894–1930), U.S. actress
10. Barbara La Marr (1896–1926), U.S. actress

5 PEOPLE WHO HAVE
TAKEN MARIANI WINE

A rare shot of Queen Victoria of England in a cheerful
mood. She took mariani wine for "medicinal purposes."

Mariani wine, a beverage made from the coca plant (from which cocaine is extracted), was once very popular for "medicinal" purposes.

1. Leo XIII (1810–1903), pope
2. Victoria (1819–1901), queen of England
3. William McKinley (1843–1901), U.S. president
4. Sarah Bernhardt (1844–1923), French actress
5. Thomas Edison (1847–1931), U.S. inventor

15 PEOPLE WHO HAVE TAKEN HASHISH OR MARIJUANA

"It sometimes happens that
your personality disappears . . ."
—Charles Baudelaire

1. Pythagoras (d. c. 497 B.C.), Greek philosopher, mathematician, and religious reformer
2. Victor Hugo (1802–1885), French writer
3. Théophile Gautier (1811–1872), French writer and critic
4. Charles Baudelaire (1821–1867), French poet
5. Fitz Hugh Ludlow (1836–1870), U.S. journalist
6. Stéphane Mallarmé (1842–1898), French poet
7. Friedrich Nietzsche (1844–1900), German philosopher
8. Alice B. Toklas (1877–1967), U.S. great and good friend of Gertrude Stein
9. Guillaume Apollinaire (1880–1918), French writer
10. Diego Rivera (1886–1957), Mexican painter
11. Mezz Mezzrow (1899–1972), U.S. jazz musician
12. Errol Flynn (1909–1959), U.S. actor
13. Gene Krupa (1909–1973), U.S. jazz musician
14. John F. Kennedy (1917–1963), U.S. president
15. Robert Mitchum (b. 1917), U.S. actor

8 PEOPLE WHO HAVE TAKEN HEROIN

"If you've beat the habit again
and kicked TV, no jail on earth
can worry you too much."
—Billie Holiday

1. Aleister Crowley (1875–1947), English mystic, writer, explorer, and cult figure
2. Alma Rubens (1897–1931), U.S. actress
3. William Burroughs (b. 1914), U.S. writer
4. Billie Holiday (1915–1959), U.S. blues singer
5. Charlie Parker (1920–1955), U.S. jazz musician
6. Lenny Bruce (1925–1966), U.S. humorist and writer
7. Stan Getz (b. 1927), U.S. jazz musician
8. Janis Joplin (1943–1970), U.S. rock singer

3 PEOPLE WHO HAVE TAKEN MORPHINE

1. Dr. William Stewart Halsted (1852–1922), father of U.S. surgery
2. Wallace Reid (1892–1923), U.S. actor
3. Hermann Göering (1893–1946), German head of the Nazi air force

Hermann Göering, Nazi morphine addict, was given
the title "marshal of the Reich" by Hitler.

13 PEOPLE WHO HAVE TAKEN LAUGHING GAS (NITROUS OXIDE)

"There are no differences but
differences of degree between degrees
of difference and no difference."
—William James, while on laughing gas

1. Thomas Wedgwood (1771–1805), English physicist
2. Samuel Taylor Coleridge (1772–1834), English poet
3. Robert Southey (1774–1843), English poet
4. Humphry Davy (1778–1829), English chemist
5. Peter Mark Roget (1779–1869), English physician and scholar, author of *Roget's Thesaurus*
6. Samuel Colt (1814–1862), U.S. inventor of Colt .45 revolver
7. William James (1842–1910), U.S. philosopher
8. Theodore Dreiser (1871–1945), U.S. novelist and editor
9. Winston Churchill (1874–1965), English statesman and author
10. Peter Ouspensky (1878–1947), Russian disciple of Gurdjieff
11. Allen Ginsberg (b. 1926), U.S. poet
12. Gregory Corso (b. 1930), U.S. poet
13. Ken Kesey (b. 1935), U.S. writer

14 PEOPLE WHO HAVE TAKEN LSD

"Such aids to perception are medicines, not diets,
and as the use of a medicine should lead on to
a more healthful mode of living, so the experiences
which I have described suggest measures we might
take to maintain a sounder form of sanity."
—Alan Watts

1. Clare Boothe Luce (b. 1903), U.S. writer, editor, ambassador
2. Anaïs Nin (1903–1977), French-U.S. writer and diarist
3. Adelle Davis (1904–1973), U.S. nutritionist, author
4. Cary Grant (b. 1904), English actor
5. Otto Preminger (b. 1906), U.S. movie producer
6. John Lilly (b. 1915), U.S. physician, investigator of dolphins and alternate consciousness
7. Alan Watts (1915–1973), English author and philosopher
8. Timothy Leary (b. 1920), U.S. educator, psychologist, writer
9. Allen Ginsberg (b. 1926), U.S. poet
10. Baba Ram Dass (Richard Alpert; b. 1931), U.S. psychologist, writer

11. Ken Kesey (b. 1935), U.S. writer
12. Peter Fonda (b. 1939), U.S. actor
13. Grace Slick (b. 1939), U.S. rock singer
14. John Lennon (b. 1940), English singer, composer

Adelle Davis, U.S. nutritionist, wrote about her
LSD experiences under the pseudonym Jane Dunlap.

16 PEOPLE WHO HAVE
TAKEN OPIUM (OR LAUDANUM)

"Certainly, no spasm of the heart or
marrow is comparable to the radiant
rape of the lungs by that black smoke."
—Claude Farrère

1. Paracelsus (1493–1541), Swiss physician and alchemist; father
   of medical pharmacology
2. Thomas Shadwell (1642?–1692), English poet laureate
3. George Crabbe (1754–1832), English poet

4. Samuel Taylor Coleridge (1772–1834), English poet
5. Thomas De Quincey (1785–1859), English author
6. Hector Berlioz (1803–1869), French composer
7. Edgar Allan Poe (1809–1849), U.S. short story writer
8. Charles Dickens (1812–1870), English novelist
9. Wilkie Collins (1824–1889), English novelist and mystery writer
10. Francis Thompson (1859–1907), English poet
11. Arthur Symons (1865–1945), English poet and critic
12. Claude Farrère (1876–1957), French naval officer and writer
13. Jean Cocteau (1889–1963), French author and filmmaker
14. Antonin Artaud (1896–1948), French writer and actor
15. Barbara La Marr (1896–1926), U.S. actress
16. Alexander King (1900–1965), U.S. writer and TV personality

15 PEOPLE WHO HAVE TAKEN PEYOTE OR MESCALINE

> ". . . everything shone with the Inner Light,
> and was infinite in its significance. The legs,
> for example, of that chair—how miraculous
> their tubularity, how supernatural their polished
> smoothness! I spent several minutes—or was
> it several centuries?—not merely gazing at those
> bamboo legs, but actually *being* them . . ."
> —Aldous Huxley

1. S. Weir Mitchell (1829–1914), U.S. neurologist and novelist; leading 19th-century brain surgeon
2. Havelock Ellis (1859–1939), English psychologist and writer
3. W. B. Yeats (1865–1939), Irish dramatist and poet
4. Hermann Hesse (1877–1962), German novelist and poet
5. Aldous Huxley (1894–1963), English novelist and critic
6. Antonin Artaud (1896–1948), French actor and writer
7. Henri Michaux (b. 1899), French writer and painter
8. Don Juan Mattus, Yaqui Indian shaman
9. John Blofeld (b. 1913), Buddhist scholar
10. Alan Watts (1915–1973), English author and philosopher
11. Jack Kerouac (1922–1969), U.S. writer
12. Neal Cassady (1924–1968), U.S. writer and "beat generation" personality
13. Allen Ginsberg (b. 1926), U.S. poet and eccentric
14. Carlos Castaneda (b. 1935), U.S. anthropologist and writer
15. Hunter S. Thompson (b. 1939), U.S. journalist

—A.W. & J.BER. (with the cooperation
of the Fitz Hugh Ludlow Memorial Library,
San Francisco, Calif., in all nine of these lists)

THE 10 TOP-SELLING
PRESCRIPTION DRUGS IN THE U.S.

Ampicillin and tetracycline are generic names. All other drugs included on this list are brand names of drugs manufactured by specific companies.

1. VALIUM®

Prescribed as a tranquilizer for mild anxiety.

2. PREMARIN®

A mixture of naturally occurring estrogens most commonly prescribed for menopausal symptoms.

3. AMPICILLIN*

A broad-spectrum antibiotic commonly used in treating urinary tract infections; respiratory symptoms or bronchitis in chronic lung disease patients; and infections in children (particularly ear infections).

4. LASIX®

A potent diuretic (a drug that increases the discharge of urine, and thus the loss of body water) prescribed especially for patients with congestive heart failure and high blood pressure.

5. TETRACYCLINE HCl*

A broad-spectrum antibiotic prescribed for chronic bronchitis; acne; cholera; and gonorrhea (as an alternative to penicillin when the patient is allergic to penicillin).

6. DARVON COMPOUND-65®

A mild analgesic (painkiller) prescribed for a large variety of illnesses.

7. LIBRIUM®

A mild tranquilizer prescribed for mild anxiety or disabling neuroses.

8. EMPIRIN COMPOUND WITH CODEINE®

An analgesic (painkiller) that contains codeine (a narcotic). Prescribed for pain for everything from a toothache to an infected toe or finger.

9. V-CILLIN K®

An oral penicillin V most commonly prescribed for streptococcal sore throats and for streptococcal and pneumococcal middle-ear infections.

10. ALDOMET®

In conjunction with a diuretic, commonly prescribed for the treatment of high blood pressure.

*Both tetracycline and ampicillin are sometimes prescribed for viral infections on which they have no effect.

—P.D.L.

11 FAMOUS TOBACCO SMOKERS

1. WINSTON CHURCHILL (British prime minister)

Rationed himself to 15 cigars a day. He once wrote, "How can I tell that my temper would have been as sweet or my companionship as agreeable if I had adjured from my youth the Goddess of Nicotine?"

2. SIGMUND FREUD (Austrian founder of psychoanalysis)

Smoked as many as 20 cigars a day and continued to do so even after he developed cancer of the jaw and palate.

3. FREDERICK WILLIAM (king of Prussia)

Smoked as much as 32 pipefuls of tobacco each night.

4. ULYSSES S. GRANT (Civil War general and U.S. president)

Smoked 24 cigars on second day of the battle of the Wilderness. After his victory at Fort Donelson in 1862, he was presented with 11,000 cigars.

5. RODRIGO DE JÉREZ (Spanish explorer)

Often credited as the first European to smoke tobacco. Described by his wife as a man who "swallows fire, exhales smoke, and is surely possessed by the devil."

6. CHARLES LAMB (English essayist and critic)

When asked how he became such an avid pipe smoker, Lamb replied: "I toiled after it, sir, as some men toil after virtue."

7. THOMAS R. MARSHALL (vice-president under Woodrow Wilson)

Noted cigar smoker who coined the famous phrase, "What this country needs is a really good 5¢ cigar."

8. SIR ISAAC NEWTON (English philosopher and mathematician)

Smoked a pipe. It is reported that he once absentmindedly used his fiancée's finger as a tobacco stopper.

9. SIR WALTER RALEIGH (English navigator and historian)

A passionate pipe smoker, Raleigh is said to have been doused with water by a servant who believed that his master was on fire.

Raleigh even "took a pipe of tobacco a little before he went to the scaffold."

10. MRS. ZACHARY TAYLOR (wife of the 12th U.S. president)

Often smoked a pipe in private inside the White House.

11. MARK TWAIN (U.S. author and humorist)

Smoked cigars. Claimed that quitting was easy—he had "done it 100 times."

—D.B. & The Eds.

Mark Twain enjoying a few puffs on the porch.

THE LEAST DEADLY CIGARETTES: 10 DOMESTIC CIGARETTES WITH THE LOWEST TAR CONTENT

		Type	Tar (mg/cigarette)
1.	Carlton 70's	Regular, filter	<0.5
2.	Carlton	King, filter, menthol	1
2.	Carlton	King, filter	1
2.	Now	King, filter, menthol (hard pack)	1
2.	Now	King, filter (hard pack)	1
6.	True	King, filter	5
7.	True	King, filter, menthol	6
8.	Pall Mall Extra Mild	King, filter (hard pack)	7
8.	King Sano	King, filter, menthol	7
8.	King Sano	King, filter	7

SOURCE: Federal Trade Commission: *Report of "Tar" and Nicotine Content of the Smoke of 169 Varieties of Cigarettes.* November, 1976.

11 DOMESTIC CIGARETTES WITH THE LOWEST NICOTINE CONTENT

	Type	Nicotine (mg/cigarette)
1. Carlton 70's	Regular, filter	<0.05
2. Carlton	King, filter, menthol	0.1
2. Carlton	King, filter	0.1
2. Now	King, filter, menthol (hard pack)	0.1
2. Now	King, filter (hard pack)	0.1
6. King Sano	King, filter, menthol	0.3
7. King Sano	King, filter	0.4
7. True	King, filter	0.4
7. True	King, filter, menthol	0.4
10. Merit	King, filter	0.5
10. Merit	King, filter, menthol	0.5

SOURCE: Federal Trade Commission: *Report of "Tar" and Nicotine Content of the Smoke of 169 Varieties of Cigarettes.* November, 1976.

THE DEADLIEST CIGARETTES: 10 DOMESTIC CIGARETTES WITH THE HIGHEST TAR CONTENT

	Type	Tar (mg/cigarette)
1. Players	Regular, non-filter (hard pack)	32
2. Domino	King, non-filter	31
3. Bull Durham	King, filter	30
4. English Ovals	King, non-filter (hard pack)	29
5. Herbert Tareyton	King, non-filter	28
5. Fatima	King, non-filter	28
5. Chesterfield	King, non-filter	28
8. Stratford	King, non-filter	27
8. Mapleton	Regular, non-filter	27
10. Lucky Strike	King, filter	26

SOURCE: Federal Trade Commission: *Report of "Tar" and Nicotine Content of the Smoke of 169 Varieties of Cigarettes.* November, 1976.

12 DOMESTIC
CIGARETTES WITH THE
HIGHEST NICOTINE CONTENT

	Type	Nicotine (mg/cigarette)
1. Players	Regular, non-filter (hard pack)	2.2
2. English Ovals	King, non-filter (hard pack)	2.0
3. Bull Durham	King, filter	1.9
4. Half & Half	King, filter	1.8
4. Herbert Tareyton	King, non-filter	1.8
6. Lucky Strike	King, filter	1.6
6. Fatima	King, non-filter	1.6
6. Chesterfield	King, non-filter	1.6
6. English Ovals	Regular, non-filter (hard pack)	1.6
6. Dawn	120 mm, filter, menthol	1.6
6. Pall Mall	King, non-filter	1.6
6. More	120 mm, filter, menthol	1.6

SOURCE: Federal Trade Commission: *Report of "Tar" and Nicotine Content of the Smoke of 169 Varieties of Cigarettes.* November, 1976.

10 COUNTRIES
WHERE THE HIGHEST PERCENT
OF MEN AND WOMEN DIE
BEFORE THE AGE OF 50

MEN	%	WOMEN	%
1. Guinea	76.2	1. Guinea	74.1
2. Togo	68.3	2. Upper Volta	64.7
3. Central African Empire	66.0	3. Ivory Coast	64.5
		4. Central African Empire	61.1
4. Upper Volta	64.6		
5. Ivory Coast	64.5	5. Cameroon	58.9
6. Cameroon	61.3	6. Nigeria	58.5
7. Zaire	59.1	7. Benin	57.8
8. Burundi	58.8	8. India	57.3
9. Benin	57.8	8. Togo	57.3
10. Nigeria	57.4	10. Burundi	56.55

SOURCE: *United Nations Demographic Yearbook 1974.*

10 COUNTRIES
WHERE THE HIGHEST PERCENT
OF MEN AND WOMEN LIVE
TO BE 85 YEARS OLD

MEN	%	WOMEN	%
1. Puerto Rico	21.6	1. Puerto Rico	33.7
2. Iceland	19.1	2. Canada	33.6
3. Albania	17.9	3. Sweden	33.3
3. Sweden	17.9	4. Netherlands	32.0
5. Norway	17.3	5. Norway	31.8
6. Netherlands	16.9	6. France	31.6
6. Denmark	16.9	7. U.S.	30.8
8. Canada	16.3	8. Denmark	30.5
8. Israel	16.3	9. Bermuda	30.4
10. Greece	14.7	10. Hong Kong	30.3

SOURCE: *United Nations Demographic Yearbook 1974.*

16 OF THE OLDEST
PEOPLE IN THE WORLD

1. ZARO AGHA

He died in an Istanbul hospital on June 29, 1934, at the alleged age of 164 years. Claimed to be the oldest man in the world at that time. He worked as a porter for over a century and became a father for the last time at the age of 90.

2. THOMAS PARR ("Old Parr")

Was born in the parish of Alberbury, in Shropshire, England. Lived through the reigns of 10 English monarchs, and died on November 13, 1635, at the reputed age of 152. A simple peasant, Parr attained fame in his later years: He had his portrait painted by both Rubens and Vandyke and was presented at the court of Charles I. He is buried in Westminster Abbey.

3. MAHMUD EIVAZOV

Resident of Azerbaijan, a Caucasian republic in the U.S.S.R. Reportedly celebrated his 150th birthday in 1958. The Soviet government claimed that he was the world's oldest man. Eivazov, who did not learn to write until he was 100 years old, had a daughter said to be aged 123 and three sons who were centenarians.

4. MOHAMMED KHALIL ABDUL HAWA

Resident of Jerusalem. In 1957, when he celebrated his 136th birthday, he was reputed to be the oldest man in the Middle East.

5. GABRIEL SÁNCHEZ

At the presumed age of 135 he was among the oldest of the inhabitants of the Valley of Vilcabamba (in southeastern Ecuador). He was studied by a group of scientists who were doing research on longevity a few years ago. Still active, Sánchez continued working as a farmer—an occupation he claimed he had followed for 120 years.

6. MITCHELL WATKINS

Brought to America from Liberia as a slave when he was 12 years old, he lived to become the oldest man in the U.S. Renamed Charles Smith—after the rancher who owned him—he celebrated his 134th birthday on July 4, 1976.

7. KHFAF LASURIA

Resident of the Soviet republic of Abkhasia. A member of a troupe of performers, he was still an active dancer at the age of 131, in 1972, according to the Soviets.

8. GABRIEL ERAZO

A resident of the Vilcabamba Valley in Ecuador, where one person in every hundred claims to be a centenarian, still continued to do a full day's work in his garden at the age of 130 in 1973.

9. OSMAN BZHENIYA

Resident of the village of Lykhny in Abkhasia, in the U.S.S.R., in 1973 still continued to work part-time on a collective farm at the alleged age of 120.

10. TATZUMBIE DUPEA

Paiute Indian whose name means "Beautiful Star," died in February, 1970, at the reputed age of 120. He was born near Pine Hills, Calif., in 1849.

11. CHIEF RED CLOUD

A Sioux Indian who died at Steubenville, O., in the fall of 1962. Claimed to be 120 years old. As a young man he traveled with Buffalo Bill's Wild West show.

12. MRS. HARRY HARRISON MORAN

The oldest surviving widow of a veteran of the American Civil War, she was still receiving a pension in March, 1974, just two months before her presumed 118th birthday.

13. GEORGE FRUITS

Fought in the American Revolution, died at Alamo, Ind., on August 6, 1876, at the reputed age of 114 years.

14. MRS. DELINA FILKINS

Resident of Herkimer County, N.Y. Reached the greatest age of any human authenticated by birth records, dying on December 4, 1928, at the age of 113 years 214 days.

15. CAESAR PAUL

An Algonquin Indian, believed to be the oldest Canadian, died in Pembroke, Ont., Canada, on July 25, 1975, at the age of 112 years 103 days.

16. ALFRED ARNOLD

Britain's oldest bachelor and a practicing yogi, died in Liverpool on September 15, 1941, at the reported age of 112.

—R.S.C.

DR. DAVID DAVIES'S
10 TIPS FOR LONGEVITY

Dr. David Davies, of the Gerontological Unit of University College, London, spent two years studying the life-style and genetic make-up of the people of Vilcabamba, Ecuador, one of the longest-living groups of persons in the world. He summarized his findings in his book *The Centenarians of the Andes*. Other books by Dr. Davies include *A Dictionary of Anthropology* and *The Influence of Teeth, Diet, and Habits on the Human Face*.

1. Keep working steadily after retirement, that is if you have to retire.
2. Have absorbing hobbies to take over your mental activity after retirement.
3. Don't talk about growing old. Try to avoid those who are depressed about it.
4. Drink and smoke in moderation—if at all.
5. Get plenty of natural sleep.
6. Avoid all forms of stress—at least learn to cope with stress if unavoidable.
7. Don't worry about your children.
8. Walk at least 1 mi. a day as this is the best form of exercise. Gardening is good exercise too.
9. Eat as little meat as possible.
10. Eat as much raw food, and as little processed food, as possible.

—Exclusive for *The Book of Lists*

18
GUESS WHO'S
COMING TO DINNER

THE 13 GUESTS
AT THE LAST SUPPER

In Jerusalem it was just before the Passover, and Jesus Christ asked, "Where is the guestchamber, where I shall eat the Passover with my disciples?" An unknown host invited the party to celebrate the Seder in the upper floor of his building. Jesus and his party settled down to a dining table. There were the bitter herbs, the unleavened bread, and then the cup—to be known as the Holy Grail—and he said, "Drink ye all of it; for this is my blood of the new testament, which is shed for many . . ." It was the night of his betrayal. The Bible does not name each guest at the supper, nor does it mention the seating arrangement. It was left to Leonardo da Vinci, in 1498 when he painted *The Last Supper,* to depict the guests who attended, and to indicate where they sat (from left to right).

1. Bartholomew
2. James the Less
3. Andrew
4. Judas Iscariot
5. Peter
6. John
7. Jesus Christ
8. James the Elder
9. Thomas
10. Philip
11. Matthew
12. Thaddeus (Jude)
13. Simon

The passover feast known as the Last Supper,
depicted live in the Oberammergau passion play.

JAMES AGATE'S
11 FAVORITE DINNER GUESTS
FROM ALL HISTORY

If you had the choice of all the people in history, which 11 would you invite to dinner? James Agate, one of London's most influential drama critics and author of a nine-volume diary called *Ego*, made a journal entry in 1938 that listed the 11 persons he would have most enjoyed dining with.

1. Cheops
2. Hannibal
3. [Richard] Burbage
4. The captain [Benjamin Spooner] of the *Marie Celeste*
5. Elizabeth's Essex
6. Gilles de Rais
7. Marquis de Sade
8. Casanova
9. Billy the Kid
10. Sir Edward Marshall-Hall
11. Sir Bernard Spilsbury

Agate added a paragraph of explanation: "The point is that the first four would solve the world's four greatest mysteries: how the pyramids were built, the reason for the halt at Cannae, who wrote Shakespeare's plays, and what happened to that ship found in the middle of a dead-calm ocean with not a soul on board and the table laid for a meal. I would have included Mrs. [Julia] Wallace, the victim [in 1931] in the best of all murder cases, the Liverpool murder, but for the possibility that she was struck from behind and did not see her assailant. [Her husband, William Herbert Wallace, was accused of being her assailant, tried, found guilty, freed on appeal.] The choice of Essex is obvious. Billy the Kid was a Mexican bandit [born in New York City, sometimes operated in Mexico], was gunned down in New Mexico] with more romance about him than your Chicago gangster."

If you haven't met all of Agate's guests, here is an introduction: Richard Burbage was a friend of Shakespeare's and acted in his plays; the 2nd earl of Essex was the favorite lover of the aging Queen Elizabeth I; Gilles de Rais (or Retz) was the original Bluebeard who was executed in 1440; Sir Edward Marshall-Hall was one of England's most flamboyant and eloquent barristers and criminal defense attorneys; Sir Bernard Spilsbury dominated forensic pathology in England for three decades and helped hang Dr. Crippen.

SOURCE: James Agate, *The Selective Ego* (London: Harrap, 1976).

WILLIAM MANCHESTER'S
10 FAVORITE DINNER GUESTS
FROM ALL HISTORY

Journalist, educator, and biographer William Manchester was chosen by the Kennedy family to prepare an authorized version describing the assassination of President John F. Kennedy. Although a dispute developed as the result of differences between Mr. Manchester and the Kennedy family, a compromise was reached and the book, *The Death of a President*, became an international best seller. Other best sellers by this author include *The Arms of Krupp, The Glory and the Dream*, and *Controversy*.

1. Isaac Newton
2. Elizabeth Tudor
3. Sigmund Freud
4. Emma Hamilton
5. George Bernard Shaw

6. Oscar Wilde
7. Napoleon Bonaparte
8. Jane Austen
9. Johann Wolfgang Goethe
10. H. L. Mencken

—Exclusive for *The Book of Lists*

ARTHUR KOESTLER'S 10 FAVORITE DINNER GUESTS FROM ALL HISTORY

Internationally acclaimed author Arthur Koestler is renowned for his fiction, as well as his political and scientific essays. In 1968, he was awarded the Sooning prize at the University of Copenhagen for his contribution to European culture. The most famous of Mr. Koestler's books, *Darkness at Noon*, has been translated into 33 languages. Other books by this interdisciplinary writer include *Arrival and Departure, The Invisible Writing, The Act of Creation, Drinkers of Infinity*, and *The 13th Tribe*.

1. Pharaoh Akhenaten
2. King Solomon
3. Queen Cleopatra
4. Lucius Lucinius Lucullus
5. Genghis Khan

6. Martin Luther
7. Benjamin Franklin
8. Madame de Pompadour
9. Georges-Jacques Danton
10. Benjamin Disraeli

—Exclusive for *The Book of Lists*

FAWN M. BRODIE'S 10 FAVORITE DINNER GUESTS FROM ALL HISTORY

A graduate of the University of Utah, Fawn M. Brodie is well known for her in-depth biography *Thaddeus Stevens, Scourge of the South*, her account of Mormon prophet Joseph Smith entitled *No*

Man Knows My History, and her best-selling *Jefferson: An Intimate Biography*. She is currently teaching at the University of California at Los Angeles, and is engaged in writing a biography of Richard M. Nixon.

1. Jesus
2. William Shakespeare
3. Queen Elizabeth
4. Thomas Jefferson
5. Sally Hemings
6. Aaron Burr
7. Abraham Lincoln
8. Joseph Smith
9. Sir Richard Francis Burton
10. Richard Nixon

Sally Hemings was a slave at Monticello, Thomas Jefferson's home in Virginia. Jefferson's love for her spanned 38 years, and he was probably the father of some, if not all, of her seven children. Jefferson never issued either a private or public denial of their relationship. She outlived Jefferson by nine years and died at the age of 62 in 1835.

Fawn Brodie adds: "My choice is prompted by the mysteries, the still unanswered questions, in the lives of these 10 people."

—Exclusive for *The Book of Lists*

At the age of 24, Joseph Smith founded the Mormon Church. He introduced polygamy, and himself had 49 wives. While he was a candidate for U.S. president in 1844, he was lynched in Illinois.

ART BUCHWALD'S
11 FAVORITE DINNER GUESTS
FROM ALL HISTORY

Author, humorist, and syndicated columnist, Art Buchwald is renowned for his satires based on front-page stories. His column appears in over 500 newspapers throughout the world. He has published many books, including *And Then I Told the President*, *Washington Is Leaking*, and *I Am Not a Crook*.

1. Richard Nixon
2. John Wilkes Booth
3. Jack the Ripper
4. Adolf Hitler
5. Lizzie Borden
6. Nero
7. Joseph Stalin
8. Judas
9. Mao Tse-tung
10. Cain
11. Marquis de Sade

Buchwald adds: "I know I would have a seating problem, but I believe the conversation would be quite interesting and certainly worth a decent Château Mouton-Rothschild. How would I pay for the meal? I'd sell the pictorial rights to *Family Circle*."

—Exclusive for *The Book of Lists*

LEO ROSTEN'S
12 FAVORITE DINNER GUESTS
FROM ALL HISTORY

A popular lecturer known for his wit and humor, Leo Rosten received his doctorate from the University of Chicago and is an Honorary Fellow of the London School of Economics and Political Science. In addition to teaching, Rosten has worked as a motion picture writer. He is the author of such books as *The Education of Hyman Kaplan*, *Hollywood: The Movie Colony*, *The Joys of Yiddish*, and *Dear Herm*, and he edited *The Look Book*.

1. Aristotle
2. Erasmus
3. Mme. de Staël
4. Mark Twain
5. Lady Mary Wortley Montagu
6. Winston Churchill
7. Leonardo da Vinci
8. Samuel Johnson
9. Catherine the Great
10. Voltaire
11. Edmund Burke
12. Thomas Jefferson

—Exclusive for *The Book of Lists*

DR. A. L. ROWSE'S
10 FAVORITE DINNER GUESTS
FROM ALL HISTORY

One of the most controversial of British scholars and biographers, A. L. Rowse is a fellow of All Souls College, Oxford. Among his many books are *Christopher Marlowe: A Biography*, *Shakespeare the Man*, and *The Elizabethan Renaissance: The Cultural Achievement*. He lives in Cornwall, England.

1. William Shakespeare
2. Queen Elizabeth I
3. Jonathan Swift
4. Marcel Proust
5. D. H. Lawrence

6. Colette
7. Sir Walter Raleigh
8. Henry James
9. Christopher Marlowe
10. Flannery O'Connor

—Exclusive for *The Book of Lists*

H. R. HALDEMAN'S
10 FAVORITE DINNER GUESTS
FROM ALL HISTORY

Educated at the University of California at Los Angeles and onetime regent of the University of California, H. R. "Bob" Haldeman became vice-president of the J. Walter Thompson advertising agency. He left that position to become campaign director for Richard M. Nixon in the latter's race for governor of California in 1962. After Nixon was elected president in 1968, Haldeman served as his special assistant and chief of staff. Implicated in the Watergate scandal, Haldeman resigned in April, 1973. Found guilty of conspiring to obstruct justice, Haldeman has appealed his case. He is president of his Christian Science church.

1. Abraham Lincoln
2. John Nicolay
3. Theodore Roosevelt
4. William Loeb
5. Grigori Efimovich

6. Woodrow Wilson
7. E. M. House
8. Franklin D. Roosevelt
9. Harry Hopkins
10. Niccolò Machiavelli

Haldeman's dinner guests are all presidents of the U.S. and their aides, as well as behind-the-scenes figures in the lives of other rulers. John Nicolay was private secretary to President Lincoln and his biographer. William Loeb was President Theodore Roosevelt's chief of staff and father of the controversial present-day New Hampshire newspaper publisher. Edward M. House was President Wilson's close friend, adviser, and informal diplomatic representative. Harry

418

Hopkins was President Franklin D. Roosevelt's right-hand man. Grigori and Efimovich were the first and middle names of Rasputin (1872?–1916), the notorious Russian holy man whose influence over Czarina Alexandra gave him power over Czar Nicholas II and the nation itself. Machiavelli was, of course, the Italian statesman— under Cesare Borgia during the Renaissance—who wielded subtle and devious power.

—Exclusive for *The Book of Lists*

PETER QUENNELL'S 10 FAVORITE DINNER GUESTS FROM ALL HISTORY

An eminent English biographer, critic, and poet, Peter Quennell was educated at Balliol College, Oxford. He edited *Cornhill Magazine*, and presently is joint editor of *History Today*. His books are read worldwide, among them *Byron: The Years of Fame, Baudelaire and the Symbolists, Byron in Italy, Ruskin: The Portrait of a Prophet*, and *Samuel Johnson: His Friends and Enemies*.

1. John Wilkes
2. Charles James Fox
3. William Hickey
4. Casanova
5. Mirabeau
6. Beau Brummell
7. Byron
8. Madame de Staël
9. Sydney Smith
10. Talleyrand

William Hickey (1749–1830?) was an Anglo-Irish memoirist whose autobiography, *The Prodigal Rake*, has been widely acclaimed as a masterpiece of self-revelation.

—Exclusive for *The Book of Lists*

VINCENT PRICE'S 10 FAVORITE DINNER GUESTS FROM ALL HISTORY

Star of both stage and screen, Vincent Price is best known for his villainous roles in such horror film favorites as *The House of Wax, The Pit and the Pendulum*, and *The House of Usher*. Price is also an admired patron of the arts and noted gourmet. He is the coauthor, with his former wife Mary, of two cookbooks, *A Treasury of Great Recipes* and *The Vincent and Mary Price Cookbook*.

1. Socrates (profound—needs to be brought out)
2. George Bernard Shaw (profoundly witty—remember, he's a vegetarian)
3. Oscar Wilde (wise and witty—will eat anything)
4. James McNeill Whistler (witty and wise—picky eater)
5. Noel Coward (kind, witty and wise and funny—fastidious)
6. Coral Browne (my wife—witty and sly—a good eater)
7. Tallulah Bankhead (sly, delightful, and loud—liquid diet)
8. Diana Rigg (beautiful—loves good food and men)
9. Any of the D'Este or Borgia girls (these girls make you remember what you've eaten—you'd better remember or you may never forget)
10. Lorenzo de' Medici (you need a title—especially when backed up with taste and money. Besides, he dresses so well! And he has the perfect nose to look down if anyone gets out of line—and most of them will by dessert)

Vincent Price adds: "The wine should preferably be from a recently discovered Greek amphora in the sea. If not, Californian will do or South African."

British playwright and wit Oscar Wilde lounging after dinner.

THE MENU

1. *Hors d'oeuvres:* caviar straight with aquavit—maybe onion and egg
2. *Soup du jour:* depending on the day—vegetable broth for George Bernard Shaw
3. *Salad:* celeriac in remoulade
4. *Main course:* swan stuffed with goose, which is in turn stuffed with duck, veal, and finally larks. Or roast bison with very wild rice. Or, if weather permits—braised antelope

5. *Vegetables:* everything in season for George Bernard Shaw
6. *Cheeses:* Brie, Camembert, and Walnut Gourmandise
7. *Fruits:* Chinese gooseberries, guavas, passion fruits, mangoes, peaches, mandarin oranges, papayas, etc., etc., etc. The fruits surround a figure of the host or hostess carved in ice. Or a nude ice carving of Socrates (should be a conversation piece . . . what for?)
8. *Haitian coffee,* or *Turkish sweet*
9. *Hemlock*
10. *B. & B. . . .* or *B. or B.*
11. *Haitian rum:* served in sugar cane

—Exclusive for *The Book of Lists*

BEVERLEY NICHOLS'S
10 FAVORITE DINNER GUESTS
FROM ALL HISTORY

After attending Balliol College, British author Beverley Nichols began writing books and has never stopped. Some of his successes

Mary Baker Eddy, discoverer and founder of Christian Science.

include *The Star-Spangled Manner, Evensong, Cry Havoc! A Case of Human Bondage,* and *Down the Kitchen Sink.* Also a composer and playwright, he has had eight of his shows staged.

1. Tolstoy
2. Karl Marx
3. Doctor Johnson
4. Oscar Wilde
5. Voltaire
6. Pasteur
7. Florence Nightingale
8. Mary Baker Eddy
9. Chopin
10. Toulouse-Lautrec

Nichols adds: "The dinner party would be, to some extent, a party of opposites, Tolstoy would certainly strike sparks off Karl Marx, Wilde would be a match for Johnson, Pasteur would be violently irritated by Mary Baker Eddy, etc. It would probably end in tears, but Chopin might bring it to a harmonious conclusion and Toulouse-Lautrec could record it for posterity."

—Exclusive for *The Book of Lists*

W. A. SWANBERG'S
10 FAVORITE DINNER GUESTS
FROM ALL HISTORY

Winner of the Pulitzer prize in nonfiction, W. A. Swanberg is the author of such notable biographies as *Sickles the Incredible, Citizen Hearst, Dreiser,* and *Luce and His Empire.*

1. Attila
2. Henry VIII
3. Cesare Borgia
4. Hitler
5. Nero
6. Heliogabalus
7. Rasputin
8. Machiavelli
9. Jack the Ripper
10. Dr. Henry Kissinger

—Exclusive for *The Book of Lists*

JOHN TOLAND'S
10 FAVORITE DINNER GUESTS
FROM ALL HISTORY

A best-selling author and historian, John Toland is renowned for such books as *The Last 100 Days, The Battle of the Bulge,* and *Hitler.* His book *The Rising Sun* won a Pulitzer prize in nonfiction in 1970.

1. Jesus
2. Marx
3. Marco Polo
4. Gandhi
5. Marat
6. Napoleon
7. Ben Franklin
8. Cromwell
9. Disraeli
10. Lenin

Toland adds: "For coffee—I'd like to talk to Hitler—but not while I'm eating."

—Exclusive for *The Book of Lists*

MARY HEMINGWAY'S
10 FAVORITE DINNER GUESTS
FROM ALL HISTORY

Former war correspondent and journalist, Mary Hemingway gave up her writing career to become the fourth and final wife of novelist Ernest Hemingway. What was it like being married to the Nobel prizewinning author? That is what she recorded in her new book, *How It Was*.

1. William Shakespeare
2. Alexander the Great
3. Lady Mary Wortley Montagu
4. Karl von Clausewitz
5. Goya
6. Pëtr Ilich Tchaikovsky
7. Dr. Samuel Johnson
8. Eleanor Roosevelt
9. Robert Benchley
10. Ernest Hemingway

—Exclusive for *The Book of Lists*

DAVID WALLECHINSKY'S
10 FAVORITE DINNER GUESTS
FROM ALL HISTORY

David Wallechinsky is the coauthor of five books, including *Chico's Organic Gardening and Natural Living*, *The People's Almanac*, and *The Book of Lists*. His favorite foods are mangoes, fresh berries, and ice cream.

1. Gautama, the Buddha
2. Percy Bysshe Shelley
3. Leo Tolstoy
4. Mohandas K. Gandhi
5. George Bernard Shaw
6. Pythagoras
7. Lao-tzu
8. John Muir
9. Leonardo da Vinci
10. Henry David Thoreau

Adds Wallechinsky: "Because I cook only vegetarian meals, I have invited only people who were confirmed vegetarians at some time in their lives. If fictional characters accepted dinner invitations as readily as deceased real people, I would add one more vegetarian to my list—Dr. Dolittle."

IRVING WALLACE'S
12 FAVORITE DINNER GUESTS
FROM ALL HISTORY

Irving Wallace's books have sold over 100 million copies worldwide. Among his best-selling novels are *The Prize*, *The Man*, and *The R Document*. He is one of the authors of *The Book of Lists*.

1. Cleopatra
2. George Gordon, Lord Byron
3. Samuel Johnson
4. Richard Francis Burton
5. Abraham Lincoln
6. Oscar Wilde
7. Giovanni Giacomo Casanova
8. Dr. Joseph Bell
9. Alexandre Dumas père
10. Victoria Woodhull
11. Daniel Defoe
12. Charles Fort

Adds Wallace: "Perhaps three of my guests need an introduction to the others. A. Conan Doyle studied under Dr. Joseph Bell at Edinburgh, and it was the deductive genius of Bell that inspired the creation of Sherlock Holmes. Victoria Woodhull, who advocated free love and birth control, ran for president of the U.S. in 1872. Charles Fort, a strange and brilliant American eccentric who died in 1932, collected phenomena that science could not explain and authored such works as *The Book of the Damned* and *Lo!*"

U.S. author Charles Fort collected and recorded
unusual events that scientists could not explain. Among his
admirers were Theodore Dreiser, Ben Hecht, Tiffany Thayer.

AMY WALLACE'S
13 FAVORITE DINNER GUESTS
FROM ALL HISTORY (POTLUCK)

Amy Wallace is a coauthor of *The Two* and *The Book of Lists*.

1. Arthur Rimbaud
2. James Dean
3. Emma Goldman
4. Jesus Christ
5. Oscar Wilde
6. Hassan i Sabbah

7. James Thurber
8-9. Violet and Daisy Hilton
10. Ezra Pound
11. Aleister Crowley
12. D. D. Home
13. Lao-tzu

Hassan i Sabbah was the founder of the Bavarian Illuminati, a bizarre anarchist cult. Violet and Daisy Hilton were a Siamese twin vaudeville act. D. D. Home was a 19th century British psychic and medium.

James Dean for dinner.

10 PEOPLE NOT
TO INVITE TO DINNER

1. ALFERD PACKER

Alferd Packer was the only person in U.S. history ever to be convicted of cannibalism. On February 9, 1874, he and five mining companions set out on a 75-mi. trek across the Rockies. On April 16, Packer arrived alone at the destination, the Los Pinos Ute Agency. Those at the agency pressured Packer into a confession and he offered several, finally insisting that cotraveler Shannon Wilson Bell had killed the others and that he, in turn, killed Bell in self-defense. Then, to stay alive for two months in temperatures that often fell to −50°F., he ate the flesh of his dead companions. Packer served 17 years in prison but died a free man at age 65 in 1907. In May, 1968, the student body of the University of Colorado voted to name the new grill room in their cafeteria "Alferd Packer Grill."

2. MARY MALLON

She was better known as "Typhoid Mary" because her body was loaded with typhoid. She was the first carrier of the contagious disease in American history. She was a walking epidemic. From 1906 to 1915, she worked as a cook in the New York City area, and the food she touched infected many of the people who ate it. She was responsible for 54 persons' contracting typhoid: three of them died and some of the survivors passed the disease on to others. She refused to be treated, refused to be confined to hospitals, until she was finally arrested and isolated on North Brother Island. She died in 1938 at the age of 70—not from typhoid but from a stroke.

3. EUGÈNE-MARIE CHANTRELLE

A language teacher in Edinburgh, he seduced a 15-year-old schoolgirl in his art class and married her when she became pregnant. In 1877, after insuring her for £5,000 against accidental death, he poisoned her with a good-night drink of lemon juice made lethal by the addition of opium. The next morning he contrived a gas pipe and filled the bedroom with gas before he called the police. Dr. Joseph Bell, the original of Sherlock Holmes, found a trace of her saliva on her pillow which showed the lemon drink had been the source of the opium poison. Chantrelle cheerfully went to the gallows.

4. GABRIELE D'ANNUNZIO

The Italian author, lover, and military leader claimed that he had once eaten a roasted baby and drunk wine from the skull of a virgin. He died in 1938.

5. MARY BLANDY

In 1751, finding her married lover unacceptable to her father, she persuaded the lover to supply her with a love philter to change her parent's mind. As a letter she wrote showed, she knew the powder to be arsenic, and she used it in her father's tea. "Gentlemen," she said on the scaffold, "do not hang me high, for the sake of decency."

6. FRITZ HAARMANN

He was a food smuggler in Hanover, Germany, immediately after W.W. I, when the country was suffering famine. In 1919 he found a new way of getting meat out on the black market. He murdered 28 persons—possibly 50—between the ages of 13 and 20, dismembered them, and sold the meat as sausages. He was caught in 1924 and, after a two-week trial, was sentenced to death by decapitation.

7. SAWNEY BEANE

This 15th-century Scottish cannibal lived with his wife in a cave on the Galloway coast where they grew fat on the flesh of travelers unfortunate enough to pass within earshot of their home. Over the course of 25 years, the Beane clan grew to include 8 sons, 6 daughters, 18 grandsons, and 14 granddaughters—who would often hunt as a unit. By the time the law caught up with them in 1435, the Beanes had slaughtered and devoured over 1,000 people.

One person definitely *not* to invite for dinner. An American Kwatiutl Indian —member of the only known cannibal tribe to inhabit North America —enjoying an hors d'oeuvre. Photographed by Edward S. Curtis in 1910.

8. ALBERT FISH

An innocuous-looking house painter in New York City, he killed and ate at least 15 children. The last victim was a 10-year-old girl. After murdering her, he cooked her as a stew—with onions and carrots—and took nine days to consume her. Fish was arrested in 1934, tried, found guilty, and executed.

9. GEORGE HENRY LAMSON

In 1882, he poisoned his nephew (a cripple away at boarding school) by injecting a raisin with aconitine, inserting it in a slice of cake, and giving it to the boy under the eye of the headmaster. Sentenced to die on April 2, his execution was postponed on receipt of a cable from U.S. president Chester A. Arthur, but the execution was carried out 26 days later.

10. LEWIS KESEBERG

In 1846, he was a member of the George Donner party of 20 wagons heading into the U.S. West. The Donner party was overtaken by early snows in the High Sierras and forced to kill its cattle for food. Some members perished. Keseberg was one who survived. He was accused of murdering six members of the party and eating their flesh. While denying murder, Keseberg admitted to having indulged in cannibalism. He stated later: "It has been told that I boasted of my shame—said that I enjoyed this horrid food, and that I remarked human flesh was more palatable than California beef. This is a falsehood . . . This food was never otherwise than loathsome, insipid, and disgusting."

—I.W., B.F., J.BE., N.C.D., & D.W.

19
AH, SWEET MYSTERIES
OF LIFE

JEANE DIXON'S
10 GREATEST PSYCHICS
OF ALL TIME

The uncanny ability to predict accurately political and world-wide events has earned Jeane Dixon the title of "Seeress of Washington." Her recent books include *The Call to Glory* and *My Life and Prophecies*. Believing her psychic abilities to be divinely inspired, Ms. Dixon donates her earnings from books and lectures to the non-profit charity Children to Children.

1. John the Evangelist, writer of the Book of Revelation.
2. Gautama, the Buddha.
3. Isaiah the prophet, who foresaw the deliverance of Israel from Babylonian captivity and the restoration of Jerusalem to glory.
4. Pharaoh Amenhotep IV, called Akhnaton, who introduced monotheism—the worship of only one god—into ancient Egypt.
5. Simeon, priest of the temple of Jerusalem, and . . .
6. Anna, humble servant of the God of Israel. Together, they greeted the infant Jesus and his mother at the temple and hailed him as the deliverer of his people.
7. St. Theresa, an extraordinary mystic and one of the most forceful women in the history of Europe.
8. Nostradamus, seer of the Renaissance, whose views of the future are still studied for their insights into our time and ages yet to come.
9. Emanuel Swedenborg, philosopher and theologian of the 18th century, whose writings introduced millions to the realm of the spirit.
10. Leo Nikolaevich Tolstoy, the Russian novelist and mystic, whose search for truth and holiness prefigured that of Aleksandr Solzhenitsyn in our own day.

Jeane Dixon adds: "I suspect that some of the names I have chosen will come as surprises. I believe, however, that the designation 'psychic' must be used in its highest spiritual sense, rather than as it is sometimes popularly applied."

—Exclusive for *The Book of Lists*

RUTH MONTGOMERY'S
10 LEADING PSYCHICS
IN HISTORY

The winner of numerous journalism awards, Ruth Montgomery is prominent both as a psychic and as an author. Among her widely read books are *A Gift of Prophecy*, *A World Beyond*, *Born to Heal*, and *The World Before*.

1. Jesus of Nazareth, the greatest psychic of all time
2. Gautama Buddha
3. Joan of Arc and numerous other Catholic saints such as St. Francis of Assisi and St. Theresa of Avila of 16th-century Spain
4. Emanuel Swedenborg of 18th-century Sweden (many Swedenborgian churches have been founded in his name in the U.S. and abroad)
5. Paramahansa Yogananda, the great yogi from India who died in Los Angeles in 1952
6. Edgar Cayce of Virginia Beach, Va.
7. Daniel Dunglas Home of 19th-century England
8. "Margery," the wife of Dr. L. R. G. Crandon, a professor of surgery at Harvard Medical School
9. Eileen J. Garrett
10. Arthur Ford

—Exclusive for *The Book of Lists*

60 CELEBRATED PERSONS AND
THEIR BRAIN RADIATION LEVELS

Oscar Brunler (1892–1952) was a physician, inventor, and diplomat. Among his accomplishments were the Brunler flame, which burns underwater, and Surf, one of the first detergents. The latter part of his life was devoted to psychic investigation. He developed a system for measuring the evolutionary process of the individual soul as it is reincarnated in a human body. Applying the basic methodology of radionics, a system of divination which uses a pendulum and is similar to dowsing, he measured the brain radiation of thousands of people, alive and deceased, and placed these measurements along the Brunler brain radiation scale, which he considered to be an accurate accounting of personal evolutionary progress. The great majority of persons tested (95%) rated below 300 on the scale, while "genius" was 500 or above. The following list is a small sampling from his results, given in biometric units (50 b.u. = approximately 1 cm).

		Biometric Units
1.	Leonardo da Vinci	720
2.	Michelangelo	688
3.	Cheiro (palmist)	675
4.	Mme. Helena Blavatsky	660
5.	Titian	660
6.	Frederick the Great	657
7.	Raphael	649
8.	Francis Bacon	640
9.	Rembrandt van Rijn	638
10.	Peter Paul Rubens	633
11.	Francisco Goya	613
12.	Johann Wolfgang von Goethe	608
13.	Napoleon	598
14.	William Blake	580
15.	Paul Cézanne	570

Leonardo da Vinci, most evolved soul.

16.	Annie Besant	568
17.	Pëtr Ilich Tchaïkovsky	567
18.	Frédéric Chopin	550
19.	El Greco	550
20.	Greta Garbo	538
21.	Richard Wagner	538
22.	Franz Liszt	538
23.	Claude Monet	538
24.	Alice Bailey	538
25.	Grigori Rasputin	526
26.	Laurence Olivier	525
27.	Noel Coward	520
28.	Mary Pickford	520
29.	Jawaharlal Nehru	520
30.	Pablo Picasso	515
31.	George Washington	512
32.	Salvador Dali	495
33.	Francisco Franco	490
34.	Edgar Allan Poe	489
35.	Woodrow Wilson	485
36.	Edgar Cayce	482
37.	Mohandas K. Gandhi	477
38.	Herbert Hoover	477
39.	Benito Mussolini	470
40.	Thomas Edison	470
41.	Albert Einstein	469
42.	Abraham Lincoln	462
43.	Queen Victoria	458
44.	H. G. Wells	448
45.	Henry Ford	448
46.	A. Conan Doyle	426
47.	Krishnamurti	423
48.	Duke of Windsor	422
49.	John F. Kennedy	421
50.	Bertrand Russell	420
51.	Sigmund Freud	420
52.	Charles de Gaulle	418
53.	Walter Winchell	407
54.	Billy Graham	406
55.	Jacqueline Kennedy Onassis	391
56.	Georges Gurdjieff	385
57.	C. G. Jung	385
58.	Chiang Kai-shek	375
59.	Alfred Kinsey	360
60.	King Farouk I	307

—A.W.

8 CASES OF
SPONTANEOUS COMBUSTION

These cases are taken from the book *Fire from Heaven, or How Safe Are YOU from Burning?* by Michael Harrison (London: Sidgwick and Jackson, 1976), a work devoted to the study of an inexplicable phenomenon—people catching fire without apparent cause or intention. Just you watch your step, and don't say we didn't warn you.

SPECIMEN PATHOLOGICO-MEDICUM
INAUGURALE
DE
INCENDIIS CORPORIS HUMANI
SPONTANEIS,
QUOD,
FAVENTE SUMMO NUMINE,
Ex Auctoritate MAGNIFICI RECTORIS
D. DAVIDIS van ROYEN,
MEDICINAE DOCTORIS. BOTANICES IN ACAD.
LUGD. BAT. PROFESSORIS ORDINARII:

NEC NON

Amplissimi SENATUS ACADEMICI *Consensu,*
& Nobilissimae FACULTATIS MEDICAE *Decreto,*

PRO GRADU DOCTORATUS,

Summisque in MEDICINA Honoribus & Privilegiis
rité ac legitimé consequendis,

Eruditorum Examini submittit

IONAS DUPONT,
AMST. BAT.

Ad diem 16. *Decembris* M. D. CC. LXIII. *H. L. Q. S.*

Intima pars homini vero flagravit ad ossa:
Flagravit stomacho flamma, ut fornacibus intus.
LUCRET.

LUGDUNI BATAVORUM,
Apud THEODORUM HAAK, Bibliop.

The classic on spontaneous combustion in human beings, published in 1763, was the first scientific study of this phenomenon.

433

1. COUNTESS CORNELIA DI BANDI

The 62-year-old countess of Cesena, Italy, combusted in the 18th century, exact date unknown. Her neighbors had noticed a "yellowish, utterly loathsome half-liquid smoke" exuding from the windows of the countess's room. The maid discovered her remains in the morning: ". . . 4 ft. from the bed there was a heap of ashes," wrote Sir David Brewster. "Her legs, with the stockings on, remained untouched . . . Nearly all the rest of the body was reduced to ashes. The air in the room was covered with floating soot." Neither the furniture nor the floor was burned. Oddly enough, two tallow candles standing on a bedside table had melted, but the cotton wicks remained intact.

2. MR. "H"

A professor of mathematics at the University of Nashville, Tenn., Mr. H was walking home on a winter's day in 1835 when he felt a sharp pain in his left leg. When he looked down, he observed that a flame several inches high was spouting from his leg. Slapping at the flame failed to extinguish it, so he cupped his hands around it to cut off the supply of oxygen, and it went out. A tiny hole had been burned in his underwear, but there was no corresponding hole in his pants. The burn on Mr. H's leg took an unusually long time to heal.

3. MR. AND MRS. PATRICK ROONEY

Mr. and Mrs. Rooney died together on Christmas Eve, 1885. Mrs. Rooney combusted spontaneously and Mr. Rooney, a Seneca, Ill., farmer, died of asphyxiation from the smoke in the air.

4. EUPHEMIA JOHNSON

This 68-year-old widow, living in England in 1922, combusted while drinking her afternoon tea. She blazed so quickly that her remains, "a pile of calcinated bones," were lying within her unburned clothes. The surrounding furniture was barely singed.

5. PHYLLIS NEWCOMBE

Miss Newcombe, a 22-year-old British girl, combusted before a roomful of people while waltzing in a dance hall on August 7, 1938.

6. MARY HARDY REESER

This 67-year-old resident of St. Petersburg, Fla., combusted in her easy chair on the night of July 1, 1951. Her neighbor, a Mrs. Carpenter, awoke the next morning to the smell of smoke. The doorknob of Mrs. Reeser's apartment was too hot to be touched by bare hands, and when the door was finally opened a gust of hot air blew out. According to Harrison, "Within a blackened circle about 4 ft. in diameter were a number of coiled seat springs and the remains of a human body . . . and a small pile of blackened ashes." Mrs. Reeser's case was much investigated, and is perhaps the most famous in the history of spontaneous combustion. Stated Police Chief J. R. Reichart: "As far as logical explanations go, this is one of those things that just couldn't have happened, but it did. The case is not closed and may never be closed to the satisfaction of all concerned."

7. MRS. ANNA MARTIN

This West Philadelphia, Pa., matron combusted in her 69th year, on May 18, 1957. Only her extremities burned, leaving her torso—and, mysteriously, her shoes—intact.

8. BILLY THOMAS PETERSON

A 27-year-old welder in Pontiac, Mich., combusted on December 14, 1957. He was discovered by a passing motorist, smoldering in his car which was parked in his garage. He had either just committed suicide by inhaling carbon monoxide, or was still trying to do so, when he combusted. His left arm, genitals, and some of his face were badly burned, and a plastic religious statue on the dashboard had melted. However, the hairs on his body, his eyebrows, and the top of his head were unharmed. None of his clothes were so much as singed.

—A.W.

10 PEOPLE WHO HAD STIGMATA

Stigmata, spontaneously formed wounds corresponding to those suffered by Christ on the cross, have appeared on the bodies of more than 330 people, most of whom were nuns, monks, and priests prone to brooding about the Crucifixion. Authorities in the Roman Catholic Church are cautious about recognizing stigmata as miraculous and cite conscious or unconscious suggestion as one of the possible causes.

1. ST. FRANCIS OF ASSISI (Italian saint; 1182–1226)

First person known to evidence stigmata. This gentle saint was born to a rich merchant family; was a profligate teenager, then converted to a pious life of poverty and emulated Christ. Famous for his love of all creatures. In 1224, two years before his death on Mount Alverno, in the Apennines, he saw a radiant fiery angel with six wings carrying a crucified man. Went into an ecstatic trance and stigmata appeared. It was as if long, pointed nails were in his hands and feet, and a spear wound in his side. Stigmata attested to by two popes: Gregory IX and Alexander IV.

2. ST. CATHERINE OF SIENA (Italian nun and visionary; 1347–1380)

Was a volunteer nurse at age 19. Grew to have great political power in affairs of both Church and state; wrote letters to kings and to Pope Gregory XI, calling him "dear little Babbo." Lived on a handful of herbs a day, two hours of sleep a night. Had stigmata, but chose to keep them hidden. Stigmata not shown on statues of her by order of Pope Sixtus IV. Died at 33, Christ's age when he was crucified.

3. ST. RITA OF CASCIA (Italian saint; 1381–1457)

Forced as a 12-year-old child to marry a rich nobleman who was brutal to her. Through patient affection, changed him into a loving mate, but he was killed 18 years after their marriage. Entered Augustinian convent in Cascia in 1452. Prayed to feel Christ's passion after hearing a missionary preach about it. Felt crown of thorns on her forehead. Developed wounds, possibly smallpox, which became wormy and fetid; was isolated as a leper. Supposedly her puncture wounds sent out holy rays when she died.

4. ST. VERONICA GIULIANI (Italian nun; 1660–1697)

At age 33, on Good Friday, saw vision of Christ nailed to the cross. Developed stigmata when rays went from his wounds to her hands, feet, and sides. Suffered from wounds alternately healing and bleeding—a spear puncture on her side constantly bled. She drew a picture to show heart wounds that were verified after her death.

5. ANNA KATHARINA EMMERICH (German nun; 1774–1824)

Born to a peasant family; was a cow keeper. Entered the convent of Agnetenberg in 1803; was continually ailing but spent her nights making clothes for the poor. At age 37, developed wounds on hands, side, and feet; had punctures from the crown of thorns and a double cross on her breast. Healed after prayer but always bled on Fridays.

6. MARIA VON MÖRL (German; 1812–1868)

Stigmata on hands, feet, and side, seen by more than 40,000 people.

7. LOUISE LATEAU (French seamstress; 1850–1883)

Daughter of working-class family. Nursed sick in hometown of Bois d'Haine during cholera epidemic of 1866. Had miraculous recovery from illness. In 1868, developed stigmata, which appeared every Friday between 1:00 and 2:00 P.M. and 4:00 and 5:00 P.M.

8. ST. GEMMA GALGANI (Italian saint; 1878–1903)

As a child, lived with relatives because of tuberculosis in family. At age 20, lost father; lived in extreme poverty. Had tuberculosis of the spine, but was saved by a miracle. After seeing vision of St. Gabriel Possenti, wanted to join Passionist convent but was refused. Worked as a housekeeper. At age 21, wounds appeared on hands, feet, side, and forehead; scourge marks on body—all occurring on Fridays. Taunted for her piety. Canonized by Pope Pius XII in 1940.

9. PADRE PIO (Italian priest, miracle worker, and clairvoyant; 1887–1968)

Entered Capuchin monastery at 17. Nine years later felt pains in hands, feet, and side—no apparent medical reason. Three years later, collapsed while praying; stigmata appeared. Kept hands covered in public, but one photograph of him showed a bloody palm raised to bless a congregation. Suspended from duties by Vatican twice because of embarrassing attention paid him. Received large

Padre Pio of Italy suffered bleeding from wounds or
stigmata similar to Christ's. He died in 1968.

sums of money from the faithful; used $7 million of it to build a hospital. Presently being considered for canonization.

10. THERESE NEUMANN (German; 1898–1962)

Most recent case of stigmata on record. In 1918, aged 20, helped put out a fire—an experience which broke her health. One year later, became blind and bedridden, but had miraculous recovery. In 1926, developed stigmata below eyes, heart, and hands. In 1927, took no real nourishment except for Holy Communion. Could "read" consciences. Was focus of Good Friday pilgrimages, at which time Roman Catholics were allowed to view her wounds. Considered by many to be a saint. Stigmata attributed by doctors to nervous disorder. Died at age 64 in Konnersreuth, Germany.

—A.E.

10 EYEWITNESS ACCOUNTS OF LEVITATION

1. COLIN EVANS

English medium Colin Evans is shown "in flight" in a photograph in Hill and Williams's *The Supernatural*.

2. "THE FLYING WITCH OF NAVAREE"

A woman known only by this designation, "after sliding halfway down a tower like a lizard, flew into the air in the sight of all," according to P. de Sandoval in *La Historia de la Vida y Hechos del Emperador Carlos V*.

3. "DON GENARO" AND "DON JUAN"

Anthropologist Carlos Castaneda reported seeing an informant whom he called Don Genaro, a Mexican Indian sorcerer, fly through the air, walk horizontally up the side of a tree, and fly back. He also claimed to have seen both Don Genaro and Don Juan jump off a cliff, twirl slowly in the air, reach bottom, and float back up to the top. According to Castaneda, Don Genaro described one of his experiences as "something . . . like nothing I can tell . . . We spun through the air with such speed and force that I couldn't see anymore. Everything was foggy. The spinning went on, and on, and on."

4. DANIEL DUNGLAS HOME

Home was a British psychic who is said to have effected his own levitation. Wrote Lord Adare in the late 1860s: "We heard Home go into the next room, heard the window thrown up, and presently Home appeared standing upright outside over a window; he opened the window and walked in quite coolly." This window was on the third floor and had no balcony. A published critic of mediums and

There have been a number of actually witnessed cases of human levitation in history. Here is an imagined one, "Levitating Nun," drawn by Fernando Botero in 1976.

frauds, the Rev. C. M. Davies, wrote a piece for the magazine *Belgravia* in which he described having seen Home float around Mrs. Samuel Carter Hall's drawing room for five minutes.

5. JUAN DE JESÚS

The flights of Juan de Jesús of San Diego in the Canary Isles are attested to in Chapter 18 of A. Abreu's *Vida del Ven. Siervo de Deo N. Juan de Jesús.* Abreu, teacher and officer of the Inquisition, apparently backed the account with documentary evidence.

6. ST. JOSEPH OF CUPERTINO

Prospero Lambertini (Pope Benedict XIV), in an 18th-century treatise, wrote: "Whilst I was discharging the office of *promotor fidei,* the cause of the venerable servant of God, Joseph of Cupertino, was discussed by the Congregation of Sacred Rites, and eyewitnesses of unexceptionable integrity reported on the celebrated levitations and remarkable flights of this servant of God when in a condition of ecstatic rapture." Nuns of St. Ligorio, who had been attending mass at the Church of St. Gregory of Armenia in Naples, claimed to have seen St. Joseph rise into the air and land upon the altar amid burning candles. "He will catch fire!" the nuns had screamed out, but St. Joseph flew back down to the ground, unharmed. Other eyewitnesses included Pope Urban VIII, Johann Friedrich (the duke of Brunswick and employer of philosopher G. W. Leibniz), the Infanta Maria (daughter of Charles Emmanuel the Great, duke of Savoy), and Francesco Pierpaoli, St. Joseph's physician during his final illness.

7. CARLO MIRABELLI

Mirabelli, a Brazilian faith healer, is shown "in flight" in a photograph in Guy Lyon Playfair's *The Unknown Power.* An eyewitness report of one of his levitations "before several members of the Academy Cesare Lombroso" is given in Nandor Fodor's *Encyclopedia of the Psychic Sciences.*

8. M. STAINTON MOSES

Moses was an Oxford professor whose levitation was attested to by E. Myers of the Society for Psychical Research.

9. EUSAPIA PALLADINO

Numerous eyewitness reports exist of levitation by Eusapia Palladino, a 19th-century medium. One account is in Hereward Carrington's *Eusapia Palladino and Her Exploits* (1909).

10. WILLY SCHNEIDER

Schneider, a European medium, "rose horizontally and seemed to rest on an invisible cloud. He ascended to the ceiling and remained five minutes suspended there, moving his legs about rhythmically. The descent was as sudden as the uplifting. The supervision was perfect." This was reported by Baron Albert von Schrenk-Notzing and quoted by Sudre in *Introduction à la Métapsychique* and requoted in Fodor's *Encyclopedia of the Psychic Sciences.*

—M.W.J. & D.B.

9 POSSIBLE VISITATIONS FROM OUTER SPACE

1. THE GOLD AIRPLANE

A pre-Columbian gold artifact from South America, made more than 1,000 years ago, looks very much like the model of a delta-winged jet. Though it has been identified as a representation of a devilfish, it does not look much like one. How to explain the upright triangular tail and the cockpitlike gash in its "head"? Were South Americans visited by extraterrestrials traveling in jetlike vehicles long ago? And did they make a model of one of the vehicles to commemorate the occasion?

2. EZEKIEL'S WHEEL

Ezekiel was exiled from Israel in 597 B.C. and five years later had a "vision of God," when an aerial chariot containing four-winged monsters and traveling on wheels within wheels arrived before him in a storm wind with flashes of fire. Were the wings the rotors of four linked helicopters manned by creatures from outer space? Were those creatures superior beings who gave Ezekiel "the word" to upgrade the morality of earthlings?

3. THE GREEN CHILDREN

In August, 1887, two children with bright green skin and slanted eyes came out of a Spanish cave. They wore clothes made of a strange material, and spoke a language which experts from Barcelona were unable to identify. The boy died. The girl learned to speak Spanish, and said she had been transported to the cave by a whirlwind which had carried her off from a country which was always in twilight. Was that country another planet? Was she transported here by a time or space warp, some phenomenon involving parallel worlds or the fourth dimension?

4. SIGHTINGS OF UFOS IN 1897

Several times during 1897, flying objects were seen in different parts of the world. On April 19, Alexander Hamilton, a Kansas farmer, saw a 300-ft. cigar-shaped airship hovering over his cow pasture at a height of about 30 ft. The carriage under the hull seemed to be made of a glasslike material, and strange beings inside it were talking a foreign language. The beings lassoed one of the farmer's cows with a cable, and pulled it inside their spacecraft. On March 27, a large object had been seen flying over Topeka, Kans., by 200 people, including the governor. "I don't know what the thing is, but I hope it may yet solve the railroad problem," said the governor in an unusual response to the event.

5. THE SIBERIAN EXPLOSION

An explosion as powerful as a hydrogen bomb shook Siberia on June 30, 1908. Some witnesses reported seeing a pillar of fire or kind of "mushroom cloud." There was nothing to account for it. In 1927, Soviet scientists found the site—a charred piece of earth about 25 ft. across—and said there was no evidence that a meteorite had caused the explosion. Other possible causes suggested by scientists: a collision between earth and antimatter from space (how did the antimatter get through earth's atmosphere?), a comet (none was seen), a piece of a black hole, a laser beamed from another planet. Aleksander Kazantsev, a Russian metallurgist and weapons engineer, thinks the explosion was caused by the crash of a spaceship manned by extraterrestrials on a reconnaisance flight over earth.

6. THE 1913 UFOS

On February 9, 1913, strange flying objects traveling horizontally in groups, more slowly than meteorites, were observed by farmers and astronomers in Canada, Bermuda, Brazil, and Africa. Astronomer W. F. Denning reported seeing lighted windows in one of them.

7. THE HILLS' VISIT TO A SPACESHIP

On September 19, 1961, while driving through a deserted summer resort in New Hampshire, Betty and Barney Hill were stopped by a disk-shaped flying object. It was approximately 65 ft. across and carried five creatures who were about 5 ft. tall, had big eyes, no noses, and grayish skin. When the creatures approached, the Hills lost their willpower; they were dragged into the craft and given physical examinations. The spacemen communicated with the Hills through a kind of ESP; among themselves, they spoke an odd language. The Hills were told by the beings to forget what had happened to them, and then they were released, but under hypnosis they remembered everything. This event was taken so seriously that it was the subject of a TV special in 1975.

8. INTELLIGENT RADIO SIGNALS

Astronomers have intercepted what may be radio signals coming from celestial objects designated CTA-21 and CTA-102 (one in Pegasus and the other in Aries). Soviet astronomer Nikolai S. Kardashev believes that the signals are being sent by a race of superior beings from another planet. Other related speculations: that the northern and southern lights are signals from another world; that pulsars are artificial beacons to guide spaceships in their travels from one star to another.

9. THE NEW JERSEY UFO

In a report discussed by J. Allen Hynek and Jacques Vallee in *The Edge of Reality,* ABC newsman Robert Le Donne is quoted as saying that he saw a UFO on the night of June 4, 1974, in Woodcliff Lake, N.J. It made no sound and looked like "a brilliant oval of lights" in the southeastern sky. Le Donne stopped his car and watched it approach, flying very low, from about ¼ mi. away. It appeared to have yellow lights revolving from front to rear and a red light in back. It was, he said, "as garish as a Ferris wheel in the sky." The police, to whom he reported the sighting, said they had seen a UFO which looked like a "flying pan" about two months before. Le Donne unsuccessfully tried to convince himself that the UFO was a helicopter.

—A.E.

9 GREAT UNSOLVED MYSTERIES

1. "MAN-MADE" OBJECTS CREATED BEFORE THE ADVENT OF MAN ON EARTH

In 1885, a metal cube—whose symmetry and composition led experts to believe it could have been man-made—was found embedded in coal formed more than 12 million years ago. Glass lenses, metal nails, chains, a fossil screw, and a battery have been discovered inside geological formations. Bulletlike objects have been taken from the bones of prehistoric animals. Where did these objects, many of them technologically advanced, come from? Possibly from civilizations which existed on earth very early, then were completely wiped out? Or, perhaps, extraterrestrials who made a visit to this planet and left behind some of their "junk"?

2. THE PYRAMID OF CHEOPS

Built by the Egyptian pharaoh Cheops more than 45 centuries ago, the great pyramid presents more than one mystery. It took 22 years to construct, using an incredible labor force of 100,000 common workers during the three months of each year when the Nile River flooded. How these laborers moved stones that weighed up to 2½ tons is one of the mysteries. Another mystery is the significance of the pyramid. Could Cheops have been so vain as to require this large monument to memorialize himself, or did it mean more? Its height—146.6 meters—may be related to the distance between the earth and the sun—148,208,000 kilometers. Did the Egyptians know this distance? It was not calculated accurately in recent times until the 19th century. Is the pyramid a huge calendar, an astronomical calculator?

3. STONEHENGE

Begun in 2200 B.C. and rebuilt sometime around 1600 B.C.—a time span of about 600 years—the great double ring of stones known as Stonehenge stands in what is now Wiltshire, England. The first builders left behind the huge 35-ton Heel Stone, brought from 24 mi. away. Its purpose is unknown. Years later, giant bluestones were brought from Prescelly Mountains, 135 mi. away. Eventually the pillars were topped with lintels. Outside the circle are 56 small pits known as the Aubrey Holes. How did the builders move those gigantic stones? Why did they invest 1.5 million days of manpower? For worship? Or, as we now think, to make a huge observatory and calendar? A recent computer study has revealed several correlations between the position of the stones and the position of the sun and moon in 1500 B.C. Which brings us to another mystery—how did these primitive people know enough about the movements of the heavenly bodies to place the stones so precisely?

4. THE NAZCA LINES

On a plateau in the Peruvian desert there are yellow lines which were drawn in the dark earth between the years 400 and 1200 A.D. From the air, the lines—some 40 mi. long—portray geometric figures, animals, insects, flowers, and gods. Who "wrote" these messages to the sky? And why? Do the lines comprise a desert calendar? Were they made by creatures from outer space using a spaceship? Or by primitive Indians using a much smaller blueprint?

5. THE LOCH NESS MONSTER

In 565 A.D., the abbot St. Columba saw in Loch Ness a "fearsome beast . . . something like a huge frog but not a frog." Since then, the beast—which by all subsequent reports is more like a sea serpent than a frog—has been seen by nearly 200 people, including divers, tourists, local residents, and scientists using submarines, echo sounders, and other sophisticated equipment. Pictures and movies—many of them fuzzy in outline—have been taken of "Bobby" (as the locals call the monster), or "Nessie" (as named by scientists who think "it" is female). "She" is about 90 ft. long with a sinuous body, a tail, and a snakelike head and neck. Does she really exist in that long (24 mi.), narrow (1½ mi.), deep (750 ft.) Scottish lake? If so, what is she? An "extinct" plesiosaur, a species which flourished 70 million years ago? A giant newt? A sea slug? How did she get in the lake? Were her ancestors landlocked there when ocean waters receded, or does she even now enter and leave the lake through a secret passage connecting Loch Ness with the ocean?

6. EASTER ISLAND'S STATUES

Easter Island lies about 2,000 mi. west of the coast of Chile. Only 35 mi. in circumference, it was discovered in 1722—on Easter Day—by the Dutch navigator Jacob Roggeveen. Even then the statues, which have made it famous, were there—statues of small-bodied, large-headed, long-eared, naked men—all Caucasians with ruthless expressions. Some are as high as a three-story house and weigh 60 tons. Their topknots of red stone have fallen off—were they intended to portray redheads? One hundred of them are complete—another 150 were left unfinished. Native legend says that about 475 A.D., 300 "long ears" landed on the uninhabited island after a 120-day voyage from the east. Twenty generations later, the "short ears" (a contingent of Polynesians) came and were forced by the long ears to work on the statues until the 17th century, when the short ears revolted against their masters. That men could have crossed thousands of miles of the Pacific that long ago has been proved by Thor Heyerdahl's famous voyage on his raft *Kon-Tiki*. But the question remains: Who were those Caucasian long ears? Europeans who, long before the Vikings landed in North America, found their way to South America and then could not get back?

7. ZIMBABWE

Who built the ancient ruined city of Zimbabwe in Rhodesia? Arabs, Phoenicians, Indians, Chinese, Egyptians, Israelites, Bantus? Was it the ancient city of Ophir? Did its gold mines belong to King Solomon? Some archaeologists now believe it may have been built in the 15th century by native Africans—but not the Bantus—who then moved away. If so, who were those Africans?

8. THE YETI

In Tibet, high in the Himalayas, there may be what the native Sherpas call yeti and what others have nicknamed the abominable snowmen. These are beings 5–8 ft. tall, with long brown hair, pointed heads, humanoid faces, who walk upright on two legs. Since the 1880s, footprints 12–20 in. long have been seen and even photographed by mountain climbers, among them New Zealander Sir Edmund Hillary, conqueror of Everest. If yeti do exist, what are they —monkeys, bears, or missing links that are related to man? And if they exist, why hasn't one been captured? What about other "man-apes" reported in central Asia, Sumatra, New Guinea, and the American Northwest (where they are called Sasquatch, or Big Feet)?

9. THE FATE OF THE ROMANOVS

After the Bolsheviks took over Russia, they supposedly murdered the ex-Czar Nicholas Romanov, his wife Alexandra, and their five children—Alexei (a hemophiliac), Olga, Maria, Tatiana, and Anastasia—in the cellar of a house in Ekaterinburg on July 19, 1918. Sitting on a row of chairs, the Romanovs were, it was claimed, shot to death by a firing squad, along with the family physician and three servants. However, another story exists—that while the czar and his son were killed, the Romanov women were taken to a safe place, and were known to be alive six months after the czar's death. Many people have claimed to be members of that ill-fated family. The most widely publicized claimant has been a woman who—as a teenager in 1920—was fished out of a Berlin canal. She had tried to commit suicide and, when rescued, said that she was Anastasia. According to "Anastasia," she was wounded while in the cellar but escaped with the help of one of the members of the firing squad—a man she later married. Evidence exists both for and against her story. No one has yet been able to obtain the Romanov money, which amounts to millions of dollars.

—A.E.

Czar Nicholas and family on the roof of
a greenhouse in Ekaterinburg, Siberia, during their
captivity in 1918. (L to R) Grand Duchess Olga, Grand Duchess
Anastasia, Czar Nicholas, his son, and Grand Duchess
Tatiana. Standing: Grand Duchess Maria.

10 GHASTLY GHOSTS

1. THE GHOST OF ANNE BOLEYN

Anne Boleyn is said to have been born at Blickling Hall in Norfolk. She certainly spent part of her childhood there, and her ghost returns every year on May 19, the anniversary of her execution in 1536. She sits in a coach drawn by four headless horses and driven by a headless coachman—she carries her own head on her knees. The coach drives slowly up the avenue to the house and vanishes at the front door. She also haunts the Tower of London, both the chapel of St. Peter-ad-Vincula where she officially lies buried, and the White Tower. (There is a tradition that her body was secretly removed to Salle and laid under a black marble slab without any inscription.)

2. THE GHOST OF CATHERINE HOWARD

The haunted gallery at Hampton Court Palace echoes with the shrieks of Catherine Howard. She rushes along the gallery and passes through the door at the end, which leads into the chapel. She also haunts Eythorne Manor, Hollingbourne, Kent. She was beheaded on February 13, 1542, after 18 months of marriage to King Henry VIII.

3. THE VERMILION PHANTOM

This ghost has appeared at various critical junctures in the history of France. A tall well-built figure, wrapped in a red cape, with a beard also of a red hue, he appeared to Henry IV on May 13, 1610, in the king's bedchamber, and predicted, "Tomorrow you will die." Henry sent for his counselors immediately, and discussed with them the manifestation and the message. Within 12 hours the king was assassinated by François Ravaillac, a Catholic visionary who believed that Henry's conversion to Catholicism was politically motivated. The vermilion phantom appeared four times to Napoleon Bonaparte. On the third occasion, in January, 1814, Count Mole-Nieuval was a witness to the tall red apparition. Dr. Antomarchi saw the figure at Napoleon's bedside on May 5, 1821—the fourth visitation—on the day of Napoleon's death.

4. THE FLYING DUTCHMAN

In 1680, a Dutch East Indies ship captained by Hendrick Van der Decken sailed from Amsterdam for Batavia. Near the Cape of Good Hope a sudden gale battered the vessel. The legend of the spectral ship was well known before Wagner wrote his opera *Der Fliegende Holländer*. Any ship that sights the phantom is said to meet with bad luck soon after. In March, 1939, some 60 people on Glencairn beach at the tip of South Africa saw a fully rigged 17th-century merchantman sail steadily toward destruction on the sands of the strand, with all her sails drawing well although there was not a breath of wind. As excitement rose in the group of spectators, the ship vanished as mysteriously as it had appeared.

5. THE EPWORTH POLTERGEIST

In 1716, the Rev. Samuel Wesley—the father of John Wesley—lived at Epworth Rectory in Lincolnshire, England. According to John Wesley's account, the hauntings began on December 2, 1716, when Robert Brown, a servant, heard a knock on the door, followed by a groan, about 10:00 P.M. He opened the door, expecting to see a Mr. Turpine, who apparently had a habit of groaning, but found no one there. This happened three times. Feeling somewhat alarmed, Brown and the other servants went to bed. At the top of the garret stairs, Brown saw a handmill turning by itself, and when in bed he heard noises like a turkey gobbling and someone stumbling over shoes. The next day, one of the maids heard a knocking on the dairy shelf for which she could find no apparent cause, and she was so frightened that she flung down the trayful of butter that she was carrying and fled from the room. The high moral standard of the Wesley family is one of the reasons why the ghost is perhaps one of the most celebrated poltergeists in history.

6. THE DRURY LANE THEATRE GHOST

The Drury Lane Theatre ghost, a young dandy murdered in 1780, is said to bring extraordinary acting success to those who see it. The skeleton was found in this century when workmen opened up a wall. The shreds of a gray riding coat covered the skeleton and a dagger was sticking in its ribs. In 1939, the ghost hunter J. Wentworth Day sat up to watch for the specter. All he saw was a very peculiar bluish light which came out of the wall, flickered round the back of the upper circle, then vanished. However, he has recorded conversations with people who have seen the ghost, which was hatless and dressed in gray.

7. THE GHOST OF CHARLES ROSMER

The ghost story which started spiritualism—and perhaps the most important ghost story in the 19th century—took place in a broken-down wooden house in the small rural community of Hydesville in Wayne County, N.Y. There lived John D. Fox, a poor Canadian farmer who had come to the U.S. with his wife and three children: Margaret, Catherine, and Leah. All the members of the family were devout Methodists. On a March morning in 1848, strange rappings and knockings were heard in the house. They continued throughout the following days and nights, growing in intensity, until by the end of the month the whole building was literally being shaken to its rickety fundations. Quite by chance while the noises were occurring, Catherine—age 7—clapped her hands. Almost immediately there was an answering clap. She snapped her fingers. Back came a snapping sound. The 10-year-old Margaret clapped—and was similarly answered. She ran in amazement to get her parents. John Fox and his wife followed the lead of their daughters and attempted to communicate with the ghost by means of a series of raps. In return the spirit conveyed to them the message that he was the ghost of Charles Rosmer, an itinerant peddler who had been murdered on the property. The Fox sisters toured America and were admired by such luminaries as Horace Greeley and James Fenimore Cooper.

8. THE ANGELS OF MONS

Following the battle of Mons, Belgium, on August 26, 1914, the British Expeditionary Force was in retreat and pursued by a unit of German cavalry. Expecting certain death, the British turned and saw to their astonishment a squadron of phantom cavalry between them and the German cavalry. The German horses were terrified and stampeded in all directions. From the German side came an account that their men refused to charge a point (where the British line was broken) because of the presence of a large number of troops. According to Allied records, there was not a single British soldier in the area. An army chaplain recorded that he had heard accounts of the apparition from a brigadier general and two of his officers. The retreat was successfully accomplished, and soldiers of both armies believed that they had seen a spectral army of angels.

9. THE BORLEY GHOST

The ghost of Borley Rectory was "Marie Lairre," a nun who died in 1667. The rectory was built in 1863 in Borley, on the Essex-Suffolk border. Prior to 1929, the ghost appeared to over a dozen witnesses. She was in nun's habit and invariably sad. Harry Price, a noted ghost hunter, became interested in the rectory in 1929 and lived there for 10 years. He published two books, *The Most Haunted House in England* and *The End of Borley Rectory,* which won international acclaim. In a series of table-tapping séances conducted by an associate of Price, Marie Lairre disclosed that she was sad because she had been interred in the rectory grounds without a Christian burial. When the building was razed in 1944, a brick hovered unassisted in the air for a period of time and sounds were heard which were thought to be unconnected with the work in progress.

10. THE WHITE HOUSE GHOST

Abraham Lincoln's ghost haunts the White House. (When he was alive he used to hold séances there, as he was interested in psychic research.) Mrs. Eleanor Roosevelt has recorded: "I was sitting in my study when one of the maids burst in on me in a state of great excitement. I looked up from my work and asked her what was the trouble. 'He's up there—sitting on the edge of the bed, taking off his shoes!' she exclaimed. 'Who's up where, taking off his shoes?' I asked. 'Mr. Lincoln!' the maid replied." Among others to have seen the ghost was Queen Wilhelmina of the Netherlands during a state visit in 1945.

—P.C.J.

PRESERVING OUR HERITAGE
—21 BEST-KNOWN STUFFED OR
EMBALMED HUMANS AND ANIMALS

1. TUTANKHAMEN

In 1922, while excavating in the Valley of the Kings, English archaeologist Howard Carter discovered the tomb of Tutankhamen, a king of the 18th Dynasty of Egypt who flourished about 1348 B.C. The mummy of the pharaoh was encased in a 6-ft. coffin containing 2,448 lbs. of gold. Over the bandages on the king's face was a lifelike gold mask inlaid with precious jewels. A dazzling assortment of rings, necklaces, amulets, and other exquisite ornaments were found among the body wrappings. The internal organs of the king had been removed, embalmed, and placed in a separate alabaster chest. The mummy, coffin, and other valuables from the tomb are currently at the Egyptian Museum in Cairo.

2. CHARLEMAGNE

This ruler of the Holy Roman Empire died in 814. Embalmed, he was dressed in his royal robes, a crown placed on his head, a scepter placed in his hand, and thus he was propped up in a sitting position on his marble throne. His preserved body remained on that throne for 400 years. At last, in 1215, Holy Roman Emperor Frederick II removed the corpse, which was found to be in excellent condition. It was buried in a gold and silver casket in the cathedral at Aix-la-Chapelle.

3. EL CID (Rodrigo Díaz de Bivar)

Spanish leader in the war against the Moors, he established the independent kingdom of Valencia. Wounded in battle in 1099 and dying, El Cid's last wish was that his body be embalmed, and then seated on his horse, Babieca, during the next battle. When the next battle came—an attack on Valencia by King Bucar of Morocco—and the Spanish were on the verge of defeat, the preserved corpse of El Cid, mounted on his horse, appeared at the head of the troops. Heartened, the Spanish troops rallied, and were victorious.

4. INÉS DE CASTRO

When King Pedro of Castile was a young prince, he fell in love with Inés de Castro. His father, fearing political complications, trumped up a charge against Inés and had her beheaded. Pedro waited until he had become king after his father died, then had the hearts torn out of the assassins and ordered Inés's body exhumed. Her corpse was dressed, placed on the throne, and officially crowned queen. All the dignitaries were forced to pay homage by kissing her hand and treating her like a living monarch. Pedro died in 1369.

5. RICHARD II

This English king was deposed in 1399 and probably murdered in 1400. In 1413, Henry V had Richard's body embalmed and put on public display in full royal regalia. Three days later Henry was the chief mourner at Richard's second funeral, during which Richard was interred in Westminster Abbey. At one time there was a hole in the side of the tomb through which visitors could put their hands to touch the king's head. In 1776, an enthusiastic schoolboy thrust his hand in and stole Richard's jawbone. The boy's descendants kept the relic until 1906, when it was finally restored to its rightful resting place.

6. CATHERINE OF VALOIS

Henry V's queen died in 1437. Her grandson, Henry VII, made major alterations to Westminster Abbey which involved moving her embalmed body. She was placed in a crude coffin constructed of flimsy boards and left above ground. There she remained, a public spectacle for over 200 years. Vergers used to charge a shilling to take off the lid so curious visitors could view her corpse. But seeing wasn't enough for Samuel Pepys, who went to the abbey on his 36th birthday. "I had the upper part of her body in my hands, and I did kiss her mouth, reflecting upon that I did first kiss a Queene." The body was finally removed from public view in 1776.

7. DUKE OF MONMOUTH

This English rebel was beheaded in 1685 in one of history's messiest executions (it took "five chopps"). The body and head were dispatched for burial, but at the last moment it was realized that no portrait existed of the duke. Since he had been the illegitimate son of King Charles II, it was considered important to have one painted. Body and head were returned, sewed back together, dressed—and finally painted. The portrait hangs in the National Portrait Gallery, London.

8. CHARLES BYRNE

This Irish giant lived from 1761 to 1783. He feared that his huge body would be dissected for study, so he paid a group of friends to bury him at sea. But the famous anatomist Dr. Hunter, who owned a collection of human oddities, was not to be cheated. When Byrne died, Hunter bribed the friends to deliver the body to him. He immediately set about boiling the remains before anyone discovered what had happened. The speed with which he boiled the bones turned them brown. Hunter kept his acquisition secret for over two years but finally put it on display. Byrne can still be seen in the Hunter Museum at the Royal College of Surgeons in London. His skeleton shares a glass case with the 19.8-in. skeleton of the Sicilian dwarf Caroline Crachami.

9. "THE PRESERVED LADY"

Martin van Butchell was an English eccentric who lived from 1735 to 1812. In his marriage contract there was a clause stating he could own certain articles only "while [his wife] remained above ground." When she died, he retained title to the property by having her embalmed, dressed in her wedding clothes, and placed in a glass-topped case in his drawing room. "The Preserved Lady" became a great attraction, with Butchell always introducing her as "My dear departed." When he remarried, his new wife—irritated by the competition—insisted the corpse be removed. In keeping with the provision that she remain above ground, Butchell presented her to the Royal College of Surgeons, where she remained on public view until she was cremated by a German bomb during a Luftwaffe raid in May, 1941.

10. BARRY

When the fabled Swiss St. Bernard who rescued so many travelers trapped in Alpine snowstorms (see also: 14 Celebrated Animals) died in 1814, a taxidermist stuffed and mounted him. He may be seen today, remarkably lifelike, standing in the National Museum, Bern, Switzerland.

11. JEREMY BENTHAM

English philosopher and the "Father of Utilitarianism," Bentham, who died in 1832 at the age of 84, willed his entire estate to the University College Hospital in London—on condition that his body be preserved and placed in attendance at all of the hospital's board meetings. Dr. Southward Smith was chosen by Bentham to prepare the philosopher's corpse for viewing. Smith constructed the skeleton and affixed a wax likeness of Bentham's head to it, then

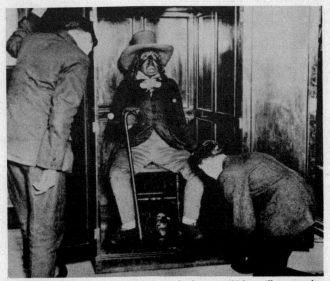

English philosopher Jeremy Bentham, dead since 1832 but still preserved.

attired the body in an appropriate suit and hat. According to Smith, "The whole was then enclosed in a mahogany case with folding glass doors, seated in his armchair and holding in his hand his favorite walking stick . . ." Thus, for the next 92 years, Jeremy Bentham never missed a board meeting.

12. JULIA PASTRANA

A freak (1832–1860), described as the ugliest woman in history, this bearded Mexican Indian was exhibited all over the world. Her manager married her "for myself alone" and when she became pregnant, made a fortune selling tickets to witness the delivery. The child was stillborn and deformed like his mother. Julia died soon after. Her husband had both mother and child embalmed and placed in a glass case, which he immediately began exhibiting around the world. Her body, still on display, was in Norway at last report.

13. JUMBO

Phineas T. Barnum's famous giant elephant, 10 ft. 9 in. at the shoulder, was hit by a freight train and killed in 1885. (see also: 14 Celebrated Animals.) The showman had Jumbo's carcass stuffed —sending his skeleton to the Smithsonian Institution in Washington, D.C.—and put the mounted animal on permanent exhibit in Barnum Hall, Tufts University, Medford, Mass. In April, 1975, a fire swept Barnum Hall and destroyed Jumbo's remains.

14. COMANCHE

When the U.S. Army horse who survived Custer's Last Stand (see also: 14 Celebrated Animals) died a national hero, it was decided to preserve and mount him. A University of Kansas naturalist, Prof. Lewis Dyche, was paid $450 to do the job. Comanche's insides were given a military funeral. His outsides were preserved, shown at the Columbian Exposition in Chicago in 1893, then permanently placed in the University of Kansas Museum of Natural History in Lawrence. In 1947, Gen. Jonathan Wainwright tried to get Comanche back to be a U.S. Army exhibit in Fort Riley, but failed. In 1950, to save his hide from expanding and contracting, Comanche was placed in an airtight glass case with humidity control, and set against an artificial "sunbaked" setting of soil and grass.

15. TIM

Tim was a small mongrel dog who came to Paddington Station in London in 1892 to meet the trains. Attached to his collar was a collection box into which departing passengers dropped coins for a British railroad's fund for widows and orphans. After a decade's work, Tim died in 1902. He was stuffed, and his preserved body— complete with collar and collection box—was placed in a glass case in Paddington Station to continue his good works.

16. ANDERSON McCREW

In 1913, a one-legged Negro hobo died after falling off a moving freight train in Marlin, Tex. Anderson (also known as Andrew) McCrew was dead, but he did not rest in peace for 60 years. The morning after his death, he was taken to a funeral parlor and embalmed. When no one appeared to claim the body, a traveling carnival purchased it and displayed McCrew as "The Amazing Petrified Man—The Eighth Wonder of the World." When the troupe disbanded 55 years later, McCrew remained in storage until a Dallas widow, Elgie Pace, discovered him. She wanted to give him a decent burial because, as she said to her sister, "He's a human being. You just can't throw a body in a ditch." However, she was unable to afford the cost of burial, so she nicknamed him "Sam" and kept him in the basement. Eventually, a local black undertaker volunteered to give McCrew a funeral. The service was "beautiful, and very dignified," reported Elgie, and Anderson McCrew was finally laid to rest. Several months later, folksinger Don McLean wrote a song, "The Legend of Andrew McCrew," which inspired a radio listener to purchase a gravestone for McCrew. The stone reads: "Andrew McCrew, 'The Mummified Man,' Born 1867/Died 1913/Buried 1973."

17. VLADIMIR ILYICH LENIN

On January 21, 1924, Lenin died, reportedly of a stroke, but possibly of poisoning. The deification process began at once. Lenin's brain was removed, cut into 20,000 sections for study by the Soviet Brain Institute, and then his body was embalmed. It was a poor job, and the face became wrinkled and shrunken. By 1926, a Russian doctor, using new embalming fluid which he claimed was based on that used by the ancient Egyptians, re-embalmed the body. A younger, more ascetic look was restored to the face. In 1930, a mausoleum composed of red Ukrainian granite and Karelian porphyry was built in Red Square to contain Lenin's body enclosed in a glass sarcophagus. There, wearing a khaki jacket buttoned to the neck and trousers, Lenin rests today, on display to the world.

18. CHIH HANG

This roly-poly Chinese Buddhist monk was much loved by his followers in Taiwan. As his death grew near, he feared that he was

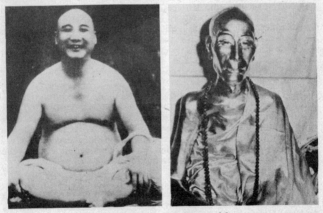

The Buddhist monk Chih Hang in life . . .
and five years after, preserved in gold.

unworthy of his people's love. He decided upon an unusual test of his holiness: He asked that when he died his body be placed in a large urn for three years. If, at the end of this time, his body had not decayed, it was to be painted with pure gold and enshrined forever. After five years, when enough money had been saved to buy the gold, the urn was opened. There was Chih Hang's body—thinner, to be sure, but intact. The body was taken to a shrine in Taipei to be gilded, and to receive offerings and incense from the constant stream of pilgrims. Today, Chih Hang sits on display in a Taipei pagoda.

19. EVA PERÓN

When the wife of Argentine president Juan Perón died in 1952, her husband had the body embalmed. Perón planned to build a mausoleum for his wife, but his government was overthrown in 1955 and he was forced into exile in Spain. Eva Perón's body disappeared and it was assumed that she was buried in an Italian cemetery under a different name. However, by 1971 Perón had retrieved the body and, according to a friend who dined with Perón, the body was present every evening at the dinner table along with Perón and his new wife Isabel. In late 1974, at Isabel's request, Eva Perón was returned to Argentina, where she was placed in an open casket beside the closed casket of her husband.

20. TRIGGER

The world's most famous animal actor, Trigger costarred with Roy Rogers in 88 motion pictures and 100 television shows. An unusually intelligent horse, Trigger was able to untie knots with his teeth and count to 20. Upon his death in 1965 at the age of 33, Trigger was stuffed and mounted. He is on display at the Roy Rogers Museum in Victorville, Calif., as is Dale Evans's horse, Buttermilk.

21. MAO TSE-TUNG

After Mao, chairman of the Chinese Communist party, died at 82 on September 9, 1976, he was embalmed. His corpse was placed in a crystal sarcophagus to be displayed permanently to the public in a mausoleum in Peking.

—I.W., J.BE., A.W., & D.W.

12 GRAVESTONE EPITAPHS THAT NEVER WERE

Many famous persons have announced—usually tongue in cheek—what epitaphs they would like carved on their gravestones after their deaths. Here are the epitaphs 12 celebrities chose for themselves. To our knowledge, not one was actually used.

1. **W. C. FIELDS** (comedian)

"On the whole I'd rather be in Philadelphia."

2. **GEORGE BERNARD SHAW** (author)

"I knew if I stayed around long enough, something like this would happen."

3. **CLARK GABLE** (film actor)

"Back to silents."

4. **ERNEST HEMINGWAY** (author)

"Pardon me for not getting up."

5. **ROBERT BENCHLEY** (comedian and author)

"This is all over my head."

6. **JEAN HARLOW** (film actress)

"Of this quiet and peace/I'm very fond;/No more remarks—'She's a/Platinum blonde.' "

7. **FREDRIC MARCH** (film actor)

"This is just my lot."

8. **WILLIAM HAINES** (film actor and decorator)

"Here's something I want to get off my chest."

9. **EDDIE CANTOR** (comedian)

"Here in nature's arms I nestle,/Free at last from Georgie Jessel."

10. **DR. ALBERT SCHWEITZER** (Nobel peace prizewinner)

"If cannibals should ever catch me/I hope they will say:/'We have eaten Dr. Schweitzer/And he was good to the end . . . /And the end wasn't bad.' "

11. **RUBE GOLDBERG** (cartoonist)

"Dear God: Enclosed please find Rube Goldberg, Now that you've got him, what are you going to do with him?"

12. **GEORGE ARLISS** (stage and film actor)

"All my old junk gone to the storehouse,/Here I am, God, starting for your house./In order to prevent possibility of ruction/Am bringing you back your original production."

25 DEATHS FROM STRANGE CAUSES

1. ZEUXIS (Greek painter; 5th century B.C.)

Laughed so hard at his own painting of an old hag that he broke a blood vessel and died.

2. AGATHOCLES (tyrant of Syracuse; 361–289 B.C.)

Died as the result of choking on a toothpick.

3. ALEXANDER THE GREAT (Macedonian king and conqueror; 356–323 B.C.)

Died from a fever contracted during a two-day period of drinking and carousing.

4. MARCUS LICINIUS CRASSUS (Roman financier and politician; 115?–53 B.C.)

According to one story, this notorious Roman leader and moneylender met his death at the hands of Parthian soldiers who poured molten gold down his throat.

5. CLAUDIUS I (emperor of Rome; 10 B.C.–54 A.D.)

Claudius choked to death on a feather. His physician Xenophon shoved the feather down Claudius's throat in an effort to induce vomiting (Claudius's wife had been serving him poisoned mushrooms). Some say the feather was also poisoned.

6. JOHN (king of England; 1167?–1216)

Died of an intestinal illness resulting from an overindulgence in lampreys.

7. FULK FITZWARINE IV (English baron; 1230?–1264)

Retreating from the battle of Lewes, Fulk suffocated in his own armor when his horse became bogged down in a swamp.

8. GEORGE, DUKE OF CLARENCE (English nobleman; 1449–1478)

Reputedly died when his brother, Richard III, had him drowned in a barrel of wine.

9. JAMES DOUGLAS, EARL OF MORTON (regent of Scotland; 1525?–1581)

Was beheaded by the "maiden," a guillotine-type device which he himself had introduced into Scotland.

10. JOHN WHITSON (British adventurer; 1557–1629)

At the age of 72, Whitson fell from a galloping horse and neatly impaled his head on a nail that had been standing upright outside a blacksmith's shop.

11. FRANCIS BACON (English philosopher and writer; 1561–1626)

On a sudden impulse to discover whether snow would delay putrefaction of a dead body, Bacon stopped his carriage, purchased a hen, killed it, and stuffed it with snow. He was later seized with a sudden chill which resulted in his death.

12. THOMAS MAY (English historian; 1595–1650)

As he grew fatter and fatter, May found it expedient to tie up his drooping chins with strips of cloth. This arrangement finished him off one day when he swallowed too much and choked to death.

13. THOMAS OTWAY (English dramatist; 1652–1685)

A poor man, Otway had gone days without food and was driven by hunger to begging. He was given a guinea, bought a roll with it—and choked to death on the first mouthful.

14. GÉRARD DE NERVAL (French romantic writer; 1808–1855)

Committed suicide by hanging himself from a lamppost by an apron string.

15. ALLAN PINKERTON (founder of U.S. detective agency; 1819–1884)

Stumbled during his morning constitutional, bit his tongue, and died of gangrene.

16. COUNT ERIC MAGNUS ANDREAS HARRY STENBOCK (English nobleman and writer; 1860–1895)

Stenbock died when he fell into his fireplace while attacking a friend with a poker in a drunken rage.

17. ARNOLD BENNETT (British novelist; 1867–1931)

Died in Paris of typhoid contracted from a glass of local water—which he drank to demonstrate that the water in Paris was perfectly safe.

18. LIONEL JOHNSON (British critic and poet; 1867–1902)

Died of injuries incurred when he fell off a barstool.

19. YOUSOUF ISHMAËLO (Turkish wrestler; d. 1898)

This colorful behemoth came to the U.S. in 1897, defeated former wrestling champion Evan Lewis easily, and then won over Greco-Roman champion Ernest Roeber. Ishmaëlo converted all his winnings into gold coins, which he kept—day and night—in a belt around his waist. Returning home on *Le Bourgogne* in 1898, his ship collided with a British vessel off Nova Scotia and began to sink. Ishmaëlo refused to discard his money belt and, still wearing it, he went overboard. Although a good swimmer, he was too weighted by gold coins to stay afloat. He sank to his death at the bottom of the sea.

The colorful Turkish wrestler Yousouf Ishmaëlo.

20. GRIGORI EFIMOVICH RASPUTIN (Russian holy man; 1871?–1916)

Consumed poisoned tea cakes and wine, was shot twice, but died from drowning after being bound and thrown into the Neva River.

21. ISADORA DUNCAN (U.S. dancer; 1878–1927)

Was strangled to death when, while riding in a car, her long scarf became entangled in a rear wheel and her neck was broken.

22. JEROME NAPOLEON BONAPARTE (the last American Bonaparte; 1878–1945)

Died of injuries sustained when he tripped over the leash of his wife's dog in Central Park, New York, N.Y.

23. RODOLFO FIERRO (Mexican revolutionary general; c. 1880–1917)

While marching toward Sonora with Pancho Villa's troops, Fierro decided to take a shortcut. Unfortunately, his horse became entrapped in quicksand, and Fierro was so loaded down with gold that he sank to his death.

24. LANGLEY COLLYER (U.S. collector and eccentric recluse; 1886–1947)

Mr. Collyer was crushed to death in his own home by his own booby trap. While carrying food to his equally reclusive brother Homer, Collyer tripped his burglar trap and was buried under bundles of old newspapers, three breadboxes, a sewing machine, and a suitcase filled with metal. His brother starved to death, and the two bodies were not found for three weeks.

25. ALEXANDER (king of Greece; 1893–1920)

Was bitten by a pet monkey and died from blood poisoning.

—R.H., F.B.F., & B.F.G.

THE 10 DISEASES
WHICH TAKE THE MOST LIVES

1. HEART DISEASE

According to the best available data, heart disease is the undisputed number one killer in North America, Europe, and Oceania. It is emerging as a formidable threat around the world as more of the population lives longer. In the U.S. alone, more than 750,000 people die from it each year. In one country a reduction in smoking by middle-aged men resulted in more than an 8% decrease in the incidence of the disease, a saving of 10,000 lives per year.

2. MALIGNANT NEOPLASMS (cancerous tumors)

In the broad sense this category refers to a group of more than 100 different diseases. Virtually no country in the world escapes the clinical and financial effects of cancer. Viruses are viewed with great suspicion as possible causes of cancer in man. However, at present the only positively identified viral tumor of man is the common wart, hardly a significant cause for concern. Cancer has been pinpointed as the leading cause of death among American women aged 30–54. Because of the multiplicity of cancer forms, researchers believe numerous cures rather than a single cure will have to be found.

3. CEREBROVASCULAR DISEASE (apoplexy or stroke)

Formation of a blood clot in the lining of a cerebral artery can lead to a great reduction in blood flow to some portion of the brain, or bleeding inside the brain. This cause of death ranks high around the world. Its increasing incidence is attributed to increased human life spans, since it frequently strikes the elderly.

4. ENTERITIS (and other diarrheal diseases)

Accounts for high mortality rates in many underdeveloped countries, especially among infants and the elderly. Enteritis is an inflammatory disease of the intestine, usually the small intestine. Chronic enteritis, also known as terminal ileitis, may stay with the victim for years. A major danger wherever public health standards are poor or nonexistent. Its causes include chemical or food poisoning, emotional upset, allergies, or it may result from such infectious diseases as dysentery and typhoid.

5. INFLUENZA and PNEUMONIA

The leading causes of death in Mexico and Chile, these killers are common throughout the world. In medieval times, influenza was believed to be a visitation from heaven. Although the exact area of its origin remains a mystery, experts believe it was widely spread by the Crusades. In one short period, 1918–1919, a worldwide epidemic claimed an estimated 20–30 million lives. Pneumonia (inflammation of the lung) is still cause for serious concern although it usually responds to modern treatment methods.

6. BRONCHITIS, EMPHYSEMA, and ASTHMA

Medical evidence indicates that the greatest single cause of bronchitis is cigarette smoke. Dust and various other air pollutants seem to contribute to its prevalence. It is four times more likely to show up in men than women. Once a real killer, especially in Britain, it was dubbed the English disease. The greatest incidence of emphysema occurs among heavy cigarette smokers, especially those who breathe polluted air. Asthma can be brought about by some of the same causes as hay fever, in addition to the consumption of foods such as shellfish, nuts, eggs, and chocolate, though to a lesser extent.

7. DIABETES MELLITUS

A disorder caused by an insufficient production of and/or utilization of insulin. It may develop at any age. Although there are various causes for the various forms, complete recovery is almost never realized. Insulin injections usually are highly successful in treating this disease. There is a body of evidence which suggests there may be a genetic tendency toward the disorder, but that environment, as with some varieties of mental illness, plays a big part in its development.

8. CIRRHOSIS OF THE LIVER

This worldwide killer causes irreversible change in the normal tissue of the liver that results in the degeneration of living, working cells and their replacement with fibrous connective tissue. The most widespread form is brought about by excessive and chronic consumption of alcohol. A recent study concluded that vitamin deficiencies, once considered a factor in the development of the disease because alcoholics have poor eating habits, play an insignificant role. It is a more prevalent cause of death in North America and Europe than in Africa, South and Central America, and Asia.

9. TUBERCULOSIS

Caused by the bacillus *Mycobacterium tuberculosis*, this disease may affect any tissue of the human host, but appears in the lungs most commonly. By the 19th century it was one of the most dreaded diseases in the world. Discoveries of tubercular lesions in the bones of Egyptian mummies and of a Neolithic man indicate the disease is ancient. Among those infected, the death rate is highest among children. A major disease of the poor in the world today, it shows up most frequently in poverty-stricken and overcrowded areas.

10. DISEASES AT BIRTH

Although still a matter of concern in the industrial world, birth diseases (including birth injuries) are especially common in the underdeveloped nations where prenatal care and advanced medical care are not always readily available. In fact, in many underdeveloped countries, parents are accustomed to the arrival of 8, 10, or even more children with the expectation that fewer than half of them will survive past infancy.

NOTE: While accidents and suicides generally are considered to be among the top 10 causes of death in the world, they are omitted from this list because they are not diseases.

—J.T.

10 COUNTRIES WITH THE LOWEST INFANT DEATH RATES

(based on latest estimates)

		Infant Deaths per 1,000 Live Births
1.	Sweden	9.2
2.	Finland	10.1
3.	Netherlands	11.0
4.	Japan	11.3
5.	Iceland	11.4
6.	Norway	11.8
7.	France	12.1
8.	Denmark	12.2
9.	Switzerland	13.2
10.	Luxembourg	13.5

The U.S. ranks 17th.

SOURCE: "World Population: Recent Demographic Estimates for the Countries and Regions of the World" (U.S. Bureau of the Census, International Statistical Programs Center, 1975).

10 COUNTRIES WITH THE HIGHEST INFANT DEATH RATES

(based on latest estimates)

		Infant Deaths per 1,000 Live Births
1.	Upper Volta	263
2.	Gabon	229
3.	Guinea	220
4.	Niger	200
5.	Central African Empire	190.5
6.	Chad	190
7.	Mauritania	186

8.	Congo	180
9.	Nigeria	178
10.	Tanzania	165

SOURCE: "World Population: Recent Demographic Estimates for the Countries and Regions of the World" (U.S. Bureau of the Census, International Statistical Programs Center, 1975).

THE 10 MOST COMMON
METHODS OF SUICIDE (WORLDWIDE)

Suicide statistics, as well as the means of computing them, change from year to year. This list ranks worldwide trends according to the most recent available information.

1. POISONING BY SOLID AND LIQUID (MAINLY ANALGESIC AND SOPORIFIC) SUBSTANCES

Ranks first for females, third for males. Since many overdose cases are not listed as suicides, actual figures may be higher than statistics indicate. (Ranks second in the U.S.)

2. HANGING, STRANGULATION, and SUFFOCATION

Until last decade, leading method of suicide. Now down from almost one-third of all suicides to one-quarter. Still the most common method for males, third for females. (Ranks third in the U.S.)

3. FIREARMS and EXPLOSIVES

Second most common for males worldwide. (Most common method in the U.S., accounting for almost half of all suicides.)

4. POISONING BY GASES

Motor vehicle gas (carbon monoxide) accounts for 90% of suicides by gas poisoning. Has jumped 3% in last decade. (Is on an upward trend in the U.S.)

5. ELECTROCUTION, STARVATION, FREEZING, SELF-IMMOLATION (BURNING), CRUSHING BY MACHINERY

These and other more exotic methods of dying are lumped by the World Health Organization into one unspecified category which numbers a fairly consistent 3%. (U.S. figures for this multiple category show a decline from the turn-of-the-century high of 6.5%.)

6. SUBMERSION (DROWNING)

Down from fourth place in 1965, but is now second most-common method for females, worldwide.

7. JUMPING FROM HIGH PLACES

Increased worldwide urbanization is a probable factor. (Now ranks fourth in the U.S., up from last place in 1901.)

8. USE OF CUTTING OR PIERCING INSTRUMENTS

Ranks about 2% worldwide. (Also 2% in the U.S., down from almost 6% in 1901.)

9. AUTOMOBILE "ACCIDENTS"

Suicidal intention is difficult to determine in most cases, and statistical evidence is lacking. (In the opinion of most investigators, this fourth-most-common cause of death in the U.S. probably ranks among the highest-frequency methods of suicide.)

10. "CHRONIC SUICIDE"

A label for long-term self-destruction, officially unrecognized as suicide but considered significant by increasing numbers of psychologists and suicide researchers. Includes compulsive behaviors resulting from drug abuse, alcoholism, smoking, obesity, and other less apparent means. The degree of unconscious intentionality is hard to define and measure, but chronic suicide may rank highest of all in actual frequency. Benjamin Franklin estimated in 1749 that "nine men in 10 are suicides." More than 200 years later, many researchers think that's still a good guess.

—J.EA.

THE PEOPLE'S ALMANAC'S
15 FAVORITE ODDITIES
OF ALL TIME

1. COINCIDENCE

On December 5, 1664, the first in the greatest series of coincidences in history occurred. On this date, a ship in the Menai Strait, off north Wales, sank with 81 passengers on board. There was one survivor—a man named Hugh Williams. On the same date in 1785, a ship sank with 60 passengers aboard. There was one survivor—a man named Hugh Williams. On the very same date in 1860, a ship sank with 25 passengers on board. There was one survivor—a man named Hugh Williams.

2. THE MOST REALISTIC MOVIE IN HISTORY

In 1914, a Hollywood motion-picture company signed a contract with Mexican revolutionary leader Pancho Villa in which he agreed to fight his revolution according to the studio's scenario in return for $25,000. The Hollywood crew went down to Mexico and joined Villa's guerrilla force. The director told Pancho Villa where and how to fight his battles. The cameraman, since he could only

Mexican guerrilla leader Pancho Villa and his band of
irregulars (known as the Division of the North) staging
a real revolution for a Hollywood film studio in 1914.

463

shoot in daylight, made Pancho Villa start his fighting every day at 9:00 A.M. and stop at 4:00 P.M.—sometimes forcing Villa to cease his real warring until the camera could be moved to a new angle. When the completed film was brought back to Hollywood, it was found too unbelievable to be released—and most of it had to be reshot on the studio lot.

3. THE ABYSSINIAN ELECTRIC CHAIR

On August 6, 1890, the first electric chair in history was put into use in the death chamber of Auburn Prison in New York. In distant Abyssinia—now called Ethiopia—Emperor Menelik II (1844–1913) heard about it and decided that this new method of execution should become part of his modernization plan for his country. Immediately, he put in an order for three electric chairs from the American manufacturer. When the chairs arrived and were unpacked, the emperor was mortified to learn they wouldn't work—Abyssinia had no electricity. Determined that his investment not be completely wasted, Emperor Menelik adopted one of the electric chairs for his imperial throne.

4. GANGSTER JOHN DILLINGER DIED BEFORE THE FBI KILLED HIM

America's Public Enemy No. 1 John Dillinger, with a $10,000 reward on his head, died peacefully under anesthetic 26 days before FBI agent Melvin Purvis and fellow agents shot him down outside the Biograph Theater in Chicago on July 22, 1934. Dillinger had gone to Drs. Wilhelm Loeser and Harold B. Cassidy and paid them $5,000 to alter his facial features and get rid of his fingerprints. Given an overdose of ether, Dillinger died during the operation. Said FBI director J. Edgar Hoover, "It was only through prompt action on the part of Loeser that he was resuscitated."

5. THE MOST INCREDIBLE ENGINEER IN THE WORLD

Oddity hunter John Hix told one of the authors of this book about the world's most incredible engineer: "A 300-ft. suspension bridge of old junk, across the Snake River, in Wyoming, was engineered by Charles McCrary, a traveling odd-job man, who had never seen such a structure in his life. A postcard picture of the San Francisco Bay Bridge served as the blueprint. And though government engineers said it would cost $10,000, it was built for $750."

6. THE MAN WHO DID NOT OWN HIS BODY

In 1890, a Swedish gentleman who was desperately in need of money signed a contract with the Caroline Institute in Stockholm—a medical academy that awards the Nobel prize in medicine—promising its staff doctors his body for dissection purposes after his death. In return, he was given the cash he needed. In 1910, this same gentleman inherited a large sum of money. Now he decided he did not want to leave his body for dissection. He tried to buy back the contract from the doctors of the institute. They refused to sell. The gentleman then sued the institute and went to court. The gentleman not only lost the suit and future possession of his body—but he had to pay damages to the institute's doctors because he had had two of his teeth pulled without their permission.

7. THE POPE WHO ISSUED A DECREE AGAINST A COMET

On June 29, 1456, a date when Halley's comet could be seen in the sky at night and mankind feared it could bring on a plague, famine, or some other disaster, Pope Calixtus III, who had been enthroned for one year, issued a papal bull or official decree against the comet. His decree asked Christendom to pray that the comet—or symbol of "the anger of God," as he put it—be fended off or that, as Bartolomeo Platina wrote in 1479, the comet "be entirely diverted against the Turks, the foes of the Christian name."

8. THE MYSTERY OF LITTLE MISS NOBODY

On July 6, 1944, the Ringling Brothers and Barnum & Bailey circus was giving a performance in Hartford, Conn., before 7,000 paid customers. A fire broke out: 168 persons died in the blaze and 487 were injured. One of the dead, a small girl thought to be six years old, was unidentified. Since no one came to claim her, and since her face was unmarred, a photograph was taken of her and distributed locally, and then throughout the U.S. Days passed, weeks and months passed, but no relative, no playmate, no one in the nation came forward to identify her. She remains unknown to this day.

9. THEY ROWED ACROSS THE ATLANTIC OCEAN

On June 6, 1897, Frank Samuelson, a 36-year-old American, and George Harvo, a 31-year-old Norwegian, set out in a small open rowboat from New York Harbor to row across the Atlantic Ocean. Their boat, the *Richard K. Fox*, was 18 ft. long with a 5-ft. beam. They carried no mast, no sails, only five spare pairs of oars. Together, each at an oar, they pulled constantly for 55 days, crossed the vast ocean, 3,075 mi. in all, and made it safely to St. Mary's in the Scilly Islands off southwest England—an unbelievable achievement.

10. HE HAD A DREAM

John Wesley, the founder of Methodism, an evangelist who preached 40,000 sermons, left behind his *Journal* covering the years 1735–1790, much of it written in an indecipherable code. No one in the years that followed was able to solve the code. In 1909, Rev. Nehemiah Curnock, of Rayleigh, England, was poking through a secondhand bookstore when he came across a treasure—John Wesley's personal Bible, with marginal handwritten notes by Wesley in the same mysterious code. The reverend bought the Bible, studied it, then forgot about it. One night, shortly after, while deep in sleep, Reverend Curnock had a dream—he saw Wesley's *Journal*, and on one page the code was deciphered. Waking, he had the key. Remembering his dream, he examined Wesley's code writing in the Bible, and unlocked the mystery. He proceeded to "translate" Wesley's *Journal* and published the results between 1909 and 1916 in four volumes.

11. THE CAVALRY THAT CAPTURED A FLEET OF SHIPS

The most famous instance of a company of cavalry actually defeating and capturing a fleet of ships occurred in the Netherlands on January 20, 1795. In that period, the French Army was pitted against the Dutch, British, and Austrians. French Gen. Charles

Pichegru led his cavalry unit of hussars into Amsterdam in freezing weather. He found the Dutch fleet off the island of Texel, frozen into immobility by heavy ice. Gen. Pichegru immediately ordered his horsemen over the ice-covered waters, overwhelmed the Dutch ships and sailors, and captured them. With that, the Dutch government surrendered.

12. FUNERAL FOR A FLY

Publius Vergilius Maro or Vergil (70–19 B.C.), the Roman poet known for the *Aeneid*, one of the great epic poems in history, sponsored a lavish funeral for a fly, a common housefly he claimed was a favorite pet. The funeral ceremony was held in Vergil's splendid mansion on Esquiline Hill in Rome. An orchestra was on hand to soothe the paid mourners. Many celebrities attended, among them Vergil's patron, Maecenas, who gave a long and moving eulogy to the fly. To cap it off, Vergil himself wrote several poems for the occasion and read them. The fly was buried in a special mausoleum. The entire extravaganza cost Vergil 800,000 sesterces—about $100,000. What motivated this funeral to a fly? Two possibilities. Vergil loved the bizarre, and this may have been an attention-getting put-on. Or he may have known in advance that the government—the Second Triumvirate of Octavius, Lepidus, and Mark Antony—planned to confiscate the property of the rich and parcel it out to war veterans. One exception was that no grounds containing burial plots were to be touched. When this law came to pass, Vergil sought exemption because there was a mausoleum on his land. Exemption was granted, and Vergil's fly had saved his master's property.

13. HOW TO BECOME A WRITER

Victor Hugo (1802–1885), leading French romantic writer, normally had little trouble producing such books as *The Hunchback*

Victor Hugo, author of *Les Misérables*, while he was *not* writing.

of Notre Dame and *Les Misérables*. But sometimes he did run into difficulties and was tempted to do things other than write. At such times he forced himself to work by having his servant take away all of his clothes, with instructions not to return them for several hours. Left with his own nude self, and pen and paper, there was nothing to do but sit down and write.

14. THE WORLD SOLD AT AUCTION

In 193 A.D., Rome dominated or controlled all of the so-called civilized world. In that year, the Roman praetorian guard—the 12,000-member personal bodyguard of the Caesars—turned on the reigning Emperor Pertinax and murdered him. To fill his seat, one guardsman suggested that the leadership of Rome and the world be auctioned off. On March 28, 193, the public auction was held. There were two bidders. One was the assassinated emperor's father-in-law. The other was the wealthiest senator in Rome, 61-year-old Didius Julianus. After spirited bidding, Julianus won the throne with a bid of 300 million sesterces. Didius Julianus was unpopular with both the Senate and the public; his reign lasted only 66 days. The Roman general Severus in Pannonia, hearing of the infamous auction, led his troops back to Rome, sought out the emperor, and had him beheaded.

15. THOU SHALT NOT KILL

In the seventh century, the Toltecs, an agricultural people, moved from northern Mexico down into the vicinity of Mexico City. In all of history, there was never a people more civilized or humane. According to the old histories, the Toltecs went to war with wooden swords—so that they would not kill their enemies.

—I.W.

MARSHALL McLUHAN'S
10 MOST POTENT EXTENSIONS OF MAN

Author, educator, and communications expert Marshall McLuhan is responsible for introducing new concepts in the study of the media. His book *Understanding Media* won him the Albert Schweitzer chair in the humanities at Fordham University, as well as his own TV special and numerous offers from private industry to serve as a consultant.

1. Fire
2. Clothing
3. The wheel
4. The lever (Archimedes: "Give me but one firm spot on which to stand, and I will move the earth.")
5. Phonetic alphabet (extension of language)
6. The sword

7. Print (everyone a reader. Contrast Xerox: everyone a publisher)
8. Electric telegraph (predecessor of telephone)
9. Electric light
10. Radio/TV (extensions of the central nervous system)

Professor McLuhan adds: "It is very difficult to restrict the extensions of man to these 10, but they may prove controversial and interesting."

—Exclusive for *The Book of Lists*

JIMMY THE GREEK'S
FINAL ODDS ON 12 MAJOR EVENTS

His legal name is Jimmy Snyder, but everyone knows him as Jimmy the Greek. He is not a bookmaker or gambler. He is the world's foremost oddsmaker. As scientifically as possible he sets the odds on the outcome of certain events—football games, elections—and he announces these odds in his column, which is syndicated to 240 newspapers and broadcast over 360 radio stations of the Mutual network. He also heads a public relations firm in Las Vegas. Howard Hughes was once a client, paying $175,000 a year for Jimmy's services. Snyder's autobiography is entitled *Jimmy the Greek*.

		Winner
1976	Ford 6-5 to beat Carter	Carter
1972	Nixon 1,000-1 to beat McGovern	Nixon
1970	Super Bowl: Minnesota 8 points over Kansas City	Kansas City
1969	Super Bowl: Baltimore 17 points over New York Jets	New York Jets
1968	Nixon 4-1 to beat Humphrey	Nixon
1964	Johnson 1,000-1 to beat Goldwater	Johnson
1960	Kennedy 2-1 to beat Nixon	Kennedy
1956	Eisenhower 5-1 to beat Stevenson	Eisenhower
1952	Eisenhower 2-1 to beat Stevenson	Eisenhower
1948	Truman 11-10 to beat Dewey	Truman
1944	Roosevelt 3-1 to beat Dewey	Roosevelt
1940	Roosevelt 3-1 to beat Willkie	Roosevelt

—Exclusive for *The Book of Lists*

HANK MESSICK'S
10 GREATEST GAMBLERS IN HISTORY

A onetime college professor, investigative reporter, consultant to law enforcement agencies, Hank Messick has written such books as *The Private Lives of Public Enemies, The Beauties and the Beasts,* and *The Only Game in Town* (with Burt Goldblath).

1. Samson, who murdered 30 men to pay off a gambling debt
2. Arnold Rothstein, who fixed the 1919 World Series
3. Meyer Lansky, who put casino gambling on an organized basis
4. John Law, a faro expert who blew the Mississippi Bubble
5. Eleanore Dumont, who became famous as "Madame Mustache"
6. George Devol, who had the hardest head on the Mississippi
7. Gilbert Lee Beckley, king of layoff bettors until he vanished
8. Richard Canfield, who invented Canfield solitaire
9. Richard M. Nixon, who got his start gambling in the south Pacific
10. John W. "Bet-a-Million" Gates, who got rich on barbed wire and like to bet on flies

Messick adds: "I would have listed Moses Annenberg, the father of the bookie-wire service who more than any man made betting an industry, but the only chance he, personally, took was with the IRS. He lost, but his son made it big. I have left out the politician who gambles with his career, the statesman who gambles with his nation, the business executive who gambles with his millions, and the author who gambles with his self-respect."

—Exclusive for *The Book of Lists*

THE 14 WORST HUMAN FEARS

"What are you the most afraid of?" a team of market researchers asked 3,000 U.S. inhabitants. Many named more than one fear. The results may surprise you.

Biggest Fear	% Naming
1. Speaking before a group	41
2. Heights	32
3. Insects and bugs	22
3. Financial problems	22
3. Deep water	22
6. Sickness	19
6. Death	19
8. Flying	18

9. Loneliness		14
10. Dogs		11
11. Driving/riding in a car		9
12. Darkness		8
12. Elevators		8
14. Escalators		5

According to the *Sunday Times*, London, which reported this American survey: "In general, women were far more fearful than men. Twice as many were afraid of heights, insects, deep water, flying, or driving in cars; three times as many were frightened of darkness; and four times as many were frightened of elevators. They were also more fearful of dogs, of getting sick, and of dying. But if that makes it seem like a male chauvinist survey, it is worth noting the only fear which men have more often than women: the fear of financial problems."

SOURCE: *Sunday Times*, London (Oct. 7, 1973).

20 WONDERFUL BONERS

1. DAN O'LEARY'S HOME RUN

O'Leary, of the Port Huron baseball team, came to bat against Peoria with the score tied. O'Leary hit what may have been the first home run of his career. After rounding the bases, he was declared out. He had run around the bases the wrong way.

2. THE $2 MILLION COMMA

An unidentified congressional clerk was instructed to write: "All foreign fruit-plants are free from duty." Instead, he wrote: "All foreign fruit, plants are free from duty." It cost the U.S. government $2 million before a new session of Congress could rectify the error.

3. THE SWISS NAVY

William Jennings Bryan, when serving as U.S. secretary of state, invited Switzerland to send its navy to the opening of the Panama Canal.

4. THE MEMORABLE STOLEN BASE

In a baseball game, Babe Herman, the Brooklyn Dodgers' star outfielder and slugger, stole second base—with the bases loaded.

5. THE SMOKE-FILLED ROOMS

After completing construction of the Howard Hotel in Baltimore, the contractors installed boilers and started fires—before discovering they had forgotten to build a chimney.

6. THE MATERIALISTIC MINT

Many years ago, the U.S. Mint printed on a run of its gold coins: "In Gold We Trust."

7. TOPSY-TURVY ART

The U.S. National Academy of Design held an art competition and awarded second place to a work by Edward Dickinson—which the judges then learned had been hanging upside down.

8. DEFOE'S MEMORY LAPSE

In his immortal novel *Robinson Crusoe*, author Daniel Defoe had his shipwrecked castaway try to salvage some goods: "I resolved, if possible, to get to the ship; so I pulled off my clothes, for the weather was hot to extremity, and took to the water." After the naked Crusoe climbed aboard the ship: "I found that all the ship's provisions were dry; and being well disposed to eat, I went to the bread room and filled my pockets with biscuits."

9. PINTO VERSUS PINTO

During a wrestling match in Providence, R.I., Count George Zaryoff squared off against Stanley Pinto. During the proceedings, Pinto became entangled in the ringside ropes, and in trying to extricate himself his shoulders touched flat against the mat for 3 secs. He had succeeded in pinning himself and lost the match.

10. POOR DR. WATSON

According to A. Conan Doyle, creator of Sherlock Holmes, the detective's sidekick, Dr. Watson, once suffered a bullet wound during

Dr. Watson in a railway carriage with his friend Sherlock Holmes.

a military action. In *A Study in Scarlet,* Dr. Watson's wound is in the shoulder. In *The Sign of Four,* Dr. Watson's wound is in the leg.

11. LONG MAY SHE WAVE

When Emanuel Leutze painted *Washington Crossing the Delaware,* he depicted the Stars and Stripes being carried in the boat. But the Stars and Stripes were not adopted as the American flag until June 14, 1777—half a year after Washington's crossing.

12. O'NEILL'S INCREDIBLE DIRECTIONS

When Nobel prizewinner Eugene O'Neill wrote his play *Where the Cross Is Made,* he gave these stage directions for one scene: "His right arm had been amputated at the shoulder and the sleeve on that side hangs flabbily. Then he goes over to the table, and sits down, resting his elbows, his chin in his hands, staring somberly before him."

13. OVERKILL IN THE WILDERNESS

In his renowned oil painting *Israelites Gathering Manna in the Wilderness,* the painter Tintoretto armed Moses' men with shotguns. The earliest known gun did not appear until 1326, somewhat after the Exodus.

14. LINCOLN'S MOTHER'S SONG

In his biography *Abraham Lincoln—The Prairie Years,* Carl Sandburg wrote: "Lincoln's mother was standing at the door of their cabin singing 'Greenland's Icy Mountain.' " Quite a feat—the song was not written until 22 years after Lincoln's death.

15. WHO'S ON SECOND?

On Sept. 8, 1908, it was the last of the ninth inning in a crucial National League baseball game between the Chicago Cubs and the New York Giants, and the score was tied. The Giants got men on third and first. The hitter belted a single, driving in the man from third. The runner on first, Fred Merkle, started for second, saw the winning run score, stopped, and headed for the clubhouse. The Cubs' Johnny Evers retrieved the ball and touched second, which meant Merkle had been forced out and the winning run nullified. The score was tied again, but the crowd on the field made further play impossible. Later, when the game was played off, the Giants lost it—and the pennant.

16. MAD JUSTICE

In 1863, Paul Hubert, of Bordeaux, France, was convicted of murder and sentenced to life in jail. After Hubert had served 21 years in solitary confinement, his case was reopened—and only then was it found he had been convicted of murdering himself.

17. THE TWO-HATTED MAN

In one of his 3,000 portraits, Sir Joshua Reynolds painted his subject with a hat on his head—and a hat under his arm.

18. YES, WE HAVE NO BANANAS

At the Versailles Peace Conference in 1919, Lloyd George of Great Britain advised Italy that it could make up its commercial losses by increasing the production of its banana crop. The Italians were not heartened—Italy has no banana crop.

19. THROW OUT THE GAUNTLET

In a portrait of his patron, Charles I of England, Anthony Vandyke painted the king in full armor with two gauntlets (or medieval gloves)—both for the right hand.

20. MORE TOPSY-TURVY ART

The Museum of Modern Art in New York City, displayed Henri Matisse's *Le Bateau* in 1961—and it took 47 days before some-one discovered it was being shown upside down.

—I.W.

COALS TO NEWCASTLE:
7 GREAT BRITISH EXPORT SALES

In 1975, G. and J. Greenhall Distillers of Warrington and the *Export Times* of London sponsored the Vladivar Vodka Incredible Export Award to honor British capitalistic ingenuity. Here are the winners, along with several honorable mentions.

1. TOM-TOMS TO NIGERIA

The Premier Drum Co. of Leicester won first prize with their sale of four shipments of tom-toms to Nigeria, including complete kits for the Nigerian Police Band and the country's top band (Dr. Victor Oliyia and his all-star orchestra). Premier also sold maracas to South America and xylophones to Cuba.

2. OIL TO THE ARABS

Second place went to Permaflex Ltd. of Stoke-on-Trent, which exports £50,000 of petroleum a year to the Arab states in the form of lighter fluid.

3. SPAGHETTI TO ITALY

Associated Health Foods of Godalming, Surrey, sold 100 tons of whole wheat pasta to nutrition-minded Italians.

4. SAND TO ABU DHABI

Eastern Sands and Refractories of Cambridge shipped 1,800 tons of sand to sand-rich Abu Dhabi, which needed sand grains of a special shape for water filtration.

5. CHOW MEIN TO HONG KONG

One hundred cases of Batchelor's Vesta (Ready Meal) chow mein were sold in Hong Kong by representatives of Unilever Export Ltd.

6. FRENCH BISTRO TO PARIS

Ayala Designs Ltd., a Suffolk-based construction company, received a £90,000 order to design and construct a French bistro and café in the middle of Paris.

7. SNOWPLOW TO ARABIA

The defense force of the Arab sheikhdom of Dubai purchased from Bunce Ltd. of Ashbury, Wiltshire, one snowplow. It is to be used to clear sand from remote roads.

Timothy Dexter (1747–1806), an American merchant prince and eccentric who once published a book without punctuation, actually sent a shipload of coal to Newcastle, known as a center for shipping coal *out*. The coal arrived just as Newcastle was paralyzed by a coal strike and there was a shortage of fuel for the citizenry. Dexter came away with enormous profits.

SOURCE: *Export Times,* London (1975).

15 MOST MEMORABLE ARTICLES EVER INSURED

1. The San Francisco-Oakland Bay Bridge ($40,000,000)
2. The *Titanic* ($3,019,400)
3. The voice of N.Y. Metropolitan Opera star Risë Stevens ($1,000,000)
4. The legs of dancer Fred Astaire ($650,000)
5. The crossed eyes of comedian Ben Turpin ($500,000)

A half-million-dollar insurance policy was taken on movie comedian Ben Turpin's eyes—in case they uncrossed.

6. The ice skates (five pairs) of skater Sonja Henie ($250,000)
7. Comedy team of Bud Abbott and Lou Costello: against disagreement between them, for a period of five years ($250,000)
8. The legs of actress Betty Grable ($250,000)
9. Washington, D.C., shopkeepers against failure of Harry S Truman to arrive for his 1949 inauguration ($200,000)
10. The nose of comedian Jimmy Durante ($140,000)
11. Loch Ness monster: its capture and delivery alive ($56,000)
12. Actress Julie Bishop took a seven-year policy with Lloyd's against gaining 4 in. around the hips or waist ($25,000)
13. The Scottish Tailoring Mercery Co. of Sydney, Australia took a policy from Lloyd's of London against "death caused by accident" due to the falling of a Soviet satellite ($22,400)
14. The special elasticized wool trousers (four pairs) of flamenco dancer José Greco ($3,920)
15. Talking myna bird in cookbook promotion ($500)

—J.L.L.

35 COUNTRIES
AND WHEN THEY EXTENDED
THE VOTE TO WOMEN

1.	New Zealand	1893	19.	South Africa	1930
2.	Australia	1902	20.	Spain	1931
3.	Finland	1906	21.	Brazil	1932
4.	Norway	1913	22.	Thailand	1932
5.	Denmark	1915	23.	Turkey	1933
6.	U.S.S.R.	1917	24.	Philippines	1937
7.	Austria	1918	25.	France	1944
8.	Canada	1918	26.	Italy	1945
9.	Germany	1918	27.	Japan	1945
10.	Poland	1918	28.	Yugoslavia	1945
11.	Belgium	1919	29.	Bulgaria	1947
12.	Great Britain	1919	30.	China	1947
13.	Netherlands	1919	31.	Israel	1948
14.	Ireland	1919	32.	Indonesia	1955
15.	Sweden	1919	33.	Iran	1963
16.	U.S.	1920	34.	Switzerland	1971
17.	India*	1926	35.	Jordan	1973
18.	Pakistan*	1926			

* Allowed to vote only in provincial elections.

10 FAMOUS LIBRARIANS

1. GOTTFRIED VON LEIBNIZ (1646–1716)

German philosopher, mathematician, diplomat, and intellectual giant of his time, Leibniz was appointed librarian at Hanover in 1676 and at Wolfenbüttel in 1691.

2. DAVID HUME (1711–1776)

British philosopher, economist, and historian, Hume spent the years 1752–1757 as librarian at the Library of the Faculty of the Advocates at Edinburgh, where he wrote his *History of England.*

3. CASANOVA (GIOVANNI GIACOMO CASANOVA DE SEINGALT; 1725–1798)

At the climax of his career in 1785, the inestimable womanizer began 13 years as librarian for the Count von Waldstein in the château of Dux in Bohemia.

4. AUGUST STRINDBERG (1849–1912)

The Swedish author of the classic drama *Miss Julie* was made assistant librarian at the Royal Library in Stockholm in 1874.

5. POPE PIUS XI (Achille Ambrogio Damiano Ratti; 1857–1939)

After 19 years as a member of the College of Doctors of the Ambrosian Library in Milan, he was appointed chief librarian. In 1911 he was asked to reorganize and update the Vatican Library and four years later became prefect of the Vatican Library. From 1922 until his death in 1939, the former librarian served as pope.

6. SAM WALTER FOSS (1858–1911)

Poet, author, and columnist for the *Christian Science Monitor,* Foss became librarian in 1898 of the public library in Somerville, Mass.

7. ARCHIBALD MacLEISH (b. 1892)

Playwright, poet, lawyer, assistant secretary of state, winner of three Pulitzer prizes, and a founder of the United Nations Educational, Scientific, and Cultural Organization (UNESCO), MacLeish was appointed by President Franklin D. Roosevelt as librarian of Congress in 1939 for five years.

8. MAO TSE-TUNG (1893–1976)

In 1918 he worked as an assistant to the chief librarian of the University of Peking. Overlooked for advancement, he decided to get ahead in another field and eventually became chairman of the Chinese Communist party.

9. J. EDGAR HOOVER (1895–1972)

His first job as a young man was that of messenger and cataloger in the Library of Congress.

10. JOHN BRAINE (b. 1922)

Author of the British novel *Room at the Top* (1957), Braine worked as assistant librarian at Bingley Public Library (1940–1951), branch librarian at Northumberland County Library (1954–1956), and branch librarian at West Riding of Yorks County Library (1956–1957).

—S.S.

DR. MARGARET MEAD'S 10 BEST ANTHROPOLOGY BOOKS OR STUDIES

American anthropologist Dr. Margaret Mead is curator emeritus of ethnology at the American Museum of Natural History in New York City. Noted for her studies of the nonliterate peoples of Oceania as well as her studies of current social issues, she is past president of the American Anthropological Association. Her numerous books include *Coming of Age in Samoa, Growing Up in New Guinea,* and *Blackberry Winter.*

1. Gregory Bateson, *Naven* (Cambridge, England: Cambridge University Press, 1936)
2. Ruth Benedict, *Patterns of Culture* (Boston: Houghton Mifflin, 1934)
3. Franz Boas, *The Mind of Primitive Man* (New York: Macmillan, 1911)
4. Ruth L. Bunzel, *The Pueblo Potter,* Columbia University Contributions in Anthropology, no. 8 (New York: Columbia University Press, 1929)
5. George Devereux, *Reality and Dream* (New York: International Universities Press, 1951)
6. Clifford Geertz, *Islam Observed* (New Haven: Yale University Press, 1969)
7. Alfred L. Kroeber, *The Nature of Culture* (Chicago: University of Chicago Press, 1952).
8. Claude Lévi-Strauss, *Structural Anthropology,* trans. C. Jacobson and B. G. Schoepf (New York: Basic Books, 1963)
9. Bronislaw Malinowski, *Argonauts of the Western Pacific* (London: Routledge, 1922)
10. Edward Sapir, *Language* (New York: Harcourt, Brace, 1921)

—Exclusive for *The Book of Lists*

10 TOP FINANCIAL
CONTRIBUTORS TO THE U.N.

	% of Total U.N. Budget
1. U.S.	25.00
2. U.S.S.R.	12.97
3. Japan	7.15
4. W. Germany	7.10
5. France	5.86
6. People's Republic of China	5.50
7. United Kingdom	5.31
8. Italy	3.60
9. Canada	3.18
10. Ukrainian S.S.R.	1.71

SOURCE: John Paxton, *The Statesman's Year-Book* 1976/1977 (New York: St. Martin's, 1976).

10 COUNTRIES WHICH HAVE
GONE THE LONGEST WITHOUT
A CENSUS OR POPULATION SURVEY

1. Oman	No census ever.
2. Qatar	No census ever.
3. Laos	No census ever; last estimate 1958.
4. N. Korea	No information available.
5. San Marino	Sept. 28, 1947; enumerated pop. 12,100.
6. Bolivia	Sept. 5, 1950; it is estimated that the population of Bolivia has more than doubled since then.
7. People's Republic of China	June 30, 1953; enumerated pop. 582,603,417. Although censuses have been held since 1953, they are considered inaccurate. In rural areas of China ancestor worship is so strong that it is common practice to retain the names of clan members on official registers after they die.
8. Andorra	November, 1954; the population of Andorra has quadrupled since, and is now over 26,000.
9. Guinea	October, 1954–April, 1955; reported pop.

2,570,000—considered a gross underestimation.

10. Zaire   May, 1955–February, 1958.

Notable also-rans include Nigeria, which has held four censuses since 1952, but none has been considered accurate enough to allow publication of the results; and Saudi Arabia, which held a census in 1962–1963, but the results were repudiated by the government. (Another census was held in September, 1974, but the official results have not been made public.)

SOURCE: "World Population: Recent Demographic Estimates for the Countries and Regions of the World" (U.S. Bureau of the Census, International Statistical Programs Center, 1975).

23 TYPICAL JOBS
RATED ACCORDING TO BOREDOM

Based on interviews with 2,010 workers performing 23 different jobs, the Institute for Social Research at the University of Michigan drew up "boredom factors" for each occupation. The average was considered to be 100, and the higher the rating the more boring the job.

	Boredom Rating
1. Assembler (work paced by machine)	207
2. Relief worker on assembly line	175
3. Forklift-truck driver	170
4. Machine tender	169
5. Assembler (working at own pace)	160
6. Monitor of continuous flow goods	122
7. Accountant	107
8. Engineer	100
9. Tool- and diemaker	96
9. Computer programmer	96
11. Electronic technician	87
12. Delivery service courier	86
13. Blue-collar supervisor	85

18 UNNATURAL LAWS

Have you ever received a phone call the minute you stepped outside and locked your door? Has the bus you were waiting for ever appeared from behind a parked truck the instant you lit up a cigarette? Certain astute individuals have noticed that such events are not the exception but, rather, the rule. Men like Murphy, Peter, and Parkinson have made it their lifework to ferret out the operating principles—the laws—that govern the frustrating lives we mortals live. Here is a small sampling of these laws from Arthur Bloch's *Murphy's Law—and Other Reasons Why Things Go Wrong* (Los Angeles: Price/Stern/Sloan Publishers, 1977):

1. MURPHY'S LAW

If anything can go wrong, it will.

2. O'TOOL'S COMMENTARY ON MURPHY'S LAW

Murphy was an optimist.

3. THE UNSPEAKABLE LAW

As soon as you mention something . . .
. . . if it's good, it goes away.
. . . if it's bad, it happens.

4. NONRECIPROCAL LAWS OF EXPECTATIONS

Negative expectations yield negative results.
Positive expectations yield negative results.

5. HOWE'S LAW

Every man has a scheme that will not work.

6. ZYMURGY'S FIRST LAW OF EVOLVING SYSTEMS DYNAMICS

Once you open a can of worms, the only way to recan them is to use a larger can.

7. ETORRE'S OBSERVATION

The other line moves faster.

8. SKINNER'S CONSTANT (FLANNAGAN'S FINAGLING FACTOR)

That quantity which, when multiplied by, divided by, added to, or subtracted from the answer you get, gives you the answer you should have gotten.

9. LAW OF SELECTIVE GRAVITY

An object will fall so as to do the most damage.

9A. JENNING'S COROLLARY

The chance of the bread falling with the buttered side down is directly proportional to the cost of the carpet.

10. GORDON'S FIRST LAW

If a research project is not worth doing at all, it is not worth doing well.

11. MAIER'S LAW

If the facts do not conform to the theory, they must be disposed of.

12. HOARE'S LAW OF LARGE PROBLEMS

Inside every large problem is a small problem struggling to get out.

13. BOREN'S FIRST LAW

When in doubt, mumble.

14. THE GOLDEN RULE OF ARTS AND SCIENCES

Whoever has the gold makes the rules.

15. BARTH'S DISTINCTION

There are two types of people: those who divide people into two types, and those who don't.

16. SEGAL'S LAW

A man with one watch knows what time it is. A man with two watches is never sure.

17. NINETY-NINETY RULE OF PROJECT SCHEDULES

The first 90% of the task takes 90% of the time, and the last 10% takes the other 90%.

18. FARBER'S FOURTH LAW

Necessity is the mother of strange bedfellows.

10 GREAT IMPOSTORS

1. GEORGE PSALMANAZAR (b. southern France; 1679?–1763)

In 1703, Psalmanazar—whose real name is unknown—appeared in London and claimed to be a native of the island of Formosa (now Taiwan) and a recent convert to Christianity. Despite his distinctly occidental appearance, the 25-year-old Frenchman induced British authorities to hire him to teach "Formosan" (which he invented from A to Z) at Oxford and translate the Bible into his "native" tongue. His best-selling book *The Historical and Geographical Description of Formosa* (1704) described the island's religion and customs: Formosans supposedly ate raw meat, including the flesh of legally executed criminals, and annually offered to God a burnt offering of 18,000 hearts cut from the breasts of native boys under nine. Psalmanazar later regretted the hoax and confessed all in his last will and in a book that was published posthumously.

2. SARAH WILSON (b. Staffordshire, England; 1750–?)

A servant to one of Queen Charlotte's ladies-in-waiting, Wilson was caught in the act of trying on the royal jewels in 1771. She was banished to the American Colonies for life. Somehow she managed to make off with a few jewels and one of the queen's dresses before boarding the convict ship bound for Maryland. After escaping from her master, the indentured servant fled south. Dressed in royal garb, she claimed to be Princess Susanna Carolina Matilda, sister of Queen Charlotte. For 18 months—until her arrest in South Carolina in 1773—she accepted gifts and lodging from dozens of Southern gentlemen and in exchange promised them appointments. During the Revolution, she again left her master, this time to marry a British Army officer.

3. MARY BAKER (b. Devonshire, England; c. 1800–?)

Unable to hold a job as a servant, Baker conspired with a sailor to perpetrate a hoax which held the interest of the British press for a year. In 1817, she appeared at the doorstep of a Gloucestershire mansion and spoke in a "foreign tongue." British linguists were unable to decipher her language until the sailor arrived and identified her as Caraboo, princess of Javasu, who had been kidnapped by pirates from Sumatra and shipwrecked off the coast of England. For a year, Baker enjoyed royal treatment. Then, because of a newspaper account that described a peculiar scar on her back, she was fingered by an old acquaintance. Thus confronted, she confessed fully, emigrated to America, and disappeared forever.

4. ARTHUR ORTON (b. London; 1834–1898)

In 1866, Orton, a butcher from Wagga Wagga, New South Wales, Australia, showed up in London and claimed to be Sir Roger Tichborne, who had been lost at sea as a young man. Lady Tichborne, unwilling to accept her son's death, ignored the obvious flaws in Orton's claim—her son (when last seen barely a decade before) weighed 125 lbs., had a long thin face, light straight hair, a tattoo, and spoke French fluently, while Orton weighed nearly 300 lbs., had a huge round face, dark wavy hair, and spoke only English. He bore no tattoo. After Lady Tichborne's death, Orton boldly laid claim to the estate. The three-year court struggle ended when the rotund impostor was put behind bars on a 14-year rap for perjury. Although he later sold his confession to a newspaper, he died penniless in London at age 64.

5. LORD GORDON-GORDON (b. Scotland; ?–1873)

During the struggle to oust railroad tycoon Jay Gould from the directorship of the Erie Railroad in 1872, Lord Gordon-Gordon came to New York and pretended to have royal connections and great wealth. Promising to help Gould retain power, the Scottish "nobleman"—whose real name is unknown—managed to bilk Gould out of $1 million in negotiable securities. Arrested two years later, Lord Gordon-Gordon extended his charade by cheerfully providing the names and addresses of well-bred friends and relatives abroad, while on the witness stand. Before these references could be checked out, Gordon-Gordon skipped bail, fled to Canada, and committed suicide.

6. ELIZABETH BIGLEY (b. Ontario, Canada; 1857–1907)

Not long after accepting a pardon from Ohio's Gov. William McKinley in 1893, convicted forger Elizabeth Bigley settled in Cleveland. There she let it be known that she was the illegitimate daughter of Andrew Carnegie and, as such, stood to inherit a portion of his millions. The tale came to be accepted as fact in Buckeye banking circles when Bigley, now known as Cassie Chadwick, began flashing bogus promissory notes from the Pittsburgh tycoon. Over a period of years, she borrowed millions from moneylenders, who expected to reap a fat interest fee after she received her inheritance. When the *Cleveland Press* exposed her checkered past in banner headlines in 1904, several northeastern Ohio banks folded. Present at her trial was Carnegie himself, who appeared pleased when his "daughter" was sentenced to the Ohio State Penitentiary for a 10-year term. Mrs. Chadwick died behind bars before her 10 years were up.

7. CONCEPCIÓN JURADO (b. Mexico City, Mexico; 1864–1931)

A soft-spoken spinster with a gift for mimicry, Jurado played the part of Don Carlos Palmori, a skirt-chasing, offensive millionaire, at private parties given at the home of her brother. For nearly 50 years, she swaggered through over 1,000 fiestas, propositioning women and intimidating men with stories of vast power and influence. At the end of each performance, Jurado would dramatically rip off her mustache, let her hair down, and announce her true identity. Her 3,000 victims, who included many prominent Mexican officials, agreed to keep her secret until her death, so that she could continue fooling batch after batch of *puerquitos* ("little pigs"). Her last performance took place in 1931, while she was dying of cancer.

8. FREDERICK EMERSON PETERS (b. New Salem, O.; 1885–1959)

Under scores of different names, Peters crisscrossed the U.S., and forged checks from 1902 until his death. Occasionally posing as the son of Theodore Roosevelt or some other well-known figure, Peters would engage a small shopkeeper in conversation, then try to cash a check for a few dollars more than the cost of the goods he purchased. Few refused the amiable Peters. Most of his time was spent in various prisons, however, where he read prodigiously and often helped establish prison libraries. On his last bad-check tour in 1959, Peters suffered a fatal stroke in New Haven, Conn., and was given a pauper's funeral by that city.

9. STANLEY CLIFFORD WEYMANN (b. Brooklyn, N.Y.; 1891)

A file clerk who commissioned himself a "lieutenant" during W.W. I, Weymann has spent his life in and out of jail for a variety of impostures, during which he almost always used his real name. "Dr." Weymann supervised sanitation conditions for an American firm in Peru in 1920, helped run a clinic at the New York Hospital for Joint Diseases in 1922, and attended to grieving actress Pola Negri at the untimely death of her betrothed—superstar Rudolph Valentino—in 1926. "Navy Lieutenant Commander" Weymann chatted with President Warren G. Harding at a 1921 White House affair for Princess Fatima of Afghanistan—an affair arranged by "Undersecretary of State" Clifford Weymann.

10. FERDINAND WALDO DEMARA, JR., (b. Lawrence, Mass.; 1921)

Known as the "Great Imposter," this high-school dropout assumed several professional roles before settling down as a legitimately ordained minister of the Gospel. During the 1940s, he posed as a Trappist monk in a Kentucky monastery, a professor of psychology at a Pennsylvania college, a biologist specializing in cancer research at an institution near Seattle, and the recreational officer at a maximum security prison in Texas. His greatest feat, however, occurred during the Korean War, when he served as a lieutenant-surgeon with the Canadian Navy. With the aid of medical books aboard ship, he pulled teeth, removed tonsils, amputated limbs, and once successfully removed a bullet lodged near the heart of a wounded South Korean soldier. Eventually discovered, he was discharged and deported to the U.S. In 1956, Maine state police arrested him for "cheating by false premises" by posing as an accredited teacher at a local school. For this offense, Demara served a few months in jail. Except for this and another 1½ years spent in a military prison for wartime desertion from the U.S. Navy in 1942, he generally managed to elude punishment. Asked why he impersonated so many people, Demara replied, "Rascality, pure rascality."

—W.A.D.

20 FAVORITE SCENTS
OF MEN AND WOMEN

In a study published in 1966 by England's R. W. Moncrieff, a fellow of the Royal Instituned of Chemistry, certain odors were shown to be much more attractive to one sex than the other. Participants selected their favorites from a group of 132 odors, and the results are as follows.

MEN'S FAVORITES

1. Honeysuckle
2. Fresh strawberries
3. Red rose
4. New Dawn rose
5. Wild rose
6. Emily Gray rose
7. Sweet pea
7. Stock
9. Mock orange (blossoms)
10. Meadowsweet (flower)

WOMEN'S FAVORITES

1. Sweet pea
2. Red rose
2. Honeysuckle
4. New Dawn rose
5. Fresh strawberries
6. Emily Gray rose
7. Stock
8. English lavender oil
9. Meadowsweet (flower)
10. French lavender oil

Other studies by Moncrieff show that men seem to prefer mock orange, honeysuckle, wild rose, musk ambrette, ilang-ilang, and lemongrass much more than women. Women prefer alpine violet perfume, bay leaf, and onions. Women also prefer perfume and food-associated odors.

—J.BER.

THE ONLY 2½ ANGELS
MENTIONED BY NAME
IN THE BIBLE

1. GABRIEL

Daniel saw this angel in a dream, and Zacharias saw him while at work and learned his wife would give him a son (John the Baptist). The angel also visited the Virgin Mary in Nazareth.

2. MICHAEL

He fought the devil over the body of Moses, and with an alliance of angels fought a dragon in heaven.

2½. LUCIFER

An ex-angel, so he can only count for half an angel. Popularly known as the fallen angel. Isaiah 14:12: "How art thou fallen from heaven, O Lucifer, son of the morning! how art thou cut to the ground, which didst weaken the nations!"

—I.W.

THE LORD THY GOD'S
10 COMMANDMENTS

Atop Mount Sinai in the Holy Land, God inscribed on two tablets of stone for Moses the 120 Hebrew words that are the 10 Commandments. There have been many versions of the commandments. This version, perhaps the oldest, is from the Book of Exodus.

1. Thou shalt have no other gods before me.
2. Thou shalt not make unto thee any graven image, or any likeness of any thing that is in heaven above, or that is in the earth beneath, or that is in the water under the earth: Thou shalt not bow down thyself to them, nor serve them: for I the Lord thy God am a jealous God, visiting the iniquity of the fathers upon the children unto the third and fourth generation of them that hate me; and shewing mercy unto thousands of them that love me, and keep my commandments.
3. Thou shalt not take the name of the Lord thy God in vain; for the Lord will not hold him guiltless that taketh his name in vain. Remember the sabbath day, to keep it holy. Six days shalt thou labour, and do all thy work: but the seventh day is the sabbath of the Lord thy God: in it thou shalt not do any work, thou, nor thy son, nor thy daughter, thy manservant, nor thy maidservant, nor thy cattle, nor thy stranger that is within thy gates: for in six days the Lord made heaven and earth, the sea, and all that in them is, and rested the seventh day: wherefore the Lord blessed the sabbath day, and hallowed it.
4. Honour thy father and thy mother: that thy days may be long upon the land which the Lord thy God giveth thee.
5. Thou shalt not kill.
6. Thou shalt not commit adultery.
7. Thou shalt not steal.
8. Thou shalt not bear false witness against thy neighbour.
9. Thou shalt not covet thy neighbour's house.
10. Thou shalt not covet thy neighbour's wife, nor his manservant, nor his maidservant, nor his ox, nor his ass, nor any thing that is thy neighbour's.

SOURCE: Exodus 20:3-17.

THE AUTHORS'
7 THOUGHTS FOR YOU,
THE READER

1. Thank you for having read this far. We hope you will write to us, if you are so moved.
2. Please tell us what you enjoyed most, and least, about this book.
3. If you come across any errors or omissions—or have any suggestions for the next edition—let us know.
4. Send us your ideas or actual lists for *The Book of Lists II*. Be sure to accompany these with a self-addressed stamped envelope.
5. If we like your ideas, we will ask you to write them for us and will pay you for your effort.
6. If you send in a *completed* list, we will compensate you if it is acceptable, or return it to you if it is not acceptable or if we already have the list or a similar one.
7. Here is how to get in touch with us. Write to:

> The Book of Lists
> P.O. Box 49699
> Los Angeles, Calif. 90049

—A.W., D.W., & I.W.

INDEX

A

Abdul Alhazred, 237
A-bomb, *illus.,* 98
Abyssinian electric chair, 464
Academy Awards, 200
Achievers at an advanced age, 3
Achilles' heel, 292
Aconitine nitrate, 84
Action Comics, #1, 234
Activities, calories burned by, 382
Actors
  best stage (Logan's), 186
  most often nominated for an Oscar, 200
Actresses most often nominated for an Oscar, 200
Acupuncture, origin of, 254
Adam, Robert, 194
Adam and Eve, 172
Adams, John Quincy, popular vote, 32
Adams of Eagle Lake (ABC), 210
Adrastea, 122
Adventure, #1, 235
"Advice to a young man," 329
Aerogenerators, 259
Aesop, 376
Africa, new lakes for, 260
Agamemnon, murder of, 272
Agate, James—dinner guests, 414
Agathocles, 455
Aglet, definition of, 162; *illus.,* 163
Agrippina, the younger, 284
Air Aces of W.W. I, 82
Airlines
  most dangerous, 154
  safest, 153
Alamo, the, 78
Alaska, 113
Alba, duchess of, 192
Albert, Jan van, 308
Albert Victor, prince, 74

Alcock, Capt. John, 150; *illus.,* 151
Alcohol drinkers, heavy (Sinclair's), 396
Alcott, Amy—greatest women golfers, 365
Aldomet, 406
Alexander, king of Greece, 457
Alexander (drink), 391
Alexander II's Lenoir, 154
Alexander III of Macedon (the Great), 173, 455; *illus.,* 80
Alexander VI, pope, 330
Alexandria, burning of, 272
Algonguin Hotel (New York, N.Y.), 375
All in the Family, 215
Amalthea, 122
Amazon basin, 113
America (airplane), 153
American Bandstand (ABC), 213
Americans, famous foreign-born, 27
American songs, *see* Popular songs
Ampère, André-Marie, 252
Ampere (unit), 252
Ampicillin, 405
Anastasia, 444
Anatomical drawings, first, 254
Anderson, John Henry, 195
Anderson, Maxwell, 198
Anderson, Paul, 351
Anderson, Sherwood, 397
Andretti, Mario—greatest auto racers, 352
Andrew's raiding party, 37
Andy Griffith Show, 215
Anesthesia, first use of, 254
Angel Falls, *illus.,* 108
Angels named in the Bible, 485
Angels of Mons, 447
Angers of Neptune, 191
Animals
  celebrated, 126

489

B

494

497

L

Muhamed (horse), 129
Muhammad Ali, 360
Muir, John, 29
Müller, Heinrich, 83
Murder mysteries, best, 230
Murders
  committed by doctors, 68
  Smith case, 274
  unusual, 472
Murphy, 1st Lt. Audie Leon, 39
Murphy's law, 480
Murrieta, Joaquin, 292
Musical idols of teenagers
  (Clark's), 181
Mussolini, Benito, 287
Mussolini, Rosa M., 287
Musters, Pauline, 310
Myllyrinne, Väinö, 309
Myra Breckinridge (film), 209
Mysteries, unsolved, 442

N

Naidu, Rama Murti, 350
Naked Maja, 192
Names
  new—for old places, 146
  unfamiliar, of objects, 162
Nanuya Levu, 106
Napoleon, 88, 105, 173, 273,
  291, 298, 332, 373, 389
Nash, John, 195
Nashnush, Sulaiman Ali, 309
Nations
  largest military expenditures
    per capita, 93
  largest percentage of persons
    in armed forces, 92
  receiving military aid from
    China, U.S.S.R., *and* the
    U.S., 94
  smallest military expenditures
    per capita, 94
  smallest percentage of persons
    in armed forces, 93
  See also Countries; Places
NATO, torture by, 65
Natural attractions, most popu-
  lar U.S., 25
Nautilus, 259

"Navaree, flying witch of," 438
Nazca lines, 442
Nazi criminals still at large, 83
Nebuchadnezzar, 255
Necronomicon, 237
Nehru, Jawaharlal, 242
Nelson, Baby Face, 53
Nelson, Horatio, 301
Neoplasms, malignant, 458
Neptune, 124
Nereid, 124
Nero, 15, 284
Nerval, Gérard de, 456
Neumann, Therese, 437
Newcomb, Simon, 250
Newcomers to the U.S., origins
  of, 29
New Guinea, 115
Newman, Paul, 42; *illus.*, 42
New names for old places, 146
Newspapers
  influential (Tebbel's), 175
  top (Merrill's), 174
Newton, Sir Isaac, 223, 253,
  321, 406
Newton (unit), 253
Nicholas II's Rolls-Royce, 154
Nichols, Beverley—dinner
  guests, 421
Nicklaus, Jack, 364; *illus.*, 364
Nicot, Jean, 165
Night Watch, The, 191
Nitrous oxide users, 402
Nivelle, Gen. Robert, 79
Nixon, Richard M., 15, 33, 61,
  126
  —all-star baseball team, 352
  enemies list, 40
Nobel prize in literature,
  nominees who lost, 246
Non-Indo-European languages,
  English words from, 168
Nonmurder cases (Belli's), 58
Northern kit fox, 136
Northern Simien fox, 136
Northern square-lipped
  rhinoceros, 137
Norway's Peer Gynt mountain
  country, 144
"Nose, The," 294
Nova, definition of, 119

R

W

PHOTO CREDITS

ABOUT THE AUTHORS

DAVID WALLECHINSKY worked on *The People's Almanac* for two years before being joined by his father, Irving Wallace, for the last two and one half years of the project. David is coauthor of *Chico's Organic Gardening and Natural Living, Laughing Gas,* and *What Really Happened to the Class of '65.* He is currently working on *The People's Almanac 2*—a million new words—to be published in 1978. David adopted the original family name of Wallechinsky when his grandfather explained that the name had been changed by a U.S. Immigration agent at Ellis Island.

AMY WALLACE, Irving Wallace's daughter, is a graduate of the Berkeley (Calif.) Psychic Institute, and has developed such psychic skills as clairvoyant reading and psychic healing. Besides coauthoring *The Book of Lists* and a new work, *The Psychic Healing Book,* she has written, with her father, *The Two,* a forthcoming biography of the original Siamese twins.

IRVING WALLACE is one of the most widely read novelists in the world, with estimated worldwide sales of his twenty books, in all editions, at 106 million copies. His first great international success was with *The Chapman Report,* followed by *The Prize, The Man, The Seven Minutes, The Word, The Fan Club, The People's Almanac* (with his son, David), and *The R Document*—all major bestsellers.

Franz Liszt